Microsoft® Word 2013: Level 1 of 3

JILL MURPHY
Custom Performance Solutions

LABYRINTH
LEARNING™

Berkeley, CA

Microsoft Word 2013: Level 1

LABYRINTH
LEARNING™

Labyrinth Learning
2560 9th Street, Suite 320
Berkeley, California 94710
800.522.9746
On the web at lablearning.com

President:
Brian Favro

Product Development Manager:
Jason Favro

Managing Editor:
Laura Popelka

Production Editor:
Margaret Young

Production Manager:
Rad Proctor

eLearning Production Manager:
Arl S. Nadel

eLearning Development:
Judy Mardar and Andrew Vaughnley

Developmental Editors:
Trisha Conlon and Sandra Rittman

Indexing:
Joanne Sprott

Cover Design:
Mick Koller, SuperLab Design

Interior Design:
Mark Ong, Side-by-Side Studio

ITEM: 1-59136-488-4
ISBN-13: 978-1-59136-488-7

Manufactured in the United States of America.

10 9 8 7 6 5 4 3 2 1

Table of Contents

WORD 2013 LESSON 4: CREATING A SIMPLE REPORT

WORD 2013 LESSON 5: WORKING WITH TABLES

Quick Reference Tables

GENERAL TASKS

PAGE SETUP TASKS

TABLE TASKS

Preface

In today's digital world, knowing how to use the most popular suite of desktop software applications is critical. Our goal is to teach new users how to take advantage of this technology and to help experienced users understand how the applications have changed from previous versions. We begin with fundamental concepts and take learners through a systematic progression of exercises, resulting in skill mastery.

An online student resource center accompanies this book. It contains Concepts Review quizzes, student exercise files, and other learning tools. The URL for the student resource center is printed on the inside front cover of this textbook.

Supplemental Options

Video Tutorials: Our easy-to-follow instructional design is complemented with hundreds of videos that demonstrate the concepts and skills covered in this textbook. All videos can be accessed online with a single license key. Videos are an option for all learners. Keys can be purchased at http://lablearning.com/Store/Shop-Videos.

eLab Course Management System: eLab is a web-based learning systems that integrates seamlessly with this textbook. eLab is an option for students enrolled in instructor-led courses that have adopted eLab as part of their course curriculum.

Visual Conventions

This book uses visual and typographic cues to guide students through the lessons. Some of these cues are described below.

`Type this text`	Text you type at the keyboard is printed in this typeface.
Action words	The important action words in exercise steps are presented in boldface.
Ribbon	Glossary terms are presented in black text with a blue background.
TIP	Tips, notes, and warnings are called out with special icons.
Command→ Command→ Command→ Command	Commands to execute from the Ribbon are presented like this: Ribbon Tab→Command Group→Command→Subcommand.
FROM THE KEYBOARD [Ctrl]+[S] to save	These margin notes present shortcut keys for executing certain tasks.
FROM THE RIBBON File→Save	These margin notes show Ribbon paths for executing certain tasks.

Acknowledgements

This textbook has benefited greatly from the reviews and suggestions of the following instructors.

Kim Anderson, *Elgin Community College*

Ann Blackman, *Parkland College*

Kristen Bogue, *Bridgerland Applied Technology College*

Jeanann Boyce, *Montgomery College, Takoma Park Campus, MD*

Margie Brunson, *Central Carolina Technical College*

Lori Collins, *Pike-Lincoln Technical Center*

Julie Davis, *Mt. Diablo Adult Ed (Loma Vista Adult School)*

Evangelina Galelgos-Garner, *South Texas Vocational Technical Institute*

Teresita Galvizo, *South East High School*

Rebecca Haney, *Isothermal Community College*

Holly Heggestad, *Madison Area Technical College*

Kathleen Holliman, *Wallace Community College Selma*

Terri Holly, *Indian River State College*

Joan Johnson, *Lake Sumter Community College*

Ronald Kaufer, *Lonestar College – Tomball*

Robin Landry, *RPCC/TEC*

Gayle Larson, *Highline Community College*

Teresa Loftis, *San Bernardino Adult School*

Tina Mazuch, *Northeast Community College*

John Mims, *Central New Mexico Community College Workforce Training Center*

Sue Mookram, *Plaza College and Queens College*

Kay Nelson, *The Lifelong Learning Center, Missoula County Public Schools*

Youcef Oubraham, *HCCC*

Monika Olsen, *Acalanes Adult Education*

Kari Phillips, *DATC*

Kate Prussing, *SERRC – The Learning Connection*

Teresa Roberts, *Wilson Community College*

Maryla Scarpa, *Vincennes University Jasper*

Rosemarie Shamieh, *Glendale Community College*

Lal Shimpi, *Saint Augustine's University*

Mary Jo Slater, *Community College of Beaver County*

Francine Smith, *Wayne Community College*

Michelle Vlaich-Lee, *Greenville Technical College*

Cynthia Wade, *CierraTEC*

Deanna Wallace, *TTC Nashville*

Ali Ware, *Humboldt County Office of Education*

Microsoft® Word 2013:
Level 1 of 3

Introducing Word Basics

LESSON OUTLINE

LEARNING OBJECTIVES

After studying this lesson, you will be able to:

- Use the Word Start screen and window
- Work with the Ribbon and Quick Access toolbar
- Open, close, and navigate in documents
- Type a new document
- Use Word Help

Microsoft Word 2013 is a dynamic word-processing program that lets you easily create and modify a variety of documents. In this lesson, you will start Word, and then you'll work with the Word interface. You will open and navigate through a multipage document, and create and save a document. Finally, you will work with Word Help, and then exit Word.

CASE STUDY

Using My Virtual Campus

My Virtual Campus is a social networking technology company. They sell their web application to colleges and universities, allowing students, alumni, faculty, and staff to use this social networking website that is closed to the public and branded for their institution. The marketing manager has asked you to create a brief summary to describe their best-selling website and how it is used. This will provide you a good opportunity to see just how easy Word 2013 is to use. And if you run into any problems along the way, you will appreciate how much help is at your fingertips.

My Virtual Campus

Our best-selling website, a social networking Intranet established specifically for college communities worldwide, has been gaining popularity at an extraordinary rate.

The website is useful for all types of networking opportunities; for example, social events and career prospects can be publicized, prospective students can check out the campus, and professors and students can participate in extended training occasions and collaborate on special projects. It also proves useful when looking for a roommate or offering items for sale. Alumni can post job opportunities for current students and other noteworthy news, and so forth.

In general, here's how it works. You join and create a profile about yourself, choosing how much personal information to enter. Then, you can invite other people to join also. You can chat in real-time with other members, post photos to share, and most importantly, you control what information others can see about you.

Security is taken very seriously by My Virtual Campus and every step has been taken to ensure your privacy and protect your confidential information.

Presenting Word 2013

Video Library http://labyrinthelab.com/videos Video Number: WD13-V0101

Word provides tools to assist you in virtually every aspect of document creation. From desktop to web publishing, Word has the right tool. For these and many other reasons, Word is the most widely used word-processing program in homes and businesses.

Starting Word

The method you use to start Word and other Office 2013 applications depends on whether you are using the Windows 7 or Windows 8 operating system.

- **Windows 7:** Click Start, choose Microsoft Office from the All Programs menu, and then choose Microsoft Word 2013.
- **Windows 8:** Locate the Word 2013 tile on the Windows Start screen; click the tile to start Word.

Viewing the Word Start Screen

The Word Start screen is the first screen you see. It offers several ways to begin working. Don't be concerned if your Start screen is arranged differently from this example. You can rearrange the templates on the right, and the appearance also depends on your screen's resolution.

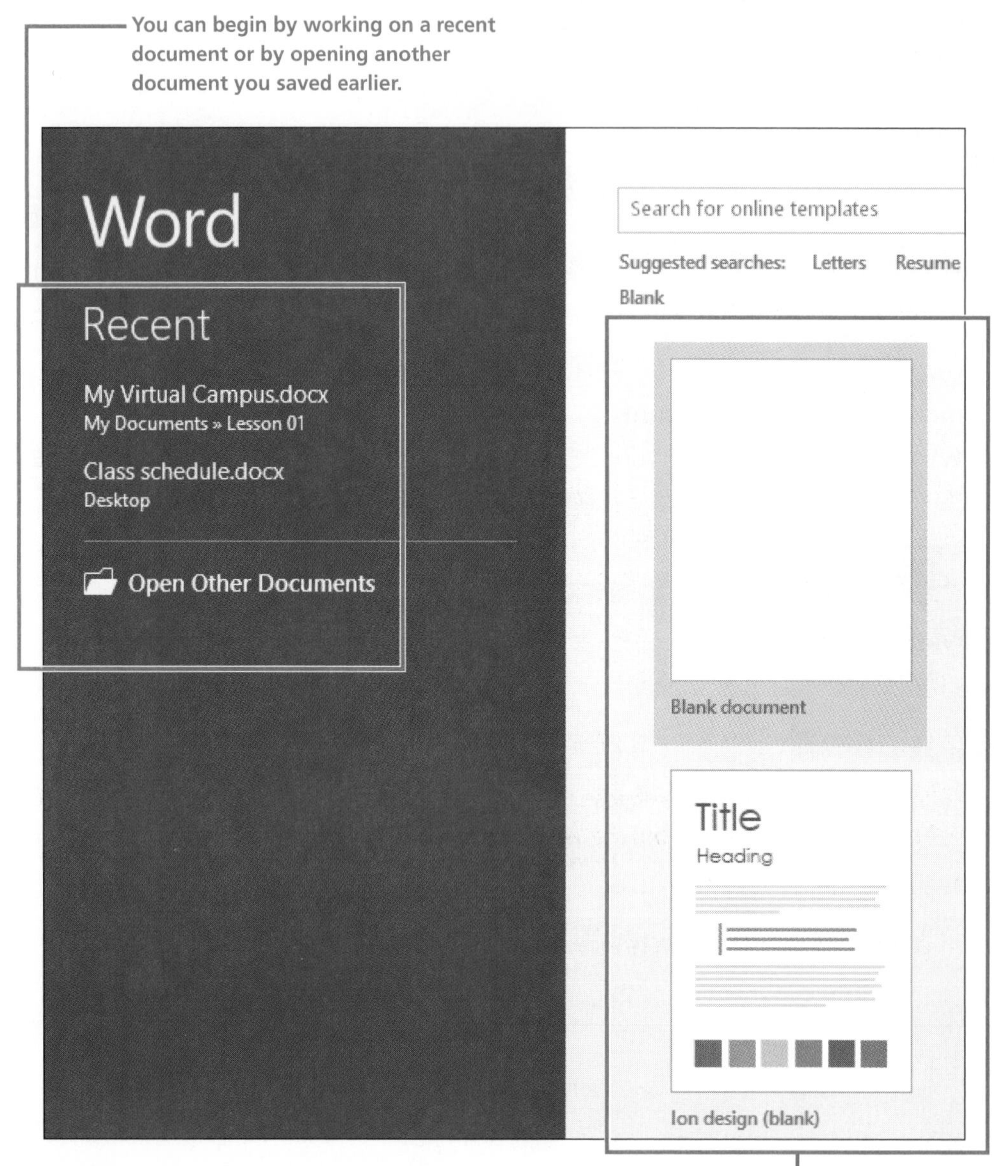

DEVELOP YOUR SKILLS WD01-D01A

Start Word (Windows 8)

Windows 7 Users: Skip to the next exercise.

In this exercise, you will start the Word program.

1. If necessary, start your computer.
   The Windows Start screen appears.
2. Locate the **Word 2013 tile**.
3. Click the tile to start Word.
   The Word program loads and the Word Start screen appears.
4. Make sure the Word window is **maximized** .
5. Click the **Blank Document** template to open the Word window.

DEVELOP YOUR SKILLS WD01-D01B

Start Word (Windows 7)

Windows 8 Users: Skip this exercise.

In this exercise, you will start the Word program.

1. If necessary, start your computer.
   The Windows Desktop appears.
2. Click **Start** at the left edge of the taskbar and choose **All Programs**.
3. Choose **Microsoft Office**, and then choose **Microsoft Word 2013** from the menu.
   The Word program loads and the Word Start screen appears.
4. Make sure the Word window is **maximized** .
5. Click the **Blank Document template** to open the Word window.

Viewing the Word 2013 Window

Video Library http://labyrinthelab.com/videos Video Number: WD13-V0102

The following illustration describes the main elements of the Word window. Don't be concerned if your document window looks somewhat different from this example. The Word screen is customizable.

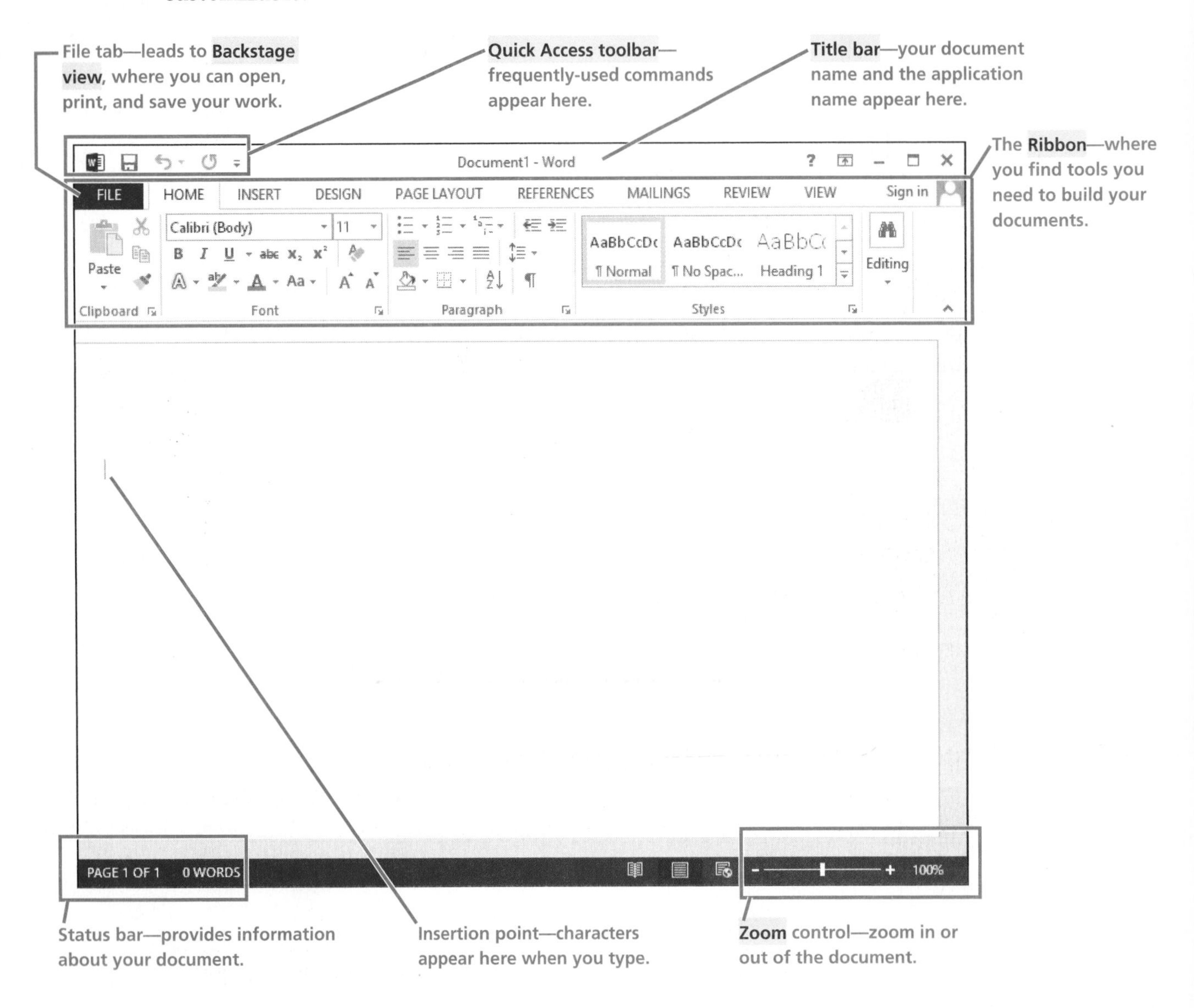

Opening Documents

Video Library http://labyrinthelab.com/videos Video Number: WD13-V0103

FROM THE RIBBON
File→Open

FROM THE KEYBOARD
[Ctrl]+[O] to open a document

In Word and other Office 2013 applications, the Open screen is where you navigate to a storage place and open previously saved documents. Once a document is open, you can edit or print it.

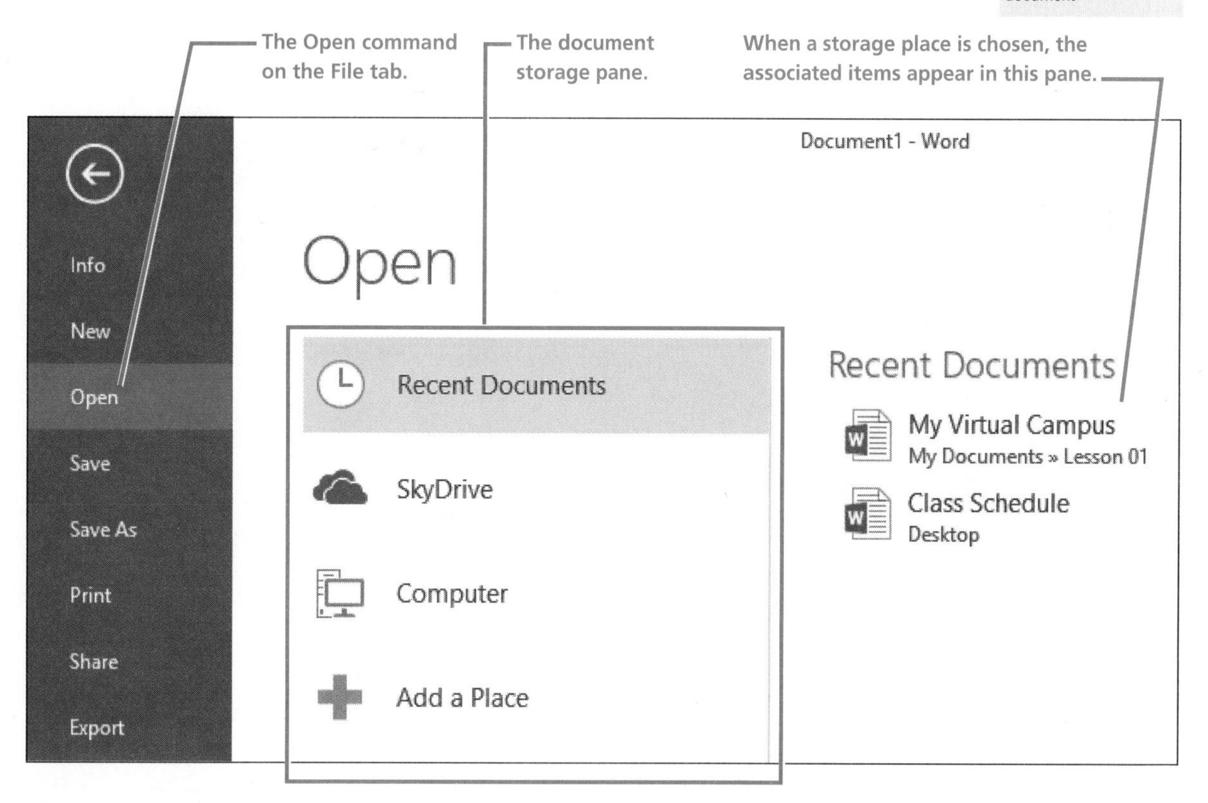

Opening Older Word Documents

If you open a document created in a previous version of an Office 2013 application (2010 and earlier), it opens in Compatibility Mode. The term appears in the Title bar. Older documents do not understand the new features in Office 2013 applications, so those features are limited or disabled.

When an older document is open, a Convert command is available in Backstage view. Use it to upgrade the file and make the new features of Office 2013 applications available. The convert process overwrites the original file.

DEVELOP YOUR SKILLS WD01-D02

Open a Document

In this exercise, you will open an existing document through the Open screen in Backstage view.

Before You Begin: Navigate to the student resource center to download the student exercise files for this book.

1. Choose **File→Open** to display the Open screen in Backstage view.
2. Double-click the **Computer** icon.
3. When the Open dialog box appears, follow these steps to open a document:

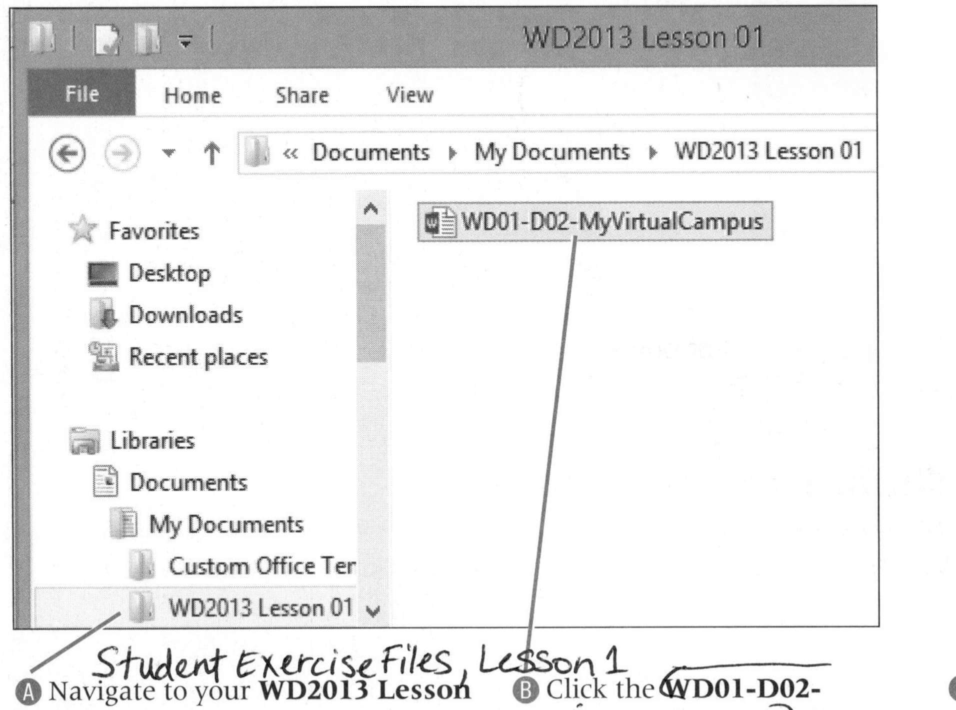

Ⓐ Navigate to your **WD2013 Lesson 01** folder. Your folder location may differ from that shown here.

Ⓑ Click the **WD01-D02-MyVirtualCampus** filename to select (highlight) it.

Ⓒ Click **Open**.

You can also double-click a filename to open the file.

4. Make sure the Word window is **maximized**.

Working with the Word 2013 Interface

Video Library http://labyrinthelab.com/videos Video Number: WD13-V0104

The band running across the top of the screen is the Ribbon. This is where you find the tools for building, formatting, and editing your documents. It consists of three primary areas: tabs, groups, and commands. The tabs include Home, Insert, Design, and so on. A group houses related commands. Groups on the Home tab, for instance, include Clipboard, Font, and Paragraph.

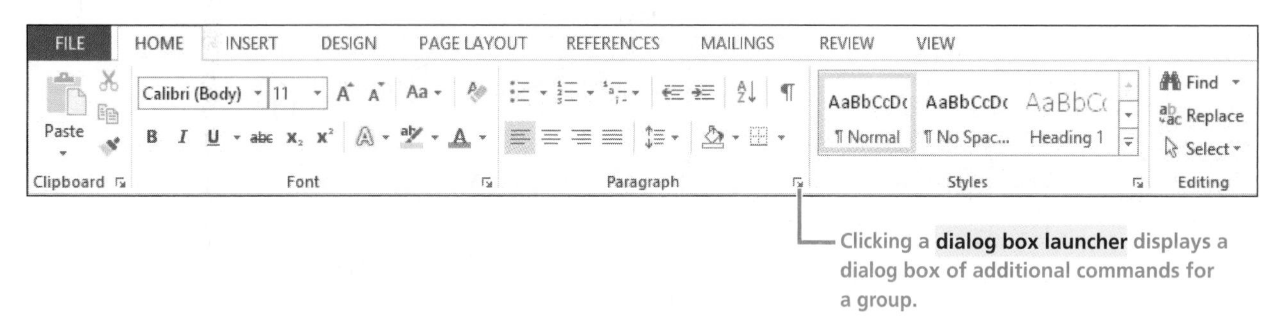

Clicking a **dialog box launcher** displays a dialog box of additional commands for a group.

The arrangement of buttons on the Ribbon can vary, depending on your screen resolution and how the Word window is sized.

FROM THE RIBBON

Right-click a tab→Collapse the Ribbon

Double-click the active tab to display the Ribbon again

FROM THE KEYBOARD

[Ctrl]+[F1] to collapse/display the Ribbon

Collapsing the Ribbon

If you want more room to work, you can collapse the Ribbon so only the tabs are visible. Clicking a tab expands the Ribbon temporarily, and then it collapses again when you work in the document.

DEVELOP YOUR SKILLS WD01-D03

X Work with the Ribbon

In this exercise, you will explore various aspects of the Ribbon, including tabs, the dialog box launcher, and collapsing and expanding the Ribbon.

1. Click the **Insert** tab on the Ribbon to display the available commands.
2. Take a moment to investigate some other tabs; return to the **Home** tab.
3. Choose **Home→Font→dialog box launcher** to open the Font dialog box.
   This dialog box provides additional tools for formatting text.
4. Click **Cancel** to close the dialog box.

Talk about the View tab
Print Layout is the default

The Ribbon
Tabs, groups, Commands

Collapse and Expand the Ribbon

5. Follow these steps to collapse and expand the Ribbon:

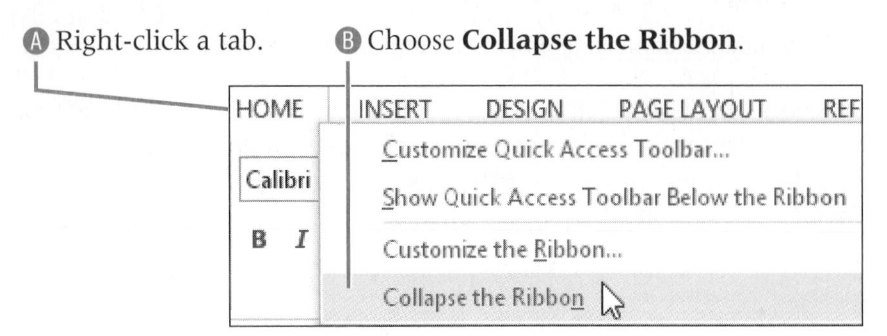

C To display the Ribbon, right-click a tab and choose **Collapse the Ribbon** to turn the feature off.

Customizing the Quick Access Toolbar

Video Library http://labyrinthelab.com/videos Video Number: WD13-V0105

The Quick Access toolbar in the upper-left corner of the Word window contains frequently used commands. You can add or remove buttons to suit your needs, and you can move the toolbar below the Ribbon if you like. If you're using a touch-mode screen, you can add a touch-mode button, which spaces buttons wider apart, making them easier to tap.

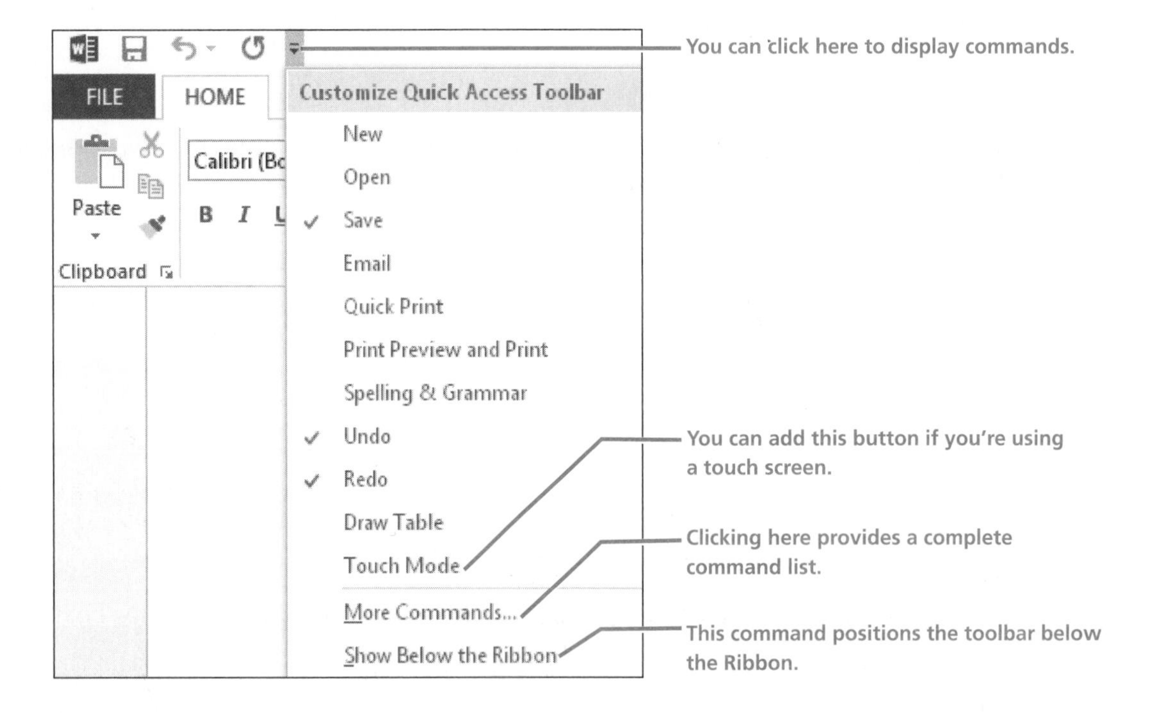

QUICK REFERENCE	WORKING WITH THE QUICK ACCESS TOOLBAR
Task	**Procedure**
Add a button	■ Click the Customize Quick Access toolbar button, and then choose a command or choose More Commands. Or, right-click a button on the Ribbon and choose Add to Quick Access Toolbar.
Remove a button	■ Right-click the button on the Quick Access toolbar you want to remove. ■ Choose Remove from Quick Access Toolbar.
Change the toolbar location	■ Click the Customize Quick Access Toolbar button. ■ Choose Show Below (or Above) the Ribbon.

DEVELOP YOUR SKILLS WD01-D04

Work with the Quick Access Toolbar

In this exercise, you will reposition the Quick Access toolbar, and then you will customize it by adding a button, and then you'll remove the button.

1. Follow these steps to move the Quick Access toolbar below the Ribbon:

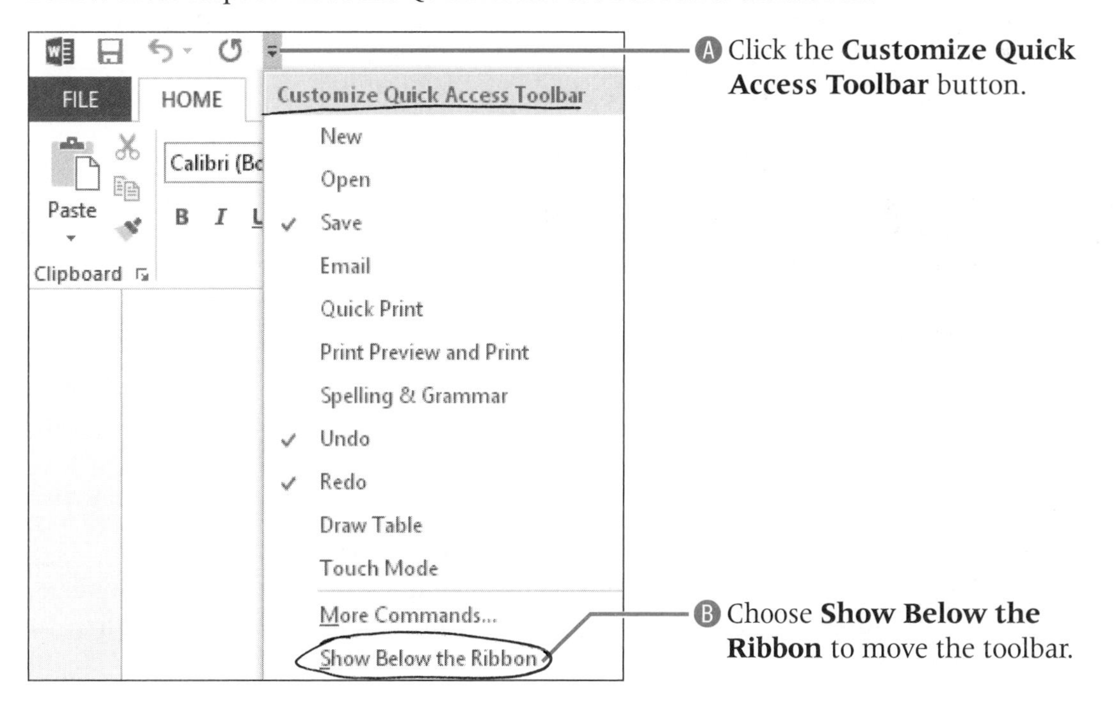

Ⓐ Click the **Customize Quick Access Toolbar** button.

Ⓑ Choose **Show Below the Ribbon** to move the toolbar.

The toolbar appears below the Ribbon. Now you will return it to its original position.

2. Click **Customize Quick Access Toolbar** again, and this time choose **Show Above the Ribbon**.
3. Make sure the **Home** tab is active.

4. Follow these steps to add the Bullets button to the toolbar:

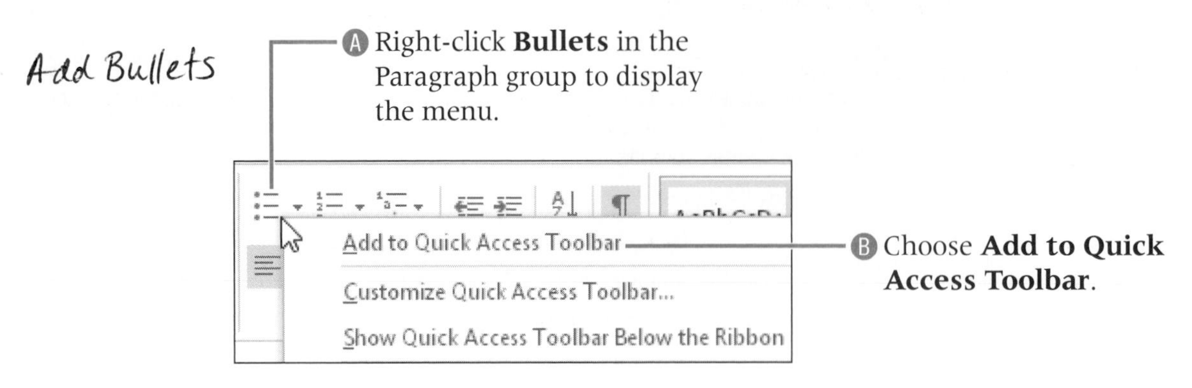

5. Follow these steps to remove the Bullets button:

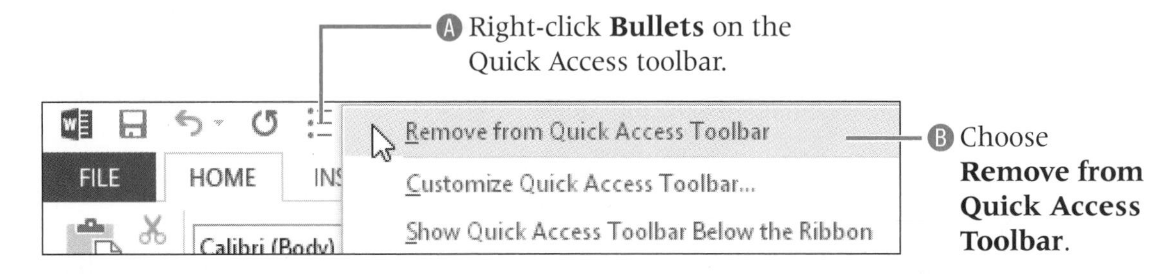

Navigating in a Word Document

Video Library http://labyrinthelab.com/videos Video Number: WD13-V0106

If you are working in a multipage document, it is helpful to know about various techniques for moving through a document. You can navigate using the scroll bar located at the right side of the screen, or you can use keystrokes.

Navigating with the Scroll Bar

The scroll bar lets you browse through documents; however, it does not move the insertion point. After scrolling, you must click in the document where you want to reposition the insertion point.

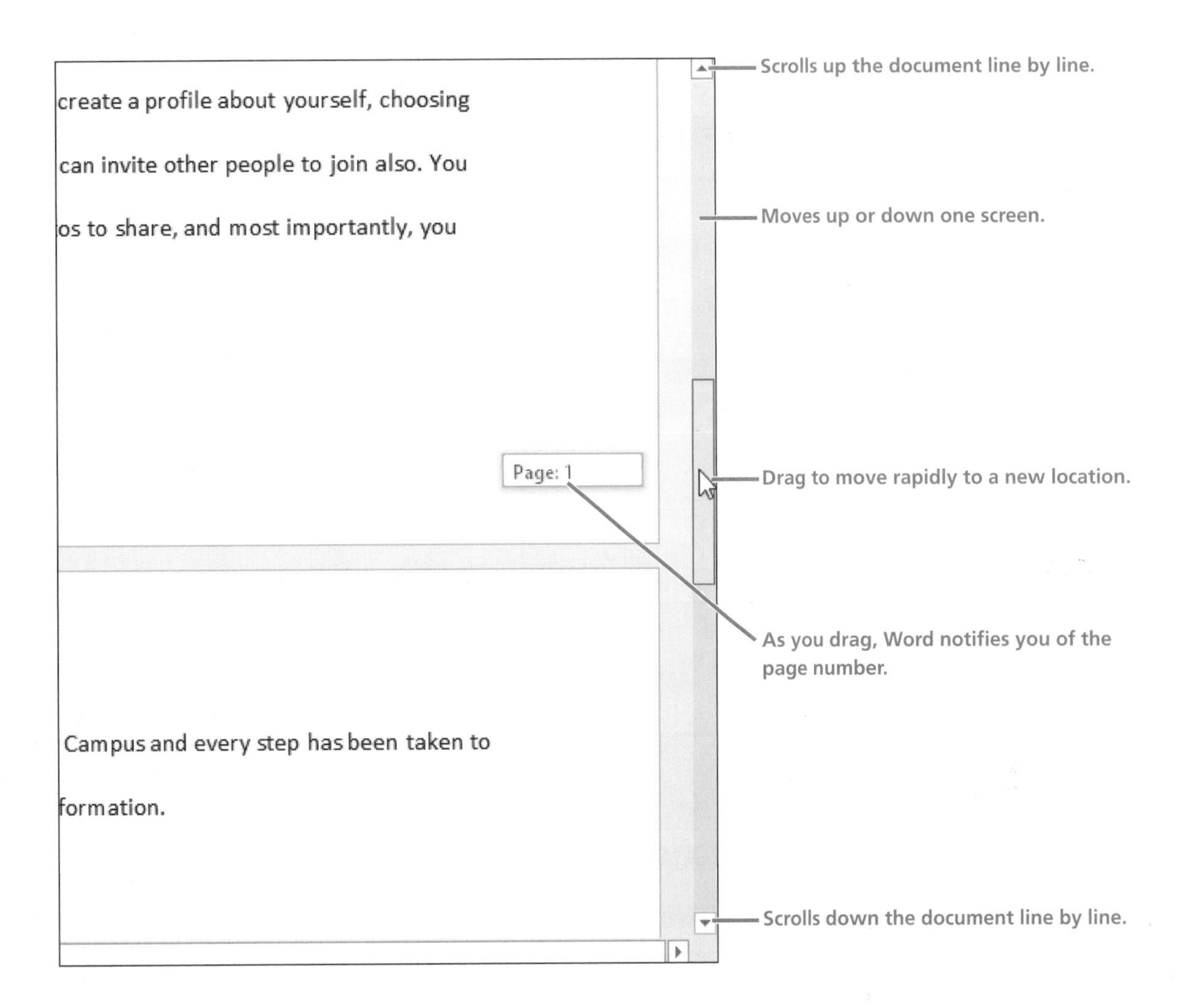

Positioning the Insertion Point

When the mouse pointer is in a text area, it resembles an uppercase "I" and is referred to as an I-beam. The insertion point is positioned at the location where you click the I-beam and it begins flashing. Wherever the insertion point is flashing is where the action begins.

DEVELOP YOUR SKILLS WD01-D05

Scroll and Position the Insertion Point

In this exercise, you will use the scroll bar to move through a document. You will also position the insertion point.

1. Follow these steps to scroll in the document:

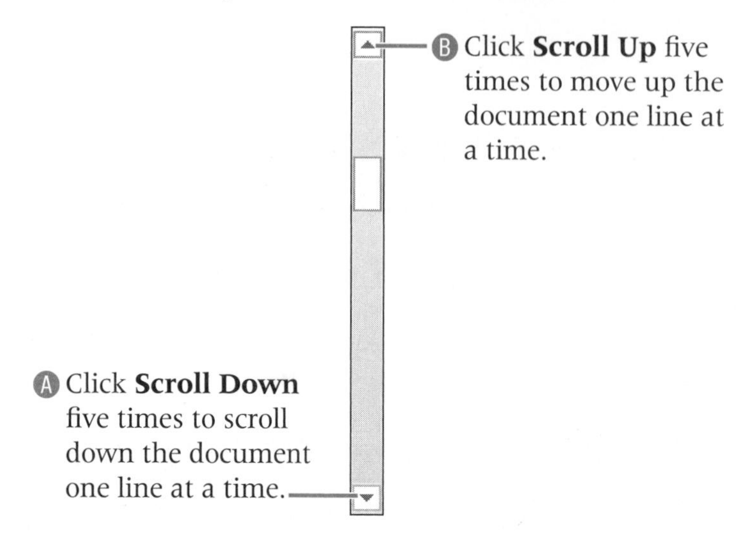

2. Place the **I-beam** mouse pointer in the body of the document.
   Notice that the mouse pointer looks like an I-beam when it's inside the document.
3. Click the **I-beam** anywhere in the document to position the blinking insertion point.
   The insertion point appears where you clicked. If the background is highlighted, you accidentally selected the text. Deselect by clicking the mouse pointer in the document background.
4. Move the mouse pointer into the left margin area.
   The white selection arrow is now visible. You'll learn more about the selection arrow later in the course.
5. Follow these steps to use the scroll bar:

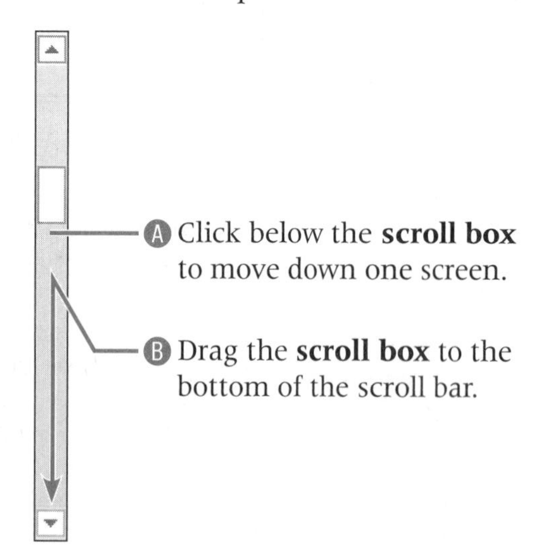

Notice that the insertion point is not blinking anywhere on the screen because all you have done is scroll through the document. You have not repositioned the insertion point yet.

6. Click the **scroll bar** above the scroll box, and then click the **I-beam** I at the end of the text to position the insertion point on the last page.
7. Drag the **scroll box** to the top of the scroll bar and click the **I-beam** I in front of the first word of the first paragraph.

Word 2013

Navigating with the Keyboard

Video Library http://labyrinthelab.com/videos Video Number: WD13-V0107

Whether you use the mouse or the keyboard to navigate through a document is up to you. Navigating with the keyboard always moves the insertion point, so it will be with you when you arrive at your destination. The following table provides keystrokes for moving quickly through a document.

KEYBOARD NAVIGATION			
Press	**To Move**	**Press**	**To Move**
→	One character to the right	Page Down	Down one screen
←	One character to the left	Page Up	Up one screen
Ctrl+→	One word to the right	Ctrl+End	To the end of the document
Ctrl+←	One word to the left	Ctrl+Home	To the beginning of the document
↓	Down one line	End	To the end of the line
↑	Up one line	Home	To the beginning of the line

DEVELOP YOUR SKILLS WD01-D06

Use the Keyboard to Navigate

In this exercise, you will use the keyboard to move through a document.

1. Click the **I-beam** I in the middle of the first line of the first paragraph.
2. Tap the right arrow → and left arrow ← three times each to move to the right and left, one character at a time.
3. Tap the down arrow ↓ and up arrow ↑ three times each to move down, and then up, one line at a time.

Use Additional Keys

Ctrl + Home

Ctrl + End

4. Press Ctrl+Home to move the insertion point to the beginning of the document.
5. Use the arrow keys to position the insertion point in the middle of the first line of the first paragraph.
6. Press Ctrl+← three times to move to the left, one word at a time.
7. Press Ctrl+→ three times to move to the right, one word at a time.

8. Tap [Home] to move to the beginning of the line.
9. Tap [End] to move to the end of the line.
10. Spend a few moments navigating with the keyboard.
11. Press [Ctrl]+[End] to move the insertion point to the end of the document.
12. Move the insertion point back to the beginning of the document.

Closing Documents

Video Library http://labyrinthelab.com/videos Video Number: WD13-V0108

FROM THE RIBBON
File→Close

FROM THE KEYBOARD
[Ctrl]+[F4] to close

Word and other Office 2013 applications offer keyboard and Ribbon options for closing a document. If you haven't saved your document, Word will prompt you to do so.

You can also use Close [×] in the upper-right corner of the Word window to close a document.

DEVELOP YOUR SKILLS WD01-D07

Close the Document

In this exercise, you will close a file.

File Close
1. Choose **File→Close**.

Don't Save
2. If Word asks you if you want to save the changes, click **Don't Save**.
3. If a blank document is open on the screen, use the same technique to close it.

Starting a New Document

Video Library http://labyrinthelab.com/videos Video Number: WD13-V0109

FROM THE RIBBON
File→New

FROM THE KEYBOARD
[Ctrl]+[N] to open a new document

In Word and other Office 2013 applications, you can start a new document using a keyboard shortcut or the Ribbon. With the keyboard shortcut, the new document is based on the Blank Document template. Using the Ribbon command offers a choice of templates in Backstage view.

DEVELOP YOUR SKILLS WD01-D08

Start a New Document (Two ways to open a new document)

In this exercise, you will open a new, blank document. There should not be any documents in the Word window at this time.

1. Press Ctrl+N to open a new document based on the Blank Document template.
   Now you will close the document and use the Ribbon command to start a new document.
2. Choose **File→Close**.
3. Choose **File→New**. - Talk about templates
   Notice that when you use the File→New command, Word gives you choices other than the Blank Document template.
4. Click the **Blank Document template** to open a new document.

Typing and Editing in Word

Video Library http://labyrinthelab.com/videos Video Number: WD13-V0110

When you insert text in an existing document, you must position the insertion point before you begin typing. When you insert text in Word, existing text moves to the right as you type. When you type paragraphs, you should not tap Enter at the end of each line. Word will automatically wrap your text to the next line when you reach the right-hand margin. You use Enter when you want short lines to remain short, such as in an inside address.

Use Backspace and Delete to remove text. The Backspace key deletes characters to the left of the insertion point. The Delete key removes characters to the right of the insertion point.

Saving Your Work

It's important to save your documents! Power outages and accidents can result in lost data, so save frequently.

You can also use Save on the Quick Access toolbar.

FROM THE RIBBON
File→Save As
File→Save

FROM THE KEYBOARD
Ctrl+S to save

Comparing Save and Save As

If the document was never saved, Word displays the Save As screen. If the document was previously saved, the Save command replaces the prior version with the edited one without displaying the Save As screen.

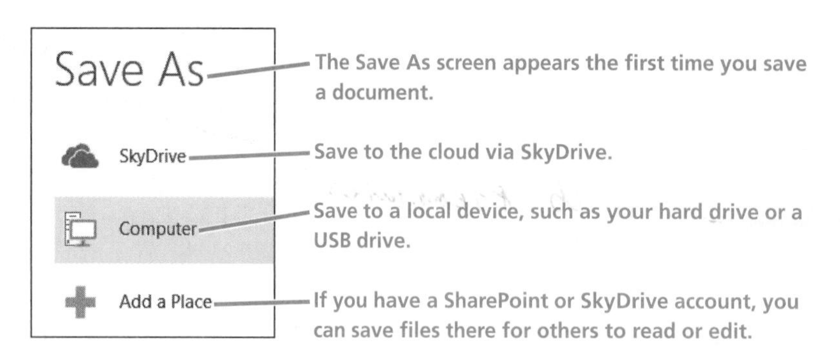

Storing documents in SkyDrive is beyond the scope of this course. You will save your files on a local device.

After choosing a place in the Save As screen, the Save As dialog box opens where you will navigate to your storage location and name and save the file.

Word's DOCX File Format

Word 2003 and earlier versions saved documents in the *doc* file format. Word 2007 introduced the *docx* file format. Users of Word 2003 and prior versions may not be able to read Word files in the *docx* format. However, you can choose to save your document in the older *doc* format to maintain backward compatibility. Also, when you open a document created in earlier Word versions, the title bar displays *Compatibility Mode* next to the title. This means certain Word 2013 features not compatible with older versions are turned off while working in the document.

DEVELOP YOUR SKILLS WD01-D09

Create and Save a Document

In this exercise, you will begin by saving your document (in this case a blank document). This technique is used throughout this course so you can start each exercise with a fresh file.

1. Click **Save** on the Quick Access toolbar.

   Since this is the first time you are saving this document, Word displays the Save As screen in Backstage view. Once you have saved the file, this button saves the current version of the file over the old version without displaying the Save As screen.

2. Double-click the **Computer** icon to open the Save As dialog box.

3. Follow these steps to save your document:

   Keep in mind that your dialog box may contain different files and folders than shown here.

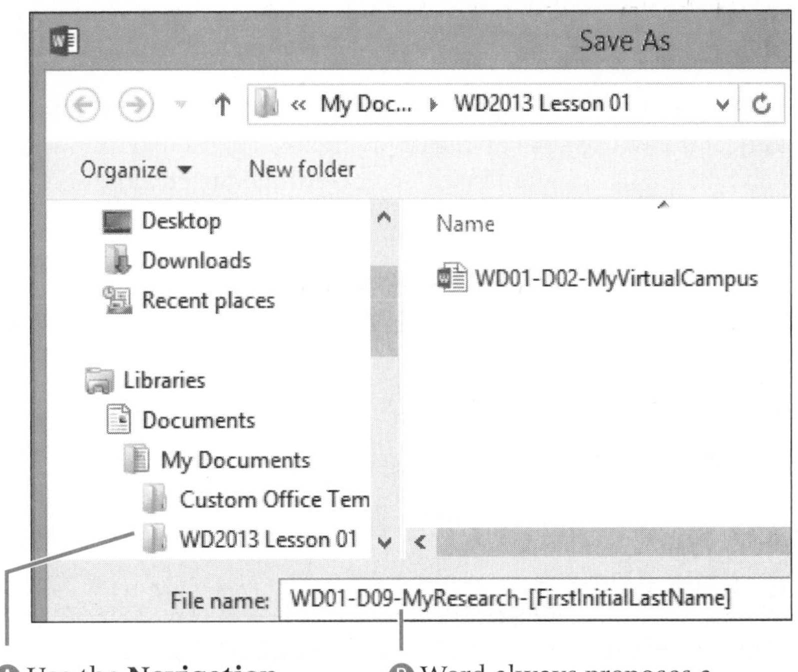

Save to My Data Folder

Ⓐ Use the **Navigation pane** to locate and open your **WD2013 Lesson 01** folder.

Ⓑ Word always proposes a filename. Replace it with **`WD01-D09-MyResearch-[FirstInitialLastName]`**.

Ⓒ Click **Save**.

   In step B, replace the bracketed text with your first initial and last name. For example, if your name is Bethany Smith, your filename would look like this: WD01-D09-MyResearch-BSmith.

4. Type the following text and let Word Wrap do its thing.

   If you make a typo, use Backspace *or* Delete *to remove it. Remember to position the insertion point next to the typo.*

   `In general, here's how it works. You join and create a profile about yourself, choosing how much personal information to enter. Then you can invite other people to join also. You can chat in real-time with other members, post photos to share, and most importantly, you control what information others can see about you.`

5. **Save** the file and leave it open.

Getting Help in Word 2013

Video Library http://labyrinthelab.com/videos Video Number: WD13-V0111

The Microsoft Word Help button appears in the upper-right corner of the Word screen and other Office 2013 application screens. The Help window contains a search box, a list of popular searches, Getting Started aids, and online training options.

FROM THE KEYBOARD
[F1] to open Help

DEVELOP YOUR SKILLS WD01-D10

Use Word Help

In this exercise, you will work with several Help techniques.

1. Click **Help** [?] in the upper-right corner of the Word window.
2. Follow these steps for an overview of Word Help:

Ⓐ Hover the mouse pointer over these buttons to display **ToolTips**.

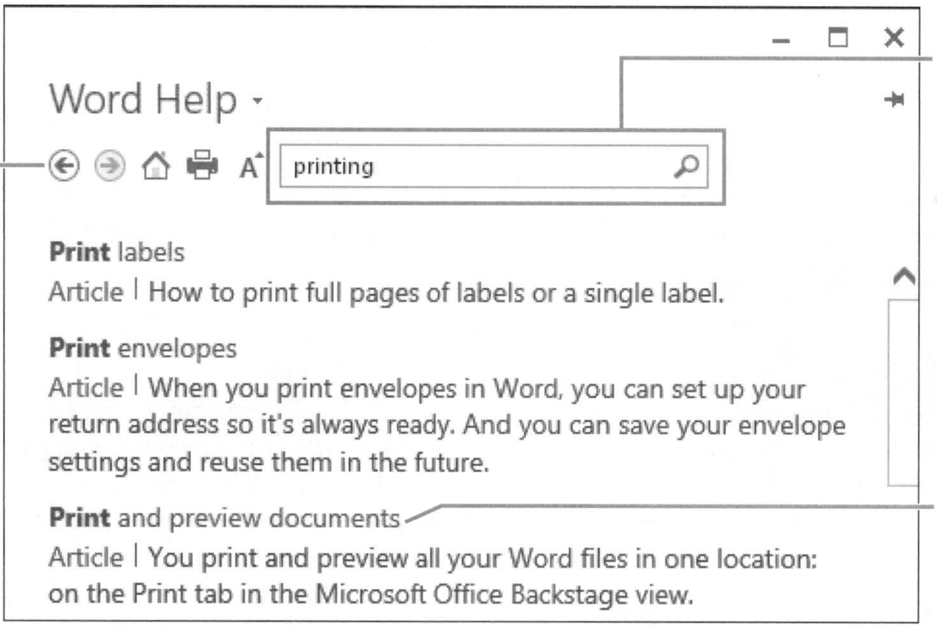

Ⓑ Position the insertion point here; type `printing`, and then click **Search Online Help** (the magnifying glass icon).

Ⓒ Click **Print and Preview Documents** and scroll down to view the instructions.

3. Take a few moments to experiment with Help. Try searching for `save` and `compatibility mode`. Feel free to explore any topics that interest you.
4. Click **Close** [×] in the upper-right corner of the Help window.

Exiting from Word

Video Library http://labyrinthelab.com/videos Video Number: WD13-V0112

You exit Word and other Office 2013 applications by clicking the Close button in the upper-right corner of the window. If you have more than one document open, you need to close each document. It's important to exit your application in an orderly fashion. Turning off your computer before exiting could cause you to lose data.

DEVELOP YOUR SKILLS WD01-D11

Exit from Word

In this exercise, you will exit from Word. Since you haven't made any changes to your document, you won't bother saving it again.

1. Click **Close** [×] in the upper-right corner of the Word window.
2. If you are prompted to save your changes, click **Don't Save**.
3. If you have more than one document open, close any remaining documents without saving.
   Word closes and the Windows Desktop appears.

Concepts Review

To check your knowledge of the key concepts introduced in this lesson, complete the Concepts Review quiz by choosing the appropriate access option below.

If you are...	Then access the quiz by...
Using the Labyrinth Video Library	Going to http://labyrinthelab.com/videos
Using eLab	Logging in, choosing Content, and navigating to the Concepts Review quiz for this lesson
Not using the Labyrinth Video Library or eLab	Going to the student resource center for this book

Reinforce Your Skills

REINFORCE YOUR SKILLS WD01-R01

Work with the Word Interface

In this exercise, you will start Word and examine the Start screen and Word window. You will use correct terminology for the Word window, and you will collapse and expand the Ribbon. Finally, you will customize the Quick Access toolbar.

Start Word and Examine the Word Start Screen

1. Start **Word** and note how the Start screen helps you begin your work.
2. Open **WD01-R01-Worksheet** from your **WD2013 Lesson 01** folder and save it as `WD01-R01-Worksheet-[FirstInitialLastName]`.
3. Refer to your worksheet and list three ways the Start screen helps you begin your work.

Word Terminology

It's important to use the correct terms when talking about Word. If you need to discuss an issue with your IT department, the staff can help you more efficiently if they are clear on what you are referring to.

4. In your worksheet, enter the correct terms for items A–F in the following illustration.

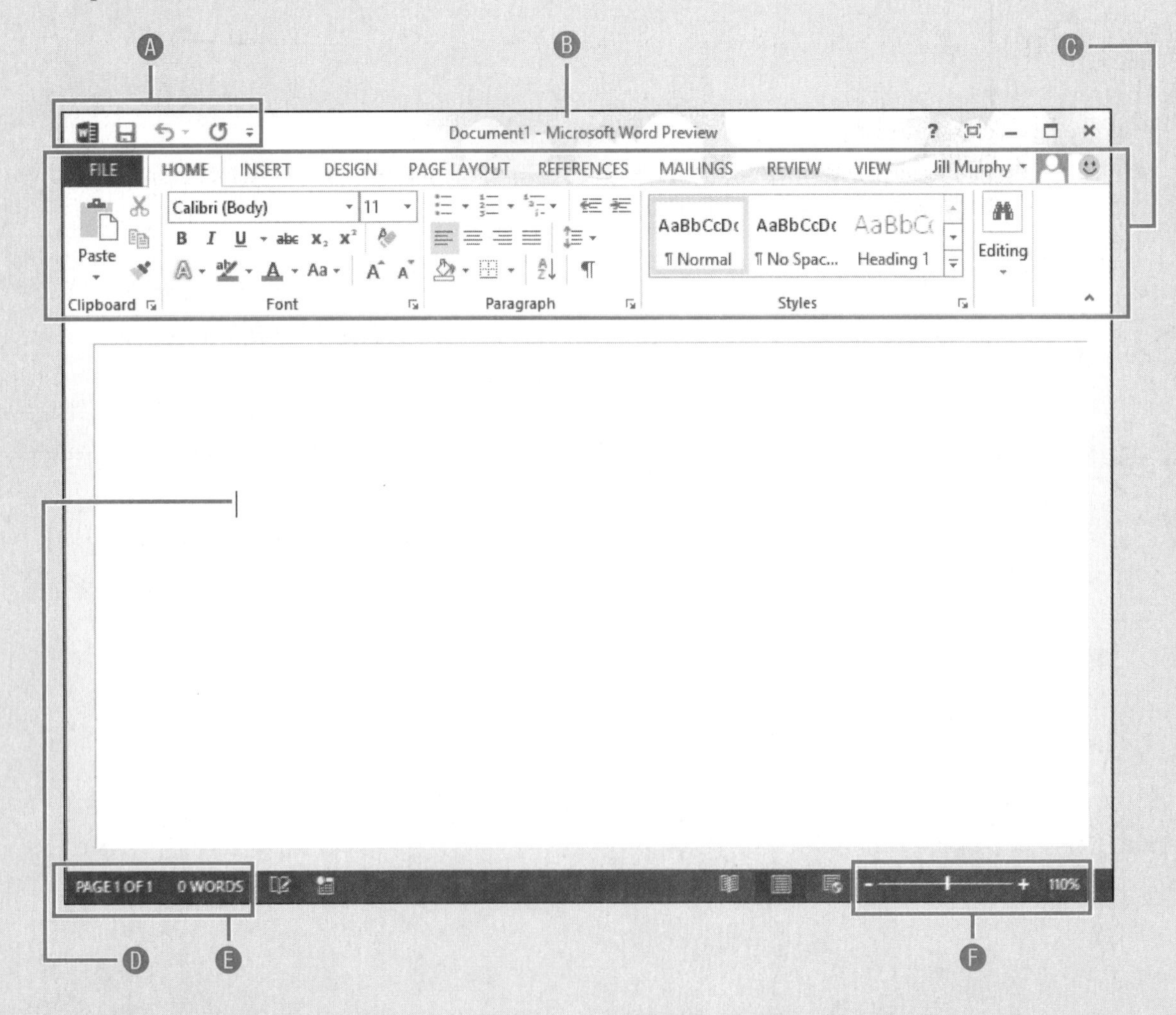

Open a Document

5. Refer to your worksheet and enter the phrase that appears in **Word's title bar** when you open a file that was created in an earlier version of Word.
6. Navigate to your **WD2013 Lesson 01** folder and open **WD01-R01-FarmersMarket**.
7. Refer to your worksheet and enter the name of the group that organized the field trip to the farmers' market.

Collapse the Ribbon

8. Collapse the **Ribbon**.
9. In your worksheet, list the steps you took to complete step 8.
10. Expand the **Ribbon**.

The Quick Access Toolbar

11. Move the **Quick Access toolbar** below the Ribbon.
12. In your worksheet, list the steps you took to complete step 11.
13. Choose **Page Layout→Page Setup** and add **Margins** to the Quick Access toolbar.
14. In your worksheet, list the steps you took to complete step 13.
15. Move the **Quick Access** toolbar back above the Ribbon.
16. Remove **Margins** from the toolbar.
17. Save your worksheet, close all files, and exit from **Word**. Submit your final file based on the guidelines provided by your instructor.

    To view examples of how your file or files should look at the end of this exercise, go to the student resource center.

REINFORCE YOUR SKILLS WD01-R02

Navigate in Word, Type a Document, and Use Help

In this exercise, you will use mouse and keyboard techniques to navigate in a multipage document. Then you will close the document, open and type in a new document, and then save your work. Finally, you will use Word's Help feature, and then exit from Word.

Navigate with the Scroll Bar and Keyboard

1. Start **Word**. Open **WD01-R02-Worksheet** from your **WD2013 Lesson 01** folder and save it as `WD01-R02-Worksheet-[FirstInitialLastName]`.
2. Open **WD01-R02-KidsNewsletter** from your **WD2013 Lesson 01** folder.
3. Follow these steps to scroll in the document:

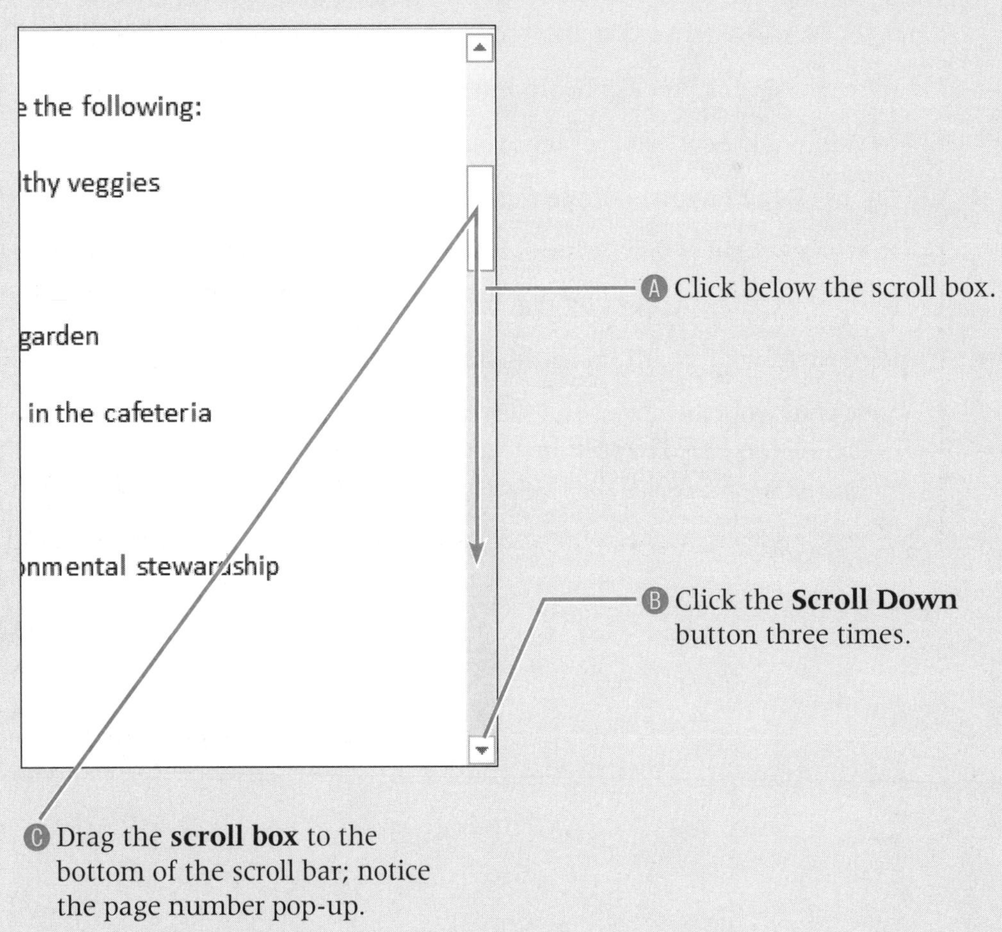

4. Hover the mouse pointer over the body of the document and notice the pointer shape, and then hover the mouse pointer in the left margin and notice its shape.

5. Press Ctrl+Home and notice the position of the insertion point.
6. Position the insertion point in the middle of the first line of the first paragraph and press Ctrl+→ three times.
7. Tap Home and notice the position of the insertion point.
8. Press Ctrl+End and notice the position of the insertion point.
9. Refer to your worksheet and answer the questions for steps 4–8.

Close the Document and Start a New Document

10. Choose **File→Close** to close **WD01-R02-KidsNewsletter**. If you are prompted to save changes, click **Don't Save**.
11. Choose **File→New** and open a new document using the **Blank Document template**.
12. Choose **File→Close** to close the new document, and then press Ctrl+N to start a new document.

    The new document is based on the Blank Document template.
13. Type the following text using Backspace or Delete to correct typos.

    The Kids for Change "Think Globally, Act Locally" program is designed to help young people develop their understanding of an increasingly interrelated world. We have an exciting guest speaker for our next monthly meeting.
14. Refer to your worksheet and answer the questions for steps 11–13.

Save Your Document

15. Choose **File→Save As** from the Ribbon and navigate to your **WD2013 Lesson 01** folder.
16. Save your document as **WD01-R02-GuestSpeaker-[FirstInitialLastName]**.

The Kids for Change "Think Globally, Act Locally" program is designed to help young people develop their understanding of an increasingly interrelated world. We have an exciting guest speaker for our next monthly meeting.

17. Choose File→Close to close the document.
18. Refer to your worksheet and answer the question for step 16.
19. Choose **File→Open**, navigate to your **WD2013 Lesson 01** folder, and open **WD01-R02-FarmVisitLtr**.

    This document was created in Word 2003, which means it is a doc *file rather than a Word 2013* docx *file. Notice the phrase to the right of the file name in the title bar.*

Explore Help and Exit from Word

20. Click **Help** [?] in the upper-right corner of the Word window.
21. Use the **Search Box** to search for `Undo`, and then click the **Undo, Redo, or Repeat an Action** link.

    Make a note of the shortcut keystrokes for Undo.
22. Use the Help **Search Box** to search for `Clipboard` and click the **Use the Office Clipboard** link. Read the first paragraph of the Help text, and make a note of what is stored in the Clipboard.
23. **Close** [×] the **Help** window. Then, choose **File→Close** to close **WD01-R02-FarmVisitLtr.**
24. Refer to your worksheet and answer the questions for steps 20–22.
25. Save your worksheet, and exit from **Word**. Submit your final files based on the guidelines provided by your instructor.

    To view examples of how your file or files should look at the end of this exercise, go to the student resource center.

REINFORCE YOUR SKILLS WD01-R03

Use the Word Interface and Work with Documents

In this exercise, you will work with the Word interface, open and navigate in an existing document, and create and save a new document. Finally, you will work with Word Help, and then exit from Word.

Do in class

Start Word and Examine the Word Start Screen

1. Start **Word**. Open **WD01-R03-Worksheet** from your **WD2013 Lesson 01** folder and save it as `WD01-R03-Worksheet-[FirstInitialLastName]`.
2. Refer to your worksheet and answer the step 2 question.

Word Window Terminology

3. Refer to your worksheet and answer the step 3 questions.

Open a Document and Collapse the Ribbon

4. Choose **File→Open** from the Ribbon and open **WD01-R03-OrgsPrtctEarth**.
5. Refer to your worksheet and answer the step 5 question.

The Quick Access Toolbar

6. In your worksheet, list the steps for removing a button from the Quick Access toolbar.

Navigate with the Scroll Bar and Keyboard

7. Refer to your worksheet and answer the step 7 questions.

Close a Document and Start a New Document

8. Choose **File→Close** to close WD01-R03-OrgsPrtctEarth.
9. Choose **File→New** and start a new document using the **Blank Document template**.
10. Type the following text:

    ```
    Organizations that are founded to protect our earth work in
    concert with nature through activities such as planting and
    caring for trees, protecting groundwater, and restoring wetlands.
    They work at the local, state, national, and international levels
    to improve policy for short- and long-term solutions. Their goal
    is to achieve a healthy planet. Kids for Change helps to connect
    kids to organizations such as these.
    ```
11. Refer to your worksheet and answer the step 11 questions.

Save Your Document in the Word DOCX File Format

12. Choose **File→Save**, navigate to your **WD2013 Lesson 01** folder, and save your document as `WD01-R03-HealthyPlanet-[FirstInitialLastName]`.
13. Refer to your worksheet and answer the step 13 question.

Get Help and Exit from Word

14. Click **Help** [?] in the upper-right corner of the Word window.
15. Refer to step 15 in your worksheet, and use **ToolTips** to identify the buttons in the upper-left corner of the Help window.
16. **Close** [×] the **Help** window.
17. Click **Close** [×] in the upper-right corner of the Word window to close the document. Close any other open documents.
18. Save your worksheet, and exit from **Word**. Submit your final files based on the guidelines provided by your instructor.

Apply Your Skills

APPLY YOUR SKILLS WD01-A01

Open a Document and Work with the Word Interface

In this exercise, you will open a document and scroll through it to determine its length. You will examine the Ribbon in some detail, modify the Quick Access toolbar, and collapse the Ribbon. Finally you will return the Ribbon and the Quick Access toolbar to their default states.

Start Word and Open a Document

1. Start **Word**. Click the **Open Other Documents** link on the left side of the Word Start screen below the Recent list.
2. Navigate to your **WD213 Lesson 01** folder, open **WD01-A01-Worksheet**, and save it as **`WD01-A01-Worksheet-[FirstInitialLastName]`**.
3. Open **WD01-A01-CorpEvents** from your **WD2013 Lesson 01** folder.
4. Refer to your worksheet and answer the question for step 4.

Work with the Word 2013 Interface

5. Refer to your worksheet, and respond to step 5.
6. Choose **Insert→Illustrations** and add the **SmartArt** button to the **Quick Access** toolbar.
7. Position the **Quick Access toolbar** below the Ribbon; then collapse the **Ribbon**.
8. Tap Prt Screen on your keyboard to capture a picture of your screen.
9. Start a blank document and paste the screen capture into the document.
10. Save the file as **`WD01-A01-ScreenShot-[FirstInitialLastName]`** in your **WD2013 Lesson 01** folder.
11. Remove the **SmartArt** button from the **Quick Access** toolbar, expand the **Ribbon**, and move the **Quick Access** toolbar above the Ribbon.
12. Choose File→Close to close **WD01-A01-CorpEvents** and **WD01-A01-ScreenShot-[FirstInitialLastName]**.
13. Save your worksheet, and exit from **Word**. Submit your final files based on the guidelines provided by your instructor.

    To view examples of how your file or files should look at the end of this exercise, go to the student resource center.

APPLY YOUR SKILLS WD01-A02

Navigate in Word, Create a Document, and Use Help

In this exercise, you will open a document and scroll through it, and then you will create and save a document. Finally, you will use Help to learn about saving a Word file as a PDF file.

Word 2013

Navigate in Word

1. Start **Word**. Open **WD01-A02-Worksheet** from your **WD2013 Lesson 01** folder and save it as `WD01-A02-Worksheet-[FirstInitialLastName]`.
2. Open **WD01-A02-UniversalEvents** from your **WD2013 Lesson 01** folder.
3. Scroll to the bottom of the document, click the **scroll box**, and then, referring to your worksheet, respond to the question for step 3.
4. Choose File→Close to close **WD01-A02-UniversalEvents** and start a new blank document based on the **Blank Document template**.

Type and Save a New Document

5. Type the following:

   `Universal Corporate Events will manage every phase of your corporate travel needs. We work directly with travelers to provide the flights that meet their needs, and we arrange ground transportation to and from all events. We have staff available 24x7 to assist travelers if any unforeseen situations arise.`

6. Save the file as `WD01-A02-Travel-[FirstInitialLastName]` in your **WD2013 Lesson 01** folder, and then close it.

Use Help

7. Open **Help** [?], search for **`Save`**, and click the **Save as PDF** link.
8. Press [Alt]+[Prt Screen] to capture a picture of the Help screen.
9. Paste the screenshot in your worksheet where indicated, and save the worksheet.
10. Close **Help**, close any open documents, and then exit from **Word**.
11. Submit your final files based on the guidelines provided by your instructor.

    To view examples of how your file or files should look at the end of this exercise, go to the student resource center.

APPLY YOUR SKILLS WD01-A03

Use the Ribbon and Use Help to Research Word Features

In this exercise, you will use the dialog box launcher on the Ribbon to open dialog boxes, and you will research terms in Word Help. Finally, you will type a document showing the results of your research.

Start a New Document and Use a Dialog Box Launcher

1. Start **Word**. Start a new document based on the **Blank Document template**.
2. Choose **Home→Paragraph→dialog box launcher**.

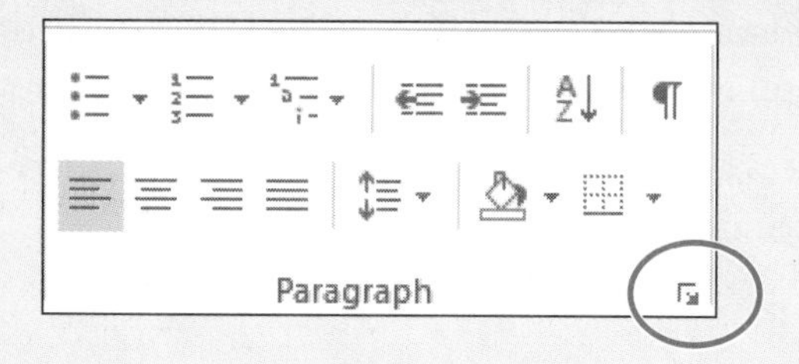

3. Click the **Line and Page Breaks** tab and notice the term Widow/Orphan Control under the Pagination heading; close the dialog box.
4. Type `HELP RESEARCH` at the top of your document and tap Enter.

Use Help

5. Open **Help** and search for `Widow/Orphan Control`.
6. Click the **Add a Page Break** link.
7. Scroll down and note what the **Widow/Orphan Control** feature accomplishes.
8. Minimize the **Help** window, and type a description of **Widow/Orphan Control** in your document.
   Minimize and restore the Help window as needed.
9. Click the **dialog box launcher** in the Font group, notice the term **Superscript** in the Effects section, and then close the dialog box.
10. Search for `Superscript` in Help and click the **"Superscript" is under "Home/Font"** link. Note the description of Superscript.
11. Type a description of superscript in your document, and then search in Help for `Save`.
12. Click the **Save Documents Online** link, and type a short description of how you save a document to the SkyDrive.
13. Save your file as `WD01-A03-HelpResearch-[FirstInitialLastName]` in the **WD2013 Lesson 01** folder.
14. Submit your final file based on the guidelines provided by your instructor.

Extend Your Skills

In the course of working through the Extend Your Skills exercises, you will think critically as you use the skills taught in the lesson to complete the assigned projects. To evaluate your mastery and completion of the exercises, your instructor may use a rubric, with which more points are allotted according to performance characteristics. (The more you do, the more you earn!) Ask your instructor how your work will be evaluated.

WD01-E01 That's the Way I See It

As an IT professional, you realize that many people need help adapting to Office 2013. You decide to start your own consulting business to fill this need. Your first client would like assistance with customizing the Quick Access toolbar in order to work more effectively. So, you will create a handout in Word that lists the steps for customizing the Quick Access toolbar.

Because your client uses a laptop, she would like to learn to collapse the Ribbon to free up space on the screen. Include instructions for collapsing the Ribbon in your handout. Finally, the client is interested in learning more about saving files "in the cloud." In the handout, include instructions for how to search Help for information on saving files in SkyDrive.

Save your handout as **`WD01-E01-WordHandout-[FirstInitialLastName]`** in your **WD2013 Lesson 01** folder. You will be evaluated based on the inclusion of all elements specified, your ability to follow directions, your ability to apply newly learned skills to a real-world situation, your creativity, and the relevance of your topic and/or data choice(s). Submit your final file based on the guidelines provided by your instructor.

WD01-E02 Be Your Own Boss

You are the owner of Blue Jean Landscaping and are also a bit of a "techie." You have decided to upgrade the company from Word 2010 to Word 2013. You want to provide online tutorials and reference materials to aid employees in the conversion. Start Word and use Help or online resources to locate three aids for this purpose (for example, opening older Word documents in Word 2013, Touch Mode, or how the Ribbon look has changed). Create a document named **`WD01-E02-WordResources-[FirstInitialLastName]`** and save it in the **WD2013 Lesson 01** folder. In the document, include the resource information and explain how each will help the employees (write three to five sentences per topic). Don't list resources without including an explanation.

You will be evaluated based on the inclusion of all elements specified, your ability to follow directions, your ability to apply newly learned skills to a real-world situation, your creativity, and your demonstration of an entrepreneurial spirit. Submit your final file based on the guidelines provided by your instructor.

Transfer Your Skills

In the course of working through the Transfer Your Skills exercises, you will use critical-thinking and creativity skills to complete the assigned projects using skills taught in the lesson. To evaluate your mastery and completion of the exercises, your instructor may use a rubric, with which more points are allotted according to performance characteristics. (The more you do, the more you earn!) Ask your instructor how your work will be evaluated.

WD01-T01 Use the Web as a Learning Tool

Throughout this book, you will be provided with an opportunity to use the Internet as a learning tool by completing WebQuests. According to the original creators of WebQuests, as described on their website (WebQuest.org), a WebQuest is "an inquiry-oriented activity in which most or all of the information used by learners is drawn from the web." To complete the WebQuest projects in this book, navigate to the student resource center and choose the WebQuest for the lesson on which you are currently working. The subject of each WebQuest will be relevant to the material found in the lesson.

WebQuest Subject: How Microsoft Word is used in business.

Submit your final file(s) based on the guidelines provided by your instructor.

WD01-T02 Demonstrate Proficiency

As the owner of Stormy BBQ, you have decided to customize the Word interface to help you work more effectively. In particular, you want to add buttons to the Quick Access toolbar that will help you in creating a brochure advertising your fresh, locally-grown vegetables and local, farm-raised pork and beef ribs.

Start Word and open a new, blank document. Examine the buttons on the Ribbon to determine which will be most useful for you. You may wish to use ToolTips or Help to determine the purpose of some of the buttons. Add five buttons to the Quick Access toolbar, and then list specific reasons for choosing each. Indicate if you prefer to have the Quick Access toolbar above or below the Ribbon and state the reason for your preference. Take a screen shot of your customized toolbar and paste it into your Word document. Reset the Quick Access toolbar to its default state when you are finished.

Save your file as **`WD01-T02-CustomizeWord-[FirstInitialLastName]`** in your **WD2013 Lesson 01** folder. Submit your final file based on the guidelines provided by your instructor.

WORD 2013

Creating and Editing Business Letters

LESSON OUTLINE

- Defining Typical Business Letter Styles
- Inserting Text
- Creating an Envelope
- Selecting Text
- Editing Text
- Working with AutoCorrect
- Copying and Moving Text
- Switching Between Documents
- Using Page Layout Options
- Working with Print and Print Preview
- Concepts Review
- **Reinforce Your Skills**
- **Apply Your Skills**
- **Extend Your Skills**
- **Transfer Your Skills**

LEARNING OBJECTIVES

After studying this lesson, you will be able to:

- Select and edit text and use AutoCorrect
- Set AutoFormat As You Type options
- Copy and move text
- Set page layout options
- Preview and print a document

In this lesson, you will create business letters while learning proper business letter formatting. You will learn techniques for entering and editing text, copying and moving text, and printing documents. In addition, you will learn to use Word's AutoComplete and AutoCorrect tools to insert frequently used text and to control automatic formatting that Word applies as you type.

CASE STUDY

Taking Care with Business Letters

You are a sales assistant at My Virtual Campus. A new prospect, Richmond University, has expressed interest in the networking website that My Virtual Campus sells. The sales manager has asked you to prepare a standard letter for potential new clients, thanking them for their interest and providing information about the website.

You start by referring to your business writing class textbook to ensure that you format the letter correctly for a good first impression and a professional appearance.

November 24, 2013

Ms. Paige Daniels
Richmond University
15751 Meadow Lane
Chester Allen, VA 23333

Dear Ms. Daniels:

Travis Mayfield referred you to us after he spoke with you about our extraordinary product. I want to take this opportunity to personally thank you for considering My Virtual Campus' social-networking website for your institution. As Travis may have mentioned, we pride ourselves in providing the latest in technology as well as excellent customer service with satisfaction guaranteed.

Enclosed you will find information to review regarding the features of the website. After reading the material, please contact our sales manager, Bruce Carter, at your earliest convenience to discuss your options. Thank you again for considering our amazing website.

Sincerely,

<your name>
Customer Service Representative
Sales Department

<typist's initials if other than sender>
Enclosures (2)
cc: Bruce Carter

Defining Typical Business Letter Styles

Video Library http://labyrinthelab.com/videos Video Number: WD13-V0201

There are several acceptable styles of business letters. The styles discussed in this text include block and modified block. All business letters contain similar elements but with varied formatting.

Block Style

The block style is the most common business-letter style. All elements are single spaced and left aligned, except for double spacing between paragraphs.

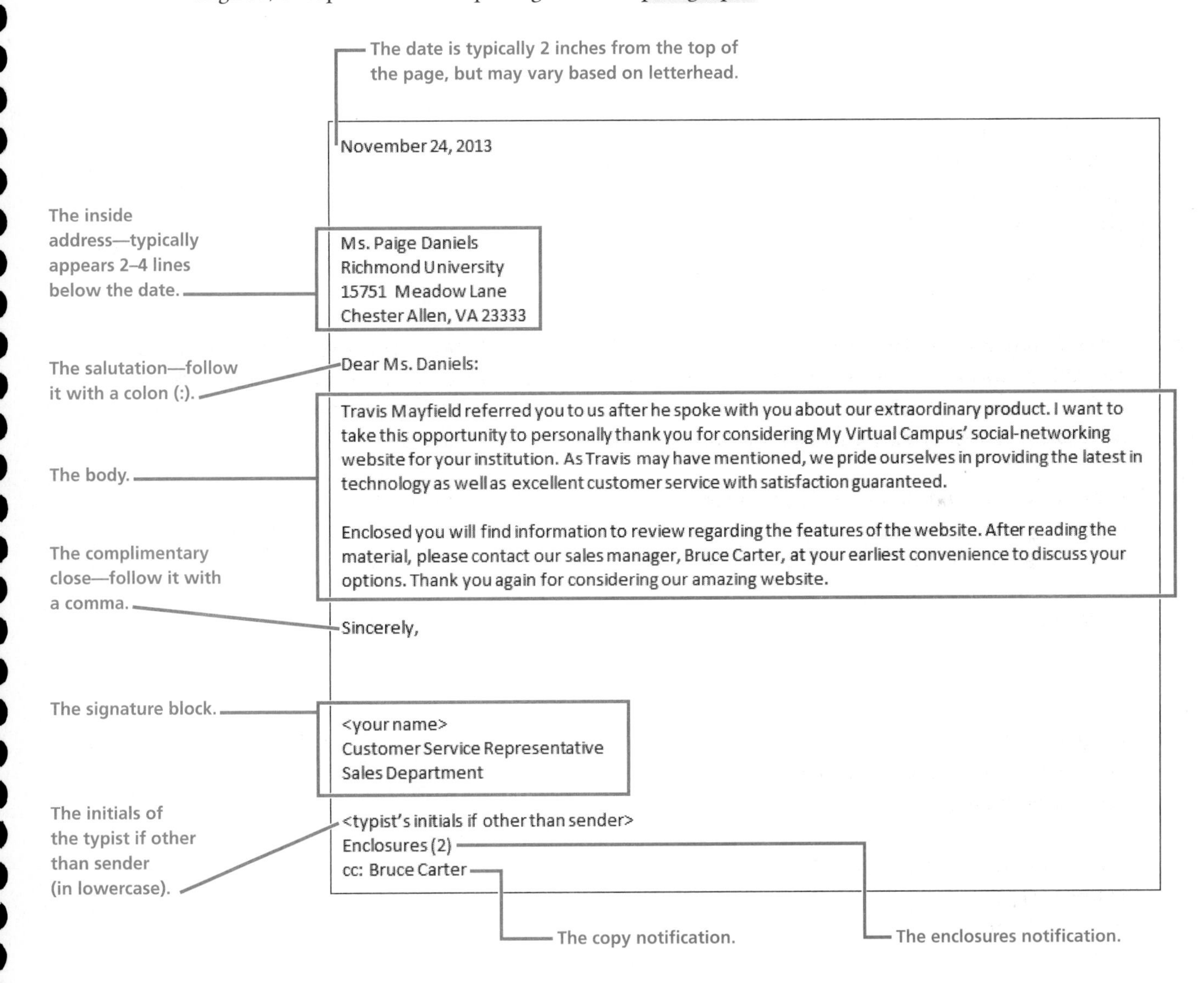

November 24, 2013

Ms. Paige Daniels
Richmond University
15751 Meadow Lane
Chester Allen, VA 23333

Dear Ms. Daniels:

Travis Mayfield referred you to us after he spoke with you about our extraordinary product. I want to take this opportunity to personally thank you for considering My Virtual Campus' social-networking website for your institution. As Travis may have mentioned, we pride ourselves in providing the latest in technology as well as excellent customer service with satisfaction guaranteed.

Enclosed you will find information to review regarding the features of the website. After reading the material, please contact our sales manager, Bruce Carter, at your earliest convenience to discuss your options. Thank you again for considering our amazing website.

Sincerely,

<your name>
Customer Service Representative
Sales Department

<typist's initials if other than sender>
Enclosures (2)
cc: Bruce Carter

Modified Block Style

Modified block is another commonly use letter format. The following illustration points out the differences in the modified block-style business letter compared to the block-style business letter.

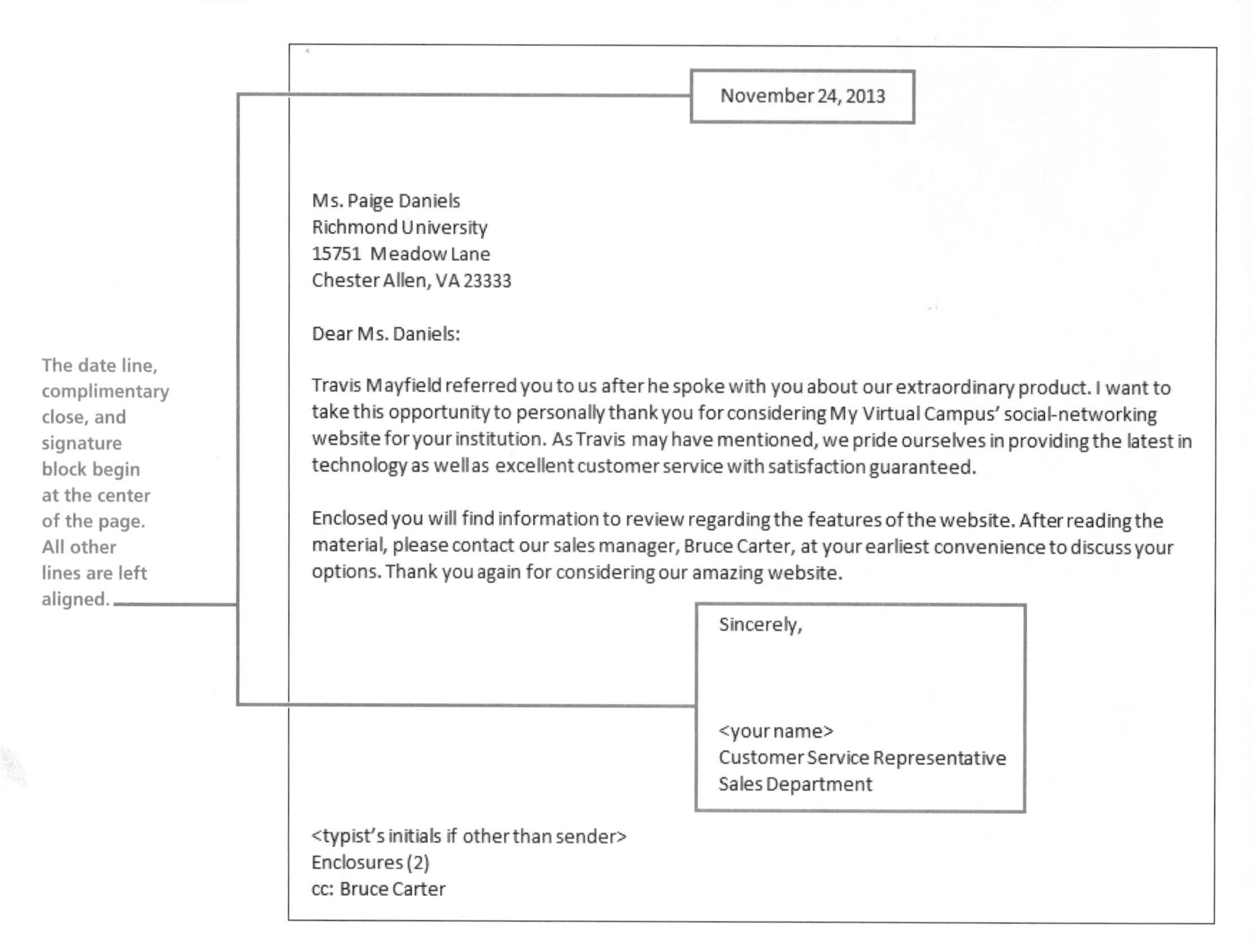

November 24, 2013

Ms. Paige Daniels
Richmond University
15751 Meadow Lane
Chester Allen, VA 23333

Dear Ms. Daniels:

Travis Mayfield referred you to us after he spoke with you about our extraordinary product. I want to take this opportunity to personally thank you for considering My Virtual Campus' social-networking website for your institution. As Travis may have mentioned, we pride ourselves in providing the latest in technology as well as excellent customer service with satisfaction guaranteed.

Enclosed you will find information to review regarding the features of the website. After reading the material, please contact our sales manager, Bruce Carter, at your earliest convenience to discuss your options. Thank you again for considering our amazing website.

Sincerely,

<your name>
Customer Service Representative
Sales Department

<typist's initials if other than sender>
Enclosures (2)
cc: Bruce Carter

Inserting Text

Video Library http://labyrinthelab.com/videos Video Number: WD13-V0202

You always insert text at the flashing insertion point. Therefore, you must position the insertion point at the desired location before typing.

Using AutoComplete

Word's AutoComplete feature does some of your typing for you. It recognizes certain words and phrases, such as names of months and days, and offers to complete them for you.

November (Press ENTER to Insert)
Nove

AutoComplete proposing the word November when *Nove* is typed.

You accept AutoComplete suggestions by tapping [Enter]. If you choose to ignore the suggestion, just keep typing; the suggestion disappears.

AutoComplete does not offer to complete the months March through July, because the names are short.

Using the Enter Key

You use [Enter] to begin a new paragraph or to insert blank lines in a document. Word considers anything that ends by tapping [Enter] to be a paragraph. Thus, short lines such as a date line, an inside address, or even blank lines themselves are considered paragraphs.

Tapping [Enter] inserts a paragraph symbol in a document. These symbols are visible when you display formatting marks.

Showing Formatting Marks

FROM THE RIBBON
Home→Paragraph→Show/Hide [¶]

Although formatting marks appear on the screen, you will not see them in the printed document. Viewing these characters can be important when editing a document. For example, you may need to see the formatting marks to determine whether the space between two words was created with the [Spacebar] or [Tab].

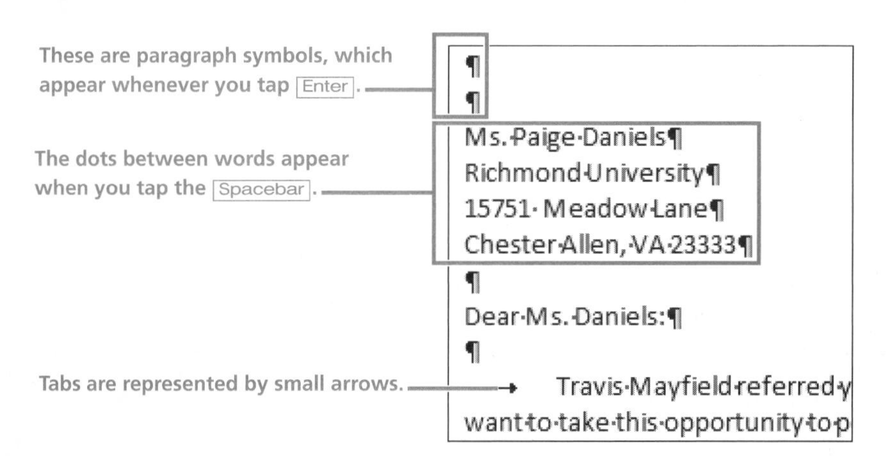

Spacing in Letters

FROM THE RIBBON
Home→Paragraph→Line and Paragraph Spacing

The default spacing in Word 2013 is 1.08 rather than the traditional single spacing. It adds an extra 8 points (a little less than an eighth of an inch) at the end of paragraphs. Therefore, rather that tapping [Enter] twice at the end of a paragraph, you just tap [Enter] once, and Word adds the extra spacing.

When you choose the Blank Document template on the Word Start screen or on the New screen, you are using the default 1.08 spacing. Some documents, however, typically require single spacing, such as business letters, reports, and proposals. Word offers these methods for applying single spacing:

- Single Spaced (Blank) template
- Line and Paragraph Spacing button

Applying Traditional Spacing Using the Single Spaced Template

Choosing the Single Spaced (Blank) template from the Word Start screen or from the New screen opens a single-spaced document. This is a good choice if the majority of your document will be single spaced. If you will use single spacing only in part of your document, the Line and Paragraph Spacing button is a good choice.

Aa

Single spaced (blank)

Changing Spacing Using the Line and Paragraph Spacing Button

If you start a new document using 1.08 spacing and then decide to apply single spacing to a portion of the document, you can choose the options indicated in the following figure. You must select (highlight) the text to be single spaced, or at a minimum, select the paragraph symbol at the end of the text before changing the spacing. Paragraph symbols carry formatting in them.

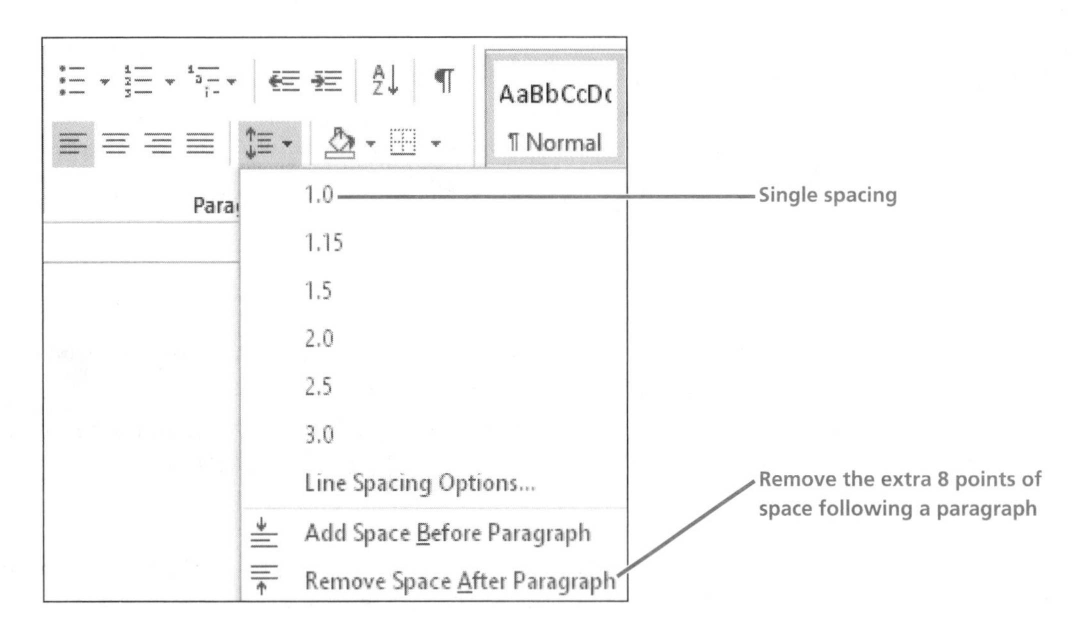

If you wish to use other spacing such as double- or triple-spacing, the Line and Paragraph Spacing button is the place to go.

QUICK REFERENCE	WORKING WITH LINE SPACING
Task	**Procedure**
Word Default Spacing	■ Choose the Blank Document template on the Word Start screen; choose File→New and choose Blank Document; or, press Ctrl+N
Single Spacing	■ Choose the Single Spaced (Blank) template on the Word Start screen; or, choose File→New and choose Single Spaced (Blank). ■ Click Create.
Other Line Spacing Options	■ Choose Home→Paragraph→Line and Paragraph Spacing.

DEVELOP YOUR SKILLS WD02-D01

X Type a Business Letter

In this exercise, you will use the Single Spaced (Blank) template to create a business letter. You will also use AutoComplete and work with the Enter *key.*

Daniels Letter
Already typed, Open + Save As to My Data

1. Start **Word** and make sure the Word window is **maximized**.
2. Click the **Single Spaced (Blank)** template to start a new single-spaced letter.
   A window appears describing the template.
3. Click **Create**.
4. Choose **File→Save** and save the document in your **WD2013 Lesson 02** folder as **`WD02-D01-DanielsLetter-[FirstInitialLastName]`**.
   Replace the bracketed text with your first initial and last name. For example, if your name is Bethany Smith, your filename would look like this: WD02-D01-DanielsLetter-BSmith.

Throughout this book, you will usually save your working document with a new name in step 1 so you can start each exercise with a fresh document.

Begin the Letter and Use AutoComplete

Show/Hide

5. Choose **Home→Paragraph→Show/Hide** ¶ to display formatting marks.
   New documents contain a paragraph symbol; you won't see it if you don't turn on the Show/Hide feature. Paragraph symbols carry formatting in them. In this example, the document formatting includes single spacing.
6. Choose **View→Show→Ruler** to display the ruler.
7. Tap Enter five times to place the insertion point 2 inches from the top of the page.
8. Type **Nove** but stop typing when AutoComplete displays a pop-up tip.
9. Tap Enter to automatically insert *November* in the letter.
10. Finish typing the date as **`November 24, 2013`**.

delete the date and have Students type to Show Auto complete

11. Continue typing the letter as shown, tapping [Enter] wherever you see a paragraph symbol. *If you catch a typo, you can tap [Backspace] enough times to remove the error, and then continue typing.*

```
¶
¶
¶
¶
¶
November·24,·2013¶
¶
¶
¶
Ms.·Paige·Daniels¶
Richmond·University¶
15751·Meadow·Lane¶
Chester·Allen,·VA·23333¶
¶
Dear·Ms.·Daniels:¶
¶
¶
```

12. Type the body paragraph as shown. Let Word Wrap do its thing and tap [Enter] twice at the end of the paragraph.

```
Travis·Mayfield·referred·you·to·us·after·he·spoke·with·you·yesterday·about·our·extraordinary·product.·I·
want·to·take·this·opportunity·to·thank·you·for·considering·My·Virtual·Campus'·social-networking·website·
for·your·institution.·As·Travis·may·have·mentioned,·we·pride·ourselves·in·providing·the·latest·in·
technology·as·well·as·excellent·customer·service.¶
¶
¶
```

If you see a wavy red line, Word thinks the word *might* be misspelled. Wavy blue lines indicate possible grammatical errors. Ignore red and blue wavy lines for now.

13. Continue typing the letter as shown, tapping [Enter] where you see a paragraph symbol. Type your name where indicated.

I·have·enclosed·information·for·your·review·regarding·the·various·features·of·the·website.·After·reading·the·material,·please·contact·our·sales·manager,·ASAP,·to·discuss·your·options.·Thank·you·again·for·considering·our·amazing·website.¶
¶
Yours·truly,¶
¶
¶
¶
<your·name>¶
Customer·Service·Representative¶
Sales·Department¶
¶
¶

14. Choose **Home→Paragraph→Show/Hide** [¶] to turn off formatting marks.

15. Choose **View→Show→Ruler** to turn off the ruler.

Feel free to turn Show/Hide and the ruler on or off as you see fit throughout this course.

16. Click **Save** [icon] on the Quick Access toolbar.
Always leave the file open at the end of an exercise unless instructed to close it.

Creating an Envelope

Video Library http://labyrinthelab.com/videos Video Number: WD13-V0203

Microsoft Word is smart and versatile when it comes to creating envelopes. When you type a business letter with the recipient's name and address at the top, Word recognizes this as the delivery address. Word gives you two options: print the address directly on the envelope or insert the envelope at the top of the document.

FROM THE RIBBON
Mailings→Create→Envelopes

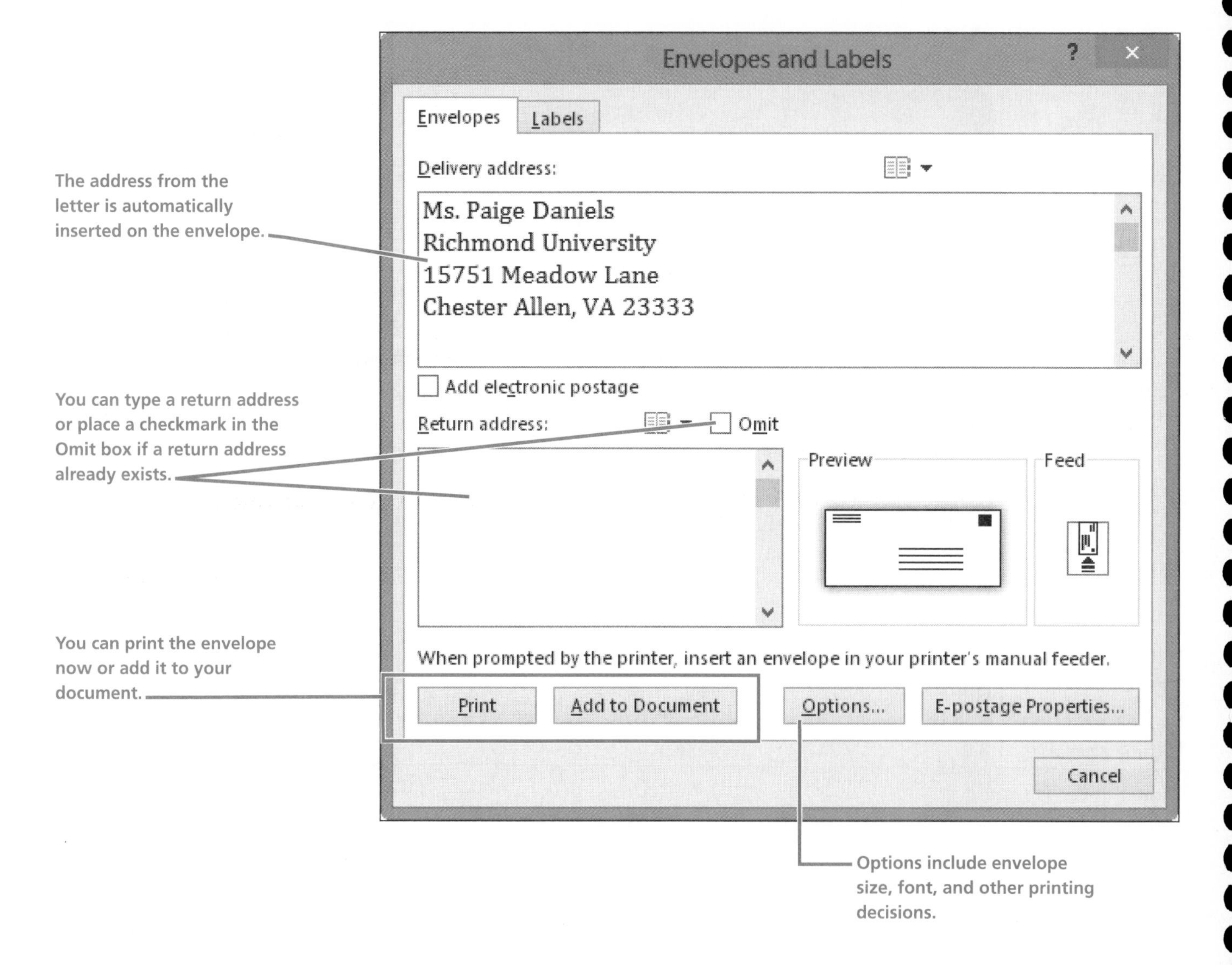

When you enter a return address, you will be prompted to save it as the default so you don't have to type it each time.

DEVELOP YOUR SKILLS WD02-D02

Create an Envelope

In this exercise, you will create an envelope and add it to your letter.

1. Press Ctrl+Home, and then choose **Mailings→Create→Envelopes**.
2. Follow these steps to add an envelope to the document:

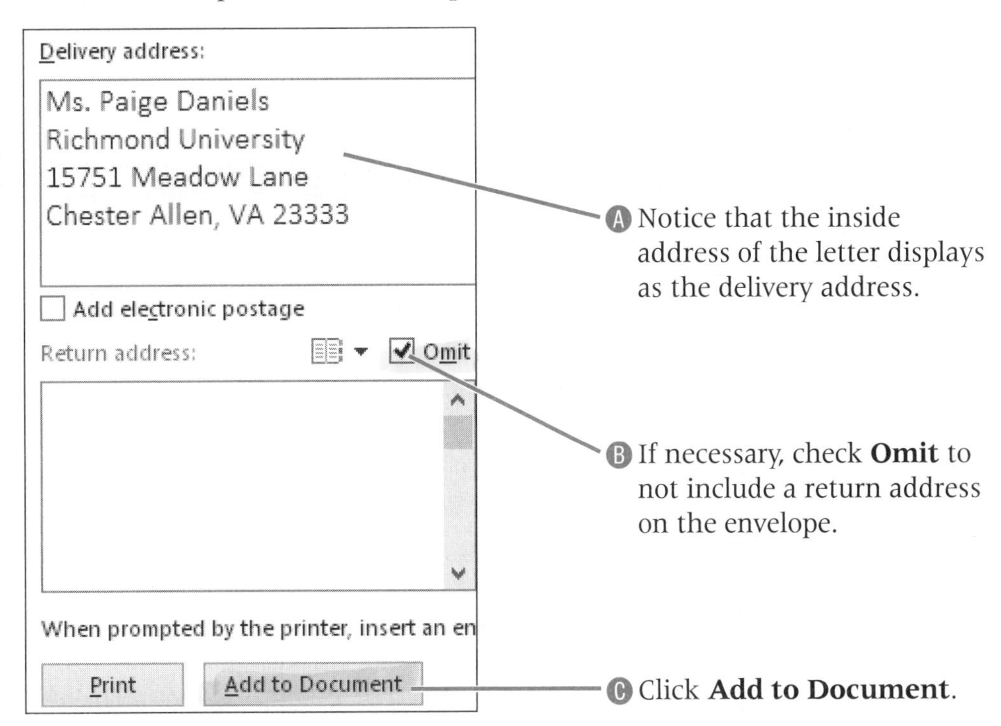

3. Observe the envelope, and then click **Undo** on the Quick Access toolbar to remove the envelope; you don't need it for this exercise.

   You'll learn more about Undo later.

Selecting Text

Video Library http://labyrinthelab.com/videos Video Number: WD13-V0204

You must select (highlight) text if you wish to perform an action on it. Suppose you want to delete a line. You select the line first, and then tap [Delete].

Word provides many mouse and keyboard selection techniques. Deselect text by clicking in the text area of the document or by tapping an arrow key. The following Quick Reference table illustrates various selection techniques.

SELECTION TECHNIQUES	
Item to Be Selected	**Mouse Technique**
One word	Double-click the word.
Continuous block of text	Hold down the left mouse button while dragging over the desired text.
A line	Place the mouse pointer selection arrow in the left margin, and click to select the line.
A sentence	Press [Ctrl] and click anywhere in the sentence.
One paragraph	Place the selection arrow in the left margin and double-click; or, triple-click the I-beam anywhere *within* the paragraph.
Multiple paragraphs	Place the selection arrow in the left margin and drag up or down; or, drag the I-beam over the desired paragraphs.
Entire document	Triple-click in the left margin; or, hold [Ctrl] and click in the left margin.
Nonadjacent areas	Select the first text block, and then hold [Ctrl] while dragging over additional blocks of text.
Item to Be Selected	**Keyboard Technique**
One word	Click at the beginning of the word, and then hold [Shift]+[Ctrl] while tapping [→].
Continuous block of text	Click at the beginning of the text, and then hold [Shift] while tapping an arrow key. Or, click at the beginning of the text block, hold [Shift], and then click at the end of the text block.
A line	Press [Shift]+[End] to select from the insertion point to the end of the line. Press [Shift]+[Home] to select from the insertion point to the beginning of the line.
Entire document	Press [Ctrl]+[A], or press [Ctrl] and click in the left margin.

The Mini toolbar appears when you select text. It contains frequently used commands. You can choose a command or ignore the toolbar and it will fade away.

DEVELOP YOUR SKILLS WD02-D03

Select Text

In this exercise, you will practice various selection techniques using the letter you just created. Selecting text causes the Mini toolbar to fade in. You can ignore it for now.

1. Follow these steps to select text using the left margin:

A Place the selection arrow in the margin to the left of the first line of the inside address; click to select the line.

B Use the selection arrow to select this line. (Notice that the previously selected line is no longer selected.)

Ms. Paige Daniels
Richmond University
15751 Meadow Lane
Chester Allen, VA 23333

Dear Ms. Daniels:

Travis Mayfield referred you to us after he spoke with you yesterday about our extraordinary product. I want to take this opportunity to thank you for considering My Virtual Campus' social-networking website for your institution. As Travis may have mentioned, we pride ourselves in providing the latest in technology as well as excellent customer service.

C Select this paragraph by double-clicking with the selection arrow.

2. Using the selection arrow, drag down the left margin to select text.
3. Click once anywhere in the body of the document to deselect.
4. Triple-click with the selection arrow anywhere in the left margin to select the entire document.
5. Click once anywhere in the body of the document to deselect.

Select Words

6. Double-click any word to select it.
7. Double-click a different word, and notice that the previous word is deselected.

Select Nonadjacent Selections

You can select multiple locations simultaneously.

8. Double-click to select one word.
9. Press and hold Ctrl as you double-click another word; release Ctrl.
   Both selections are active. You can select as many nonadjacent areas of a document as desired using the Ctrl *key.*

10. Follow these steps to drag and select a block of text:

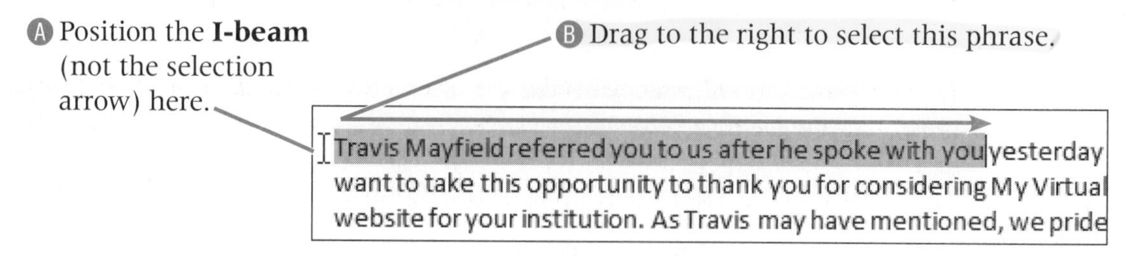

11. Click in the document to deselect.

Editing Text

Video Library http://labyrinthelab.com/videos Video Number: WD13-V0205

Word offers many tools for editing documents, allowing you to insert and delete text. You'll find Word's undo and redo features are very helpful.

Inserting and Deleting Text

Remember, you must position the insertion point before you begin typing. You can use Backspace and Delete to remove one character at a time. If you select a block of text, Backspace or Delete removes the entire block.

Using Undo and Redo

Word's Undo button on the Quick Access toolbar lets you reverse your last editing or formatting change(s). You can reverse simple actions such as accidental text deletions, or you can reverse more complex actions, such as margin changes.

FROM THE KEYBOARD

Ctrl+Z to undo the last action

Ctrl+Y to redo the last action

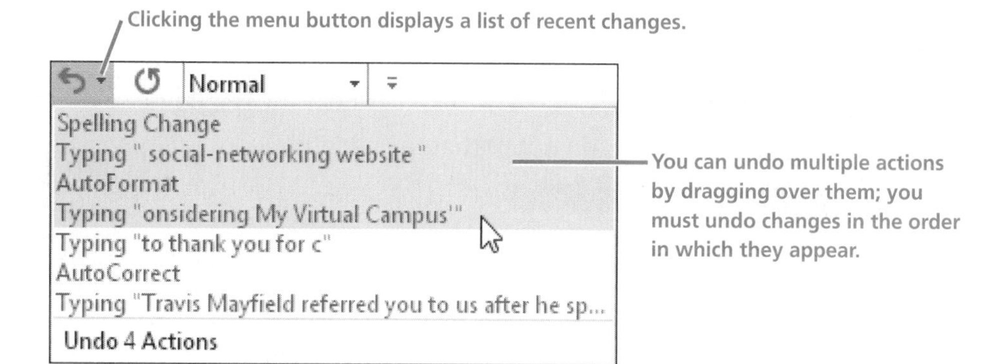

The Redo button reverses Undo. Use Redo when you undo an action and then change your mind.

DEVELOP YOUR SKILLS WD02-D04

Insert and Delete Text and Use Undo and Redo

In this exercise, you will insert and delete text. You will delete characters using both [Backspace] *and* [Delete]*, and you will select and delete blocks of text. You will also use the Undo and Redo buttons on the Quick Access toolbar. You will begin by saving your document. This technique is used throughout this course so you can start your exercise with a fresh file.*

1. Save your file in the **WD2013 Lesson 02** (My Data) folder as `WD02-D04-DanielsLetter-[FirstInitialLastName]`.
2. In the first line of the first paragraph, double-click the word *yesterday* and tap [Delete] to remove it.

spoke with you yesterday about
for considering My Virtual Camp

(1st line of 1st paragraph db click & delete "yesterday")

3. Click with the **I-beam** at the beginning of the word *thank* in the second line of the first paragraph, type **`personally`**, and tap [Spacebar].
4. Position the insertion point at the end of the first paragraph between the word *service* and the final period.
5. Tap [Spacebar] and type **`with satisfaction guaranteed`**.
6. Drag to select the first three words of the second (2nd parag.) paragraph, and then type **`Enclosed you will find`** to replace the selected text.

(Select 1st 3 words of 2nd parag. + type Enclosed you will find)

7. In the same line, position the insertion point after the word *your* and tap [Backspace] until the words *for your* are deleted; then type **`to`**. (2nd parag.)
8. Double-click the word *various* in the same line and tap [Delete].
9. In the next line, double-click *ASAP* and type **`Bruce Carter, at your earliest convenience`** in its place.
10. Delete the comma following *convenience*.
11. Place the selection arrow in the margin to the left of *Yours truly*.
12. Click once to select the line and type **`Sincerely,`** in its place.

Use Undo and Redo

13. You've decided that you prefer *Yours truly,* so click **Undo** on the Quick Access toolbar enough times to remove *Sincerely.*
14. ... after all. Click **Redo** on the Quick Access toolbar enough

2. 1st parag - Delete the word "Yesterday"
3. 2nd line - Click before the word "Thank" and type "Personally"
4. end of 1st parag - insertion point between the word "Service" and the period. Spacebar - type with Satisfaction guaranteed

Working with AutoCorrect

Video Library http://labyrinthelab.com/videos Video Number: WD13-V0206

AutoCorrect is predefined text used for automatically correcting common spelling and capitalization errors. You may have noticed AutoCorrect changing the spelling of certain words while working through previous exercises.

The AutoCorrect feature corrects more than spelling errors. For example, you can set up an AutoCorrect entry to insert the phrase *as soon as possible* when you type *asap* and tap [Spacebar] or other characters, such as a [Tab], [Comma], or [Period].

DEVELOP YOUR SKILLS WD02-D05

Use AutoCorrect

In this exercise, you will practice typing some terms that AutoCorrect will fix for you.

1. Press [Ctrl]+[End] to move the insertion point to the end of the document.
2. If necessary, tap [Enter] a few times to provide some space to practice.
3. Type **teh** and tap [Tab].
   AutoCorrect capitalizes the word because AutoCorrect thinks it is the first word of a sentence.
4. Type **adn** and tap [Spacebar]; AutoCorrect fixes the error.
5. Now select and [Delete] the words you were just practicing with.

Using the AutoCorrect Options Smart Tag

Video Library http://labyrinthelab.com/videos Video Number: WD13-V0207

Word uses smart tags, small buttons that pop up automatically, to provide menus of options that are in context with what you are doing. One of those smart tags is AutoCorrect Options.

If Word automatically corrects something that you don't want corrected, a smart tag option allows you to undo the change. For example, when Word automatically capitalizes the first C in the cc: line, you can quickly undo the capitalization.

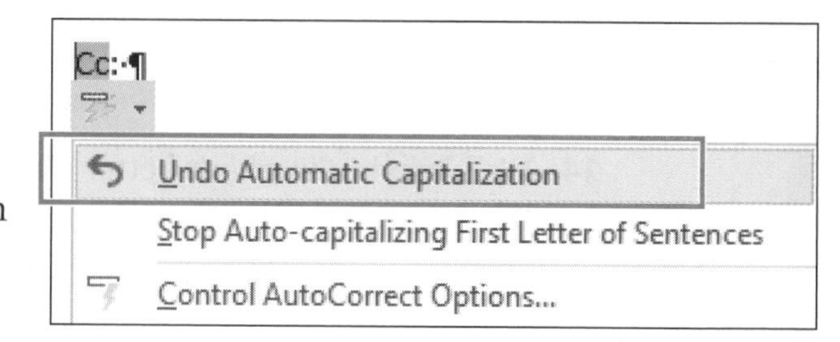

You will see many smart tags as you work. If you do not want to use a smart tag, you can ignore it and it will disappear on its own.

DEVELOP YOUR SKILLS WD02-D06

Use the AutoCorrect Smart Tag

In this exercise, you will add typist initials to the letter and use the smart tag to undo capitalization when AutoCorrect incorrectly capitalizes the first initial.

1. Save your file as **WD02-D06-DanielsLetter-[FirstInitialLastName]**.
2. Choose **Home→Paragraph→Show/Hide** [¶] to display formatting marks.
   The typist initials should appear on the second blank line following the signature block.
3. If necessary, tap [Enter] so there are at least two paragraph symbols.

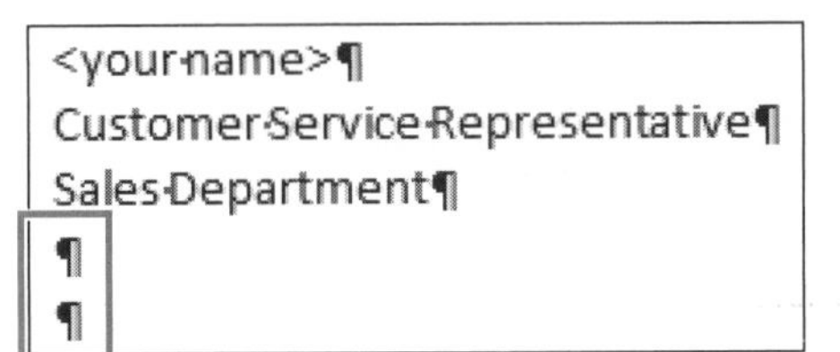

4. Follow these steps to add initials to the letter:

Ⓐ Type **ss** as the typist's initials (lowercase) and tap [Enter]. Notice that AutoCorrect incorrectly capitalized the first initial.

Ⓑ Position the mouse pointer over the first initial until you see a small blue rectangle. Slide the mouse pointer down to display the AutoCorrect smart tag.

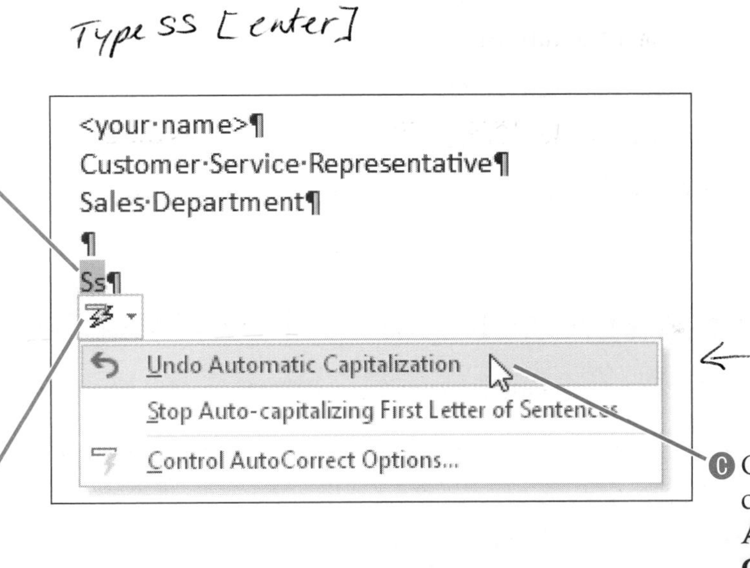

Ⓒ Click the tag and choose **Undo Automatic Capitalization**.

Word marks the initials with a wavy red line, indicating that it's a possible spelling error. You can ignore it.

5. Make sure the insertion point is on the blank line below the initials.
6. Type **Enclosures (2)** and tap [Enter].
7. Choose **Home→Paragraph→Show/Hide** [¶] to turn off formatting marks.
8. Save the document.

Customizing AutoCorrect

Video Library http://labyrinthelab.com/videos Video Number: WD13-V0208

In addition to correcting errors, AutoCorrect lets you automatically insert customized text and special characters. It's also useful for replacing abbreviations with full phrases. For example, you could set up AutoCorrect to insert the name of your company whenever you type an abbreviation for it. And you can customize AutoCorrect by deleting entries that are installed with Word; however, please do not delete any in this classroom.

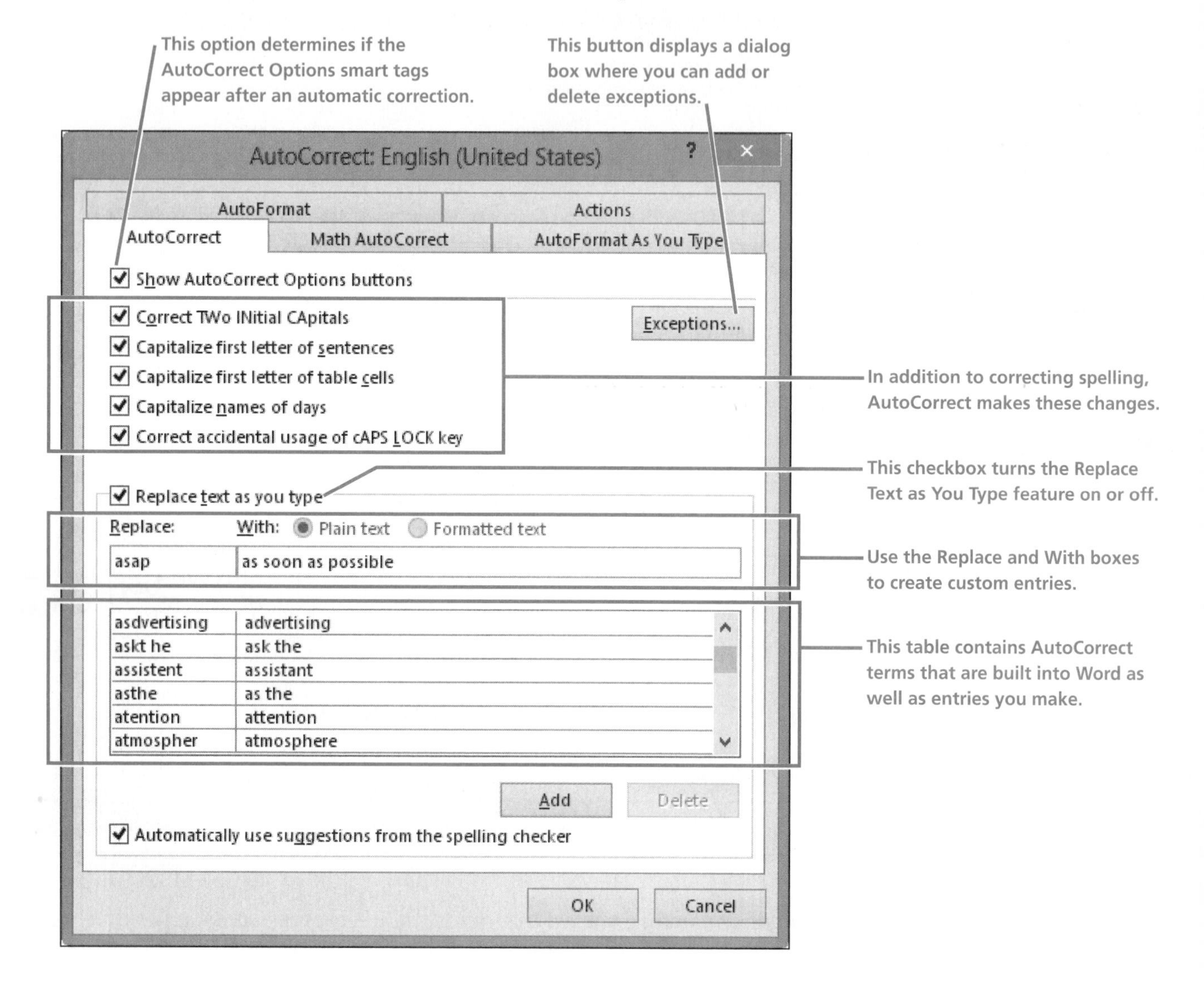

Using AutoCorrect Exceptions

You can designate exceptions to AutoCorrect when you don't want it to replace text that it normally would. For example, there is an option to capitalize the first letter of sentences. When word sees a period, it assumes that's the end of a sentence and it will capitalize the next word. However, you may not always want the capitalization to occur.

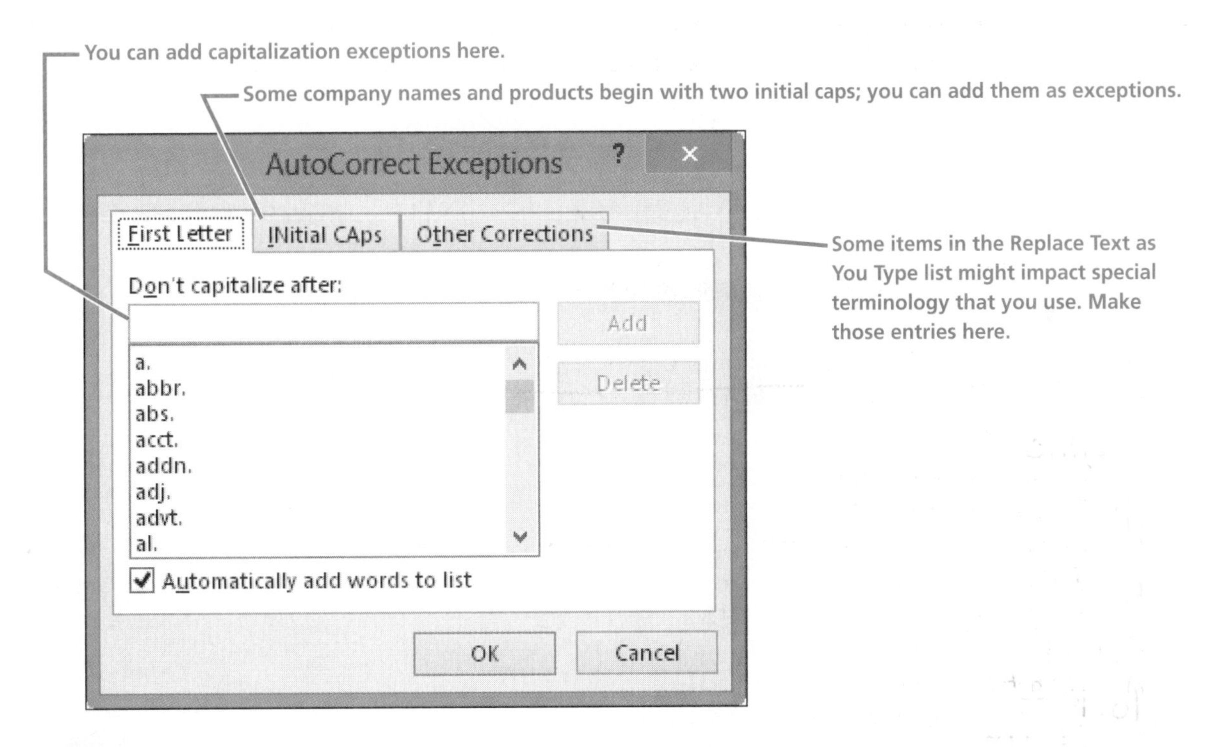

QUICK REFERENCE	USING AUTOCORRECT
Task	**Procedure**
Create a custom AutoCorrect entry	■ Choose File→Options. ■ Choose Proofing and click AutoCorrect Options. ■ Enter shortcut text in the Replace box and replacement text in the With box.
Create an AutoCorrect exception	■ Click Exceptions in the AutoCorrect dialog box. ■ Choose the appropriate tab and enter the exception.

DEVELOP YOUR SKILLS WD02-D07

Create a Custom AutoCorrect Entry

In this exercise, you will copy Bruce Carter on your memo. You need a courtesy copy notification. Since you work for him, you know you'll need to type his name frequently; therefore, it's a perfect candidate for a custom AutoCorrect entry.

1. Save your file as `WD02-D07-DanielsLetter-[FirstInitialLastName]`.
2. Choose **File→Options**.

3. Follow these steps to display the AutoCorrect dialog box:

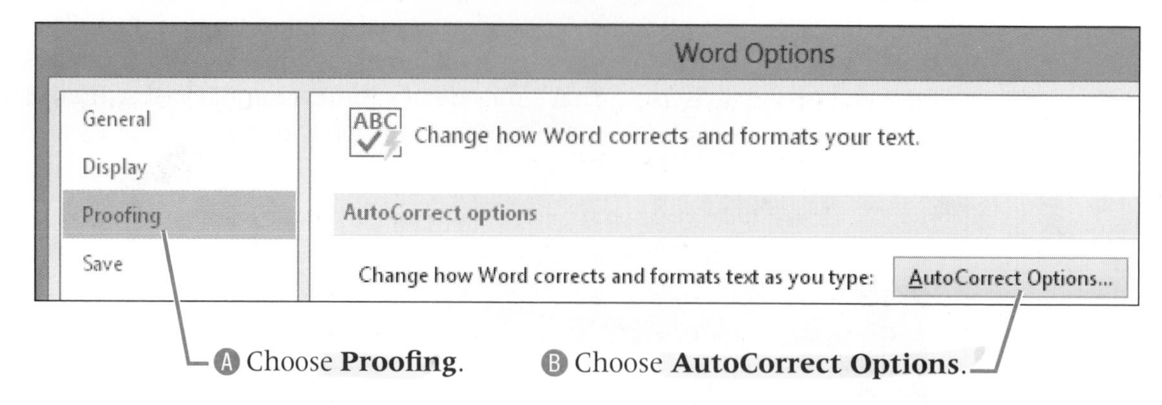

4. If necessary, click the **AutoCorrect** tab.

5. Follow these steps to add a custom AutoCorrect entry:

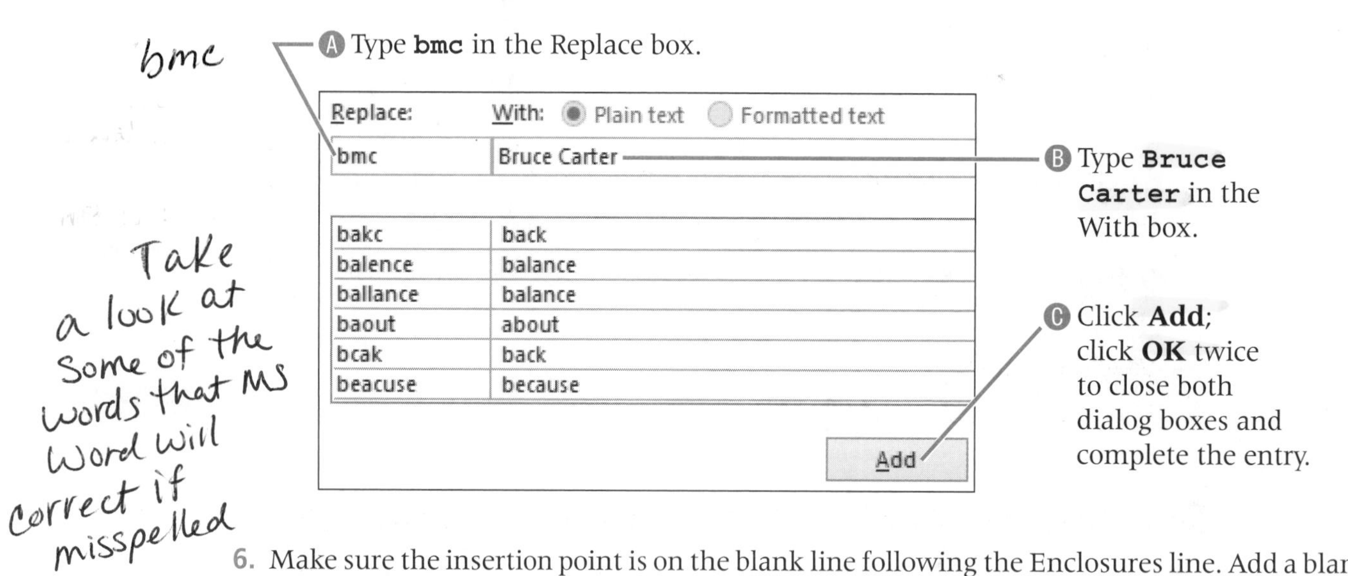

6. Make sure the insertion point is on the blank line following the Enclosures line. Add a blank line if necessary.

7. Follow these steps to add a courtesy copy notation:

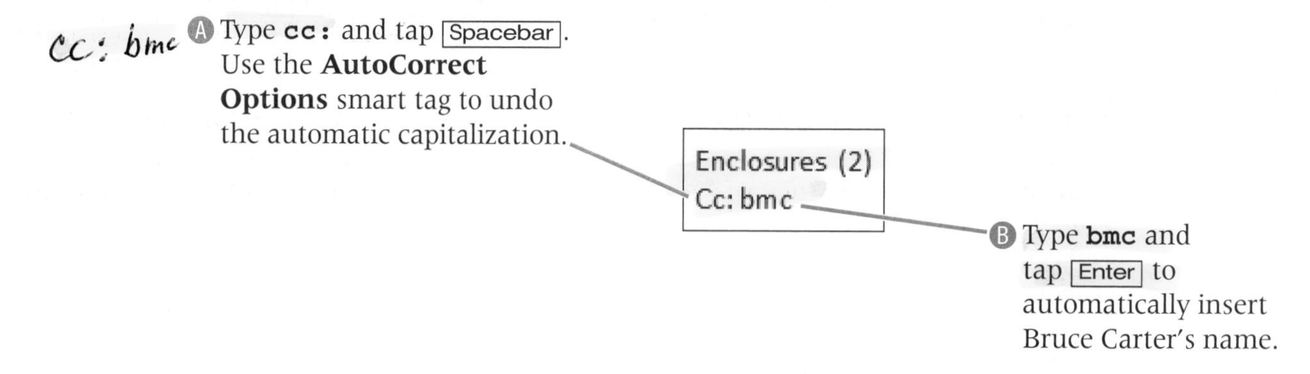

Delete the Custom AutoCorrect Entry

8. Choose **File→Options**.
9. Choose **Proofing** in the left panel, and then click **AutoCorrect Options**.
10. Follow these steps to remove the Bruce Carter entry:

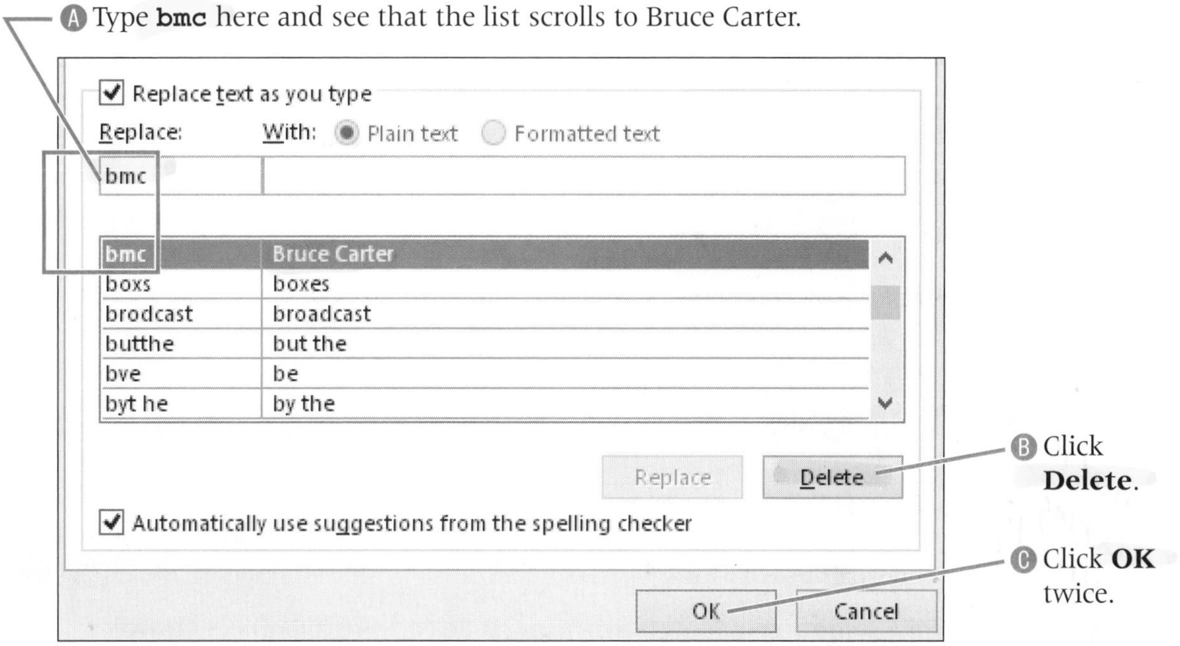

A. Type **bmc** here and see that the list scrolls to Bruce Carter.

B. Click **Delete**.

C. Click **OK** twice.

11. Save the document.

Setting AutoFormat As You Type Options

Video Library http://labyrinthelab.com/videos Video Number: WD13-V0209

One of the tabs in the AutoCorrect dialog box is AutoFormat As You Type. You may have noticed certain formatting taking place automatically; this is happening because certain options are already set for you. For example, AutoFormat will replace two typed hyphens (--) with a dash (—), an ordinal (1st) with superscript (1st), or a fraction (1/2) with a fraction character (½).

AutoFormat can also be set to create an automatic bulleted list when you start a line with an asterisk (*), a hyphen (-), or a greater than symbol (>) followed by a space or tab. Likewise, it can be set to create a numbered list when you start a line with a number followed by a period or tab.

QUICK REFERENCE CU... TYPE OPTIONS		
Task	**Pr...**	
Customize AutoCorrect	■ C...	...panel.
	■ C...	...b.
	■ T... c...	...ace box and type the
	■ C...	
Customize AutoFormat As You Type	■ C...	...panel.
	■ C... W...	...ark where you want
	■ R...	AutoFormat.
	■ Cl...	

DEVELOP YOUR SKILLS WD02-D08

Turn On Automatic Numbering

In this exercise, you will turn on the option that automatically creates a numbered list when you begin a sentence with a number.

1. Choose **File→Options**.
2. Click **Proofing** in the left panel, and then click **AutoCorrect Options**.
3. Follow these steps to turn on automatic numbering:

AutoFormat | Actions

AutoCorrect | Math AutoCorrect | AutoFormat As You Type

Replace as you type

- [x] "Straight quotes" with "smart quotes"
- [x] Ordinals (1st) with superscript
- [x] Fractions (1/2) with fraction character (½)
- [x] Hyphens (--) with dash (—)
- [ ] *Bold* and _italic_ with real formatting
- [x] Internet and network paths with hyperlinks

Apply as you type

- [x] Automatic bulleted lists
- [x] Automatic numbered lists
- [x] Border lines
- [x] Tables
- [ ] Built-in Heading styles

Ⓐ Click the **AutoFormat As You Type** tab.

Ⓑ If necessary, place a checkmark here.

Ⓒ Click **OK** twice.

4. Position the insertion point at the end of the document, tap [Enter], and then type **1.** (with a period) and tap [Spacebar].
5. Type **Item one** and tap [Enter].
   Word automatically generates the next number.
6. Select the numbered entries and tap [Delete].

Copying and Moving Text

Video Library http://labyrinthelab.com/videos Video Number: WD13-V0210

Cut, Copy, and Paste allow you to copy and move text within a document or between documents. The Cut, Copy, and Paste commands are located on the Home tab in the Clipboard group.

FROM THE KEYBOARD

Ctrl+X to cut
Ctrl+C to copy
Ctrl+V to paste

Working with the Clipboard

The Clipboard lets you collect multiple items and paste them in another location in the current document or in a different document. The Clipboard task pane must be visible on the screen to collect the items; otherwise, only one item at a time is saved for pasting.

FROM THE RIBBON

Home→Clipboard→dialog box launcher to display the Clipboard

The Clipboard holds up to 24 items. When the items you cut or copy exceed 24, the Clipboard automatically deletes the oldest item(s). By default, a pop-up appears near the right edge of the taskbar when you copy an item, notifying you of the number of items in the Clipboard.

5 of 24 - Clipboard
Item collected.

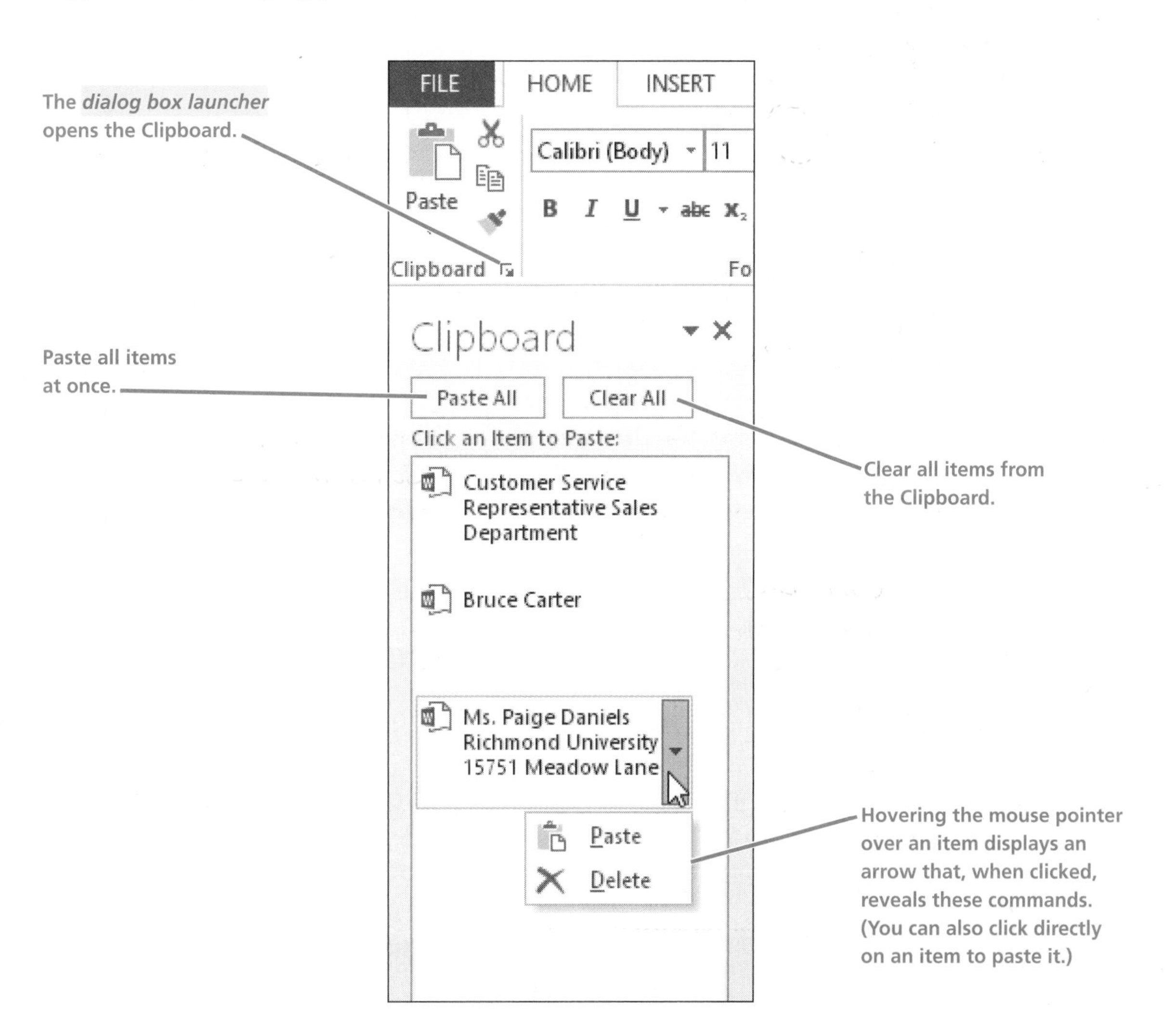

CUT, COPY, AND PASTE COMMANDS	
Command	**Description**
Cut	Removes text and places it on the Clipboard
Copy	Leaves text where it is and places a copy on the Clipboard
Paste	Inserts cut or copied text at the insertion point

DEVELOP YOUR SKILLS WD02-D09

Use Cut, Copy, and Paste

In this exercise, you will move and copy information and work with the Clipboard.

1. Save your file as `WD02-D09-DanielsLetter-[FirstInitialLastName]`.
2. If necessary, choose **Home→Paragraph→Show/Hide** to display the formatting marks.
3. Follow these steps to place the date on the Clipboard:

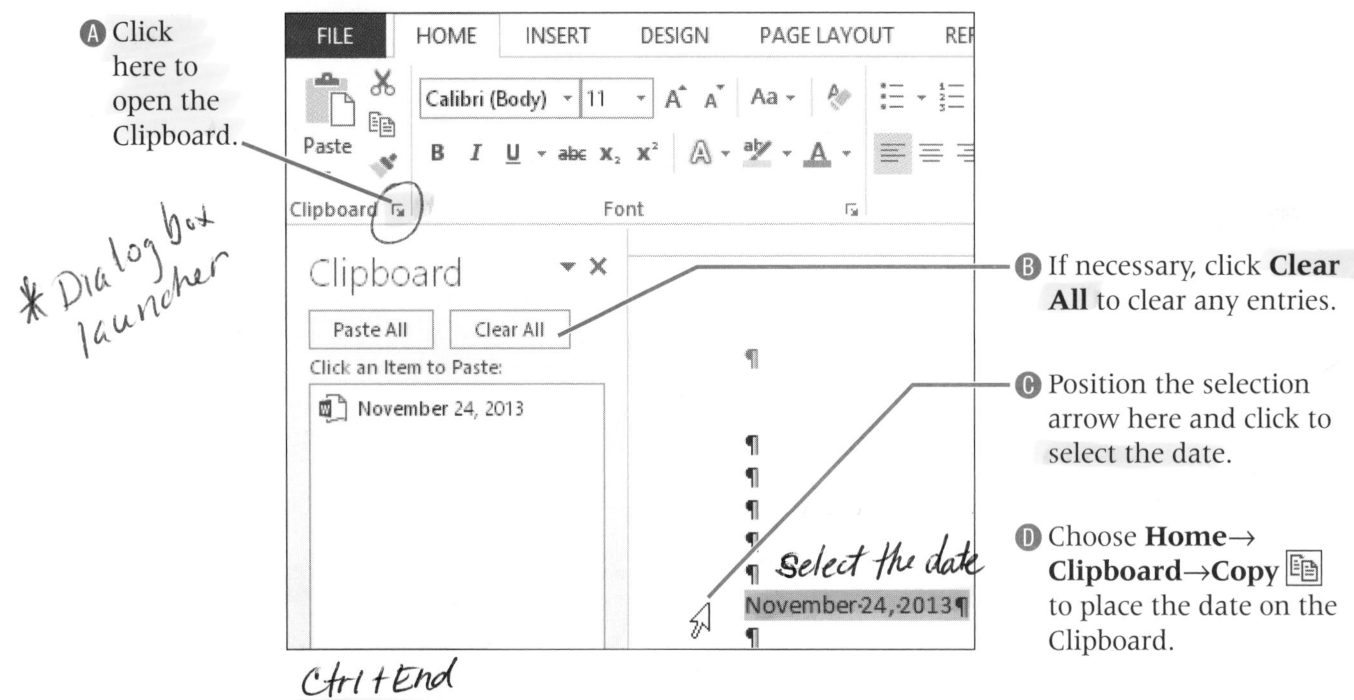

4. Press Ctrl+End to move the insertion point to the bottom of the document.

5. Follow these steps to paste the date at the bottom of the document:

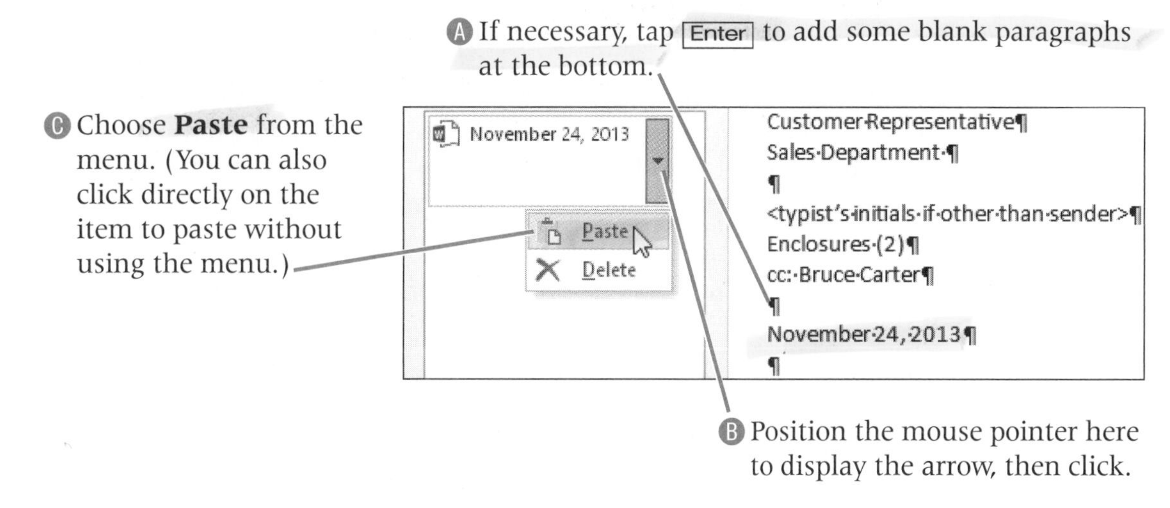

Notice the Paste Options smart tag that appears when you paste the text.

6. Click the **smart tag** to view its menu, and then click in the document to close it.
7. Tap Esc to dismiss the smart tag.

If you don't tap Esc, the button will disappear on its own.

8. Click **Undo** to undo the paste.

Move the Inside Address

9. Scroll to the top of the letter, and use the selection arrow to drag and select all four lines of the inside address.
10. Press Ctrl + X to cut the text and place it on the Clipboard.
11. Press Ctrl + End to move to the bottom of the document.
12. Click the inside address on the **Clipboard** to paste it at the insertion point.
13. Click **Close** on the **Clipboard** task pane.

    In the next exercise, you will return the inside address to its original position in the letter.

14. Save the document.

Editing with Drag and Drop

Video Library http://labyrinthelab.com/videos Video Number: WD13-V0211

The drag and drop feature produces the same result as cut, copy, and paste. It is efficient for moving or copying text a short distance within the same page. You select the text you wish to move, then drag it to the destination. If you press and hold [Ctrl] while dragging, the text is copied to the destination.

Drag and drop does not place the selection on the Clipboard task pane.

DEVELOP YOUR SKILLS WD02-D10

Use Drag and Drop

In this exercise, you will use drag and drop to move the inside address back to the top of the document.

1. If necessary, scroll so you can see both the inside address and the blank line above the salutation.
2. Save your file as **`WD02-D10-DanielsLetter-[FirstInitialLastName]`**.
3. Click and drag to select the inside address.

   Ms. Paige Daniels
   Richmond University
   15751 Meadow Lane
   Chester Allen, VA 23333

4. Position the mouse pointer over the highlighted text.
   The pointer now looks like a white arrow.
5. Follow these steps to move the selected text:

   (A) Press the mouse button, and drag the mouse pointer to the blank line above the salutation. A thick insertion point travels with the arrow. The rectangle on the arrow indicates you are in drag-and-drop mode.

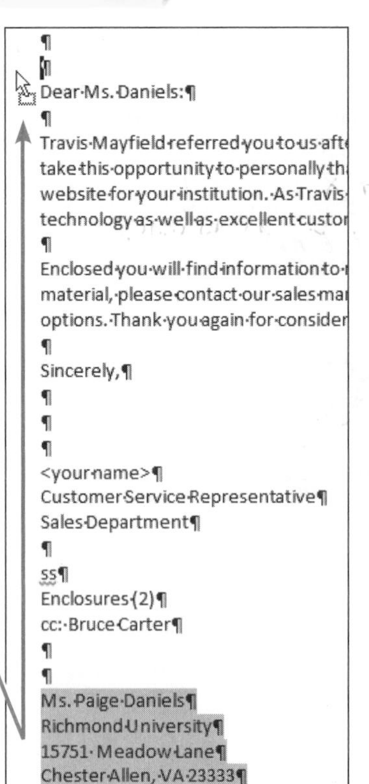

   (B) Release the mouse button to complete the move; click to deselect.

6. Save the document.

Switching Between Documents

Video Library http://labyrinthelab.com/videos Video Number: WD13-V0212

There are several techniques for switching between documents. In the next exercise, you will use the taskbar at the bottom of the screen to do it. When several documents are open at the same time, they may share one taskbar button.

A small image of each open document displays when you hover the mouse pointer over the taskbar button. Below, the Daniels letter is the active document, and you can tell because it's lighter than the others. Clicking the image opens the document on the screen.

Open Word documents

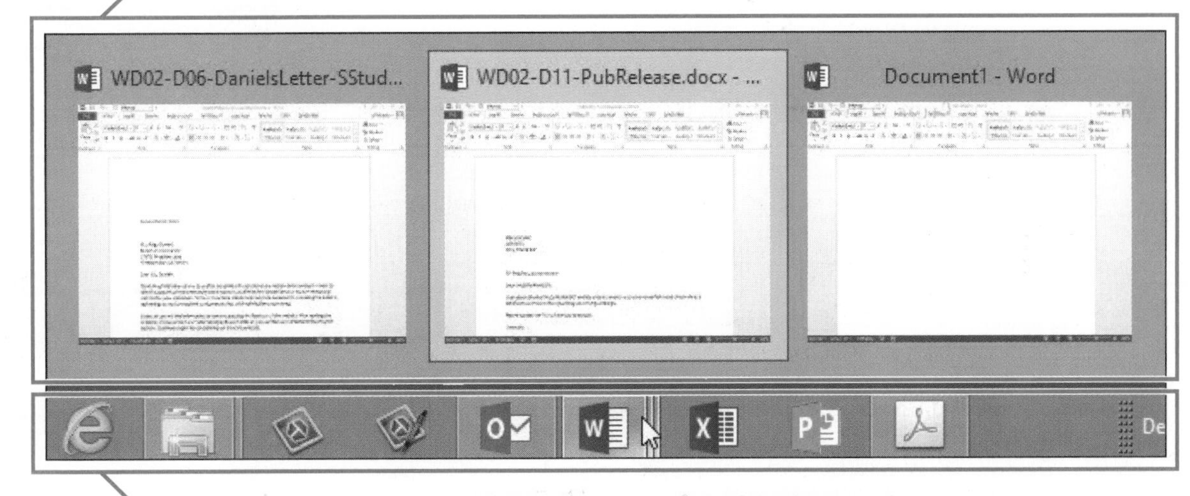

Taskbar buttons for oper ... stacked on it.)

Your buttons may be differen ... hich program buttons are displayed on you

Left off here

DEVELOP YOUR SKILLS WD02-D11

Switch and Copy Between Documents

In this exercise, you will copy and paste between two documents using the taskbar buttons to switch from one document to another.

1. Open **WD02-D11-PubRelease** from the **WD2013 Lesson 02** folder and save it as `WD02-D11-PubRelease-[FirstInitialLastName]`.
2. Follow these steps to switch to your WD02-D10-DanielsLetter-[FirstInitialLastName] file:

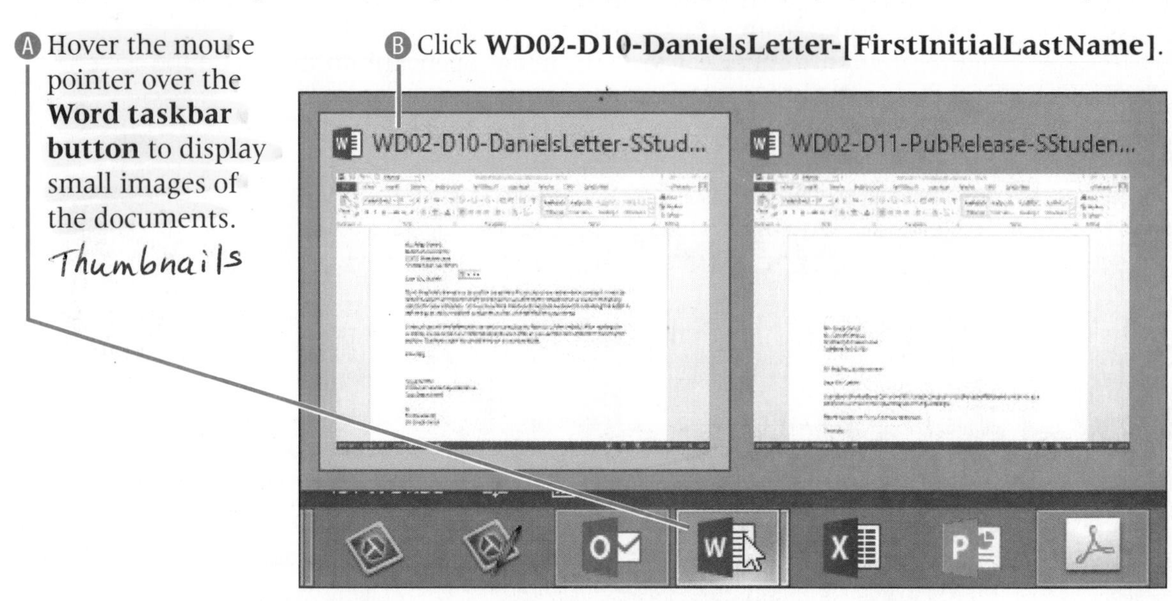

3. Select *Bruce Carter* in the second line of the second paragraph.
4. Press Ctrl + C to copy the name.

Switch Documents

5. Using the taskbar, switch to **WD02-D11-PubRelease-[FirstInitialLastName]**.
6. Select the *YOUR NAME* line in the inside address.

7. Press Ctrl + V to paste *Bruce Carter* over the selected text, and then, if necessary, tap Enter to move *ADDRESS* back to the second line.
8. Click the insertion point in front of *Bruce Carter*, type `Mr.`, and tap Spacebar.

9. Select the last two lines of the inside address and type the following:

```
My Virtual Campus
123 Cherry Blossom Lane
Salisbury, MD 21801
```

10. There should be two blank lines between the inside address and the RE: line. Add or delete blank lines as needed.

11. Select *SALES MANAGER* in the salutation and press Ctrl+V to paste *Bruce Carter* again.
12. Select *Bruce* and type **Mr.** in its place.
13. Select *SALES MANAGER* in the body paragraph and paste the name again.
14. Using the **taskbar**, switch back to the Daniels letter.
15. Select *Paige Daniels* in the inside address and press Ctrl+C to copy her name.
16. Switch back to the publicity release and paste her name over *YOUR NAME* at the bottom.
17. Save the changes you made in **WD02-D11-PubRelease-[FirstInitialLastName]**, and then close it.

Save + close Pub Release

Using Page Layout Options

Video Library http://labyrinthelab.com/videos Video Number: WD13-V0213

The three most commonly used page layout options are margins, page orientation, and paper size. All of these are located in the Page Setup group on the Page Layout tab.

Setting Margins

Margins determine the amount of white space between the text and the edge of the paper. You can set margins for the entire document, a section, or selected text. The Margins gallery displays preset top, bottom, left, and right margins. The Custom Margins option at the bottom of the gallery opens a dialog box where you can set custom margins.

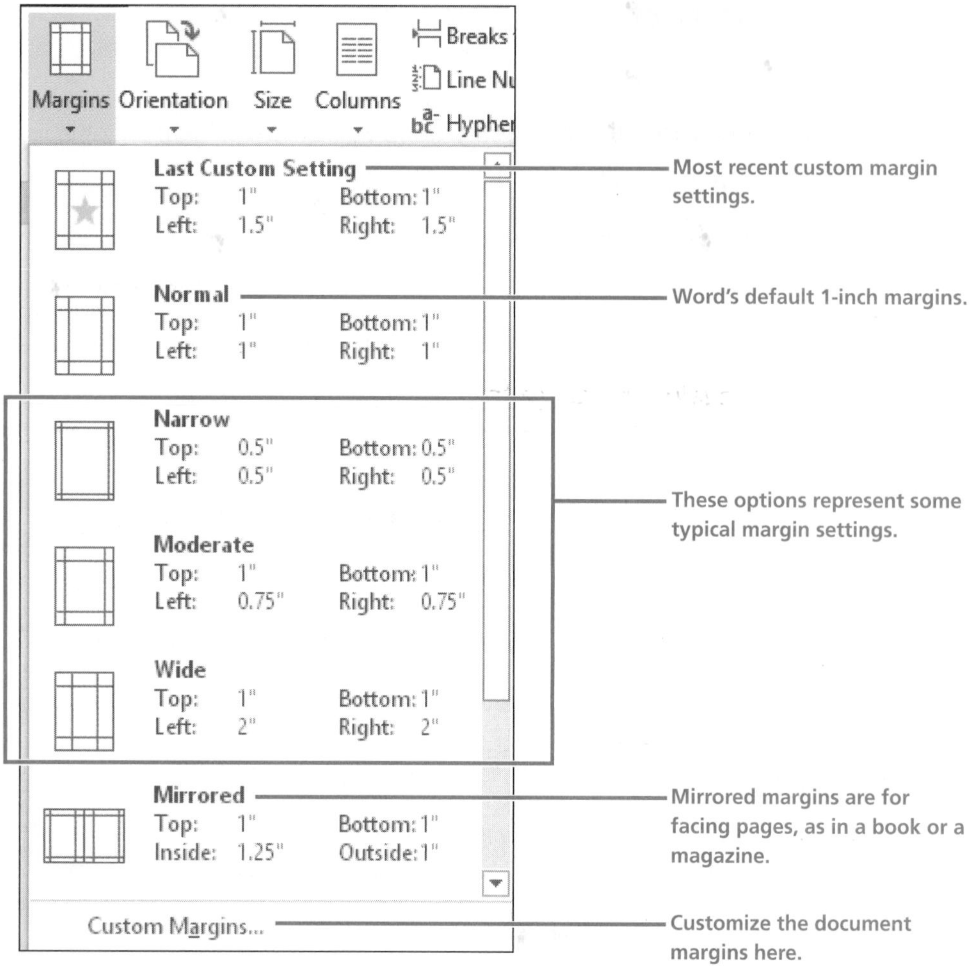

Margins Orientation Size Columns Breaks Line Nu Hypher

Last Custom Setting
Top: 1" Bottom: 1"
Left: 1.5" Right: 1.5"

Normal
Top: 1" Bottom: 1"
Left: 1" Right: 1"

Narrow
Top: 0.5" Bottom: 0.5"
Left: 0.5" Right: 0.5"

Moderate
Top: 1" Bottom: 1"
Left: 0.75" Right: 0.75"

Wide
Top: 1" Bottom: 1"
Left: 2" Right: 2"

Mirrored
Top: 1" Bottom: 1"
Inside: 1.25" Outside: 1"

Custom Margins...

Most recent custom margin settings.

Word's default 1-inch margins.

These options represent some typical margin settings.

Mirrored margins are for facing pages, as in a book or a magazine.

Customize the document margins here.

QUICK REFERENCE	SETTING MARGINS
Task	**Procedure**
Change margins from the Margins gallery	■ Choose Page Layout→Page Setup→Margins and choose a predefined margin setting.
Set custom margins	■ Choose Page Layout→Page Setup→Margins and choose Custom Margins. ■ Enter settings for top, bottom, left, and right margins.

DEVELOP YOUR SKILLS WD02-D12

Set Margins

In this exercise, you will use the Margins gallery and the Page Setup dialog box to change the document's margins.

1. Choose **Page Layout→Page Setup→Margins**.
2. Choose **Narrow** from the gallery and observe the impact on your document.
3. Click **Margins** again and choose **Wide** to see how that affects the document.
4. Open the gallery again and change the margins back to **Normal**.

Set Custom Margins

5. Display the gallery and choose **Custom Margins** from the bottom of the menu to open the Page Setup dialog box.

Clicking the dialog box launcher at the bottom-right corner of the Page Setup group also opens the Page Setup dialog box.

Notice the options for changing the top, bottom, left, and right margins.

6. Set the left and right margins to **1.5 inches**.
7. Click **OK** and notice the change in your document's margins.
8. Click **Margins** and choose **Normal**.

Setting Page Orientation and Paper Size

Video Library http://labyrinthelab.com/videos Video Number: WD13-V0214

You can set page orientation and paper size using the Page Layout tab. The page orientation determines how the text is laid out on the paper. The options are Portrait (vertical) or Landscape (horizontal). The default orientation is Portrait. Some common uses for landscape orientation include brochures, flyers, wide tables, and so forth.

Most documents use the standard letter-size paper. However, Word supports the use of many other paper sizes, including legal, and also allows you to create custom sizes.

Working with Print and Print Preview

The Print command and Print Preview feature are available in Backstage view. The left pane includes printer and page layout options; the right pane is a preview of your document showing how it will look when printed. You can experiment with different options and see the results immediately.

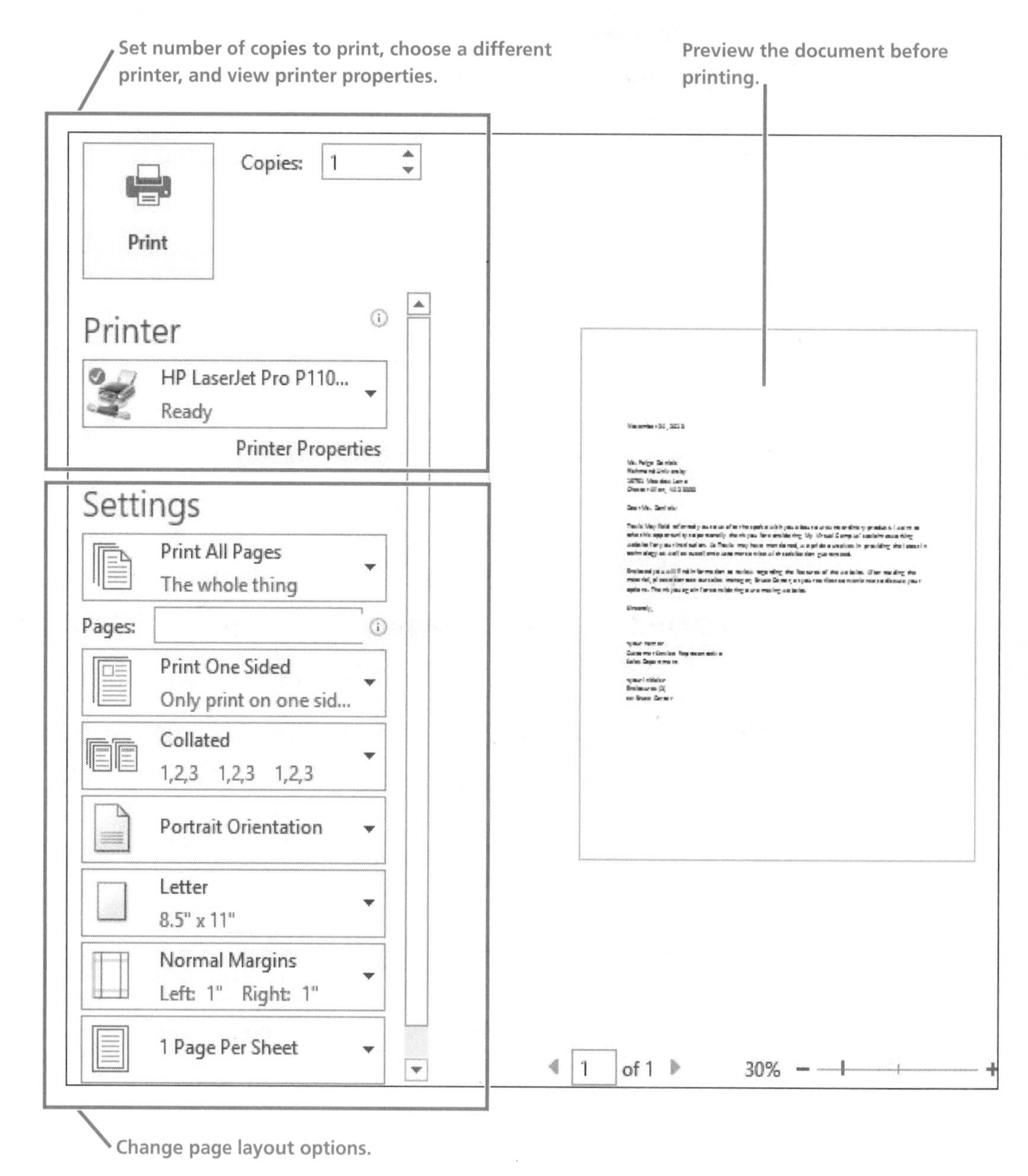

QUICK REFERENCE	SETTING PAGE ORIENTATION AND PAPER SIZE AND WORKING WITH PRINT
Task	**Procedure**
Change the page orientation	■ Choose Page Layout→Page Setup→Orientation. ■ Choose the desired orientation.
Change the paper size	■ Choose Page Layout→Page Setup→Size. ■ Choose the desired size; or, choose More Paper Sizes to create a custom paper size.
Print and Print Preview	■ Choose File→Print.

Word 2013

DEVELOP YOUR SKILLS WD02-D13

Change Page Layout and Print Options

In this exercise, you will experiment with the page orientation and paper size options. You will preview page orientation, and you will work with printing options.

Work with Page Orientation

1. Choose **File→Print**.

   The page is currently in the default Portrait orientation. Previewing the entire page allows you to see this clearly.
2. Click **Back** in the upper-left corner to close Backstage view.
3. Choose **Page Layout→Page Setup→Orientation** →**Landscape**.
4. Choose **File→Print** to preview landscape orientation.
5. Click **Back**.
6. Choose **Page Layout→Page Setup→Orientation** again, and then choose **Portrait** to change the page back to a vertical layout.

View Paper Size Options

7. Choose **Page Layout→Page Setup→Size** →**Legal**.
8. Scroll down to observe the legal paper.
9. Choose **Size** again and choose **Letter**.

Explore Print Options

10. Choose **File→Print**.
11. Set the Copies box to **2**.
12. Click below the Settings heading and choose **Print Current Page**.

Observe Page Settings Options

13. Follow these steps to view other settings in the Print screen:

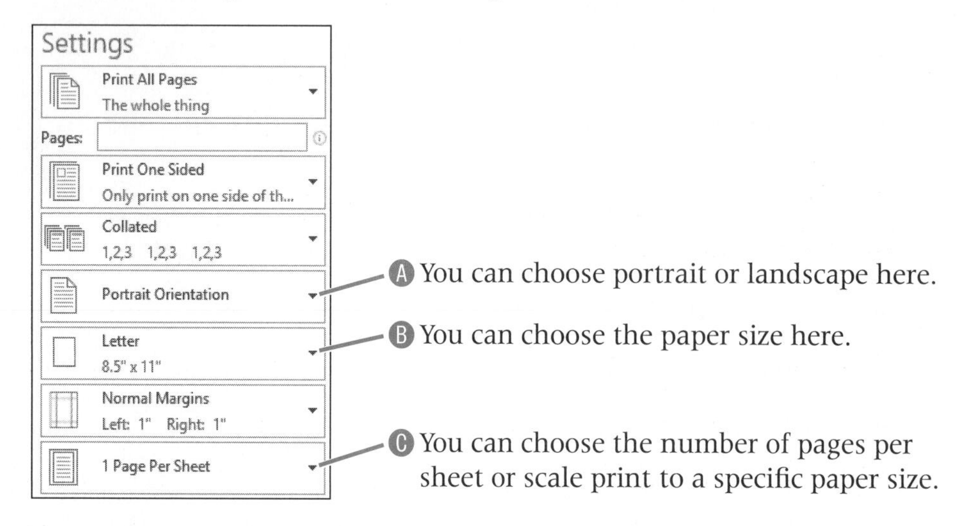

14. You won't print at this time, so click **Back**.
15. Choose **Home→Paragraph→Show/Hide** ¶ to turn off formatting marks.
16. Save and close the document, then exit from **Word**.

Concepts Review

To check your knowledge of the key concepts introduced in this lesson, complete the Concepts Review quiz by choosing the appropriate access option below.

If you are...	Then access the quiz by...
Using the Labyrinth Video Library	Going to http://labyrinthelab.com/videos
Using eLab	Logging in, choosing Content, and navigating to the Concepts Review quiz for this lesson
Not using the Labyrinth Video Library or eLab	Going to the student resource center for this book

Reinforce Your Skills

REINFORCE YOUR SKILLS WD02-R01

Create a Block-Style Letter with an Envelope

In this exercise, you will use traditional spacing in a block-style business letter and let Word Wrap and AutoComplete take effect. Then you will create an envelope for the letter.

Create a New Document and Insert Text

1. Start **Word** and create a new document based on the **Single Spaced (Blank)** template.
2. When the template description window appears, click **Create** .
3. Choose **Home→Paragraph→Show/Hide** ¶ to display formatting marks.
4. Tap Enter five times to position the insertion point approximately **2 inches** from the top of the page.
5. Type **Nove** to begin the date, tap Enter when the AutoComplete prompt appears, and then finish typing the date as **November 19, 2013**.
6. Tap Enter four times.
7. Complete the block style letter as shown on the next page, tapping Enter wherever a paragraph symbol appears.

¶

¶
¶
¶
¶
¶
November·19,·2013¶
¶
¶
¶
Current·Resident·¶
123·Peach·Blossom·Lane¶
Atlanta,·GA·30313¶
¶
Dear·Neighbor:¶
¶
I·am·the·recycling·representative·for·Kids·for·Change,·and·our·motto·is·Think·Globally,·Act·Locally.·We·know·that·recycling·large·objects·takes·extra·effort·since·they·do·not·fit·in·your·city-provided·recycle·cans.·We·would·like·to·give·you·a·hand.·¶
¶
On·Tuesday,·November·26th,·we·will·collect·oversized·recyclable·objects·in·your·neighborhood.·Please·place·your·collectables·at·the·curb·in·front·of·your·house·before·9:00·a.m.·Please·visit·http://recycleatlanta.org/·to·ensure·you·are·following·the·city's·recycling·guidelines.·¶
¶
Thank·you·for·caring·about·our·planet.¶
¶
Yours·truly,¶
¶
¶
¶
Tania·Tulip¶
Recycling·Representative¶
Kids·for·Change¶
¶

Create an Envelope

8. Press Ctrl + Home.
9. Choose **Mailings→Create→Envelopes**.
10. In the **Envelopes and Labels** dialog box, if necessary, check the **Omit** box to prevent a return address from being added to the envelope.
11. Click **Add to Document**.
12. Save the letter in your **WD2013 Lesson 02** folder as `WD02-R01-Recycle-[FirstInitialLastName]`. Close the file and exit **Word**.
13. Submit your final file based on the guidelines provided by your instructor.

    To view examples of how your file or files should look at the end of this exercise, go to the student resource center.

REINFORCE YOUR SKILLS WD02-R02

Edit a Document

In this exercise, you will edit a letter, create an AutoCorrect shortcut, and move a paragraph. You will then copy the letter into a new document, change margins and page orientation, and preview the letter.

Select and Edit Text

1. Start **Word**. Open **WD02-R02-CuyahogaCamp** from your **WD2013 Lesson 02** folder and save it as `WD02-R02-CuyahogaCamp-[FirstInitialLastName]`.
2. Make the following edits to the letter:
   - At the end of the first paragraph, replace the period with a comma and complete the sentence with the following, adding and deleting spaces as needed: **`including hiking, bird watching, tree planting, and bug hunting.`**
   - Double-click the word *sing* at the end of the third paragraph and tap [Delete].
   - Position the insertion point at the end of the fourth paragraph, and tap [Delete] twice to combine the fourth and fifth paragraphs.
   - In the last paragraph, select the *8* in *28th* and replace it with **`7`**.
   - The date of the 28th was correct after all; click **Undo** on the Quick Access toolbar, and then click in the letter to deselect the text affected by the Undo command.

Work with AutoCorrect

Cuyahoga Camp is a term you will use frequently, so you will create an AutoCorrect shortcut.

3. Choose **File→Options** and choose **Proofing** from the left panel; then click **AutoCorrect Options**.
4. Type **`cc`** in the **Replace** box, tap [Tab], type **`Camp Cuyahoga`** in the **With** box, and then click **OK** twice.

5. Position the insertion point to the right of *spend* in the first line of the first paragraph and tap [Spacebar].
6. Type this text after the space: **`a day with us at cc for`**

   Word automatically corrects cc *to* Camp Cuyahoga.
7. At the end of the sentence, select *with us* and tap [Delete].
8. Position the insertion point on the blank line following Olivia Pledger at the end of the letter, type **`cc`**, and tap [Enter].

   Olivia Pledger
   Camp Cuyahoga

   AutoCorrect corrects cc *to be* Camp Cuyahoga. *Now you will delete your AutoCorrect shortcut.*
9. Choose **File→Options**, and then choose **Proofing** from the left panel.
10. Click **AutoCorrect Options**, and type **`cc`** in the **Replace** box.

    Your shortcut is now highlighted in the list.
11. Click **Delete**, and then click **OK** twice.

Move a Paragraph

12. Position the mouse pointer in the margin to the left of the second paragraph and drag down to select the paragraph and the blank line following it.

    The selected paragraph and blank line below it are highlighted.

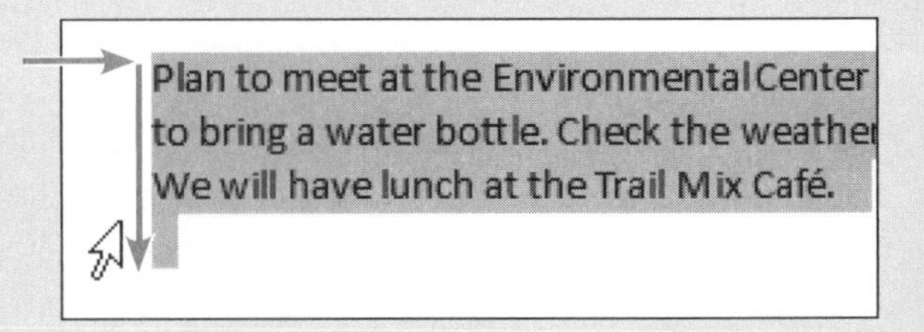

13. Press Ctrl + X to cut the paragraph.

    When you issued the Cut command, everything that was selected (paragraph and following blank line) was deleted and placed on the Clipboard, ready for you to paste it elsewhere.

14. Position the insertion point to the left of *We* in the last paragraph, and press Ctrl + V to paste the text.

Copy Text and Switch Between Documents

Since you will send this letter to other attendees, you will practice copying and pasting it into a blank document.

15. Choose **File→New**. Start a new document using the **Single Spaced (Blank)** template.
16. Click **Create** to open the blank document.
17. Use the **Word** taskbar button to switch back to **WD02-R02-CuyahogaCamp-[FirstInitialLastName]**.
18. Position the mouse pointer to the left of the word *Kids* in the first paragraph and drag down to the end of the letter.
19. Tap Ctrl + C and use the **Word** taskbar button to switch back to your new document.
20. Click in the document and press Ctrl + V.

    That was just a test; you won't save the letter now.

21. Choose **File→Close**. Click **Don't Save** when the message appears.

Use Page Layout Options and Print Preview

22. Click in the **Cuyahoga Camp** document to deselect.
23. Choose **Page Layout→Page Setup→Margins** and choose **Narrow**.
24. Choose **Page Layout→Page Setup→Orientation** and choose **Landscape**.
25. Choose **File→Print** to preview the document.

    The document looked better to begin with.

26. Click **Back**.
27. Click **Undo** twice to return the letter to its original margins and orientation.
28. Save and close the document and exit from **Word**.
29. Submit your final file based on the guidelines provided by your instructor.

    To view examples of how your file or files should look at the end of this exercise, go to the student resource center.

REINFORCE YOUR SKILLS WD02-R03

Create, Edit, and Print Preview a Letter

In this exercise, you will type a fundraising letter and an envelope and make some editing changes. You will create an AutoCorrect shortcut, and then add some text to the letter that you will copy from another document. Finally, you will preview the letter and modify the margins.

Insert Text and Use AutoComplete

You have been asked to draft a letter to send to Kids for Change members regarding the car wash fundraiser, which will be discussed at the next monthly meeting.

1. Start **Word**. Create a new document using the **Single Spaced (Blank)** template.
2. When the window appears describing the template, click **Create**.
3. Save the letter as `WD02-R03-CarWash-[FirstInitialLastName]` in your **WD2013 Lesson 02** folder.
4. If necessary, choose **Home→Paragraph→Show/Hide** ¶ to display formatting marks.
5. Type this letter, tapping Enter wherever you see a paragraph symbol. Use **AutoComplete** to help with the dates.

¶
¶
¶
¶
¶
August·6,·2013¶
¶
¶
¶
MEMBER·NAME¶
STREET·ADDRESS¶
CITY,·STATE·ZIP¶
¶
Dear·MEMBER,·¶
¶
Our·local·chapter·of·Kids·for·Change·is·planning·to·hold·a·car·wash·fundraiser·to·collect·$300·in·order·to·adopt·a·seal·at·the·Center·for·Seals.·We're·aiming·for·August·31st·as·the·car·wash·date.·The·next·monthly·meeting·will·be·a·planning·session·for·the·car·wash.·Here·are·some·things·to·think·about·before·the·meeting:¶
¶

Create an Envelope

6. Position the insertion point at the top of the document.
7. Choose **Mailings→Create→Envelopes** .
8. In the dialog box, if necessary, check the **Omit** box to prevent a return address, and then click **Add to Document**.

Select and Edit Text

Looking back over what you have typed, you see some changes you would like to make.

9. In the first line of the first paragraph, select *is planning* and replace it with **`plans`**.
10. Toward the end of the same line, select *in order* and tap [Delete].
11. In the next line, select *August 31st as the car wash date* and replace it with **`Saturday, September 7th`**.
12. Tap [Spacebar] and the suffix following 7 changes to a superscript.
13. Tap [Backspace] to remove the extra space. Save your changes.

Work with AutoCorrect

Next you will check to see if an AutoFormat as You Type option caused th *to change to a superscript.*

14. Choose **File→Options**, and then choose **Proofing** from the left panel.
15. Click **AutoCorrect Options**. When the dialog box opens, click the **AutoFormat As You Type** tab.

    The checkmark in the box next to Ordinals (1st) with Superscript is causing the superscripts. The checkmark in the box next to Automatic Numbered Lists will help you with the next part of the letter.

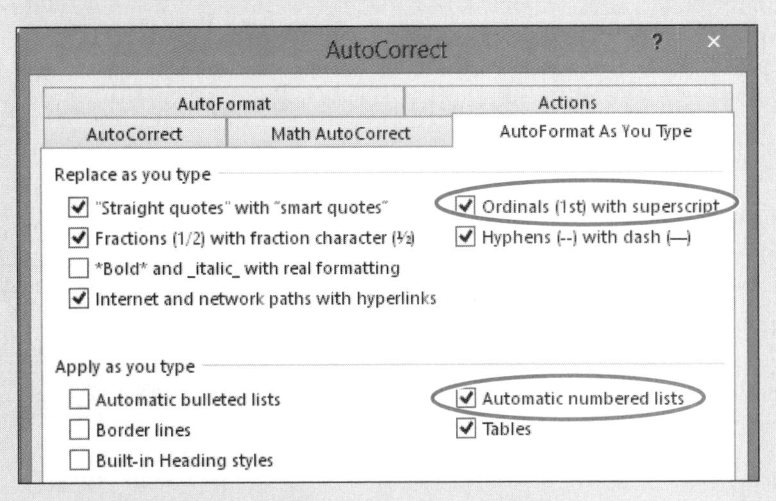

16. Click **OK** twice.
17. Hover the mouse pointer over the superscript in the September date, and drag down to display the **AutoCorrect Options smart tag**.
18. Click the tag and observe, but don't click, the Undo Superscript option.
19. Click away from the tag to close it.

20. Position the insertion point next to the paragraph symbol in the blank line following the main paragraph and tap [Enter].
21. Type **1.** and tap [Spacebar] to begin automatic numbering.
    The AutoCorrect Options smart tag appears.
22. Click the **smart tag** to see the menu options; click away from the tag to close it.
23. Type the rest of the letter as shown, tapping [Enter] where you see a paragraph symbol.
    Hint: When you finish item 5, tap [Enter] three times: twice to turn off numbering and once to generate a blank line after the list.

```
meeting·will·be·a·planning·session·for·the·car·wash.·Here·are·some·things·to·think·about·before·the·
meeting:¶
¶
    1.→Choose·a·location.·Our·options·are·the·parking·lots·at·Jake's·Gas·Station,·Beulah's·Diner,·or·Dick's·
       Grocery·Store.¶
    2.→What·hours·can·you·volunteer·on·September·7th?¶
    3.→Can·you·supply·a·hose,·vacuum,·soap,·brushes,·sponges,·or·rags?¶
    4.→Should·we·set·a·price·or·request·a·donation?¶
    5.→Can·you·design·a·flyer·to·let·people·know·that·this·is·for·a·good·cause?¶
¶
We·look·forward·to·a·great·planning·session.·See·you·at·the·meeting!¶
¶
Sincerely,¶
¶
¶
¶
Robert·Chan¶
Kids·for·Change¶
```

Copy Text and Switch Between Documents

The supervisor wants to include information about the Center for Seals so the members will know the good work this organization does. You will copy the information from a document the supervisor provided.

24. Open **WD02-R03-Seals** from your **WD2013 Lesson 02** folder.
25. Press [Ctrl]+[A] to select all and then press [Ctrl]+[C] to copy all.
26. Close the **WD02-R03-Seals** document.
    Your car wash letter will be in the foreground.
27. Position the insertion point after the space following the first sentence in the first paragraph and tap [Enter].

```
Our·local·chapter·of·Kids·for·Change·plans·to·hold·a·car·wash·fundraiser·to·collect·$300·
to·adopt·a·seal·at·the·Center·for·Seals.·¶
We·are·aiming·for·Saturday,·September·7th·for·the·car·wash.·The·next·monthly·meeting·
will·be·a·planning·session·for·the·car·wash.·Here·are·some·things·to·think·about·before·
the·meeting:¶
```

28. Position the insertion point at the end of the first paragraph and press [Ctrl]+[V].
    The Seals information is now part of the first paragraph.

Use Page Layout Options and Print Preview

Next you will preview the letter to see if it is well balanced on the page.

29. Choose **File→Print**, and preview the letter.

    You decide to widen the margins.

30. Click **Back**.

31. Choose **Page Layout→Page Setup→Margins** and choose **Custom Margins** at the bottom of the gallery.

32. Use the spin boxes to change the Left and Right margins to 1.5", then click **OK**.

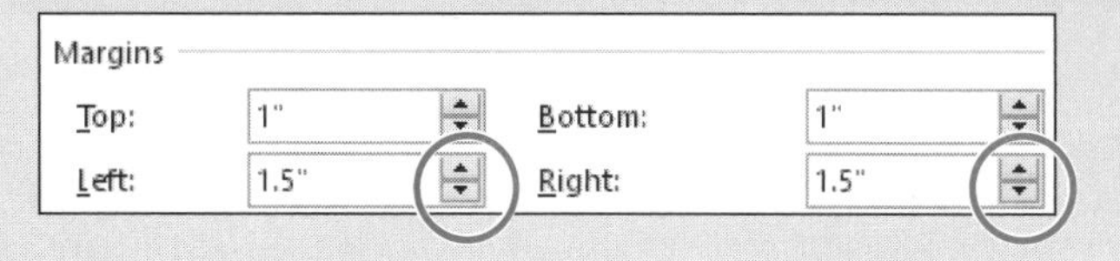

33. Choose **File→Print** to preview the letter.

    That looks better.

34. Click **Back**.

35. Save and close your letter, then exit from **Word**.

36. Submit your final file based on the guidelines provided by your instructor.

Apply Your Skills

APPLY YOUR SKILLS WD02-A01

Create a Letter and an Envelope

In this exercise, you will create a modified block-style letter, and you'll turn on the ruler to ensure the correct spacing for the date, complimentary close, and signature block. You will use AutoComplete to help you with the dates, and you will add an envelope to the letter.

Create a Block-Style Letter and Enter Text

1. Start **Word**. Create a new document using the **Single Spaced (Blank)** template.
2. Save the file in your **WD2013 Lesson 02** folder as `WD02-A01-BellLetter-[FirstInitialLastName]`.
3. Choose **View→Show→Ruler**.
4. Create the **modified block-style letter** shown in the following illustration.

Today's Date

Mrs. Suzanne Lee
8445 South Princeton Street
Chicago, IL 60628

Dear Mrs. Lee:

Congratulations on your outstanding sales achievement! Universal Corporate Events is organizing your Paris tour, which departs Saturday, October 6th and returns Wednesday, October 16th.

Please plan to attend the orientation meeting on Wednesday, September 18th in the Lake View conference room at 10:00 a.m.

We look forward to making your trip a memorable event!

Best regards,

Jack Bell
Universal Corporate Events

5. Follow these guidelines as you type your letter:
   - Space down the proper distance from the top of the page.
   - Use **AutoComplete** to help you with the dates.
   - Use Tab to align the date, closing, and signature block at **3 inches** on the ruler. (You'll need to tap Tab six times.)
   - Use correct spacing.

Create an Envelope

6. Create an envelope with no return address, and add it to the top of your letter.
7. Save and close the document; exit from **Word**.
8. Submit your final file based on the guidelines provided by your instructor.
   To view examples of how your file or files should look at the end of this exercise, go to the student resource center.

APPLY YOUR SKILLS WD02-A02

Edit a Document

In this exercise, you will make changes to a letter and copy text from another document into it. Then you will create an AutoCorrect entry, change margins, and preview your letter.

Edit Text and Work with AutoCorrect

1. Start **Word**. Open **WD02-A02-SFTours** from your **WD2013 Lesson 02** folder and save it as `WD02-A02-SFTours-[FirstInitialLastName]`.
2. Make the following editing changes, adjusting spacing as needed:
   - In the first line of the first paragraph, select *needs regarding planning your* and replace it with **`annual`**.
   - In the second line of the same paragraph, insert **`San Francisco`** to the left of *meeting*, and at the end of that sentence, Delete *in San Francisco*.
   - In the first line of the Sausalito paragraph, type **`San Francisco`** to the left of *skyline* and Delete *San Francisco* later in that sentence.
   - In the same sentence, type **`the`** to the left of *Bay*.
   - In the second sentence, type **`waterfront`** before *restaurant* and Delete *built over the water*. In the same sentence, Delete *the waterfront* and the comma that follows it.
   - In the second line of the Muir Woods paragraph, replace *wonderful* with **`majestic`**.

Switch Between Documents and Copy Text

Now you will copy some tour ideas from another document.

3. Open **WD02-A02-SiliconValley** from your **WD2013 Lesson 02** folder.
4. Select the entire document and copy it.
5. Switch back to the original letter, and position the insertion point on the second blank line following the Muir Woods paragraph.
6. Paste the copied text in the document; switch back to **WD02-A02-SiliconValley** and close it.
7. Type the current date at the top of the letter, positioning it approximately one inch from the top of the page.

8. Add the appropriate space after the date and type the following inside address:

    Ms. Addison Alexander
    Reukert Technology
    123 Apple Blossom Lane
    Detroit, MI 48217

9. If necessary, adjust the space between the address and the salutation.

Work with AutoCorrect, Margins, and Print Preview

10. Create an **AutoCorrect shortcut** for *Universal Corporate Events* using **uce** as the shortcut characters, but don't close the dialog box.
11. Press Alt+Prt Screen to take a screenshot of the dialog box showing your new entry; click **OK** twice to close the dialog boxes.
12. Paste the screenshot into a new, blank Word document and save it as **WD02-A02-ScnCap-[FirstInitialLastName]** in your **WD2013 Lesson 02** folder.
13. Close the file.
14. Change the margins in your letter to the **Narrow** setting in the Margins gallery.
15. Add the following complimentary close and signature block using your AutoCorrect shortcut for the company name, and ensure correct spacing.

    Sincerely,
    Geoff Simons
    Universal Corporate Events

16. Open the **Word Options** window, and delete the **AutoCorrect entry** you just created.
17. Save and close your file; exit from **Word**.
18. Submit your final files based on the guidelines provided by your instructor.
    To view examples of how your file or files should look at the end of this exercise, go to the student resource center.

APPLY YOUR SKILLS WD02-A03

Type and Edit a Letter, Use AutoCorrect, and Copy Text

In this exercise, you will prepare a block-style letter and an envelope to send to a Universal Corporate Events employee, and you will make editing changes to the letter and work with AutoCorrect. You will copy text from another document, and you will preview the letter.

Insert Text and Add an Envelope

1. Start **Word**. Create a new document based on the **Single Spaced (Blank)** template.
2. Save your letter as **WD02-A03-WilliamsLtr-[FirstInitialLastName]** in your **WD2013 Lesson 02** folder.

3. Type this letter.

¶
¶
¶
¶
¶
Current·Date¶
¶
¶
¶
Mr.·Bill·Williams¶
Universal·Corporate·Events·¶
14·University·Avenue¶
San·Rafael,·CA·94901¶
¶
Dear·Bill:¶
¶
You·have·been·selected·to·be·our·on-site·ambassador·at·Vaughn·Storage·Devices'·Hawaiian·event,·scheduled·for·September·1,·2013·through·September·7,·2013.·Martin·McCann·is·the·other·representative·who·will·be·working·this·event.¶
¶
You·will·be·responsible·for·helping·clients·with·airline·reservations,·hotel·arrangements,·and·side·tour·transportation.·You·will·also·coordinate·between·the·hotel·and·event·speakers·and·entertainment.·¶
¶
¶

4. Create an envelope with no return address; add it to the top of your letter.

Edit Text

5. Make the following edits to the letter:
   - In the first line of the first paragraph, change *ambassador* to **`representative`**.
   - In the same line, change *Hawaiian* to **`Kauai`**.
   - In the second line of the first paragraph, change the September dates to **`8`** through **`14`**.
   - At the beginning of the second paragraph, position the insertion point after *You*, tap [Spacebar], and type **`and Martin`**.
   - Change *entertainment* at the end of the second paragraph to **`entertainers`**.

Work with AutoFormat

Next you will type ordinals (numbers that indicate order). Word's AutoFormat feature automatically changes the ordinal suffixes to superscripts. You will turn that feature off.

6. Open the **Word Options window**, choose **Proofing** from the left panel, and click **AutoCorrect Options**.

7. Click the **AutoFormat as You Type** tab, click in the box next to **Ordinals (1st) with Superscript** to remove the checkmark, and click **OK** twice.

AutoFormat As You Type

☐ Ordinals (1st) with superscript
☑ Hyphens (--) with dash (—)

8. Position the insertion point on the second blank line at the end of the document and type the following: `The side tours will take place on September 9th, 10th, 11th, and 12th.`
9. Reset the **Ordinals** checkbox back to its original state.

Switch Between Documents and Copy Text

10. Open **WD02-A03-SideTours** from the **WD2013 Lesson 02** folder.
11. Select and copy the text.
12. Switch back to the original letter and paste the text at the end of the sentence you just typed.
13. Switch back to **WD02-A03-SideTours** and close it.
14. Add the following closing and signature block to the end of the letter; be sure to use the correct spacing.

Sincerely,

Jose Ramirez
Universal Corporate Events

Use Page Layout Options

15. Choose **Page Layout→Page Setup→Size**, and choose **Executive** from the gallery.
16. Preview the document. You may need to adjust the zoom control in the bottom-right corner of the window to see the letter and the envelope at the same time.

    You realize that executive size paper doesn't work well with a standard business envelope.
17. Change the paper size back to **Letter**.
18. Save your letter and close it; exit from **Word**.
19. Submit your final file based on the guidelines provided by your instructor.

Extend Your Skills

In the course of working through the Extend Your Skills exercises, you will think critically as you use the skills taught in the lesson to complete the assigned projects. To evaluate your mastery and completion of the exercises, your instructor may use a rubric, with which more points are allotted according to performance characteristics. (The more you do, the more you earn!) Ask your instructor how your work will be evaluated.

WD02-E01 That's the Way I See It

You have decided to start your own landscaping business, and you are going to conduct some online research to see what's involved. Your friend is studying for his MBA, and you will send him a letter containing the results of your research and ask him what he thinks of your idea.

Create a block-style letter, including a list of five landscaping tools that your research shows you will need to purchase. Then research what is involved in becoming certified as a landscape professional, and explain to your friend how you plan to earn your certification. Finally, list three tips for running a successful landscaping business. The letter should include at least three paragraphs (one to give an overview of the business, one or more to discuss certification, and one for the conclusion) and a list of three tips. The spacing in the inside address and signature block should be 1.0. Proof your work and, as necessary, use Copy and Paste or drag and drop to make changes.

Set the orientation to Landscape, and then view your letter in Print Preview. Exit Backstage view and return the orientation to Portrait. Save the file in your **WD2013 Lesson 02** folder as `WD02-E01-NewBusiness-[FirstInitialLastName]`. You will be evaluated based on the inclusion of all elements specified, your ability to follow directions, your ability to apply newly learned skills to a real-world situation, your creativity, and the relevance of your topic and/or data choice(s). Submit your final file based on the guidelines provided by your instructor.

WD02-E02 Be Your Own Boss

Blue Jean Landscaping has a new client from outside of your region who learned about your services on the Internet. She would like you to landscape her front yard. Use your imagination to decide on the client's location and climate. Conduct online research to determine what shrubs and other plants work well for the climate you chose (for example, a home in Chicago would take different plants compared to a home in San Francisco). Send the client a modified block-style letter with indented paragraphs and traditional letter line spacing to propose four plant options that would work well for her. The letter should contain both an introductory and concluding paragraph, as well as a list of four plant options, and each option should be associated with two to three sentences that explain why it is a good choice for the client's front yard. Since you will, no doubt, type "Blue Jean Landscaping" multiple times, set up an AutoCorrect entry associated with BJL.

Save the letter as `WD02-E02-NewClient-[FirstInitialLastName]` in your **WD2013 Lesson 02** folder. Proof your work and, as necessary, use Copy and Paste and drag and drop to make edits. Remove the AutoCorrect entry. Then save and close the letter. You will be evaluated based on the inclusion of all elements specified, your ability to follow directions, your ability to apply newly learned skills to a real-world situation, your creativity, and your demonstration of an entrepreneurial spirit. Submit your final file based on the guidelines provided by your instructor.

Transfer Your Skills

In the course of working through the Transfer Your Skills exercises, you will use critical-thinking and creativity skills to complete the assigned projects using skills taught in the lesson. To evaluate your mastery and completion of the exercises, your instructor may use a rubric, with which more points are allotted according to performance characteristics. (The more you do, the more you earn!) Ask your instructor how your work will be evaluated.

WD02-T01 Use the Web as a Learning Tool

Throughout this book, you will be provided with an opportunity to use the Internet as a learning tool by completing WebQuests. According to the original creators of WebQuests, as described on their website (WebQuest.org), a WebQuest is "an inquiry-oriented activity in which most or all of the information used by learners is drawn from the web." To complete the WebQuest projects in this book, navigate to the student resource center and choose the WebQuest for the lesson on which you are currently working. The subject of each WebQuest will be relevant to the material found in the lesson.

WebQuest Subject: Proper business correspondence etiquette.

Submit your final file(s) based on the guidelines provided by your instructor.

WD02-T02 Demonstrate Proficiency

As the owner of Stormy BBQ, you've decided to hold a chili cook-off to attract new clients. Use online research to learn how to have a successful cook-off, and also research rules for the chefs to ensure that they are competing on a level playing field.

Create a letter using the style of your choice (making sure to properly format it) to send out to prospective chili chefs listing three important guidelines for a successful cook-off and three competition rules for your chefs. The letter should include both an introductory and a concluding paragraph, as well as the rules that have been established. Make up the name of the first chef you wish to invite and include the information in the inside address. Create an envelope addressed to the chef with no return address.

Proof your work and, as necessary, use Copy and Paste or drag and drop to make edits. Change all margins to 0.5" and view the effect in Print Preview.

Save your letter in the **WD2013 Lesson 02** folder as **`WD02-T02-ChiliChef-[FirstInitialLastName]`**. Submit your final file based on the guidelines provided by your instructor.

Creating a Memorandum and a Press Release

In this lesson, you will expand your basic Word skills. You will create a memo, apply character formatting, and use spelling and grammar checking. You will refine your word choice with the thesaurus, and you'll learn some efficient ways to navigate in documents. Finally, you will transform PDF files into fully editable Word documents.

LESSON OUTLINE

LEARNING OBJECTIVES

After studying this lesson, you will be able to:

- Use Word's default tabs
- Insert dates, symbols, and page breaks
- Work with proofreading tools and the thesaurus
- Work with character formatting features
- Edit PDF files in Word

CASE STUDY

Preparing a Memorandum

My Virtual Campus continues to grow and add the latest advances in technology. The public relations representative has asked you to create a memorandum and attach a press release announcing the launch of MyResume, which is being integrated into the website. You understand the importance of protecting proprietary information, so you use the appropriate trademark designations in your documents.

When the marketing department decides to change the product name, the Find and Replace feature makes changing the name throughout the document a snap.

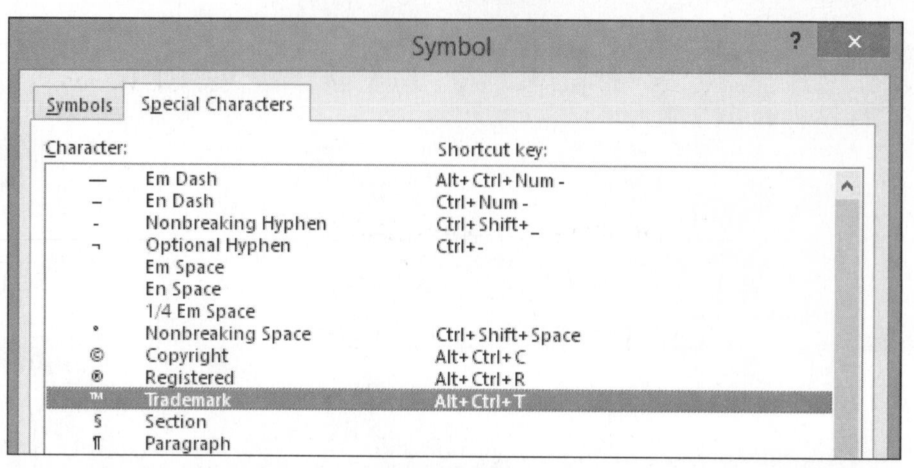

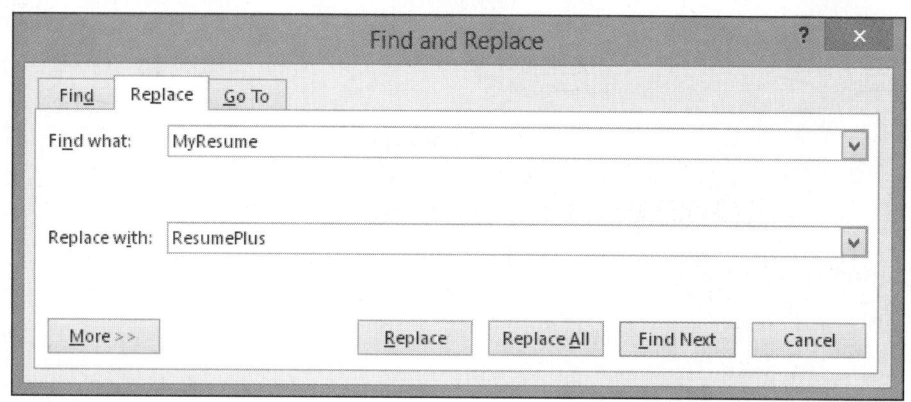

Typing a Memorandum

Video Library http://labyrinthelab.com/videos Video Number: WD13-V0301

There are a variety of acceptable memorandum styles in use today. They all contain the same elements, but with varied formatting. The style shown here is a traditional style with minimal formatting.

The introduction includes headings such as *Memo To* and *From*.

MEMO TO: Galin Rodgers

FROM: Suzanne Student

DATE: December 10, 2013

SUBJECT: My Virtual Campus Press Release

The body is next.

I have attached a press release to announce the launch of the new MyResume service. Please review the press release and let me know if you have comments or suggestions. I will submit this press release to the media organization next week.

Extras, such as attachment notations, go here.

Attachment

Introducing Default Tabs

The [Tab] key moves the insertion point to the nearest tab stop on the ruler. In Word, the default tab stops are set every one-half inch, thus the insertion point moves one-half inch when you tap [Tab]. In this lesson, you will use Word's default tab settings.

FROM THE RIBBON
View→Show→Ruler

Inserting and Formatting the Date

Word lets you insert the current date in a variety of formats. For example, the date could be inserted as 12/10/13, December 10, 2013, or 10 December 2013.

FROM THE RIBBON
Insert→Text→Insert Date and Time

FROM THE KEYBOARD
[Alt]+[Shift]+[D] to insert the date

Updating the Date Automatically

You can insert the date as text or as a field. Inserting the date as text has the same effect as manually typing the date. Fields, on the other hand, are updated whenever a document is saved or printed.

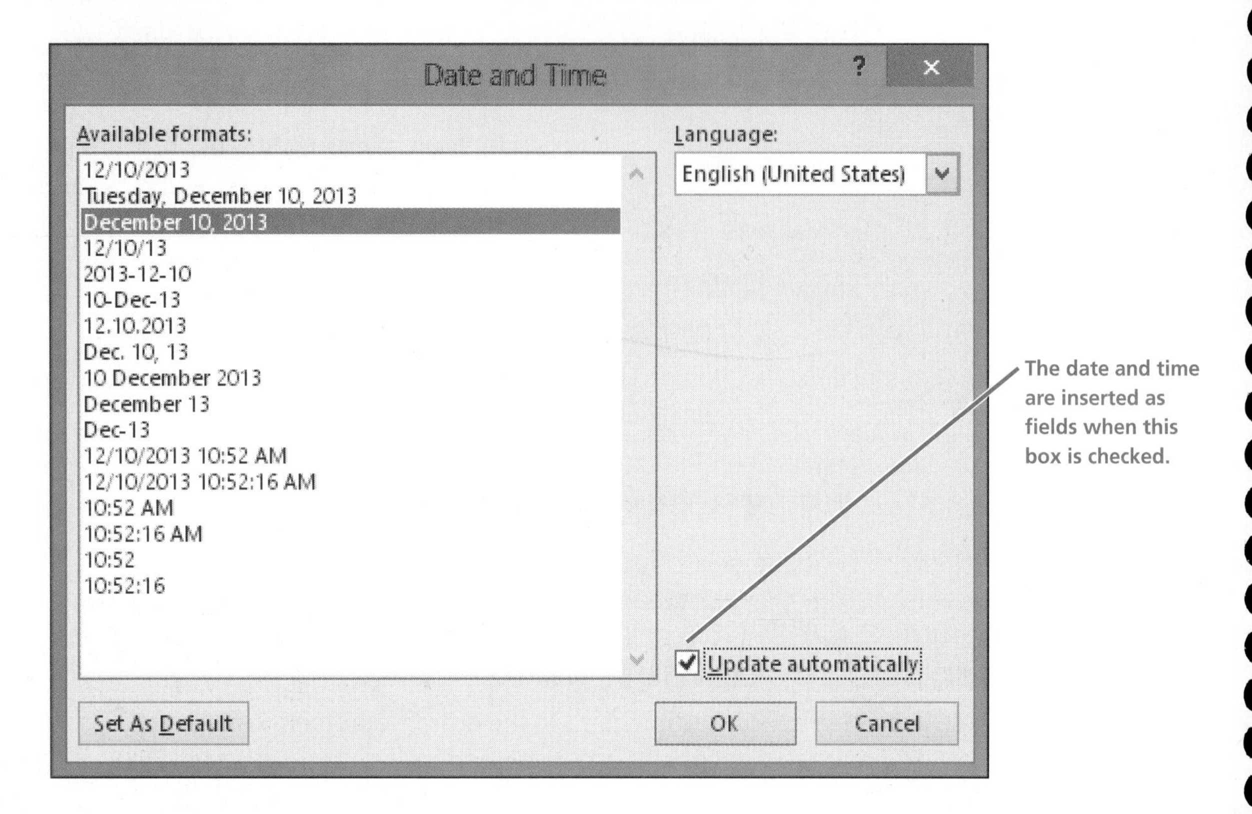

DEVELOP YOUR SKILLS WD03-D01

Set Up a Memo and Insert the Date

In this exercise, you will create a memo using Word's default tab settings and automatically insert the date. You'll also use Word's Blank Document template, which applies 1.08 line spacing with extra space following paragraphs.

1. Start a new document using the **Blank Document template**. Make sure the Word window is **maximized** .
2. Save the file in your **WD2013 Lesson 03** folder as **`WD03-D01-MartinMemo-[FirstInitialLastName]`**.

   Replace the bracketed text with your first initial and last name. For example, if your name is Bethany Smith, your filename would look like this: WD03-D01-MartinMemo-BSmith.
3. If necessary, choose **Home→Paragraph→Show/Hide** ¶ to display formatting marks.

   Next you will turn on the ruler so you can observe that Word's default tabs are set at every one-half inch.
4. If necessary, choose **View→Show→Ruler**.

   The ruler opens below the Ribbon and on the left side of the screen.

5. Follow these steps to begin the memo:

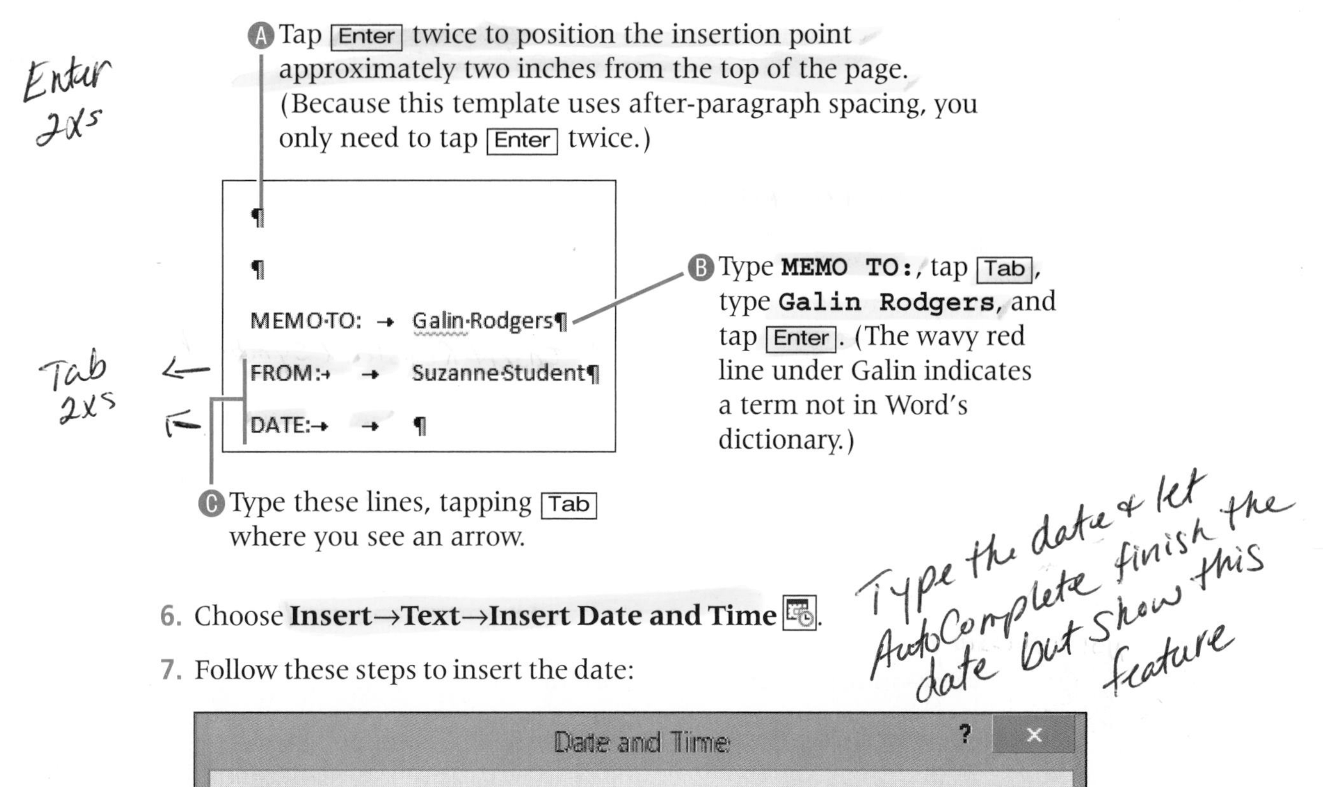

Ⓐ Tap Enter twice to position the insertion point approximately two inches from the top of the page. (Because this template uses after-paragraph spacing, you only need to tap Enter twice.)

Ⓑ Type **MEMO TO:**, tap Tab, type **Galin Rodgers**, and tap Enter. (The wavy red line under Galin indicates a term not in Word's dictionary.)

Ⓒ Type these lines, tapping Tab where you see an arrow.

6. Choose **Insert→Text→Insert Date and Time**.

7. Follow these steps to insert the date:

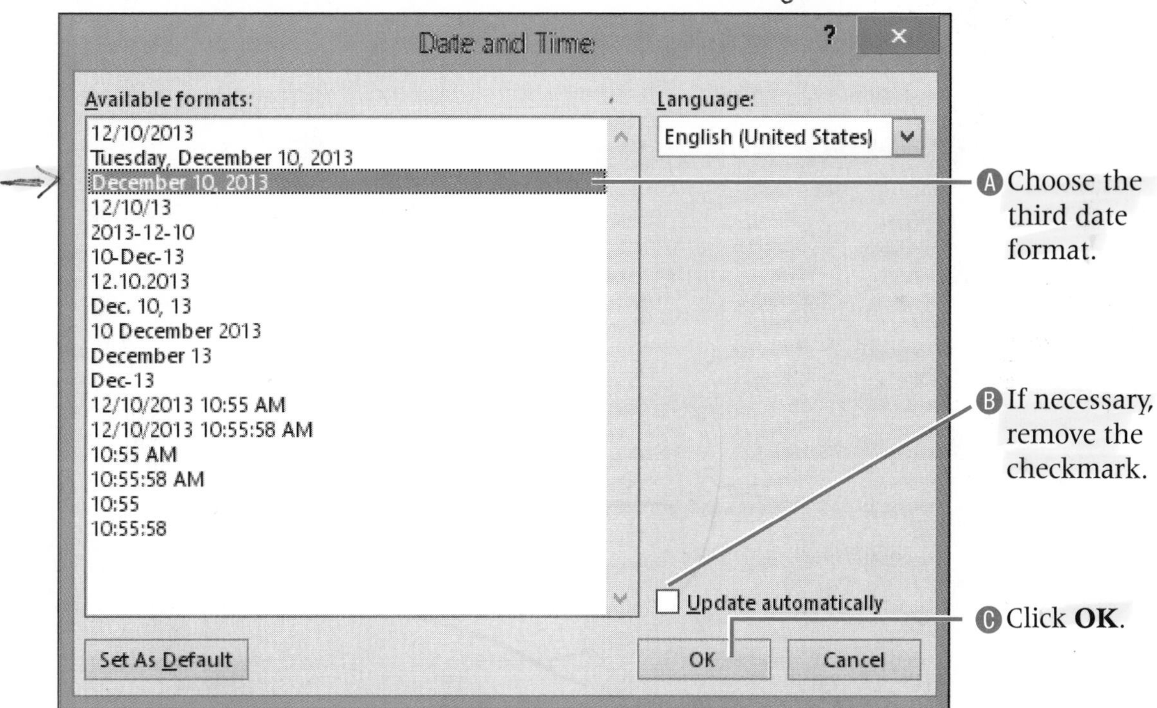

Ⓐ Choose the third date format.

Ⓑ If necessary, remove the checkmark.

Ⓒ Click **OK**.

Leaving Update Automatically checked instructs Word to insert the date as a field, which means the original date would be lost if you opened and saved the document at a later date. In this instance, you do not want the date to change.

The date shown here may differ from the current date that you use.

8. Choose **Home→Paragraph→Show/Hide** [¶] to turn off formatting marks.
9. Complete the rest of the memorandum as shown, using [Tab] to align the text in the Subject line. Bear in mind that you only need to tap [Enter] once between paragraphs due to this template's after-paragraph spacing.

MEMO TO:	Galin Rodgers
FROM:	Suzanne Student
DATE:	December 10, 2013
SUBJECT:	My Virtual Campus Press Release X *Insert Registered Symbol here*

I have attached a press release to announce the launch of the new MyResume service. Please review the press release and let me know if you have comments or suggestions. I will submit this press release to the media organization next week.

Attachment

Not necessary

? 10. Choose **View→Show→Ruler** to turn off the ruler.

11. Save the document and leave it open; you will modify it throughout this lesson.

Inserting Symbols

Video Library http://labyrinthelab.com/videos Video Number: WD13-V0302

Word lets you insert a variety of symbols and other characters not found on the keyboard. The following illustration shows the Symbol menu.

FROM THE RIBBON
Insert→Symbols →Symbol

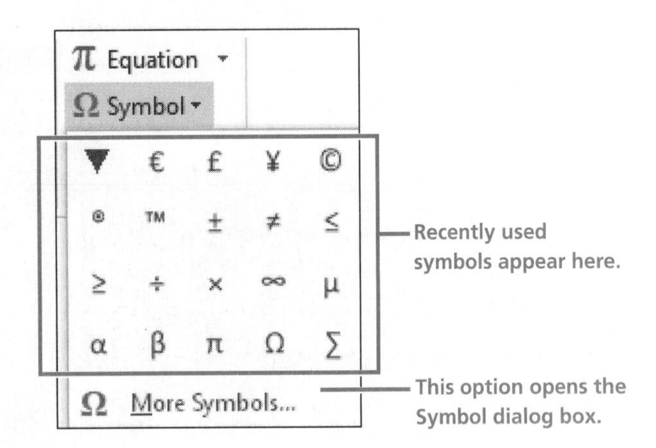

The following figure points out the main features of the Symbol dialog box.

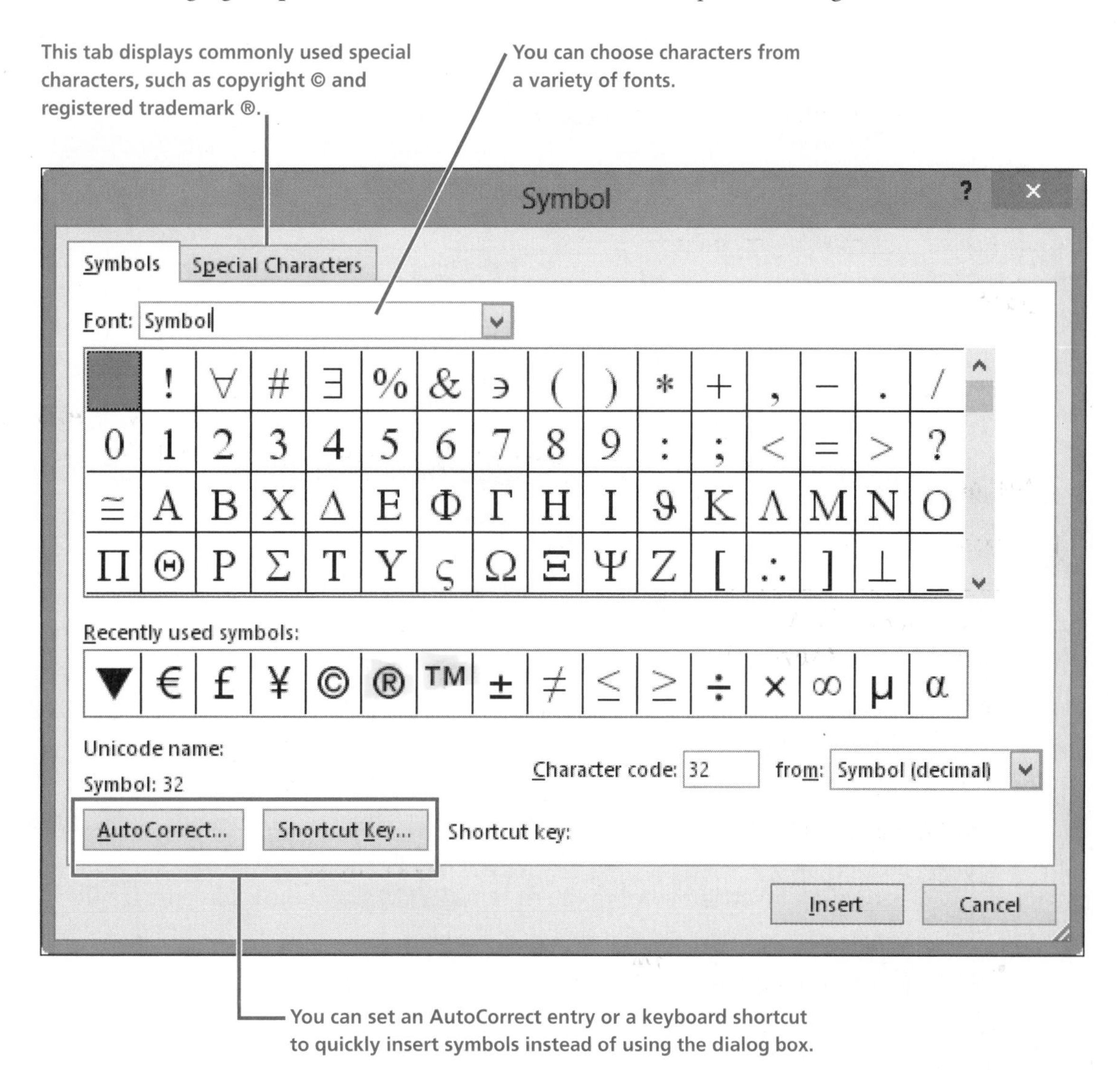

DEVELOP YOUR SKILLS WD03-D02

Insert Symbols

In this exercise, you will add a trademark symbol and a registered trademark symbol to your document.

1. Save your file as **`WD03-D02-MartinMemo-[FirstInitialLastName]`**.
2. Position the insertion point to the right of My Virtual Campus in the **Subject** line. Click after Press Release
3. Choose **Insert→Symbols→Symbol** Ω, and then choose **More Symbols** at the bottom of the menu.

4. Follow these steps to insert the registered trademark symbol:

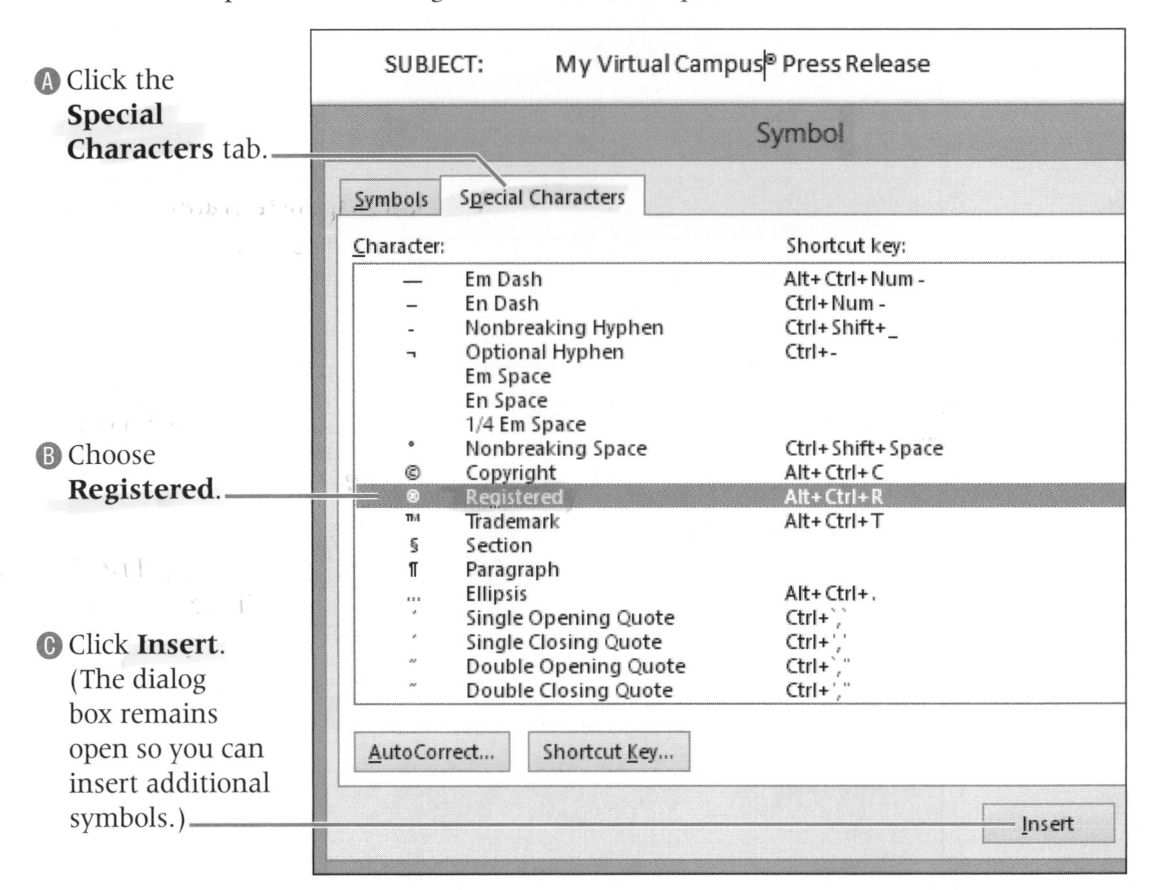

5. Position the insertion point to the right of *MyResume* in the main paragraph.

   You may need to drag the dialog box out of the way.

6. Click the **Trademark** (™) symbol, and then click **Insert**.
7. Click the **Symbols** tab and choose different fonts from the **Font** list to see other sets of symbols.
8. When you finish experimenting, click **Close**.
9. Save the memo.

Working with Page Breaks

Video Library http://labyrinthelab.com/videos Video Number: WD13-V0303

If you are typing text and the insertion point reaches the bottom of a page, Word inserts an *automatic* page break. Automatic page breaks are convenient when working with long documents. For example, imagine you are writing a report and you decide to insert a new paragraph in the middle. Word automatically repaginates the report.

A manual page break remains in place unless you remove it. You insert manual page breaks whenever you want to control the starting point of a new page.

FROM THE RIBBON
Page Layout→Page Setup→Breaks→Page

FROM THE KEYBOARD
Ctrl+Enter to insert a manual page break

Removing Manual Page Breaks

If you turn on the Show/Hide feature, you can see the page break in Print Layout view. You delete a page break the same way you delete other content in a document.

I·have·attached·a·press·release·to·annou
the·press·release·and·let·me·know·if·you
to·the·media·organization·next·week.¶

Attachment¶

..........Page Break..........¶

You can remove a page break by displaying the formatting marks, clicking to the left of the break, and tapping Delete.

DEVELOP YOUR SKILLS WD03-D03

X Work with Page Breaks

In this exercise, you will insert a page break, thereby creating a new page, so you can copy and paste a press release into the new page.

1. Save your file as **WD03-D03-MartinMemo-[FirstInitialLastName]**.

   Next you will ensure you are in Print Layout view so you can see the page break. You can see a page break in other views, but you will use Print Layout view.

2. Choose **View→Views→Print Layout**. (Already in Print Layout View)
3. Press Ctrl+End (Ctrl + End) to position the insertion point at the end of the document. If necessary, tap Enter to generate a blank line below the *Attachment* line.
4. Choose **Insert→Pages→Page Break**. Insert Page Break
5. If necessary, scroll to the bottom of page 1 to see the new page 2.
6. Scroll up until the *Attachment* line is visible.
7. If necessary, choose **Home→Paragraph→Show/Hide** ¶ to display formatting marks.
8. Position the insertion point to the left of the page break and tap Delete. Delete the page Break

9. Try scrolling down to the second page and you will see that it is gone.

10. Check to see that the insertion point is just below the *Attachment* line, and press Ctrl + Enter to reinsert the page break.

11. Choose **Home→Paragraph→Show/Hide** ¶ to hide the formatting marks.

Copy and Paste from Another Document

12. Open **WD03-D03-PressRelease** from your **WD2013 Lesson 03** folder.

    Notice that a number of terms are flagged by the spelling checker (red wavy underlines) and grammar checker (blue wavy underline). Ignore these notations for now.

13. In the press release document, press Ctrl + A to select the entire document.

14. Press Ctrl + C to copy the document.

    Now you will switch to your memo.

15. Follow these steps to switch to the memo:

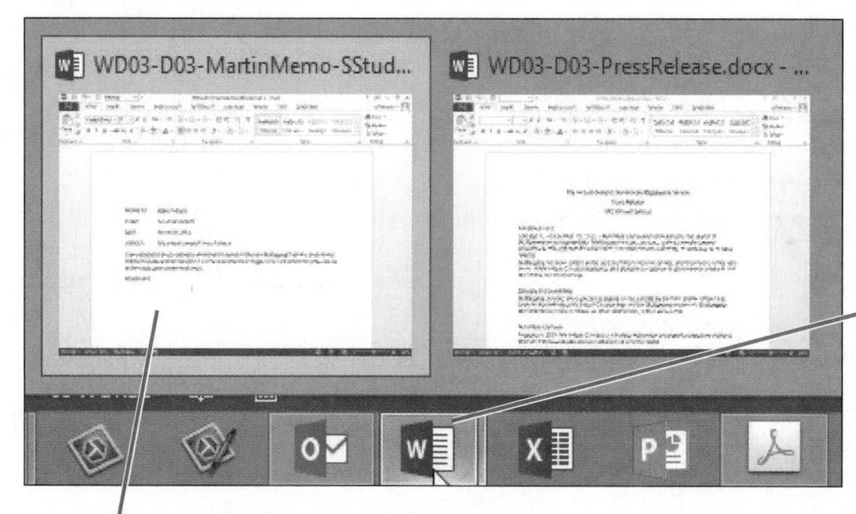

Ⓐ Hover the mouse pointer over the **Word icon** on the taskbar.

Ⓑ Click **WD03-D03-MartinMemo-[FirstInitialLastName]** to display it in the foreground.

16. Make sure the insertion point is at the top of **page 2.**

17. Choose **Home→Clipboard→Paste**.

    Now you will switch back to the press release and close it.

18. Use the taskbar button to switch to the press release document.

19. Choose **File→Close.**

    The memo document should now be in the foreground.

20. Save the file.

Working with Proofreading Tools

Video Library http://labyrinthelab.com/videos Video Number: WD13-V0304

Word's spelling and grammar tools help you avoid errors. You can choose to use the default *on-the-fly* checking, where Word marks possible errors as you type, or you can save proofing until you've completed your document. Word provides many choices allowing you to set the level of grammar and style checking from strict to casual.

Proofing tools can help polish your writing; however, they are proofreading *aids*, not the final word. You still need human judgment in a final round of proofing.

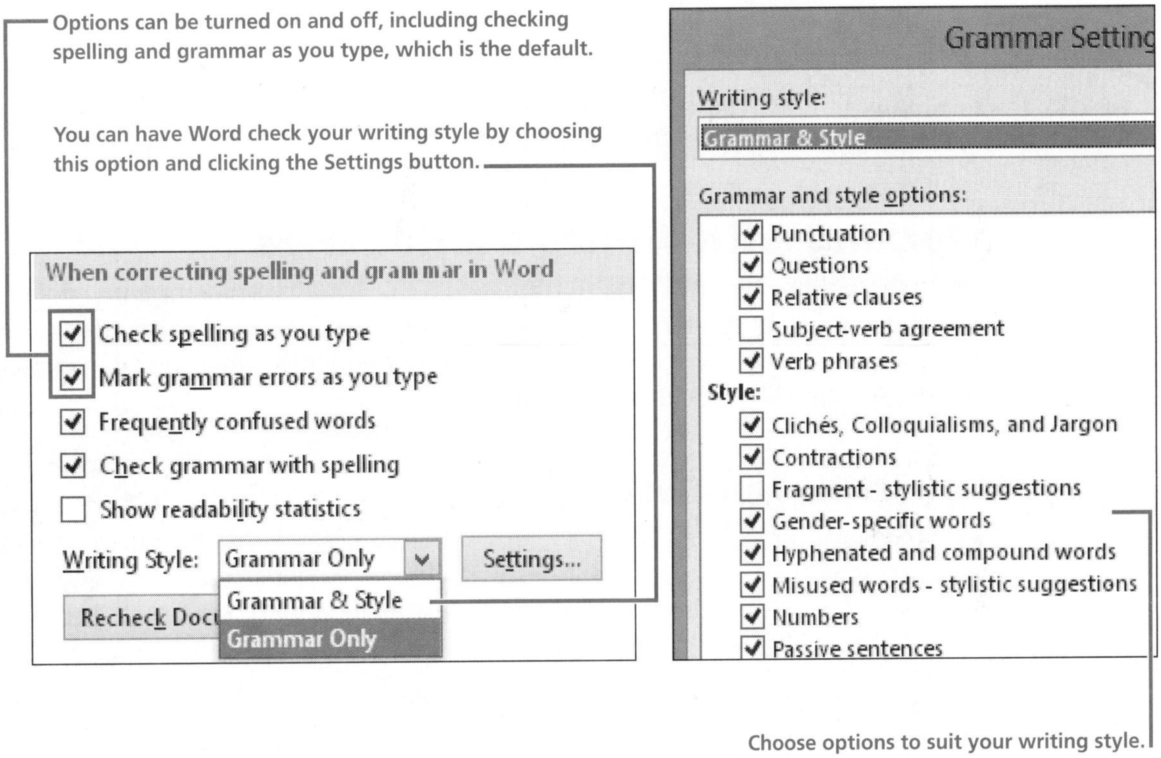

FROM THE RIBBON
Review→Proofing →Spelling & Grammar

FROM THE KEYBOARD
[F7] for proofreading tools

Options can be turned on and off, including checking spelling and grammar as you type, which is the default.

You can have Word check your writing style by choosing this option and clicking the Settings button.

When correcting spelling and grammar in Word
- [x] Check spelling as you type
- [x] Mark grammar errors as you type
- [x] Frequently confused words
- [x] Check grammar with spelling
- [ ] Show readability statistics

Writing Style: Grammar Only | Settings...
Grammar & Style
Grammar Only
Recheck Doc

Grammar Setting
Writing style:
Grammar & Style
Grammar and style options:
- [x] Punctuation
- [x] Questions
- [x] Relative clauses
- [ ] Subject-verb agreement
- [x] Verb phrases

Style:
- [x] Clichés, Colloquialisms, and Jargon
- [x] Contractions
- [ ] Fragment - stylistic suggestions
- [x] Gender-specific words
- [x] Hyphenated and compound words
- [x] Misused words - stylistic suggestions
- [x] Numbers
- [x] Passive sentences

Choose options to suit your writing style.

Using the Spelling Checker

Word can automatically check your spelling as you type. It flags spelling errors with wavy red lines. You can address a flagged error by right-clicking it and choosing a suggested replacement word or other option from the pop-up menu.

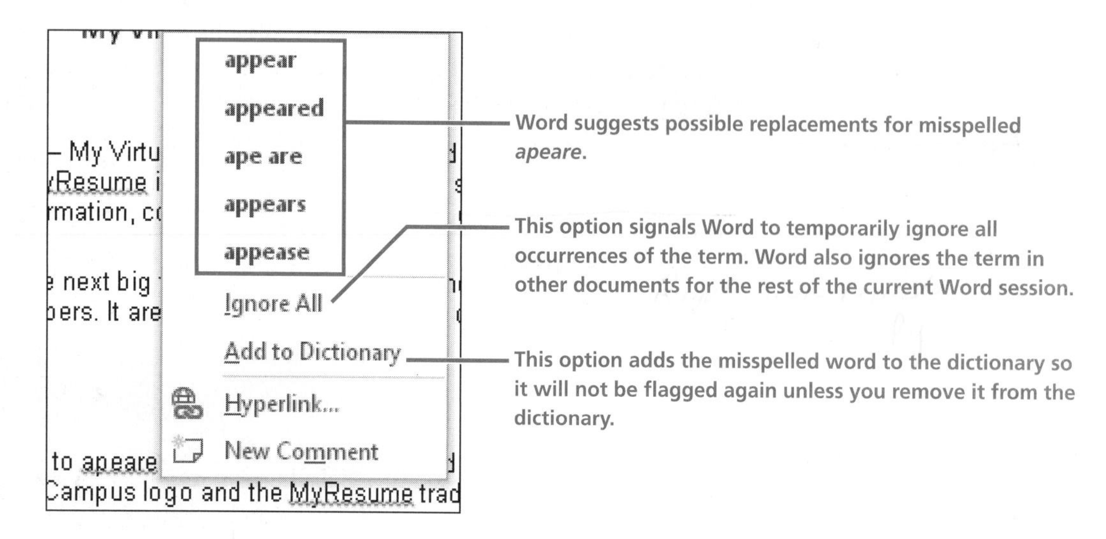

Working with Word's Dictionaries

The main Word dictionary contains thousands of common words, though it does not include all proper names, technical terms, and so forth. Word marks a term not found in the main dictionary as a possible error. If you use that term frequently, you can add it to a custom dictionary so it will not be marked as an error.

Using Dictionary Options

When Suggest from Main Dictionary Only is checked, Word only searches the main dictionary; if that option is unchecked, Word searches in custom dictionaries as well. Adding a word to the dictionary during spell checking adds it to a custom dictionary.

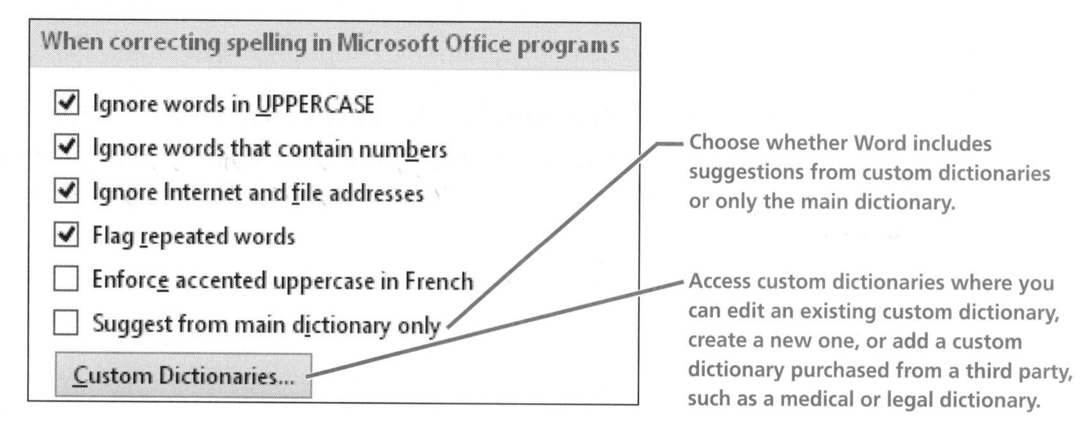

The options you set for custom dictionaries in Word apply to all Office programs.

Adding or Deleting Words in a Custom Dictionary

In addition to adding words through the spelling checker, you can add words using the Custom Dictionaries dialog box. If you add a word to the dictionary by mistake, you can remove it.

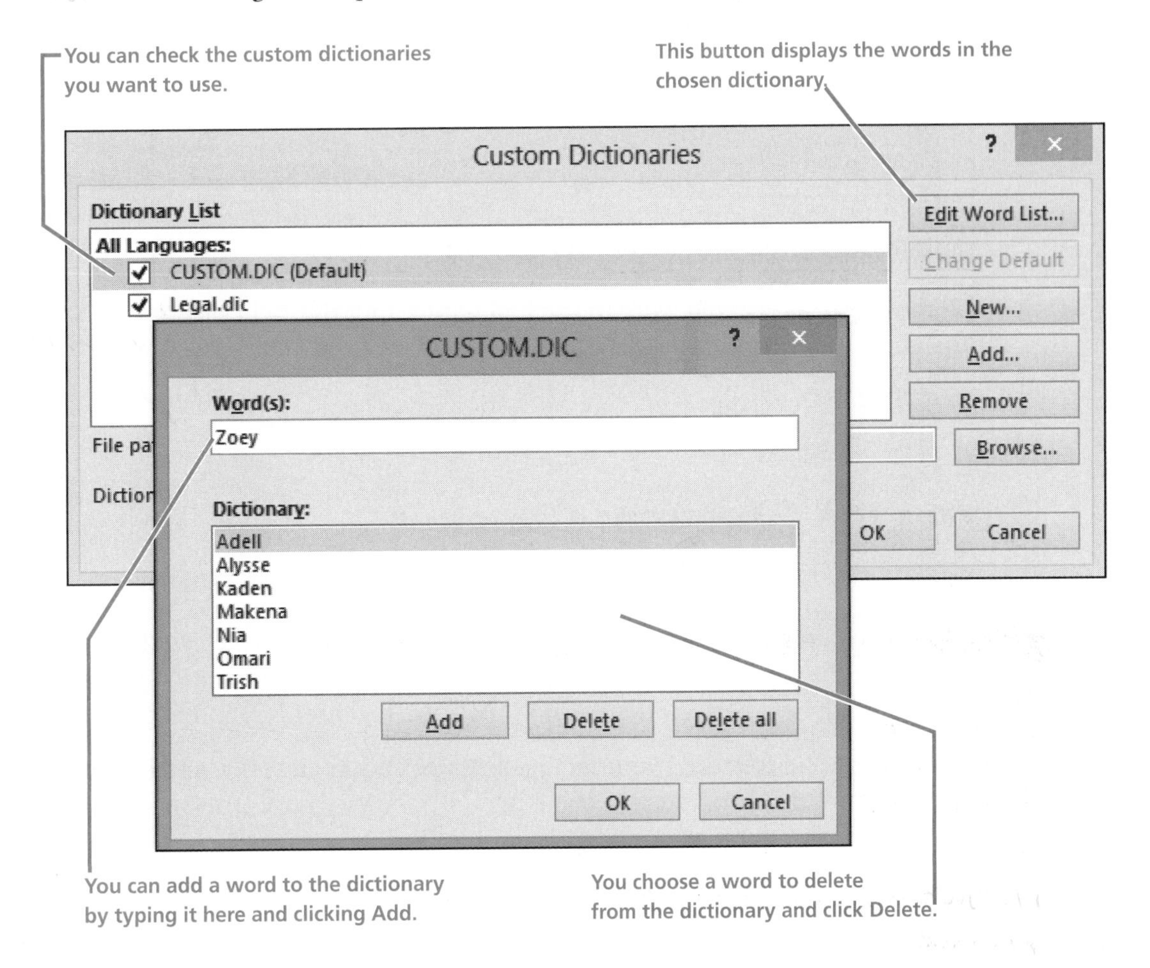

DEVELOP YOUR SKILLS WD03-D04

X **Use the Automatic Spelling Checker**

In this exercise, you will add a term to Word's dictionary. You will also delete a repeated word.

1. Save your file as **`WD03-D04-MartinMemo-[FirstInitialLastName]`**.

   Notice that the term MyResume *in the first line of page 2 has a wavy red underline.* MyResume *is spelled correctly, but it does not appear in Word's dictionary. Thus, Word flags it as a possible spelling error.*

   MyResume has a wavy red line
   Spelled correctly but not in the dictionary

2. Follow these steps to add *MyResume* to the dictionary:

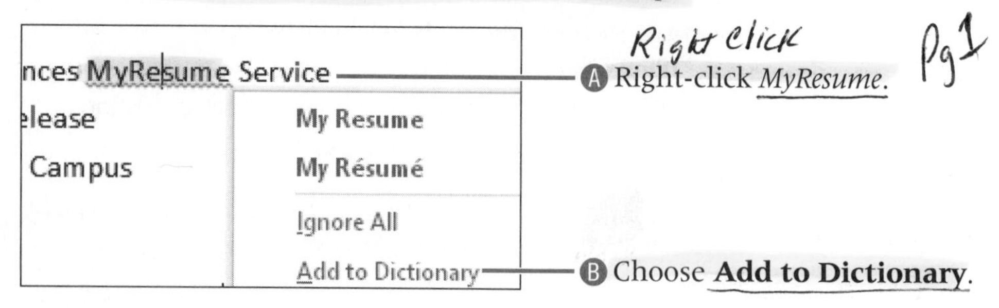

You will delete MyResume from the dictionary a little later.

3. Word flagged a repeated word in the first paragraph; right-click *our* with the wavy red line and choose **Delete Repeated Word**.
4. Save the file.

Using the Grammar Checker

Video Library http://labyrinthelab.com/videos Video Number: WD13-V0305

Word has a grammar checker that flags errors with wavy blue lines. Like the spelling checker, you right-click the error and choose a replacement phrase or other option from the menu. The grammar checker isn't perfect; there is no substitute for careful proofreading.

Like the spelling checker, the grammar checker also checks *on the fly*, and like the spelling checker, you can turn it off and save checking for later. Word uses the Spelling and Grammar task panes for making suggestions.

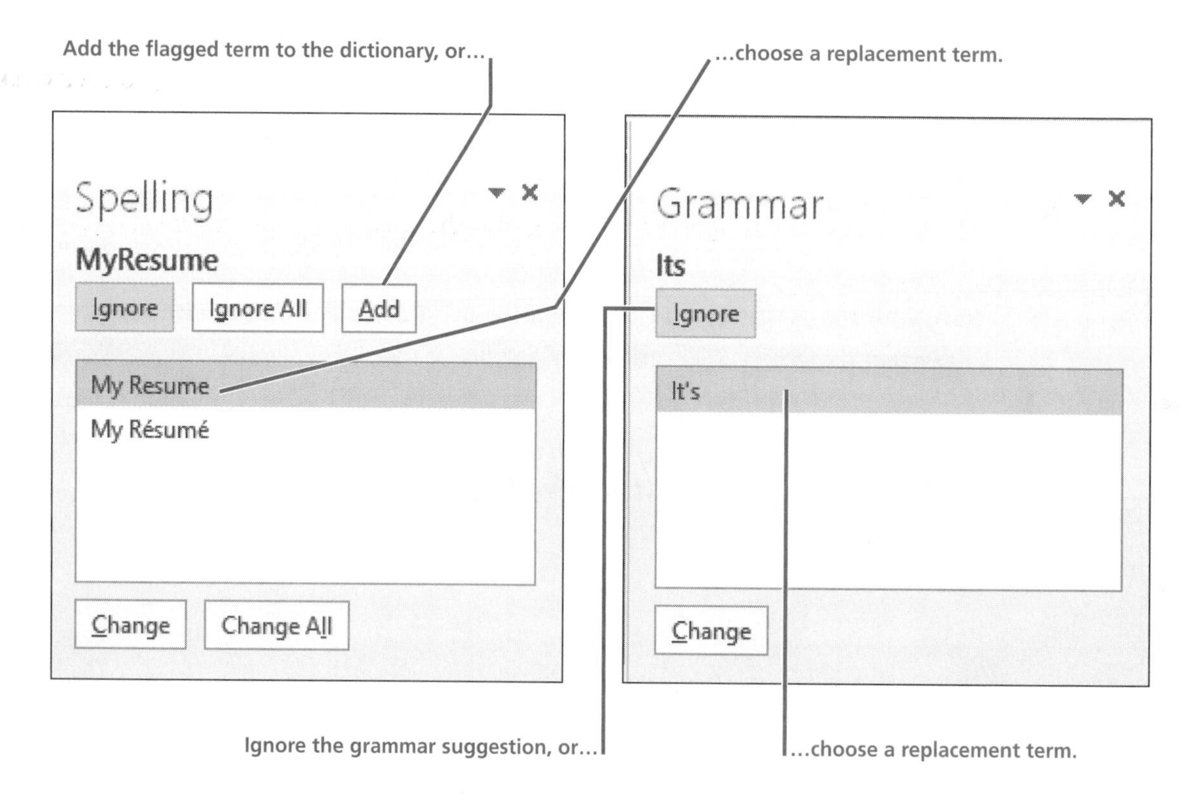

QUICK REFERENCE	USING SPELLING AND GRAMMAR OPTIONS
Task	**Procedure**
Set level of grammar and style checking	■ Choose File→Options and choose the Proofing category. ■ Choose the Writing Style and click Settings.
Work with custom dictionaries	■ Choose File→Options and choose the Proofing category. ■ Click the Custom Dictionaries button.
Turn off spelling and grammar checking as you type	■ Choose File→Options and choose the Proofing category. ■ Uncheck the options for checking spelling and marking grammar as you type.

DEVELOP YOUR SKILLS WD03-D05

X Use the Spelling and Grammar Checkers

In this exercise, you will make spelling and grammar corrections to the Martin Memo using the Spelling and Grammar task panes.

1. Save the file as **`WD03-D05-MartinMemo-[FirstInitialLastName]`**.
2. Position the insertion point at the beginning of the first line on **page 2**. Insertion point top of page 2
3. Choose **Review→Proofing→Spelling & Grammar** .
   The Spelling task pane opens, and wiht *is noted as a possible spelling error.*
4. The error is a typo, and the suggestion *with* is correct, so click **Change**.
   Now Word points out Its *as a possible grammatical error.*
5. Click **Change** to accept the grammar suggestion.
6. The next error is a spelling error, and the suggestion *Delivery* is correct, so click **Change**.
7. Finish checking the rest of the document using your good judgment regarding what changes to make. When *Galin* is flagged, click **Ignore All**.
8. When the message appears indicating that the spelling and grammar check is complete, click **OK**.

Remove a Word from the Custom Dictionary

9. Choose **File→Options** and choose the **Proofing** category.
10. Follow these steps to delete MyResume:

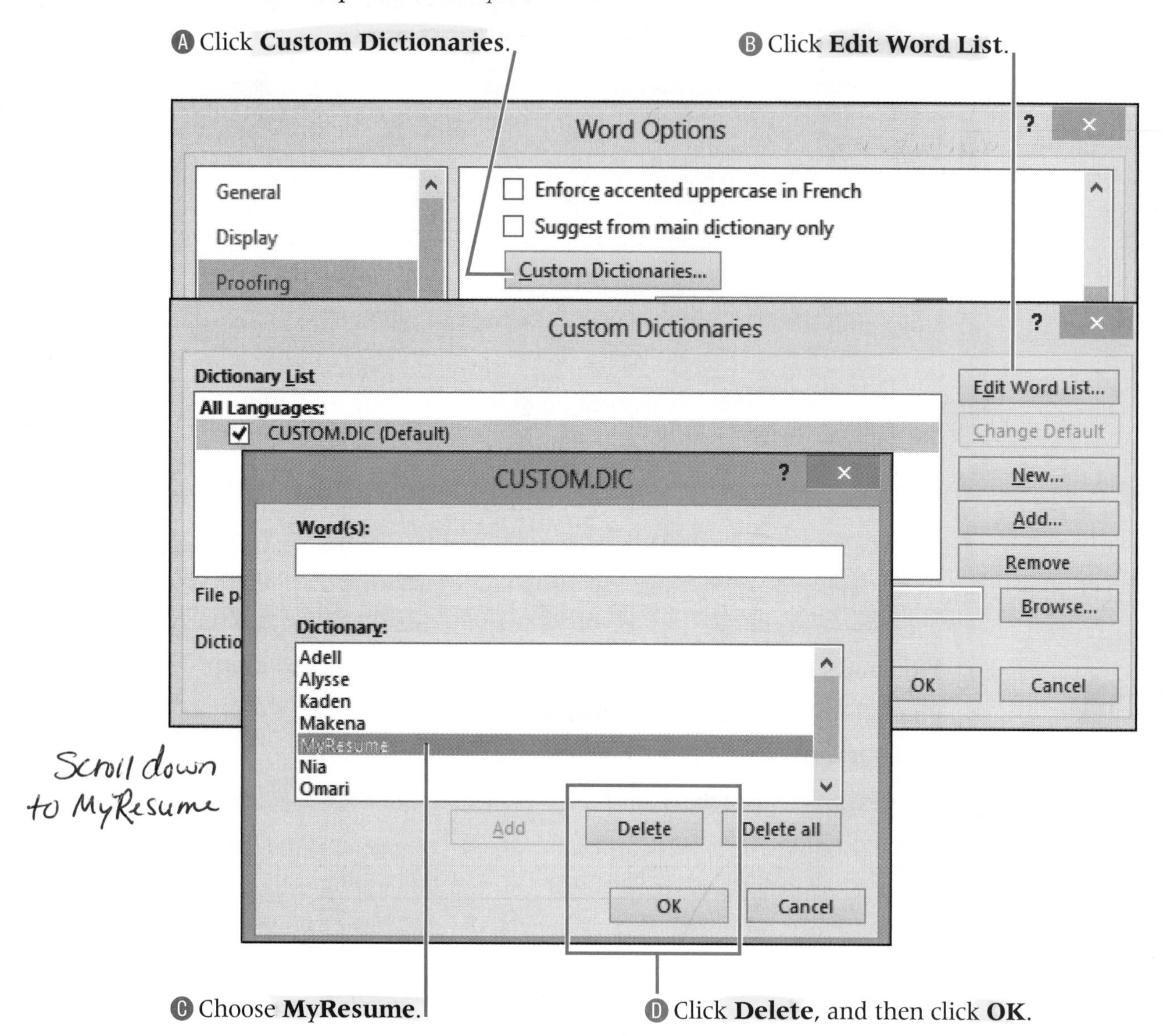

11. Click **OK** two more times.
    MyResume is flagged again, because you removed it from the dictionary.
12. Right-click *MyResume* and choose **Ignore All**.
13. Save the file.

Using the Thesaurus to Find a Synonym

Video Library http://labyrinthelab.com/videos Video Number: WD13-V0306

You can view a list of synonyms by right-clicking a word and choosing Synonyms from the menu. For a more extensive list, choose Thesaurus from the bottom of the submenu to open the Thesaurus task pane.

FROM THE RIBBON
Review→Proofing →Thesaurus

FROM THE KEYBOARD
[Shift]+[F7] to open the Thesaurus

The Thesaurus task pane goes beyond displaying a list of alternate words. As you know, a word can have different meanings depending upon the context in which it is used. For example, the word *launch* can be used to mean *presentation*, *takeoff*, *hurl*, or *open*. Using the task pane, you can look up those additional synonyms by clicking any word displayed in the results list.

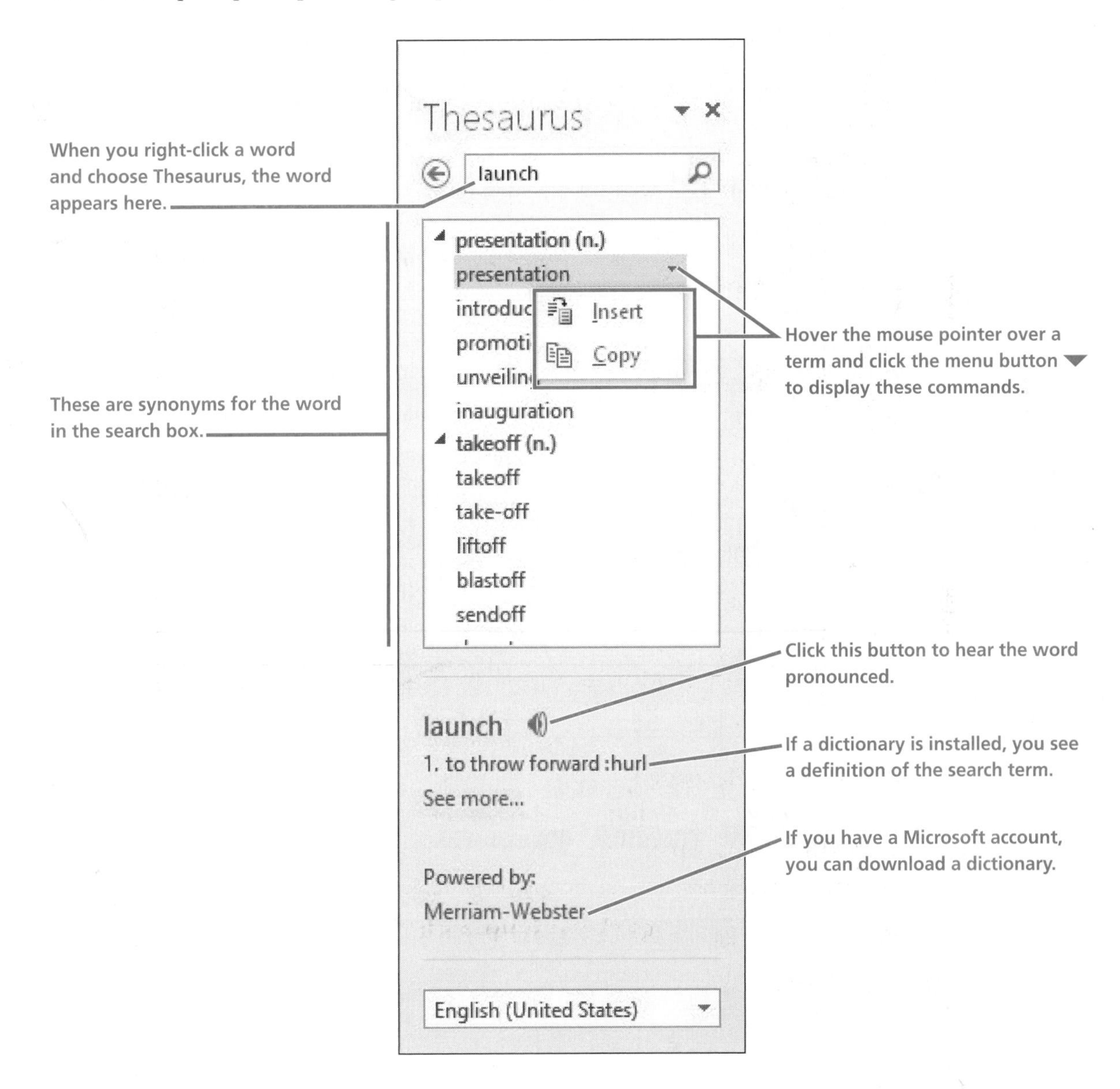

DEVELOP YOUR SKILLS WD03-D06

Use the Thesaurus

In this exercise, you will use the pop-up menu to locate a synonym. You will also use the Thesaurus task pane.

1. Save your file as **WD03-D06-MartinMemo-[FirstInitialLastName]**.
2. Scroll down to view the press release page. Pg 2
3. Right-click the word *launch* in the first sentence of the *Announcement* paragraph. First paragraph
4. Follow these steps to replace the word with a synonym:

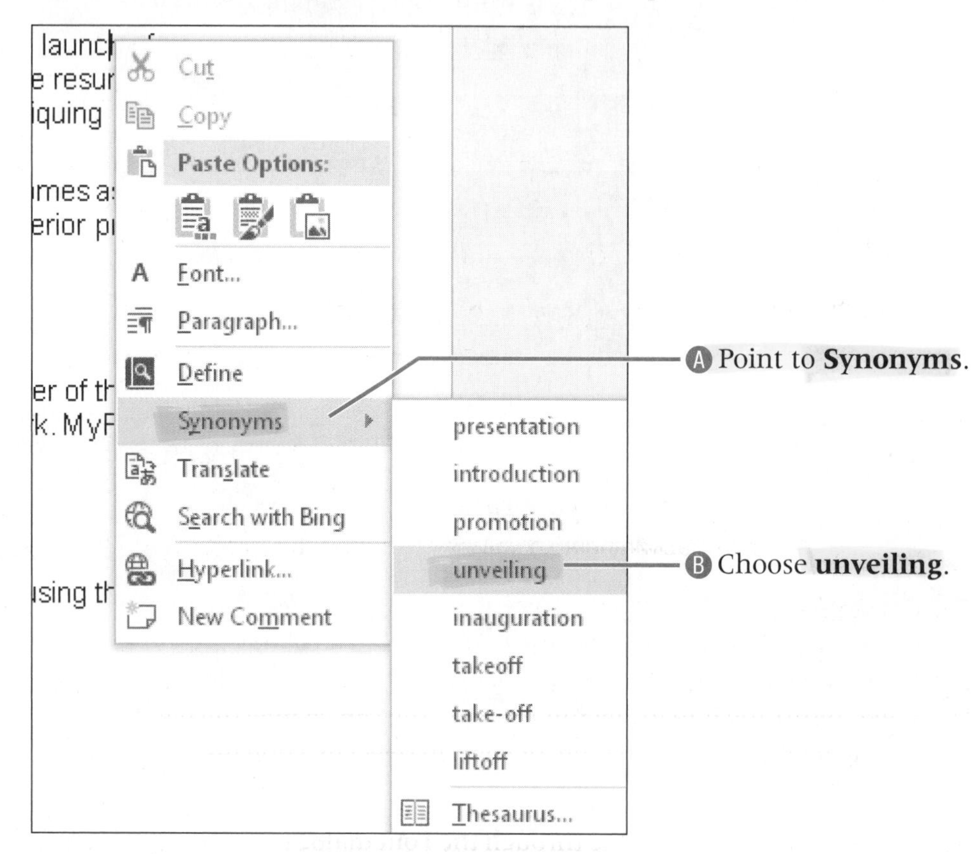

Now you'll look up synonyms in the Thesaurus task pane.

5. Choose **Review→Proofing→Thesaurus**. (Tab, Group, Command)

6. Follow these steps to re-insert *launch* in place of *unveiling*.

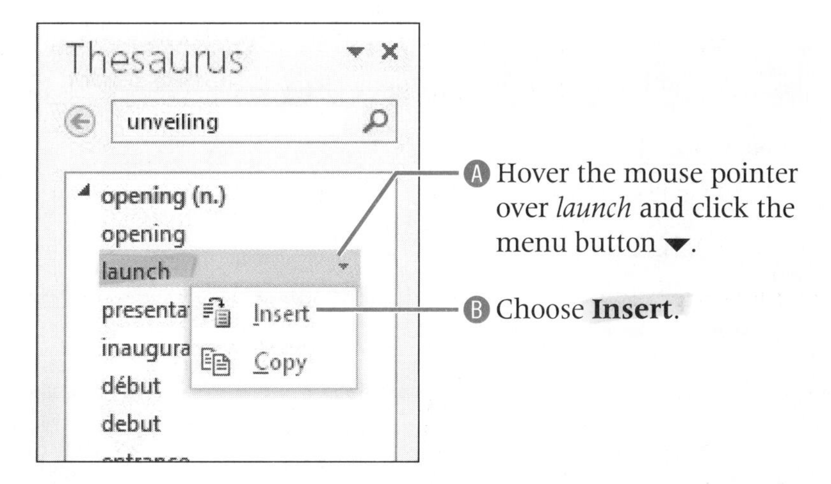

7. While the Thesaurus task pane is still open, click any word in the list to view synonyms for that word. Show the Keyboard Shortcut, Alt and click the word in the document
8. Click **Close** [×] in the upper-right corner of the Thesaurus task pane.
9. Save the file.

Formatting Text

Video Library http://labyrinthelab.com/videos Video Number: WD13-V0307

You can format text using the Font group on the Home tab. Options include changing the font, size, and color and applying various enhancements, including bold, italics, and underline. You can also clear all added formatting from text, returning it to its default formats. You can change the text formatting before you start typing, or you can select existing text and then make the changes.

FROM THE KEYBOARD
[Ctrl]+[B] for bold
[Ctrl]+[I] for italics
[Ctrl]+[U] for underline

Additional options are available through the Font dialog box. The dialog box launcher in the bottom-right corner of the Font group opens the dialog box.

Home Tab, Font Group

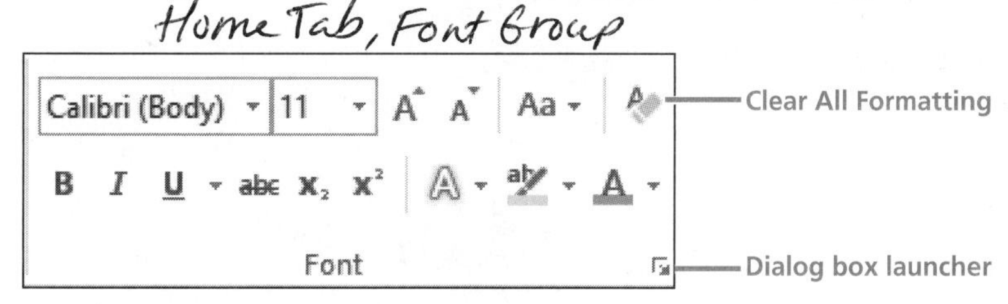

The following illustration describes the Font dialog box.

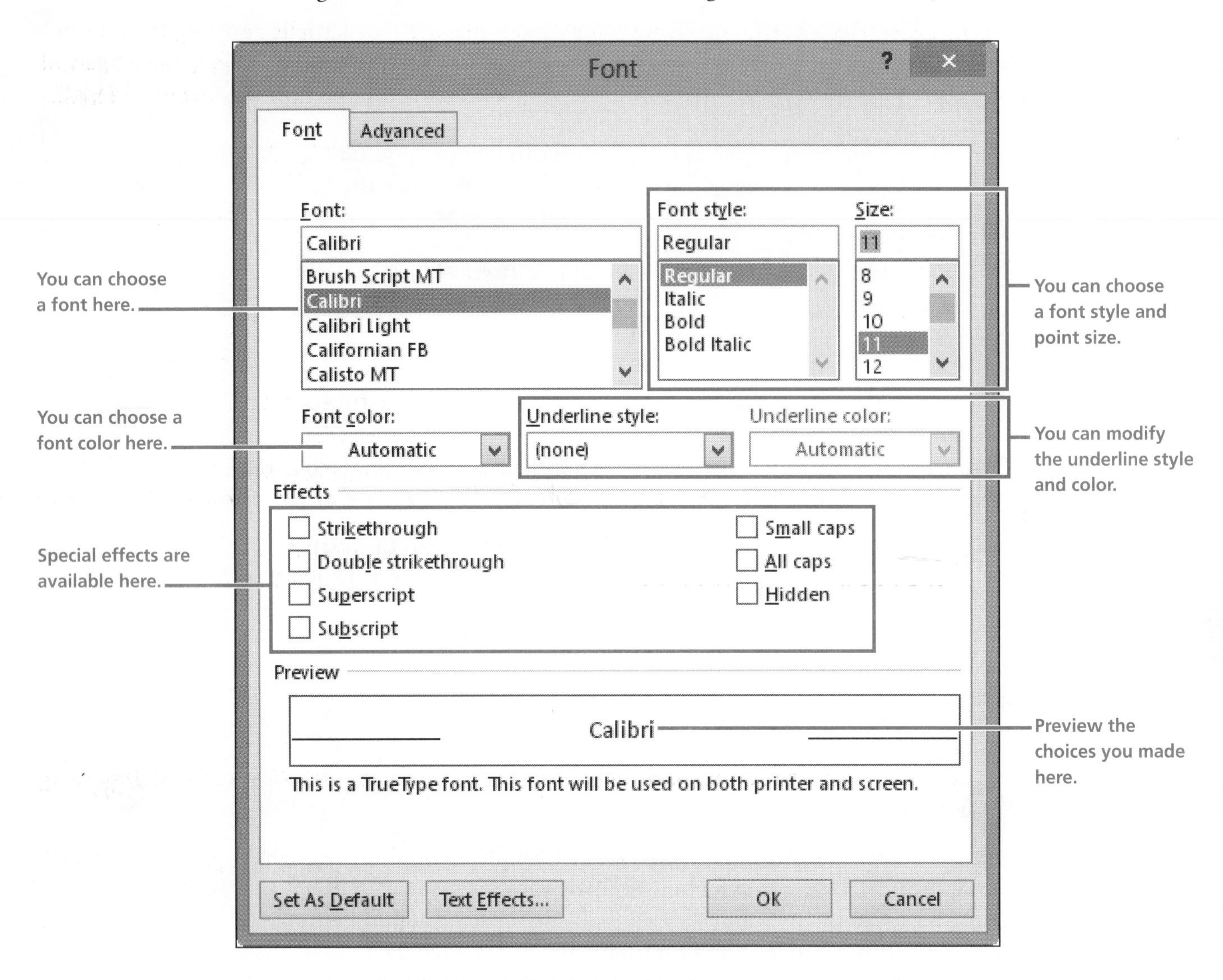

Using Live Preview

Live Preview shows what a formatting change looks like without actually applying the format. Many formatting features provide a Live Preview. In the following example, selecting a block of text and then hovering the mouse pointer over a font name previews how the text would look.

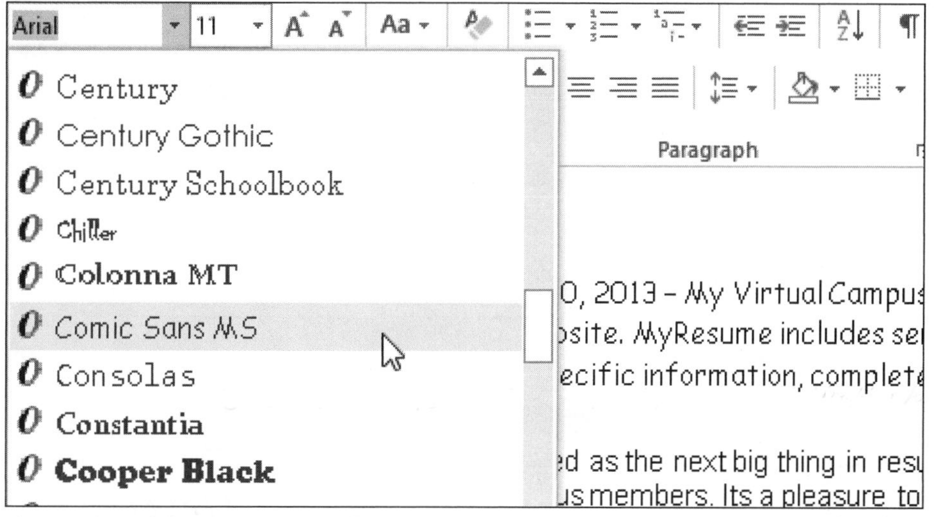

Live Preview of the Comic Sans MS font

DEVELOP YOUR SKILLS WD03-D07

X Format Text

In this exercise, you will explore fonts using Live Preview. You will use both the Ribbon and the Font dialog box to format text.

1. Save your file as **WD03-D07-MartinMemo-[FirstInitialLastName]**.
2. Scroll to the top of the second page and select the three heading lines.

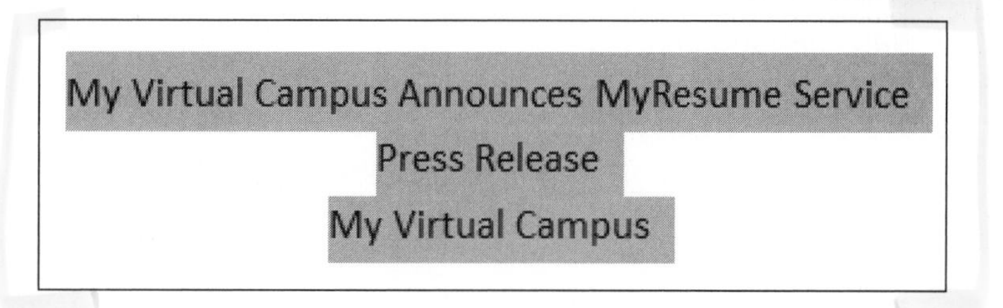

3. Choose **Home→Font** and click the drop-down arrow ▾ to the right of **Calibri (Body)**.
4. Slide the mouse pointer down the font list to see the effect of different fonts with Live Preview. Live Preview for Font Size
5. Click in the document to close the font list, and then make sure the first three lines on page 2 are still selected.

   Now you'll use the Font dialog box to change the font and font size.

Word 2013

6. Follow these steps to make the changes:

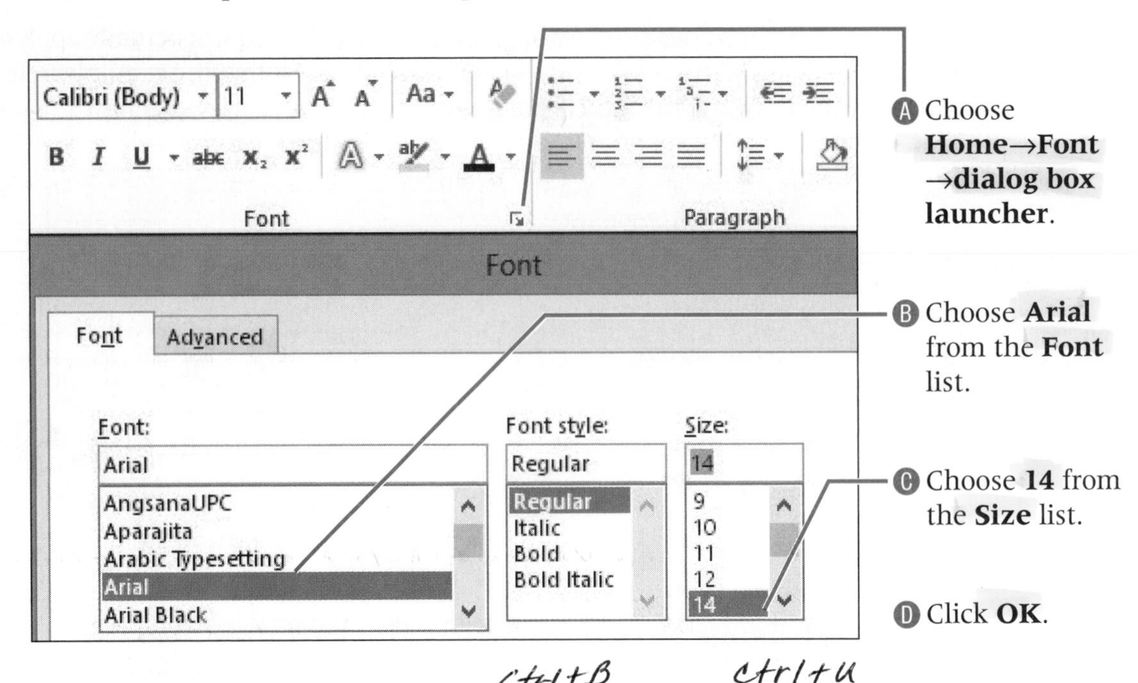

7. With the three lines still selected, press Ctrl+B and then Ctrl+U to apply bold and underline to the headings.
8. Choose **Home→Font→Underline** U to remove the underline.
9. Follow these steps to apply bold formatting to multiple selections at the same time:

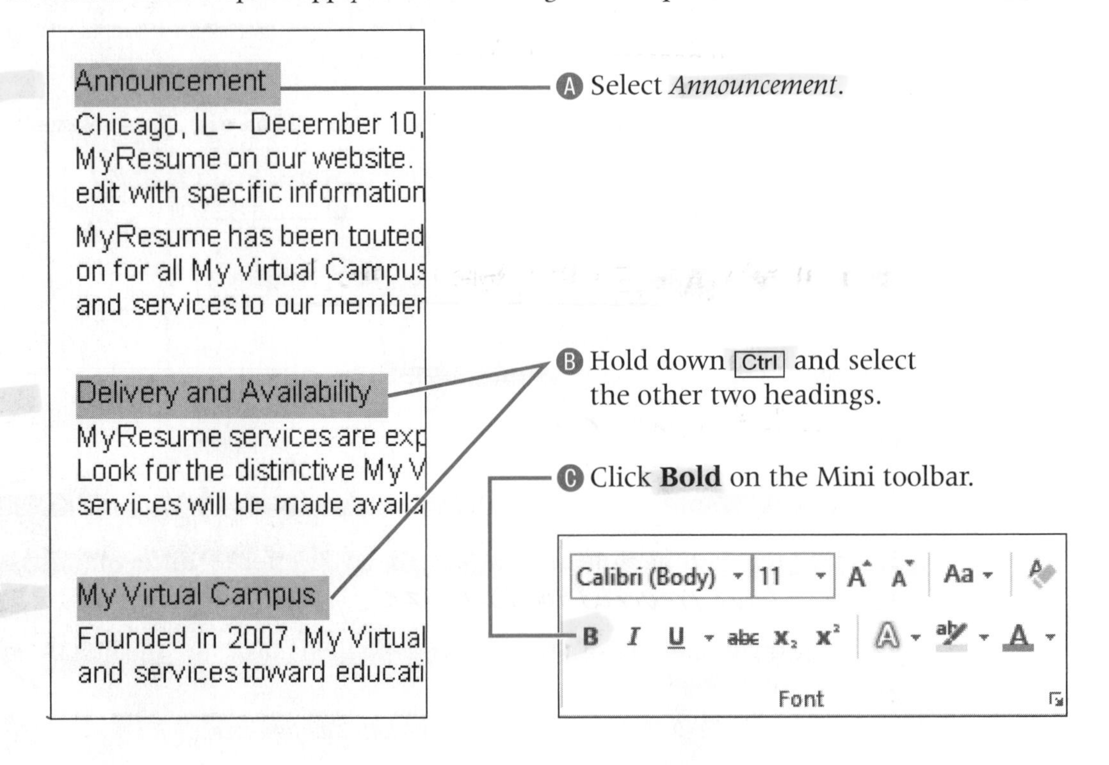

10. Save the file.

Working with the Format Painter

Video Library http://labyrinthelab.com/videos Video Number: WD13-V0308

FROM THE RIBBON
Home→Clipboard →Format Painter

FROM THE KEYBOARD
[Ctrl]+[Shift]+[C] to copy a format
[Ctrl]+[Shift]+[V] to paste a format

The Format Painter lets you copy text formats, including font, font size, and color, from one location to another. This saves time and helps create consistent formatting throughout a document. The Format Painter command is on both the Ribbon and the Mini toolbar.

QUICK REFERENCE — COPYING TEXT FORMATS WITH THE FORMAT PAINTER

Task	Procedure
Copy text formats with the Format Painter	■ Select the text with the format(s) to copy. ■ Choose Home→Clipboard→Format Painter once to copy formats to one location (double-click to copy to multiple locations). ■ Select the text location(s) to format. ■ If you double-clicked initially, click the Format Painter again to turn it off.

DEVELOP YOUR SKILLS WD03-D08

X Use the Format Painter

In this exercise, you will use both the Mini toolbar and the Format Painter to apply and copy formats. You will also copy a format and apply it to multiple blocks of text.

1. Save your file as **WD03-D08-MartinMemo-[FirstInitialLastName]**.
2. Scroll to page 2, if necessary, and select the *Announcement* heading line.
3. When the Mini toolbar appears, follow these steps to apply color to the heading line. (If the toolbar fades away, right-click the selected term to redisplay it.)

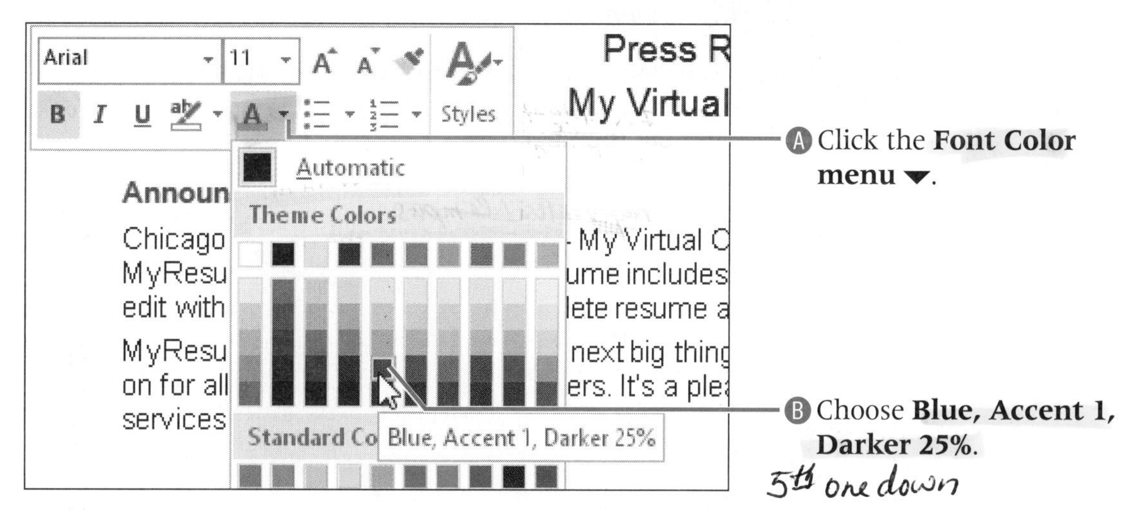

4. Keep the text selected and the Mini toolbar active, and follow these steps to apply additional formats to the text:

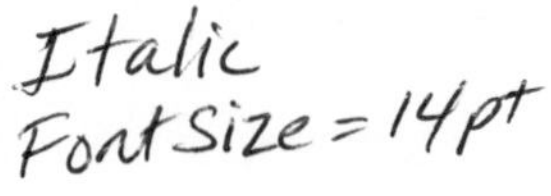

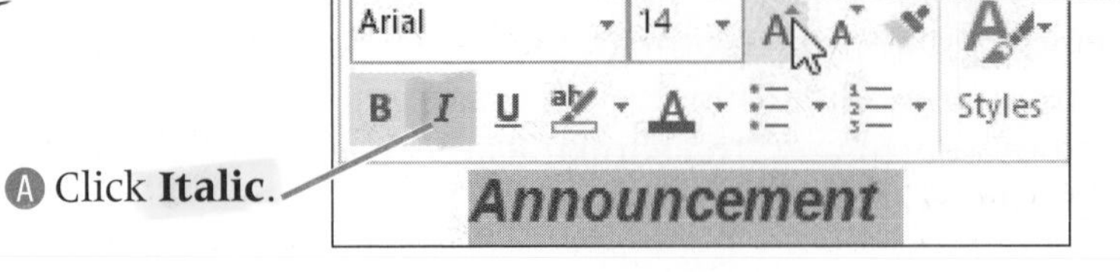

Ⓐ Click **Italic**.

Ⓑ Click **Increase Font Size** twice to change the font size to **14 point**.

Copy Formats to One Location

5. Make sure the *Announcement* heading line is selected.
6. Click the **Format Painter** on the Mini toolbar.
   A paintbrush icon is added to the mouse pointer once it is positioned over the document.
7. Drag the mouse pointer across the *Delivery and Availability* heading; release the mouse button.
   The 14 point italic blue formats should be copied to the heading.
8. Make sure the *Delivery and Availability* heading line is still selected.
9. Choose **Home→Clipboard→Format Painter**, and then select the last heading, *My Virtual Campus*, to copy the format again.

Copy Formats to More Than One Location

10. Scroll to the top of page 1 and select the heading *MEMO TO:* (include the colon).
11. Choose **Home→Font→Bold** **B**.
12. Double-click the **Format Painter** and drag over *FROM:* to apply the formatting from *MEMO TO:*.
13. Drag over *DATE:* and *SUBJECT:* to format those headings.
14. Choose **Home→Clipboard→Format Painter** to turn it off.
15. Save the file.

Using Find and Replace

Video Library http://labyrinthelab.com/videos Video Number: WD13-V0309

The Find command lets you search a document for a word or phrase. You can also search for text formats, page breaks, and a variety of other items. Find is often the quickest way to locate a phrase, format, or other item. You can use Find and Replace to search for text and replace it with something else.

FROM THE RIBBON
Home→Editing→Find
Home→Editing →Replace

FROM THE KEYBOARD
Ctrl+F for Find
Ctrl+H for Replace

Searching with the Navigation Pane

Clicking Find opens the Navigation task pane. When you search for an item, the results display in the task pane, giving you a quick view of everywhere the item appears.

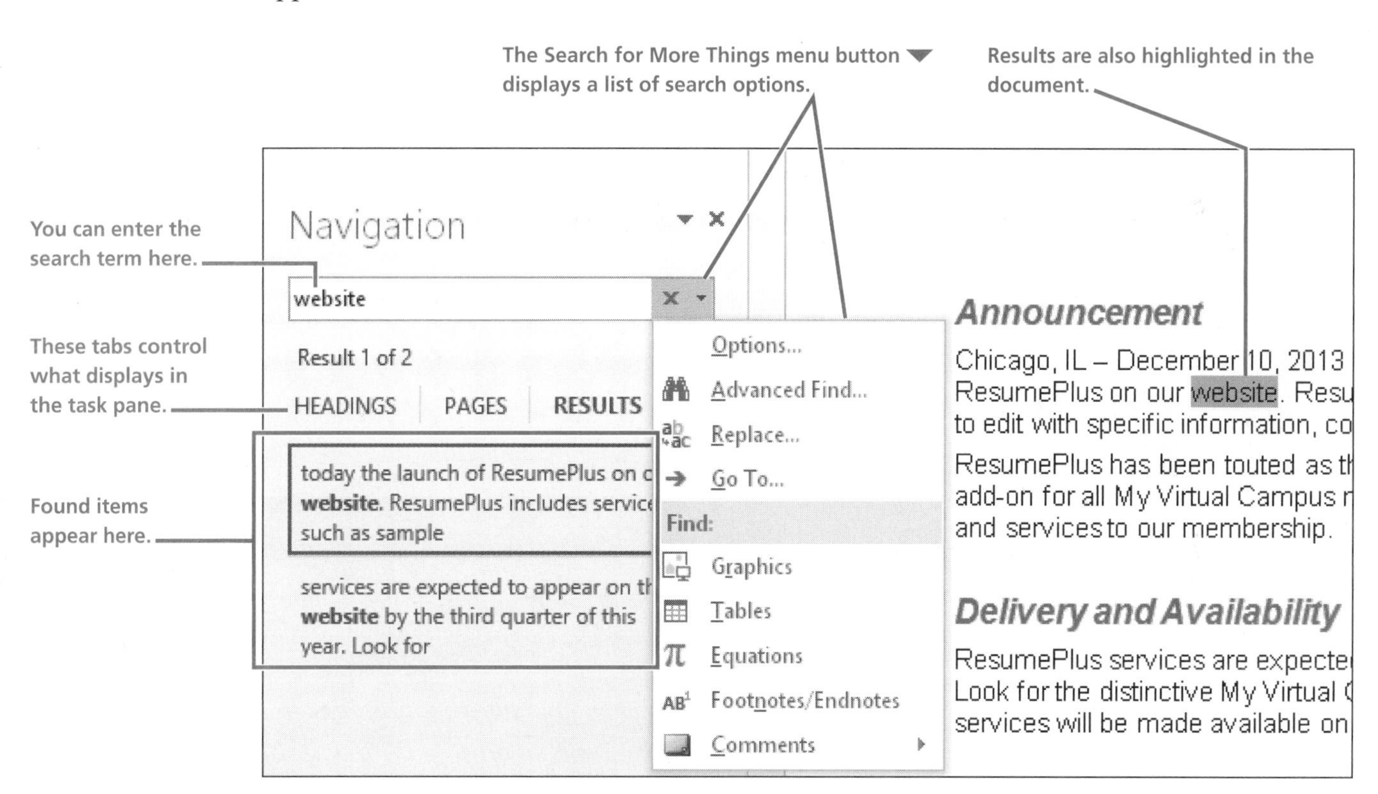

Using the Find and Replace Dialog Box

The Find and Replace dialog box includes the Find, Replace, and Go To tabs. The Find tab allows you to perform a more detailed search than the Navigation pane. The Replace tab allows you to enter a *Replace With* item to replace the *Find What* item. The Go To tab allows you to jump to a specific place in the document.

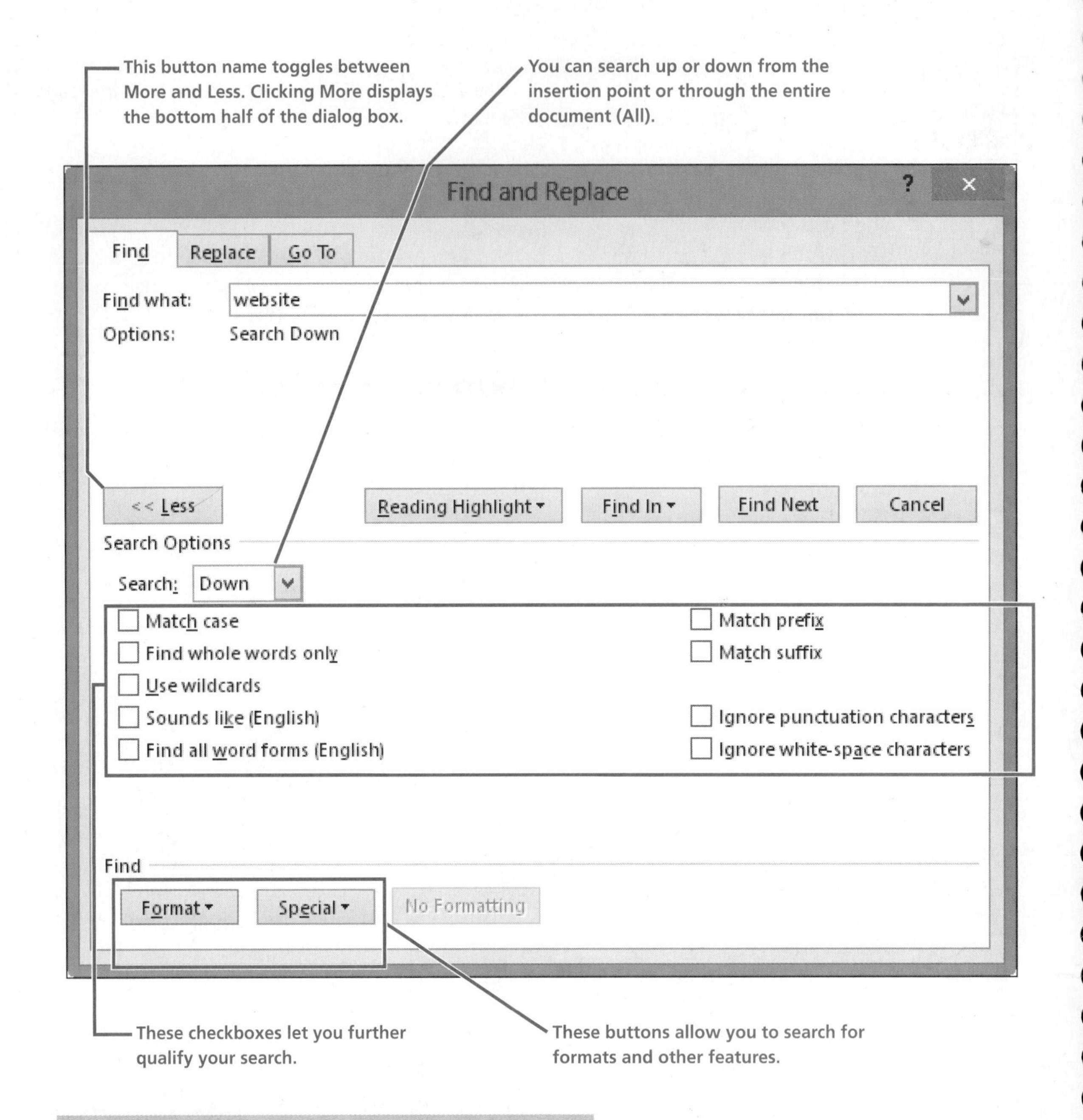

DEVELOP YOUR SKILLS WD03-D09

Use Find

In this exercise, you will search with the Navigation pane and explore search options in the Find and Replace dialog box.

1. Save your file as **WD03-D09-MartinMemo-[FirstInitialLastName]**.
2. Position the insertion point at the top of page 2, and make sure no text is selected.
3. Choose **Home→Editing→Find** to open the Navigation pane.
4. Type **website** in the search box to find all occurrences of the term.

   Notice that the search results appear in the Navigation pane, and they are highlighted in the document as well.

If you don't see the search results, click the Results tab toward the top of the task pane.

Ctrl+Home or Page Up

5. Scroll to the top of the document and position the insertion point anywhere in the first line of the memo.
6. Click in the **Navigation pane** search box, delete *website*, and type **Announce** (with a capital A) in its place.

   Word located announce *in the first paragraph of the memo with a lowercase* a, *even though you typed it in uppercase.*
7. Click the second instance in the Navigation pane results list and notice that *Announces* is highlighted in the first line of the press release.

   Word found Announce, *even though it is part of* Announces. *By default, the search feature is not case sensitive and doesn't recognize the difference between a whole word and part of a word. You will change this, however, in the next few steps.*

Use the Match Case Option

Now you will use the Search for More Things menu to display the Find and Replace dialog box, and then you will use the Match Case option.

Pg 1

8. Place the insertion point in the first line of the first page.
9. Follow these steps to display the Find and Replace dialog box and activate Match Case:

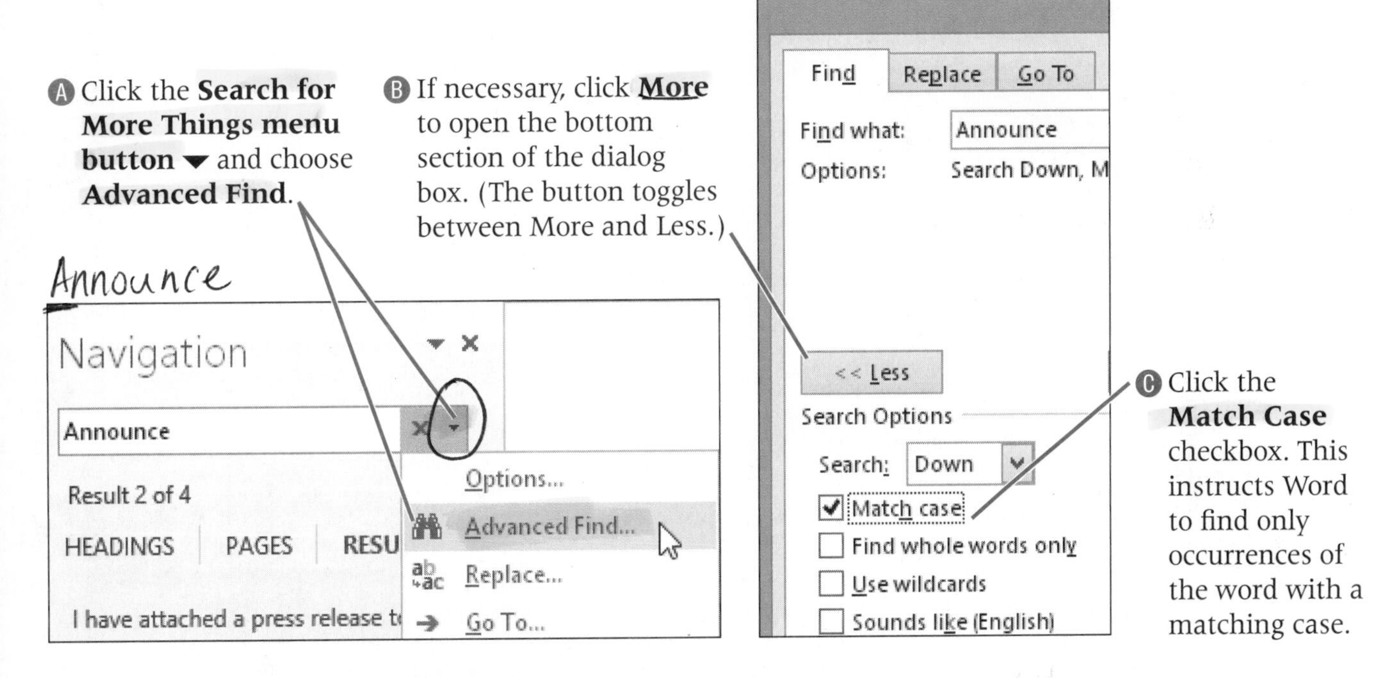

10. Click **Find Next** and Word locates the capitalized *Announces.*
11. Click **Find Next** again and Word locates the capitalized *Announcement*.
12. Click **Find Next** again and Word indicates that the entire document has been searched.

    Word skipped over the lowercase forms of announce.

13. Click **OK** in the message box; then close the Find and Replace dialog box and the Navigation task pane.
14. Save the file.

Using Replace

Video Library http://labyrinthelab.com/videos Video Number: WD13-V0310

The Replace feature allows you to replace words, formats, and other elements in a document. As an example, you could search for a particular font and replace it with another.

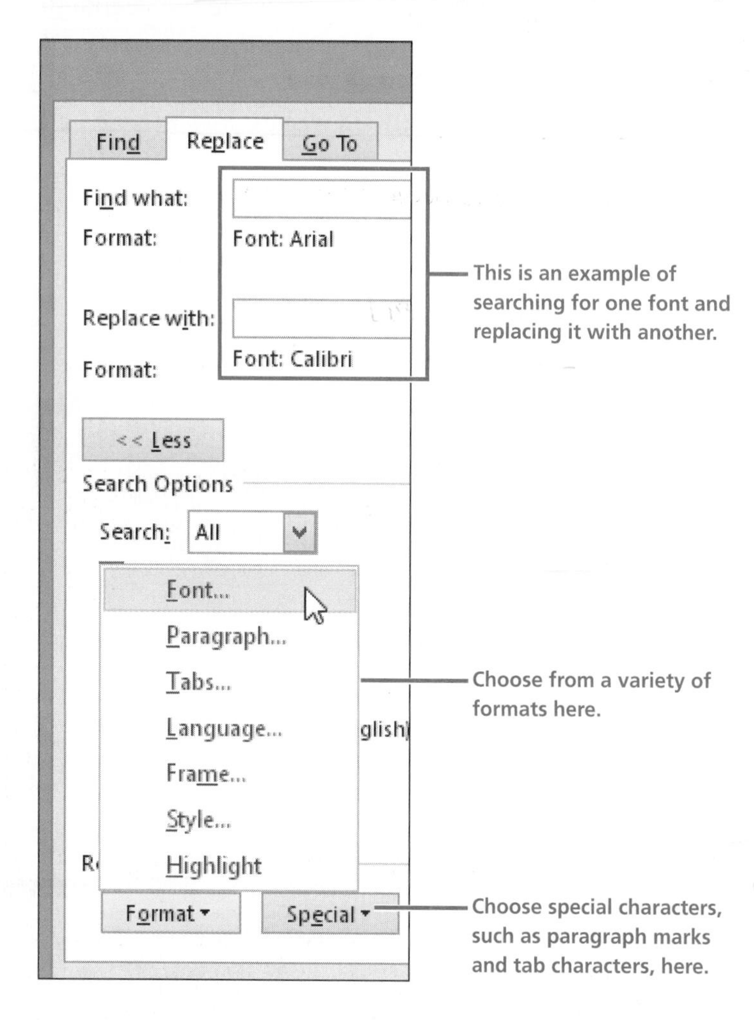

DEVELOP YOUR SKILLS WD03-D10

Use Replace

In this exercise, you will use the Replace feature. The Marketing Department decided to change the name MyResume *to* ResumePlus, *so having Word automatically make the replacements for you is a real time saver.*

1. Save your file as **WD03-D10-MartinMemo-[FirstInitialLastName]**.
2. Position the insertion point at the top of the document, and make sure no text is selected.
3. Press Ctrl + H to display the Find and Replace dialog box.
   Notice that the Replace tab is active in the dialog box.
4. If necessary, click **More** to expand the dialog box. (The button toggles between More and Less.)
   Match Case is still active from the previous exercise.
5. Uncheck **Match Case** to turn it off. Uncheck Match Case
6. Click **Less** to collapse the More options section of the dialog box.
7. Follow these steps to replace MyResume with ResumePlus:

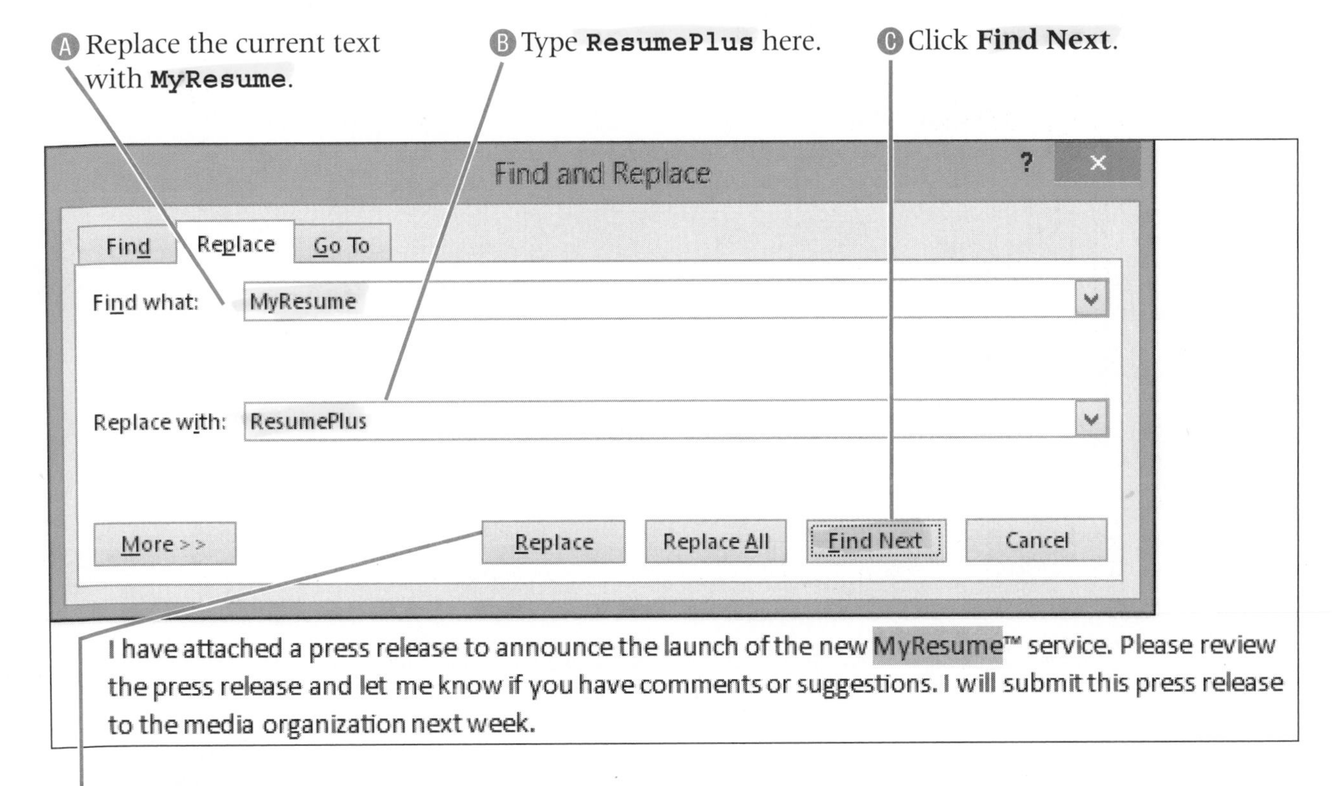

8. Click **Replace All** to make all remaining changes at once.
   The message box informs you that Word made seven replacements. 7 replacements

Use Replace All with caution. You should be confident about the replacements Word will make before you use this feature. Using *Replace* allows you to monitor each replacement.

9. Click **OK** to dismiss the message, and then close the **Find and Replace** dialog box and observe the *ResumePlus* replacements. You can ignore the wavy red lines.
10. Save the file.

Ignore All

Navigating in Documents

Video Library http://labyrinthelab.com/videos Video Number: WD13-V0311

Two highly efficient navigation methods are bookmarks and hyperlinks. You can create bookmarks to move to specific locations in a document, and you can insert hyperlinks that function just like hyperlinks in web pages. A hyperlink in Word uses bookmarks or heading styles to jump to places that are within the same document.

Using Bookmarks

You can assign a bookmark name to text or other objects in a document. Once a bookmark is set up, you can easily navigate to it by choosing the desired bookmark name from the Bookmark dialog box or the Go To tab in the Find and Replace dialog box.

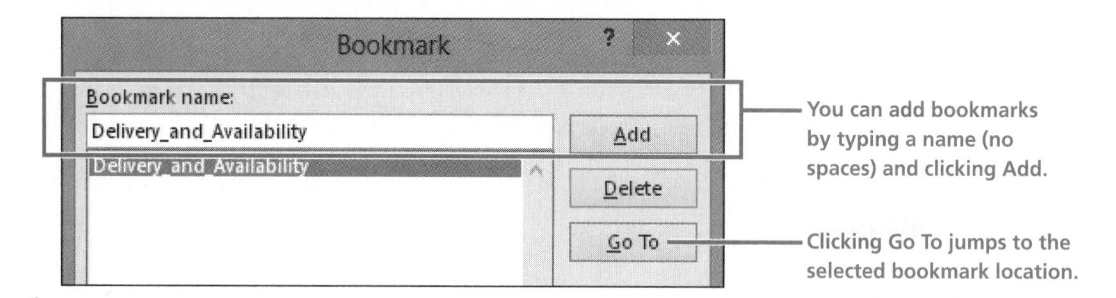

QUICK REFERENCE	USING BOOKMARKS
Task	**Procedure**
Create a bookmark	■ Select the text/object to use as a bookmark and choose Insert→Links→Bookmark. ■ Type the bookmark name (without spaces) and click Add.
Jump to a bookmark using the Bookmark dialog box	■ Choose Insert→Links→Bookmark, choose a bookmark name, and click Go To.
Jump to a bookmark using the Find and Replace dialog box	■ Choose Home→Editing→Find. ■ In the Navigation pane, click the Search for More Things menu ▼ button and choose Go To. ■ Choose Bookmark in the Go To What box, type or select the Bookmark name, and click Go To.

DEVELOP YOUR SKILLS WD03-D11

Create and Use Bookmarks

In this exercise, you will create bookmarks and use them to jump to different areas of the document. Then you will delete the bookmarks.

1. Save your file as **WD03-D11-MartinMemo-[FirstInitialLastName]**.
2. With page 2 displayed, select the word *Delivery* in the second heading.
3. Choose **Insert→Links→Bookmark**.
4. Follow these steps to create a Bookmark:

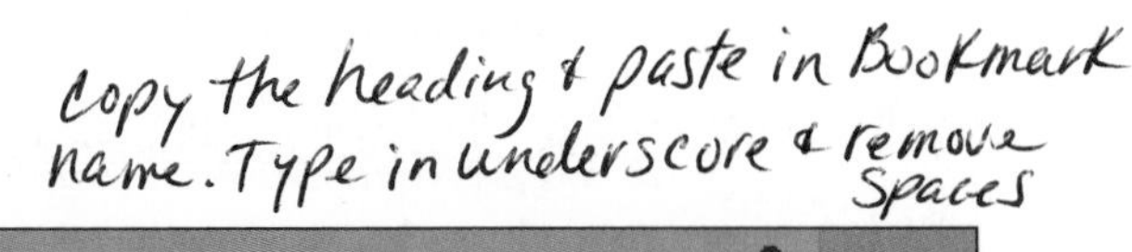

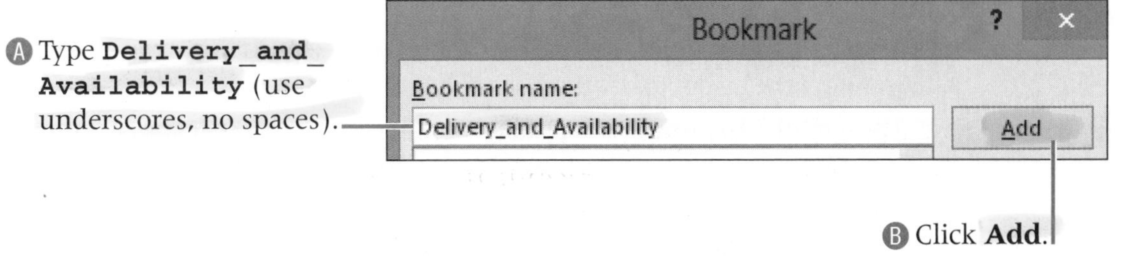

5. Scroll, if necessary, and select the *Announcement* heading. - Copy
6. Choose **Insert→Links→Bookmark**.
7. In the **Bookmark Name** box, replace the current text with **Announcement** and click **Add**.
8. Press Ctrl + Home to move to the beginning of the document.
9. Choose **Insert→Links→Bookmark**.
10. Choose **Delivery_and_Availability** and click **Go To**.
11. Close the Bookmark dialog box, then choose **Insert→Links→Bookmark**.
12. Choose **Announcement** and click **Go To**.

Delete Bookmarks

13. With *Announcement* selected in the dialog box, click **Delete**.
14. Select **Delivery_and_Availability** and click **Delete**.
15. Close the dialog box and save the file.

Using Hyperlinks

Video Library http://labyrinthelab.com/videos Video Number: WD13-V0312

A hyperlink is text or a graphic that jumps you to another place when clicked. To use a hyperlink *within* a document, the location you link to must first be set up as a bookmark or be formatted with a heading style.

There are four primary types of hyperlinks.

- **Hyperlinks to other documents or files:** A hyperlink can open another Word document or even another program, such as Excel or PowerPoint.
- **Hyperlinks to web pages:** You can create a link to jump to a web page by entering a URL address for the hyperlink.
- **Hyperlinks to areas within the current document:** This works much like a Bookmark, jumping the reader to another location in the document.
- **Hyperlinks to email addresses:** You can create a hyperlink to an email address. When the hyperlink is clicked, a new message window opens with the email address already in the To: box.

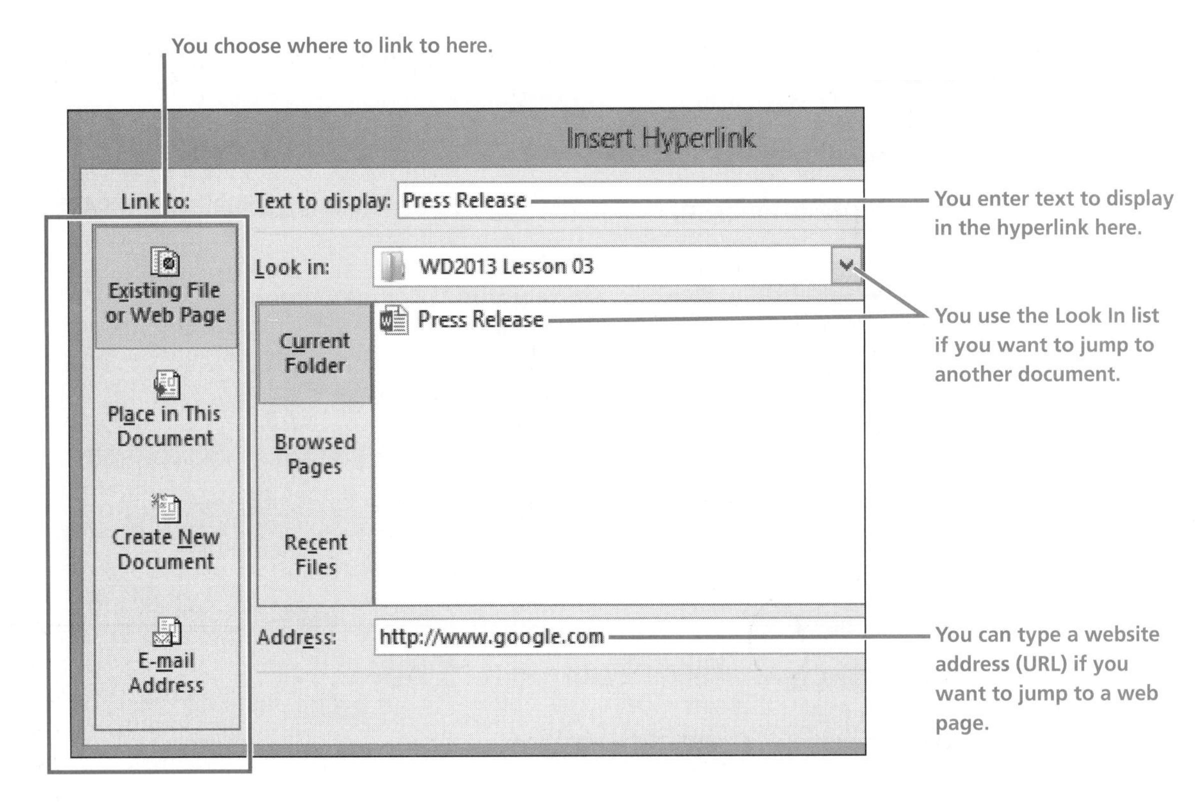

QUICK REFERENCE	CREATING HYPERLINKS
Task	**Procedure**
Create a hyperlink	■ Select the text/graphic to use as a hyperlink and choose Insert→Links→Hyperlink. ■ Choose the item to link to in the left pane. ■ In the center pane: ◆ Choose the filename if linking to a file. ◆ Type the URL in the Address box if linking to a web page. ◆ Choose a heading or bookmark name if you chose Place in This Document in the Link To list. ■ Click OK.
Remove a hyperlink	■ Click in the hyperlink, then choose Insert→Links→Hyperlink and click Remove Link; or, right-click the hyperlink and choose Remove Hyperlink.

DEVELOP YOUR SKILLS WD03-D12

Work with Hyperlinks

In this exercise, you will create a hyperlink and use it to jump to another document. Then, you will remove the hyperlink.

1. Save your file as **WD03-D12-MartinMemo-[FirstInitialLastName]**.
2. Move the insertion point to the beginning of the document. Ctrl + Home
3. Select the words *Press Release* in the **Subject** line.
4. Choose **Insert→Links→Hyperlink**.
5. Follow these steps to create a hyperlink to another document:

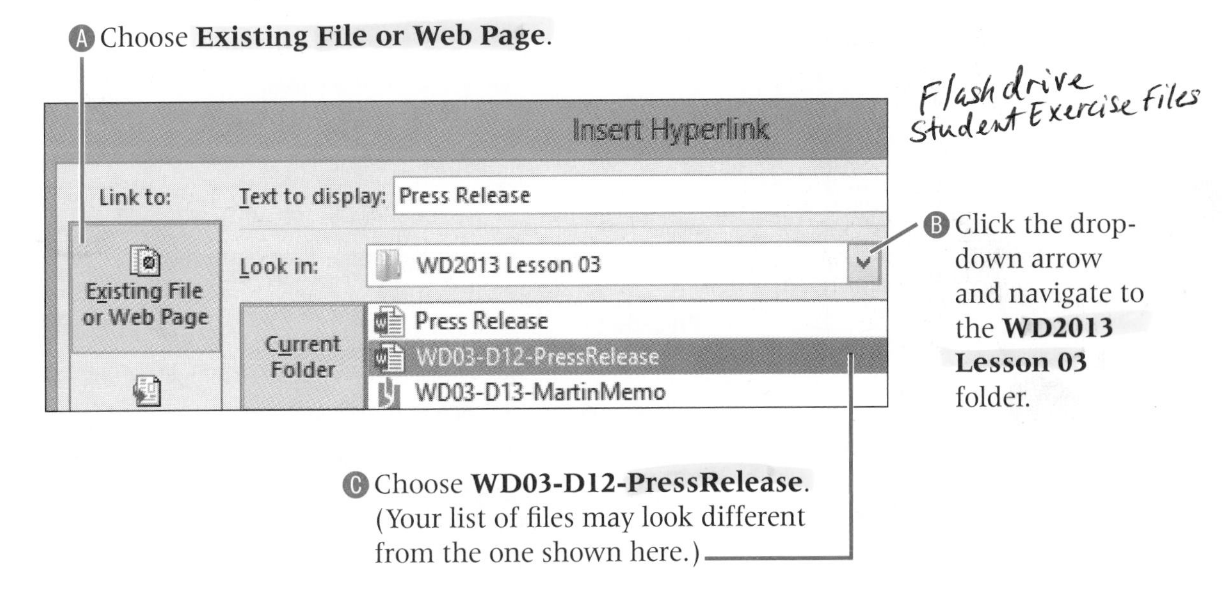

6. Click **OK** to create the hyperlink.
   The text formatting changes once this hyperlink is created.

Use and Remove the Hyperlink

7. Press Ctrl and click the link to open Press Release.
8. Close **Press Release** but leave the Martin Memo open.
   Notice that the hyperlink changes color once it is used.
9. Click anywhere in the hyperlink.
10. Choose **Insert→Links→Hyperlink**.
11. Click **Remove Link** in the bottom-right corner of the dialog box.
12. Save the memo document, then choose **File→Close** to close the document.

Opening, Editing, and Saving a PDF File

Video Library http://labyrinthelab.com/videos Video Number: WD13-V0313

You can open, edit, and save a PDF file in Word 2013 without purchasing and learning separate, and often expensive, editing software. After editing the file, you can save it as a Word or PDF file. The file you open is considered a read-only file, so you must save it under a different name.

You can optimize a PDF file based on how your audience will likely read the file. And there are additional options, such as the range of pages you want to save and the ability to create bookmarks in the PDF file.

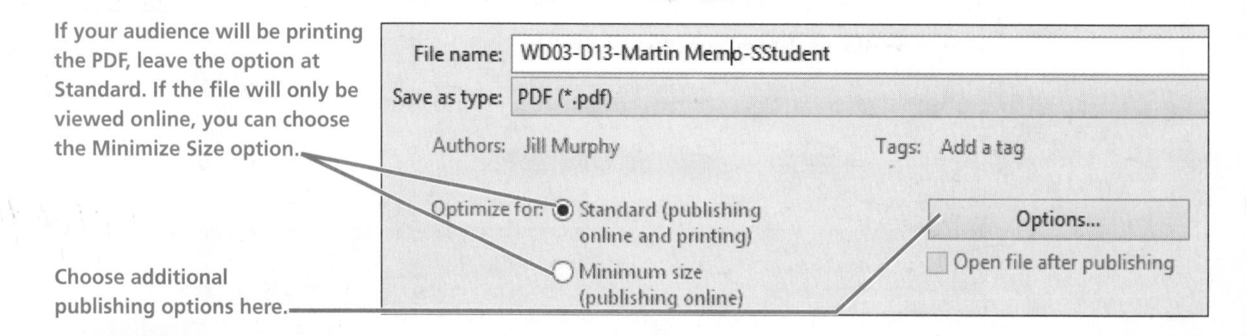

QUICK REFERENCE	OPENING PDF FILES AND SAVING AS PDF FILES
Task	**Procedure**
Open a PDF file in Word	■ Choose File→Open, navigate to the file location, and double-click the file. ■ When the message appears, click OK.
Saving a Word document as a PDF file	■ Choose File→Save As and navigate to your file storage location. ■ Choose PDF (*.pdf) from the Save as Type list and, if desired, choose optimization and publishing options.

DEVELOP YOUR SKILLS WD03-D13

Open and Edit a PDF File

In this exercise, you will open a PDF file in Word and make editing changes. You will then resave the file as a PDF.

1. Choose **File→Open**.
2. Navigate to your **WD2013 Lesson 03** folder and open **WD03-D13-MartinMemo.pdf**.
3. When the message box appears, click **OK**.
   The PDF file opens with all the Word editing and formatting tools available.

When you open a PDF in Word, there may be formatting issues. Don't worry about that now. Concentrate on opening so in the future, you know how to open and edit a PDF for which you don't have the original Word file.

4. Scroll to the top of page 2 and select the three lines at the top of the page.
5. In the Mini toolbar, click the **Font Color** A menu ▾ and choose **Blue, Accent 1, Darker 25%**.
   If the toolbar fades away, right-click the selected text to redisplay it.
6. Still using the Mini toolbar, change the Font Size to **16 point**.
7. Choose **File→Save As** and navigate to your **WD2013 Lesson 03** folder. My Data Folder
8. Append your first initial and last name to the filename: `WD03-D13-MartinMemo-[FirstInitialLastName]`.
9. Choose **PDF (*.pdf)** from the Save as Type list.
10. Click **Save** at the bottom of the dialog box. (If the PDF file opens in a PDF reader, close the PDF window.)
    Remember, the original file is read-only, so saving it under a different name saved the changes in a new file. Now you'll close the original file without saving.
11. The original file is still open in Word, so choose **File→Close**.
12. When prompted to save the file, click **Don't Save**. Exit **Word**.

Concepts Review

To check your knowledge of the key concepts introduced in this lesson, complete the Concepts Review quiz by choosing the appropriate access option below.

If you are...	Then access the quiz by...
Using the Labyrinth Video Library	Going to http://labyrinthelab.com/videos
Using eLab	Logging in, choosing Content, and navigating to the Concepts Review quiz for this lesson
Not using the Labyrinth Video Library or eLab	Going to the student resource center for this book

Reinforce Your Skills

REINFORCE YOUR SKILLS WD03-R01

Type a Memorandum

In this exercise, you will type a memorandum announcing a meeting, aligning the memo heading using the default tab grid. You will insert a page break and copy a document into page 2. Then you will use the proofreading tools to help ensure the accuracy of your memo.

Create a Memorandum Using Default Tabs

1. Start **Word** and create new a document using the **Blank Document template**.
2. Save the file as **`WD03-R01-FoodDrive-[FirstInitialLastName]`** in your **WD2013 Lesson 03** folder.
3. If necessary, choose **Home→Paragraph→Show/Hide** ¶ to display formatting marks.
4. Type the following memo, tapping Enter where you see paragraph symbols and Tab where you see arrows.

   Because you are using the default template, which has additional spacing, you only need to tap Enter *once between paragraphs.*

¶

¶

MEMO·TO: → Kids·for·Change¶

FROM:→ → Suzanne·Frost¶

DATE:→ → October·1,·2013¶

SUBJECT: → Combat·Hunger·Food·Drive¶

Think·globally,·act·locally!¶

Kids·for·Change·is·sponsoring·a·holiday·season·food·drive·in·coordination·with·our·local·community·food·bank.·The·drive·will·begin·on·November·1st,·and·we·have·lots·of·organizing·to·do·before·then.·¶

We·are·looking·for·volunteers·to·help·us·in·this·effort.·There·is·a·To·Do·list·on·the·next·page.·Look·it·over·and·see·what·you·would·like·to·volunteer·for.·We·will·discuss·the·list·and·assign·teams·during·our·October·meeting.·¶

We're·looking·forward·to·a·successful·drive·for·2013!¶

¶

¶

Work with Page Breaks and Insert a Symbol

5. Position the insertion point at the end of the memo.
6. Choose **Insert→Pages→Page Break**.
   Now you will copy a To Do list from another document into page 2.
7. Open **WD03-R01-ToDo** from the **WD2013 Lesson 03** folder.
8. Select the entire document and press [Ctrl]+[C] to copy it; close the file.
9. Make sure your insertion point is at the **top of page 2** and press [Ctrl]+[V] to paste the text.
   Now you will insert a symbol on the second page.
10. Position the insertion point after *heart* in the second line and tap [Spacebar].
11. Choose **Insert→Symbols→Symbol** and choose **More Symbols**.
12. Choose the **Webdings** font and the **heart-shaped symbol**; if necessary, use Character Code 89 to locate the symbol.
13. Click **Insert**, and then close the dialog box.

Use Proofreading Tools

There are some spelling errors in the To Do list; you will correct those now.

14. Right-click the red underlined word in the first bullet point and choose *create* from the menu.
15. Right-click the red underlined word in the third bullet point and choose *collect*.
16. Use your good judgment in making the next two spelling corrections.
    Now you will use the Thesaurus to find a synonym.
17. Select *goal* at the end of the second-to-last bullet point.
18. Choose **Review→Proofing→Thesaurus** to open the task pane.
19. Hover the mouse pointer over *objective* (the second one in the list), and then click the drop-down arrow to open the menu.
20. Click **Insert** to replace *goal* with *objective*.
21. Close the **Thesaurus task pane**.
22. Save and close your file, and exit from **Word**.
23. Submit your final file based on the guidelines provided by your instructor.
    To view examples of how your file or files should look at the end of this exercise, go to the student resource center.

REINFORCE YOUR SKILLS WD03-R02

Format a Document and Save It in PDF

In this exercise, you will format the headings in a document, use Find and Replace, and add bookmarks and hyperlinks. Finally, you will save it as a PDF file.

1. Start **Word**. Open **WD03-R02-Energy** from the **WD2013 Lesson 03** folder and save it as `WD03-R02-Energy-[FirstInitialLastName]`.

Format Text and Use the Format Painter

2. Select *Home Energy Inspector* at the top of the document.
3. Choose **Home→Font→dialog box launcher**.
4. Choose **Century Gothic**, **Bold**, **14 point**, and then choose **Small Caps** in the Effects area.
5. Click **OK** to apply the formats.
   You've decided you'd like to try some more options, so you'll clear your formats.
6. Make sure the heading is still selected.
7. Choose **Home→Font→Clear All Formatting**.
8. With the heading still selected, choose **Home→Font**. Then click the **menu button ▾** next to Calibri (Body) and choose **Comic Sans MS**.
9. Choose **Home→Font→Font Size menu button ▾** and choose **16 point**.
10. Choose **Home→Font→Bold**.
11. Choose **Home→Font→Font Color menu button ▾** and choose a **blue** color.
    Now you're ready to format the other headings.
12. Select the *What About Energy Leaks?* heading.
13. Choose **Home→Font→Font menu button ▾** and choose **Euphemia**.
14. Choose **Home→Font→Bold**.
    Next you'll use the Format Painter to copy the format to the other headings.
15. Make sure the heading is still selected.
16. Choose **Home→Clipboard** and double-click the **Format Painter**.
    Remember, double-clicking the Format Painter keeps it turned on.
17. Use the **Format Painter** to format the rest of the headings:
    - What About Appliances?
    - What Are the Best Light Bulbs?
    - What are the Worst Offenders?
    - Who Is Responsible?
18. Choose **Home→Clipboard→Format Painter** to turn off the feature.

Find and Replace

You've noticed some words you would like to change, so you will use Find and Replace to make the changes.

19. Position the insertion point at the top of the document.
20. Choose **Home→Editing→Replace** to open the Find and Replace dialog box.
21. Type `program` in the Find What box and `project` in the Replace With box.
22. Click **Find Next**, and then click **Replace**.
23. When the message appears, click **OK**.
24. Use the **Find and Replace** feature to change *offenders* to *wasters*.
    Hint: There are two occurrences of offenders.
25. When the message appears, click **OK**; close the dialog box.

Navigate with Bookmarks and Hyperlinks

Next you will create a bookmark for the last topic in the document and a hyperlink to another document.

26. Press Ctrl + End to move to the end of the document.
27. Select the last heading, *Who Is Responsible?*
28. Choose **Insert→Links→Bookmark**.

No ? mark

29. Type `WhoIsResponsible` (no spaces) in the **Bookmark Name** box; click **Add**.
30. Select the first heading at the top of the document.
31. Choose **Insert→Links→Hyperlink** to open the Insert Hyperlink dialog box.
32. Make sure **Existing File or Web Page** is chosen in the Link To area.
33. In the Look In area, navigate to your **WD2013 Lesson 03** folder, choose **WD03-R02-EnergyHelp** from the file list, and click **OK**.
34. Click **OK** again to create the hyperlink.
    The formatting changes when the hyperlink is applied. Now you'll test your hyperlink and bookmark.
35. Press Ctrl and click the hyperlink to open the Energy Help document, and then close it.
    The appearance of the hyperlink changes after it is used.
36. Choose **Insert→Links→Bookmark** from the menu.
37. Choose the bookmark and click **Go To**; close the dialog box.

Save the Document as a PDF

38. Choose **File→Save As** and navigate to your **WD2013 Lesson 03** folder.
39. Use the same file name and choose **PDF (*.pdf)** from the Save As Type menu.
40. Leave the optimization at **Standard**, and then click **Save**. (If the PDF file opens in a PDF reader, close the PDF window.)
41. Save and close the original document, and then exit from **Word**.
42. Submit your final file based on the guidelines provided by your instructor.
    To view examples of how your file or files should look at the end of this exercise, go to the student resource center.

REINFORCE YOUR SKILLS WD03-R03

Type and Format a Memorandum

In this exercise, you will create a memorandum, insert a page break, copy text, and use proofing tools. You will create a hyperlink to an external document and save your memo as a PDF file.

Type a Memo and Insert a Page Break

1. Start **Word**. Create new a document using the **Blank Document template** that is saved to the **WD2013 Lesson 03** folder as `WD03-R03-Green-[FirstInitialLastName]`.
2. If necessary, choose **Home→Paragraph→Show/Hide** ¶ to turn on formatting marks.
3. Type the following memo using these guidelines:
   - Use formatting marks as a guide for spacing.
   - Use the Insert Date and Time feature on the Insert tab to insert and format the current date, and choose not to update automatically.

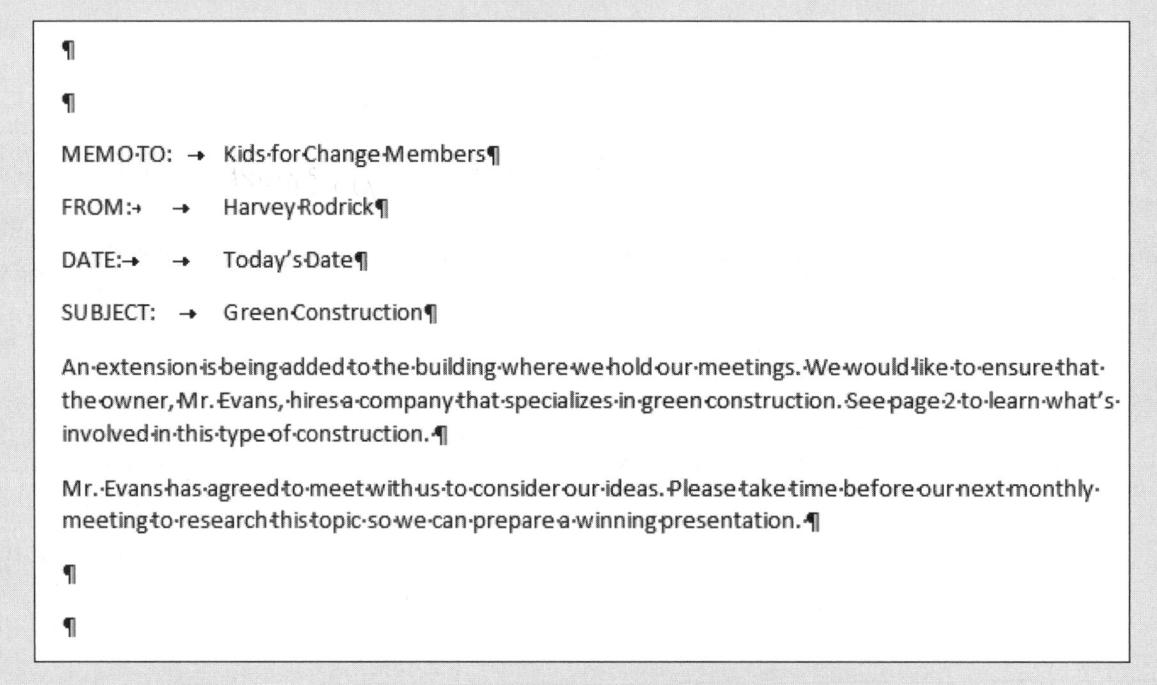

¶

¶

MEMO·TO: → Kids·for·Change·Members¶

FROM:→ → Harvey·Rodrick¶

DATE:→ → Today's·Date¶

SUBJECT: → Green·Construction¶

An·extension·is·being·added·to·the·building·where·we·hold·our·meetings.·We·would·like·to·ensure·that· the·owner,·Mr.·Evans,·hires·a·company·that·specializes·in·green·construction.·See·page·2·to·learn·what's· involved·in·this·type·of·construction.·¶

Mr.·Evans·has·agreed·to·meet·with·us·to·consider·our·ideas.·Please·take·time·before·our·next·monthly· meeting·to·research·this·topic·so·we·can·prepare·a·winning·presentation.·¶

¶

¶

4. Make sure the insertion point is at the end of the document, and then press Ctrl + Enter to insert a page break.
5. Open **WD03-R03-Construction** from the **WD2013 Lesson 03** folder.
6. Select all of contents of the document, and then press Ctrl + C to copy it.
7. Close the **Construction** document, and then paste the copied material at the top of page 2 of the **Green** document.

Use Proofing Tools

8. Tap [F7] to start proofing.

If [F7] does not work as expected, you may need to tap [F-Lock] at the top of your keyboard so [F7] behaves as a function key.

Fluoorescent *is highlighted in the Spelling task pane.*

9. Click **Change** to correct the spelling.
10. Click **Change** to correct *sustainable.*
    Daniel's last name is spelled correctly.
11. Click **Add** to add his name to the dictionary.
    The Grammar checker caught the incorrect use of a pronoun.
12. Click **Change** to make the correction, and then when the message appears, click **OK**.
    Now you will remove the name you added to the dictionary so the next student using your computer will have the same experience.
13. Choose **File→Options**, and then choose **Proofing** from the left panel.
14. Click **Custom Dictionaries**, and then in the Custom Dictionaries dialog box, click **Edit Word List**.
15. If necessary, scroll to locate *Datar* and click **Delete**, and then click **OK**.
16. Click **OK** two more times.
    Datar is flagged again because you removed it from the dictionary.

Format Text

17. Select the *Green Construction* heading at the top of page 2, format it with **Century Gothic, 14 point, Bold**; deselect the heading.
18. Scroll to the bottom of page 2, and then apply **Bold** and **Italics** to *Daniel Datar*.
19. Scroll to the top of page 1, and then apply **Bold** to the memo heading elements: *MEMO TO:*, *FROM:*, *DATE:*, and *SUBJECT:*.
20. Select *Green Construction* in the subject line, format it with a shade of green of your choice, and then apply **Bold**.
21. In the last sentence of the first paragraph on page 1, italicize *See page 2*.
22. Underline the last two words on page 1, *winning presentation*.

Use Find and Replace

23. Position the insertion point at the top of the document.
24. Choose **Home→Editing→Replace** to open the Find and Replace dialog box.
25. Type `concepts` in the **Find What** box and `ideas` in the **Replace With** box.

26. Click **Find Next**, and then when *concepts* is highlighted, click **Replace**.
27. Click **OK** when the message appears, and then close the dialog box.

    You've located some additional information on solar heating, so you will create a hyperlink to that information.

Create and Test a Hyperlink to Use for Navigation

28. Select *Solar heating* on page 2.
29. Choose **Insert→Links→Hyperlink**.
30. Make sure **Existing File or Web Page** is chosen.
31. In the Look In area, navigate to your **WD2013 Lesson 03** folder, and then choose **WD03-R03-Solar** from the list.
32. Click **OK** twice to create the hyperlink.
33. Press Ctrl and click the hyperlink to open the **Solar** document, and then close it.

Save the Document as a PDF

34. Choose **File→Save As**, and then navigate to your **WD2013 Lesson 03** folder.
35. Use the same filename, and then choose **PDF (*.pdf)** from the Save As Type menu.
36. Leave the optimization at **Standard**, and then click **Save**. (If the PDF file opens in a PDF reader, close the PDF window.)

    Next you will open and edit a PDF file. This is so you can understand the mechanics of how to do it.

When you open a PDF file in Word, there will be formatting issues. Don't worry about making the file look perfect. Concentrate more on how to open and edit, so you will be able to accomplish this task in the future when you need to edit a PDF file for which you don't have an original Word file.

Open and Edit the PDF

37. Open the **PDF** file you just saved.
38. When the message appears, click **OK**.

    The conversion to PDF misaligned the data in the FROM: and DATE: lines of the memo heading.

39. Add tabs to the *FROM:* and *DATE:* lines to realign them.
40. Change **Harvey Rodrick** in the FROM: line to `Miles Chung`.
41. Resave the file as a **PDF** in the **WD2013 Lesson 03** folder, named `WD03-R03-Green2-[FirstInitialLastName]`. (If the PDF file opens in in a PDF reader, close the PDF window.)
42. Close the original **PDF** without saving.
43. Save and close all documents; exit from **Word**.
44. Submit your final file based on the guidelines provided by your instructor.

Apply Your Skills

APPLY YOUR SKILLS WD03-A01

Create a Memorandum and a Press Release

In this exercise, you will type a memorandum, insert a page break, and copy text into page 2 of the memo. You will then insert a trademark symbol, correct spelling errors, and use the Thesaurus to find a synonym.

Type a Memorandum and Insert a Page Break

1. Start **Word**. Use the **Blank Document template** and save the file in your **WD2013 Lesson 03** folder as `WD03-A01-NewOffice-[FirstInitialLastName]`.
2. Type the following memo using proper spacing and tabs for aligning the memo head.

MEMO TO:	Malcolm Wesley
FROM:	Melissa Jones
DATE:	August 8, 2013
SUBJECT:	Bangalore Press Release

Malcolm I've attached the press release for our Bangalore announcement. Would you please look it over and let me now if you have any changes or suggestions? Thanks!

3. Insert a **page break** at the end of the memo.
4. Open **WD03-A01-BangalorePR** from your **WD2013 Lesson 03** folder and copy everything from the document and paste it into the second page of the memo. Close the Bangalore file.

Insert a Symbol and Use Proofing Tools

5. Insert the **trademark symbol** after *Universal Corporate Events* in the first line of the first body paragraph in the press release.
6. Correct the spelling errors, and then use the **Thesaurus** to replace *aspects*, in the second line of the second paragraph, with a synonym of your choice.
7. Save and close the file; exit from **Word**.
8. Submit your final file based on the guidelines provided by your instructor.

   To view examples of how your file or files should look at the end of this exercise, go to the student resource center.

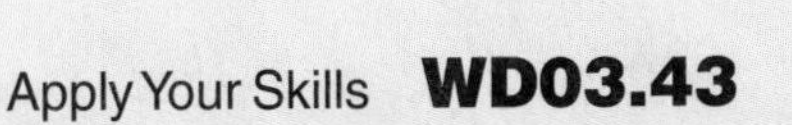

APPLY YOUR SKILLS WD03-A02

Use Formatting, Find and Replace, and a Bookmark

In this exercise, you will format headings in a document, use Find and Replace to make some editing changes, and create a bookmark to use for navigation. Finally, you will save the file as a PDF file.

Make Formatting Changes and Use Find and Replace

1. Start **Word**. Open **WD03-A02-IndiaTips** from your **WD2013 Lesson 03** folder and save it as `WD03-A02-IndiaTips-[FirstInitialLastName]`.
2. Select the first two heading lines.
3. Choose **Home→Font→Font menu button ▾**, and then use **Live Preview** to test several different fonts, and then test the **Tahoma** font.
4. Choose **Tahoma** and also apply **14 point**, **Bold**.
5. Select the *What Not to Do* heading, and then apply **Tahoma**, **Bold**, and **Italic**.
6. Use the **Format Painter** to copy the formatting to the other headings.
7. Use the Replace feature to make the following changes:
   - Replace *conversing* with *talking*
   - Replace *irritation* with *frustration*
   - Replace *another's* with *another person's*
   - Replace *appropriate* with *proper* (3 occurrences)

Navigate with a Bookmark and Save the File as a PDF

8. Select the *Dining* heading at the end of the document, and then create a **bookmark** named `Dining`.
9. Scroll to the top of the document and test your bookmark.
10. Save your file as a **PDF** using the same filename.
11. Save your original Word file and close it; exit from **Word**.
12. Submit your final file based on the guidelines provided by your instructor.

    To view examples of how your file or files should look at the end of this exercise, go to the student resource center.

APPLY YOUR SKILLS WD03-A03

Create, Format, and Navigate in a Memo

In this exercise, you will type a memo, insert a page break, and copy text into the new page. You will use the proofing tools, and then format the headings. You will use Find and Replace, insert a hyperlink, and finally, you will save the memo as a PDF file.

Create a Memorandum

1. Start **Word**. Create a new document using the **Blank Document template** and save to your **WD2013 Lesson 03** folder as `WD03-A03-HenslowMemo-[FirstInitialLastName]`.
2. Type the following memo using the appropriate spacing, automatically insert the date using the third date format, and don't check the Update Automatically feature.

MEMO TO:	Dennis Henslow
FROM:	Jordan Miller
DATE:	Today's Date
SUBJECT:	Additions to the London Trip

Dennis, since you're a Londoner, would you please take a look at the additional tours we're thinking of making available to our clients. Let me know if you agree or if you have any suggestions.

Insert a Page Break and Use Proofing Tools

3. Insert a **page break** at the end of the memo, and then open **WD03-A03-LondonTours** from your **WD2013 Lesson 03** folder.
4. Copy the content of the document, and then close it.
5. Paste the content into page 2 of your memo, and then correct the spelling and grammar. *Hint:* Cotswolds *is spelled correctly. The grammar error is in the second line of the first paragraph.*

Format Text

6. Format the heading at the top of page 2 with **Verdana**, **14 point**, **Bold**.
7. Format the *Local Excursions* heading with **Verdana**, **Bold**, and **Underline**.
8. Use the **Format Painter** to copy the formatting to the *Day Trips* heading, and then deselect the heading.

Use Find and Replace and Insert a Hyperlink

9. Use the **Replace** feature to find *St. Paul's Cathedral* and replace it with *Westminster Abbey*.
10. Select *Stonehenge*, and then insert a hyperlink to **WD03-A03-Stonehenge** in your **WD2013 Lesson 03** folder.
11. Test the hyperlink, and then close the **Stonehenge** file.

Save the File in PDF

12. Save your memo as a PDF file using the same filename.

    Next you will open and edit a PDF file. This is so you can understand the mechanics of how to do it.

When you open a PDF file in Word, there will be formatting issues. Don't worry about making the file look perfect; instead, concentrate more on how to open and edit so you will be able to accomplish this task in the future.

Open and Edit the PDF

13. Open your **WD03-A03-HenslowMemo.pdf** file. When the message appears, click **OK**.

    The conversion to PDF misaligned the FROM: and DATE: lines in the memo heading.

14. Add tabs to the *FROM:* and *DATE*: lines to realign them.
15. Scroll to page 2 and remove the **underlines** from the *Local Excursions* and *Day Trip* headings.
16. Resave the file in **PDF** to the **WD2013 Lesson 03** folder. Name the file **`WD03-A03-HenslowMemo2-[FirstInitialLastName]`**. (If the PDF file opens in a PDF reader, close the PDF window.)
17. Save and close your Word version of the Henslow memo; exit from **Word**.
18. Submit your final file based on the guidelines provided by your instructor.

Extend Your Skills

In the course of working through the Extend Your Skills exercises, you will think critically as you use the skills taught in the lesson to complete the assigned projects. To evaluate your mastery and completion of the exercises, your instructor may use a rubric, with which more points are allotted according to performance characteristics. (The more you do, the more you earn!) Ask your instructor how your work will be evaluated.

WD03-E01 That's the Way I See It

Your friend has hired you to do marketing for her local small business. You need to research what is involved in producing a press release, because her company is planning to announce a new service soon. Conduct online research to determine:

- The purpose of a press release
- The main elements that typically appear in a press release
- How to create effective content for a press release
- Three suggestions for distributing a press release

Create a new Word document named **WD03-E01-PressRel-[FirstInitialLastName]** and saved to your **WD2013 Lesson 03** folder. Then, type the information you find into the document.

Create a page break, and then type a press release for the new service (make up the service you will be promoting) using the guidelines you have discovered and documented. Make sure to format the document so it is easy to read, using the Format Painter tool as needed. Preview how the file will appear when printed, and then save it as a PDF file named **WD03-E01-PressRelPDF-[FirstInitialLastName]** in your **WD2013 Lesson 03** folder.

You will be evaluated based on the inclusion of all elements specified, your ability to follow directions, your ability to apply newly learned skills to a real-world situation, your creativity, and the relevance of your topic and/or data choice(s). Submit your final files based on the guidelines provided by your instructor.

WD03-E02 Be Your Own Boss

You are the owner of Blue Jean Landscaping. Use your imagination to determine a new service that your company plans to offer and write a press release to announce the service. Be sure to include the primary elements of a press release and explain your service in an interesting way so a reporter reading your press release will be motivated to write a good story. Indicate how you will distribute your press release.

Use the formatting skills you have learned in this lesson to make the press release visually appealing. Save your finished press release as a PDF file as **WD03-E02-BJLPressRel-[FirstInitialLastName]** in your **WD2013 Lesson 03** folder.

You will be evaluated based on the inclusion of all elements specified, your ability to follow directions, your ability to apply newly learned skills to a real-world situation, your creativity, and your demonstration of an entrepreneurial spirit. Submit your final file based on the guidelines provided by your instructor.

Transfer Your Skills

In the course of working through the Transfer Your Skills exercises, you will use critical-thinking and creativity skills to complete the assigned projects using skills taught in the lesson. To evaluate your mastery and completion of the exercises, your instructor may use a rubric, with which more points are allotted according to performance characteristics. (The more you do, the more you earn!) Ask your instructor how your work will be evaluated.

WD03-T01 Use the Web as a Learning Tool

Throughout this book, you will be provided with an opportunity to use the Internet as a learning tool by completing WebQuests. According to the original creators of WebQuests, as described on their website (WebQuest.org), a WebQuest is "an inquiry-oriented activity in which most or all of the information used by learners is drawn from the web." To complete the WebQuest projects in this book, navigate to the student resource center and choose the WebQuest for the lesson on which you are currently working. The subject of each WebQuest will be relevant to the material found in the lesson.

WebQuest Subject: Why does a company need a press kit?

Submit your final file based on the guidelines provided by your instructor.

WD03-T02 Demonstrate Proficiency

As the owner of Stormy BBQ, create a memo to your employees about a new product you will be offering. (Use your imagination to come up with a new product.) In the memo, ask your employees to review the press release and offer any changes or suggestions they have. Create the press release on page 2 of the memo, advertising the new product. Conduct online research to determine the elements required for an effective press release, if necessary. Use Spell Check to make sure all words are spelled correctly, and then format the memo and press release using the tools you have learned in this lesson to make your document visually appealing.

Save your completed work as a PDF file named **WD03-T02-NewProdPDF-[FirstInitialLastName]** in your **WD2013 Lesson 03** folder. Submit your final file based on the guidelines provided by your instructor.

Creating a Simple Report

LESSON OUTLINE

LEARNING OBJECTIVES

After studying this lesson, you will be able to:

- Use paragraph alignment settings
- Set custom tab stops
- Format lists
- Apply borders, shading, and styles
- Insert page numbers

In this lesson, you will create a simple report. Reports are important documents often used in business and education. You will format your report using various paragraph formatting techniques, including paragraph alignment, custom tab stops, and Word's indent feature. You will work with bulleted and numbered lists, and you will add interest to the report by applying borders, shading, and styles. You will be introduced to headers and footers, and you will use the Navigation pane to navigate by heading styles and to quickly reorganize your document.

CASE STUDY

Formatting a Research Report

A business analyst at My Virtual Campus has asked you to assist in researching the use of social media at universities. The report will be a useful tool for management to have as background information. It is important to understand how the "always connected" generation is using technology to pursue their education, to study, and to perform classroom activities. You will use paragraph formatting techniques such as indents, styles, and bullets and numbering to prepare an easy-to-read, properly formatted, and professional-looking document.

My Virtual Campus

SOCIAL MEDIA IN UNIVERSITIES

Universities today are engaging constantly-connected Millennials through social media. Use of Facebook, YouTube, Twitter, blogging, and podcasting have all experienced double-digit increases on campus in the last year. Students are checking out universities through student-run blogs, and recruiters are checking out students on Facebook and LinkedIn.

The Net Generation

In her article appearing in The Teaching Professor, August/September 2009, Dalton State College psychology professor Christy Price makes the following observations:

> "...the ideal learning environment was Millennials' preference for a variety of teaching methods, as opposed to a "lecture only" format."
>
> "Respondents thought professors who involved them in class with a variety of methods (not just lecture) as more connected to millennial culture."

Formatting Reports

Video Library http://labyrinthelab.com/videos Video Number: WD13-V0401

There is a variety of acceptable report formats. Different formats can be used for marketing publications and other types of business and educational documents. The following example shows a traditional business report in unbound format.

The title is positioned at approximately 2 inches from the top of the page and centered.

The title is in uppercase and bold; you can also apply a distinctive font to the title.

SOCIAL MEDIA IN UNIVERSITIES

Universities today are engaging constantly-connected Millennials through social media. Use of Facebook, YouTube, Twitter, blogging, and podcasting have all experienced double-digit increases on campus in the last year. Students are checking out universities through student-run blogs, and recruiters are checking out students on Facebook and LinkedIn.

The Net Generation

In her article appearing in The Teaching Professor, August/September 2009, Dalton State College psychology professor Christy Price makes the following observations:

> "...the ideal learning environment was Millennials' preference for a variety of teaching methods, as opposed to a "lecture only" format."
>
> "Respondents thought professors who involved them in class with a variety of methods (not just lecture) as more connected to millennial culture."

The body is double-spaced with paragraphs indented to ½ inch.

Quotations and other text you want to emphasize are indented on the left and right.

Formatting Paragraphs

Paragraph formatting includes paragraph alignment, line spacing, and bullets and numbering, to mention a few. In Word, a paragraph is created anytime you tap Enter. In other words, a paragraph could consist of several lines that end with Enter or just one line, such as a heading, that ends with Enter. Tapping Enter to generate a blank line creates a paragraph, even though there is no text in it. What's more, Word stores formats in the paragraph symbol.

Each of these is a paragraph because each ends with a paragraph symbol (heading, blank lines, text paragraph).

Social·Media·Benefits·for·Students¶
¶
Technology·can·be·used·to·reach·the·Net°Generation·in·an·effective·way.·They·consider·technology·a·natural·way·to·pursue·their·education,·to·study,·and·to·perform·classroom·activities.·¶
¶
◆→ Search·for·classes·online¶
o→ Locate·desired·subjects,·dates,·and·times¶
o→ Review·syllabi¶

Each of these lines is a paragraph.

Comparing Paragraph Formatting to Character Formatting

Selecting paragraphs for formatting purposes is a little different from selecting characters. With character formatting, you typically select the entire block of text you want to format, which is necessary in the majority of cases. With paragraph formatting, you need only click in the paragraph to *select* it. On the other hand, if you want to apply formatting to more than one paragraph, you must select at least part of each paragraph.

Using Paragraph Alignment

Paragraph alignment determines how text aligns between the margins. Left alignment gives paragraphs a straight left margin and ragged right margin. Center alignment is usually applied to headings. Right alignment generates a straight right and ragged left margin. Justify provides straight left and right margins.

FROM THE RIBBON

Home→Paragraph→Alignment Option

FROM THE KEYBOARD

Ctrl+L align left
Ctrl+E center
Ctrl+R align right
Ctrl+J justify

Here's how the different paragraph alignment settings look in Word.

Left-aligned — Centered — Right-aligned

SOCIAL MEDIA IN UNIVERSITIES

SOCIAL MEDIA IN UNIVERSITIES

SOCIAL MEDIA IN UNIVERSITIES

Justified — Universities today are engaging constantly-connected Millennials through social media. Use of Facebook, YouTube, Twitter, blogging, and podcasting have all experienced double-digit increases on campus in the last year. Students are checking out universities through student-run blogs, and recruiters are checking out students on Facebook and LinkedIn.

DEVELOP YOUR SKILLS WD04-D01

Align Text

In this exercise, you will use the alignment buttons in the Paragraph group of the Home tab to align your report heading.

1. Start **Word**. Create a new, blank document using the **Blank Document template** and make sure the Word window is **maximized**.
2. Save the file as `WD04-D01-SocMediaRprt-[FirstInitialLastName]` in your **WD2013 Lesson 04** folder.

   Replace the bracketed text with your first initial and last name. For example, if your name is Bethany Smith, your filename would look like this: WD04-D01-SocMediaRprt-BSmith.
3. Tap [Enter] twice to position the insertion point approximately **2 inches** from the top of the page.
4. Turn on [Caps Lock], and then choose **Home→Font→Bold** [B].
5. Type the report title, `SOCIAL MEDIA IN UNIVERSITIES`.
6. Choose **Home→Font→Bold** [B] and then tap [Caps Lock] to turn both off.
7. Tap [Enter] twice to provide blank lines before the body of the report, which you will add shortly.
8. Position the insertion point in the report heading.

Align the Heading

9. Choose **Home→Paragraph→Align Right**.
10. Choose **Home→Paragraph→Align Left**.
11. Choose **Home→Paragraph→Center**.
12. Save the file and leave it open; you will modify it throughout the lesson.

Adding Hyphenation

Video Library http://labyrinthelab.com/videos Video Number: WD13-V0402

FROM THE RIBBON
Page Layout→Page Setup→Hyphenation

Typically, when you create a document, you let Word Wrap do its thing; that is, it adds all of the text it can on a line until it comes to a word that won't fit, and then it wraps down to the next line. Sometimes this can cause your right margin to appear too ragged. You can use hyphenation to create a more even margin.

- **Automatic:** The entire document is hyphenated automatically, and as you edit or revise the document hyphenation continues.
- **Manual:** Manual hyphenation searches for words you might want to hyphenate and provides a prompt where you can accept, modify, or reject the hyphenation.

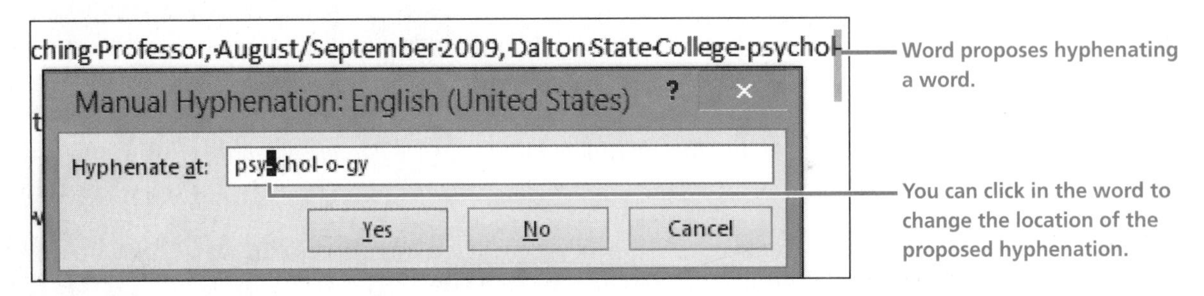

DEVELOP YOUR SKILLS WD04-D02

Use Manual Hyphenation

In this exercise, you will copy the content for your report from another document, and then you will use manual hyphenation to smooth out the right-hand margin.

1. Save your file as **`WD04-D02-SocMediaRprt-[FirstInitialLastName]`**.
2. If necessary, choose **Home→Paragraph→Show/Hide** [¶] to turn on formatting marks.
3. Open **WD04-D02-RprtContent** from your **WD2013 Lesson 04** folder.
4. Press [Ctrl]+[A] to select all content, and then press [Ctrl]+[C] to copy it.
5. Close **WD04-D02-RprtContent**.
   You will now paste the copied document in the Social Media Report document.

6. Follow these steps to paste the document into the report:

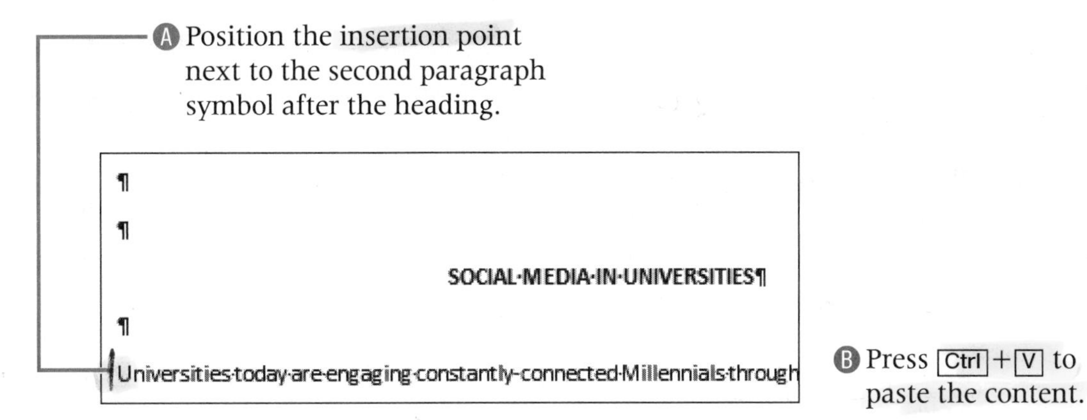

7. Choose **Home→Paragraph→Show/Hide** ¶ to turn off formatting marks.
8. Press Ctrl+Home.

Hyphenate Words

9. Choose **Page Layout→Page Setup→Hyphenation** and choose **Manual** from the menu.
10. When Word proposes hyphenating *Facebook*, click **No**.
    In this example, we prefer to keep Facebook as one word even though it could be hyphenated.
11. When Word proposes hyphenating *psychology*, click **Yes** to accept the suggestion.
12. When Word proposes hyphenating *opposed*, click **Yes** to accept the suggestion.
13. When Word suggests hyphenating *increases*, click **Cancel** to end Manual hyphenation.
14. Save the report.

Inserting a Nonbreaking Hyphen or Space

Video Library http://labyrinthelab.com/videos Video Number: WD13-V0403

Word allows you to keep terms together that should remain together on one line, such as dates or hyphenated names. You use nonbreaking hyphens and nonbreaking spaces to accomplish this.

FROM THE KEYBOARD

Ctrl+Shift+Hyphen to add a nonbreaking hyphen

Ctrl+Shift+Spacebar to add a nonbreaking space

QUICK REFERENCE — **USING NONBREAKING HYPHENS AND SPACES**

Task	Procedure
Insert Nonbreaking Hyphens	■ Choose Insert→Symbols→Symbol, and then choose More Symbols. ■ Click the Special Characters tab, choose Nonbreaking Hyphen, and click Insert.
Insert Nonbreaking Spaces	■ Choose Insert→Symbols→Symbol, and then choose More Symbols. ■ Click the Special Characters tab, choose Nonbreaking Space, and click Insert.

DEVELOP YOUR SKILLS WD04-D03

Insert Nonbreaking Hyphens and Spaces

In this exercise, you will insert nonbreaking hyphens and spaces in your document. Then you will test to see if the words stay together as one term.

1. Save your file as **`WD04-D03-SocMediaRprt-[FirstInitialLastName]`**.
2. Scroll to the top of the document.
3. Follow these steps to insert a nonbreaking hyphen in double-digit:

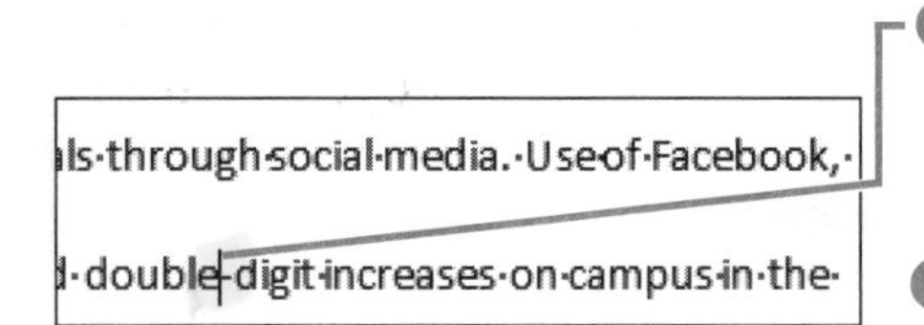

Ⓐ Click here to position the insertion point to the left of the hyphen.

Ⓑ Tap [Delete] to remove the hyphen.

4. Choose **Insert→Symbols→Symbol** [Ω].
5. Choose **More Symbols** from the menu, and when the Symbol dialog box opens, click the **Special Characters** tab.
6. Choose **Nonbreaking Hyphen**, click **Insert**, and close the dialog box.
7. Position the insertion point to the left of *double-digit*.
8. Tap [Spacebar] several times to move double-digit to the right until it wraps to the next line as a single term.

   Notice the nonbreaking hyphen you inserted kept the hyphenated word together.
9. Click **Undo** [↶] on the Quick Access toolbar to undo the spaces you inserted.

Insert and Test a Nonbreaking Space

10. Scroll to the end of the document.
11. Follow these steps to insert a nonbreaking space:

Technology can be used to reach the Net Generation

natural way to pursue their education, to study, and t

Ⓐ Position the insertion point to the right of *Net* and tap [Delete].

Ⓑ Press [Ctrl]+[Shift]+[Spacebar] to insert a nonbreaking space.

12. Position the insertion point to the left of *Net* and tap [Spacebar] until *Net Generation* wraps to the next line as one term.

    The nonbreaking space kept the words together as one term.
13. Click **Undo** [↶] on the Quick Access toolbar.
14. Save the report.

Indenting Text

Video Library http://labyrinthelab.com/videos Video Number: WD13-V0404

Indents offset text from the margins. You can set indents by using the buttons on the Ribbon or by dragging the indent markers on the ruler.

FROM THE RIBBON

Home→Paragraph→Decrease/Increase Indent

FROM THE KEYBOARD

[Ctrl]+[Shift]+[M] to decrease the indent

[Ctrl]+[M] to increase the indent

Adjusting Indents with the Ribbon

The Increase Indent and Decrease Indent buttons adjust the indent of an entire paragraph (or one or more selected paragraphs) and they affect the left indent only. They adjust the indent based on the default tab stops, which are set at every half inch.

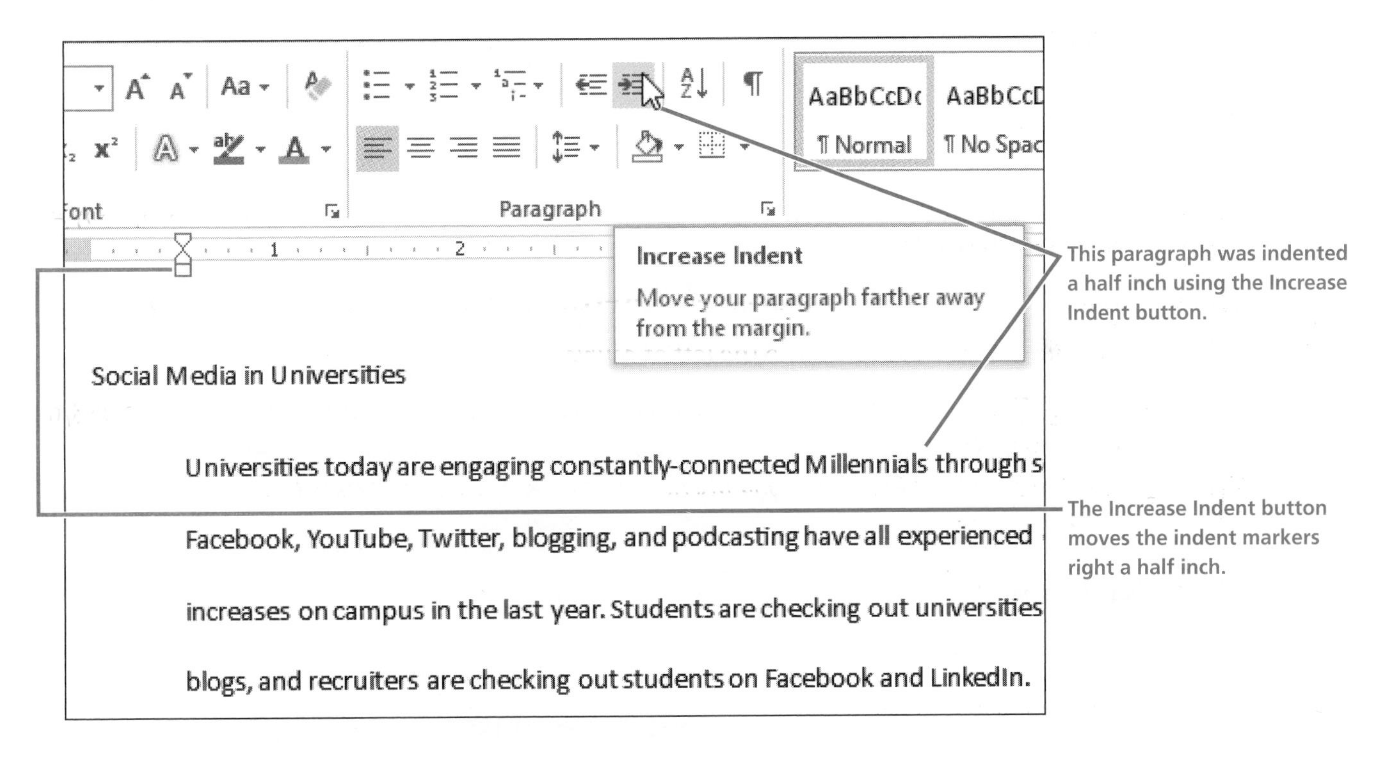

This paragraph was indented a half inch using the Increase Indent button.

The Increase Indent button moves the indent markers right a half inch.

DEVELOP YOUR SKILLS WD04-D04

Experiment with Left Indents

In this exercise, you will use the Increase Indent button to indent quotations to one inch. Then you will use the Decrease Indent button to return the quotations to the left margin.

1. Save your file as `WD04-D04-SocMediaRprt-[FirstInitialLastName]`.
2. If necessary, choose **View→Show→Ruler** to turn on the ruler.

3. Follow these steps to indent multiple paragraphs:

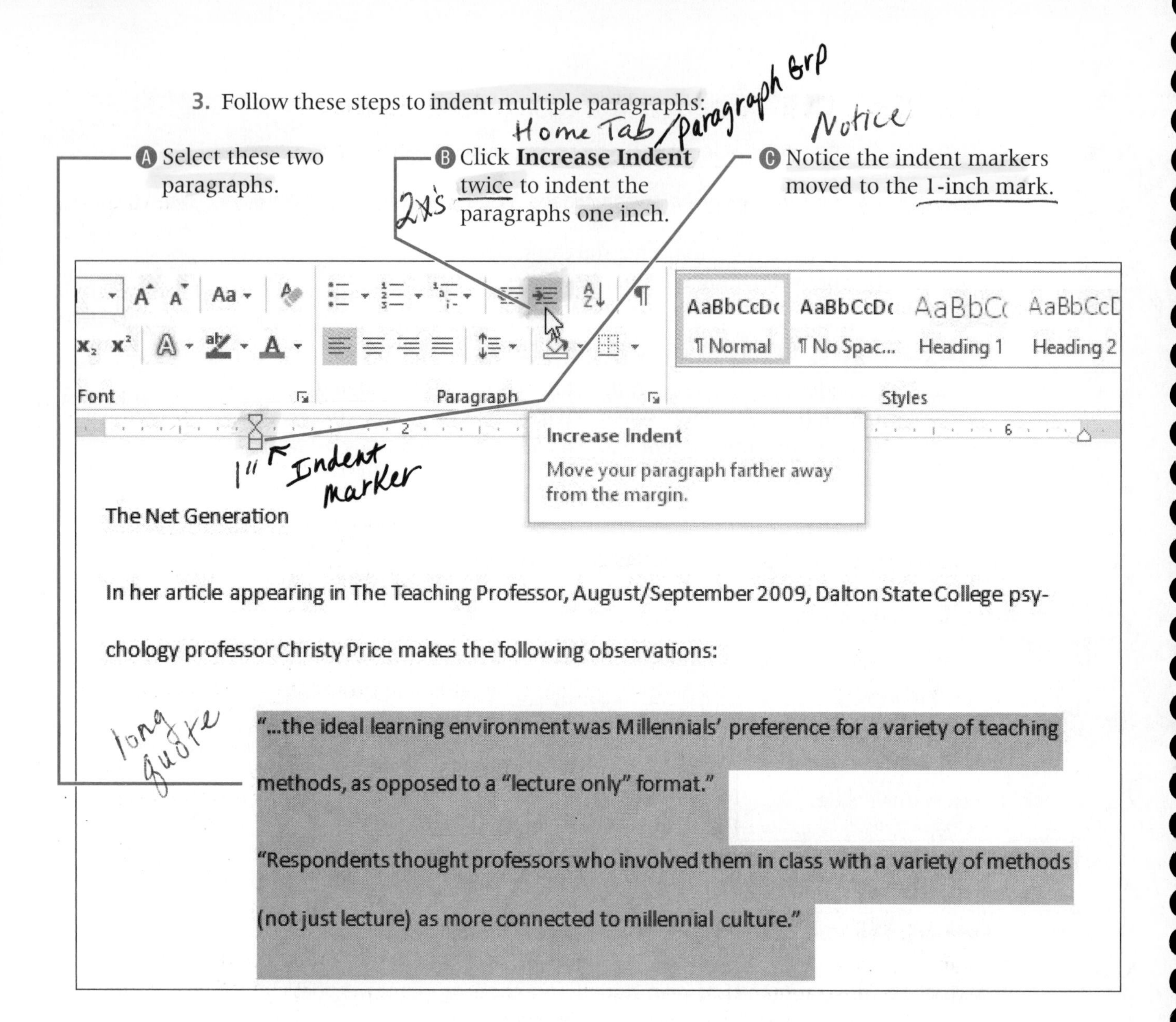

4. Make sure the paragraphs are still selected.
5. Choose **Home→Paragraph→Decrease Indent** twice to return the paragraphs to the left margin.
6. Save the report.

Setting Custom Indents on the Ruler

Video Library http://labyrinthelab.com/videos Video Number: WD13-V0405

You can set indents by dragging the indent markers on the horizontal ruler. The following illustration shows the ruler and the indent markers.

INDENT MARKERS	
Item	**Description**
First Line Indent	Indents the first line of the paragraph.
Hanging Indent	This triangle is *attached* to the Left Indent rectangle. Place the mouse pointer in the triangle and drag right to indent everything except the first line.
Left Indent	This rectangle is *attached* to the Hanging Indent triangle. Place the mouse pointer in the rectangle and drag left/right to position all lines simultaneously. Whether the triangles are aligned with each other or separated, dragging the rectangle positions both triangles simultaneously.
Right Indent	Drag to indent the entire paragraph from the right.

Using Hanging Indents

Hanging indents are not often used, thus many people are not familiar with the term. The following illustration shows an example of a hanging indent, where the first line is *outdented* and the remaining lines of the paragraph are *indented*.

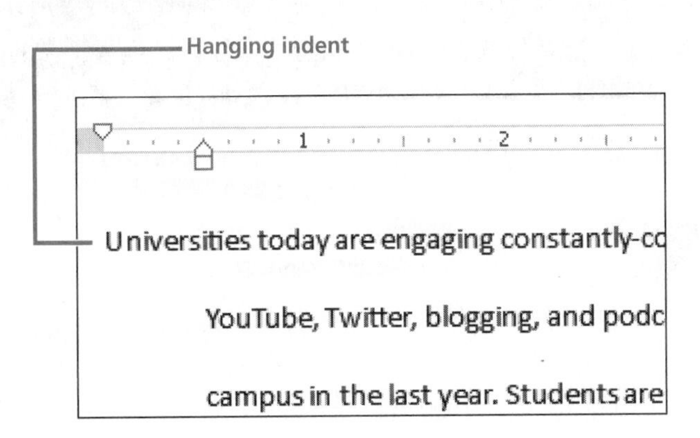

DEVELOP YOUR SKILLS WD04-D05

Use the Indent Markers to Indent Paragraphs

In this exercise, you will use the indent markers on the horizontal ruler to indent the quotations from both the left and right. You will also use the First Line Indent marker to indent the first line of the other paragraphs.

1. Save your file as **WD04-D05-SocMediaRprt-[FirstInitialLastName]**.
2. Follow these steps to adjust the left and right indents:

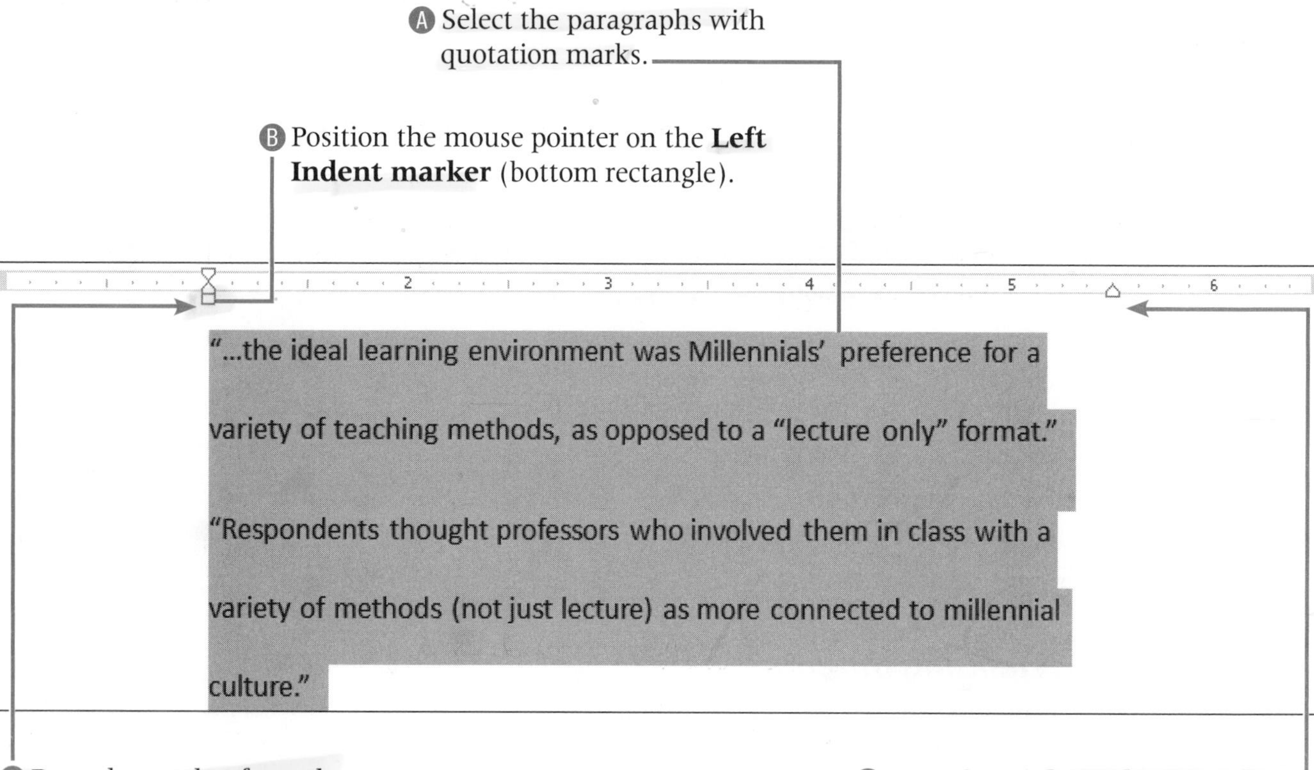

3. Follow these steps to indent the first line of paragraphs:

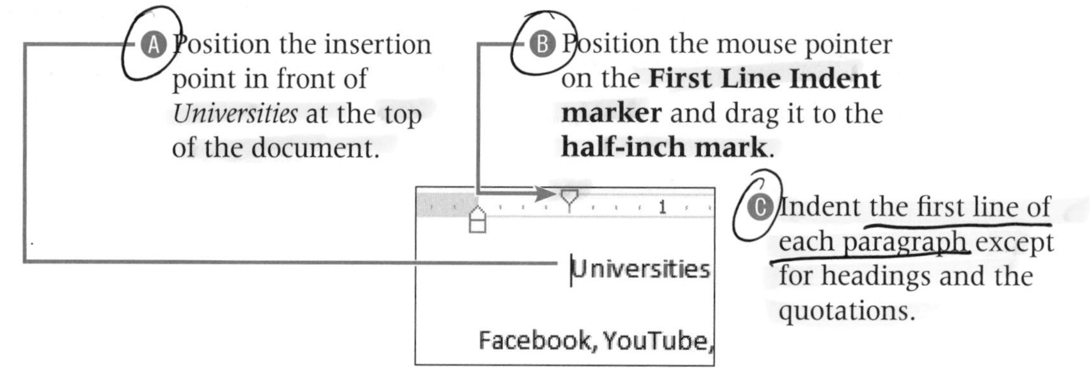

4. Save the report.

Using Custom Tab Stops

Video Library http://labyrinthelab.com/videos Video Number: WD13-V0406

Default tab stops are set every one-half inch, so the insertion point moves one-half inch whenever you tap [Tab]. You can customize tab stops if you want other settings, or if you want to use a special tab, such as one that center aligns.

Never use the spacebar to line up columns of text. Even if it looks right on the screen, it most likely will not print correctly.

Setting Custom Tab Stops with the Ruler

Word has four types of custom tab stops: left, right, center, and decimal. You can set all four types using the horizontal ruler. It is critical that you position the insertion point on the line where you plan to set tabs. Tab settings are carried inside the paragraph symbol to the next paragraph when you tap [Enter].

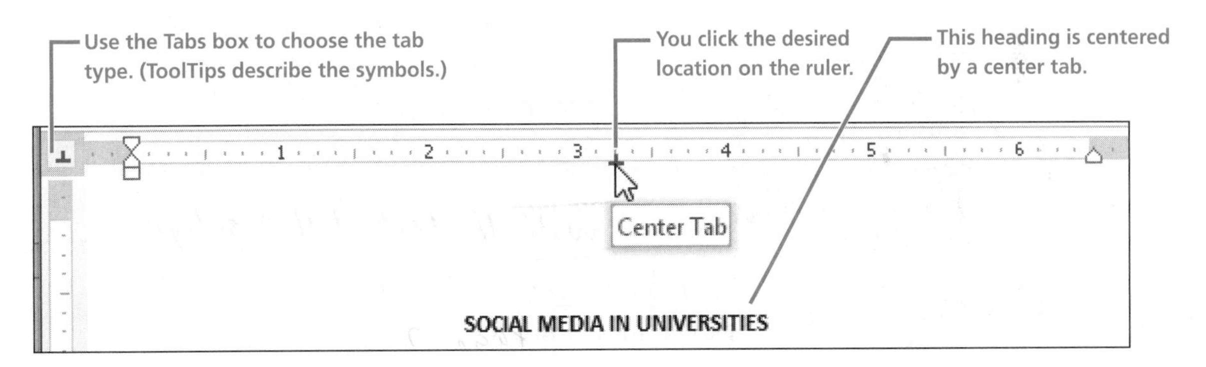

DEVELOP YOUR SKILLS WD04-D06

Set Tabs Using the Ruler

In this exercise, you will use custom tabs to set up text in a columnar format.

1. Save your file as `WD04-D06-SocMediaRprt-[FirstInitialLastName]`.
2. If necessary, choose **Home→Paragraph→Show/Hide** [¶] to display formatting marks.
3. If necessary, choose **View→Show→Ruler** to turn on the ruler.

4. Follow these steps to set tabs for the heading line of your table:

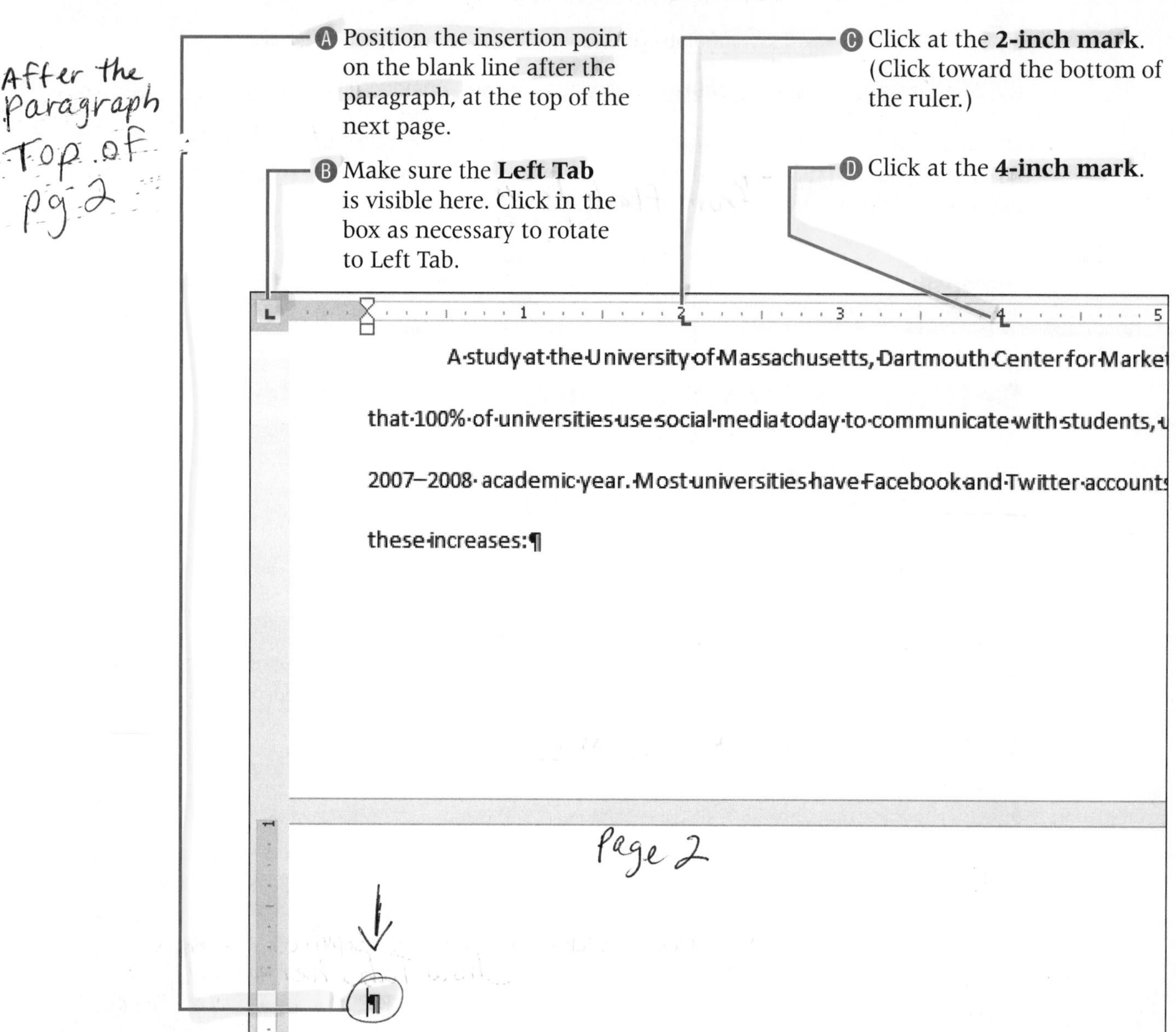

5. Type the following heading line, tapping [Tab] where you see small arrows.

6. Tap [Enter] at the end of the line, and notice that the ruler still reflects the tabs you set in the previous line.
7. Save the report.

Working with the Tabs Dialog Box

to set multiple tabs

Video Library http://labyrinthelab.com/videos Video Number: WD13-V0407

You can set custom tab stops in the Tabs dialog box. You can specify precise positions for custom tabs, choose the type of tab (alignment), clear custom tab stops, and set leader tabs.

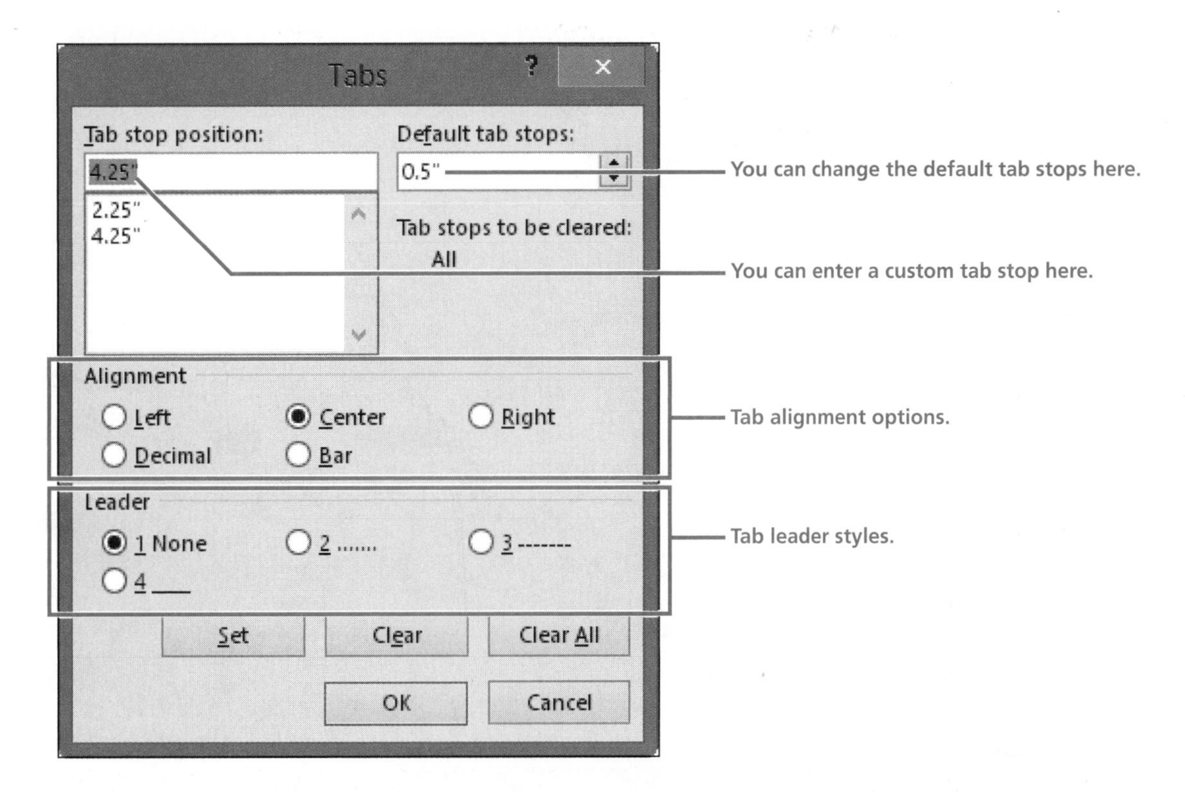

QUICK REFERENCE	USING THE INDENT MARKERS
Task	**Procedure**
Set tabs	■ Choose the desired tab in the Tabs box and click the desired location on the ruler; or, choose Home→Paragraph→dialog box launcher and click Tabs. ■ Enter the settings in the Tab Stop Position field, choose the Alignment, and click Set.
Modify tab settings	■ Drag the tab(s) to a new location on the ruler; or, in the Tabs dialog box, clear the tab(s) you want to change, enter new settings in the Tab Stop Position field, and click Set.
Clear tabs	■ Drag the tab(s) off the ruler; or, use the Clear or Clear All button in the Tabs dialog box.

DEVELOP YOUR SKILLS WD04-D07

Use the Tabs Dialog Box

In this exercise, you will use the Tabs dialog box to clear tabs that were set for the table's heading line and to set custom tabs for the body of the table.

1. Save your file as **WD04-D07-SocMediaRprt-[FirstInitialLastName]**.
2. Follow these steps to clear all tabs:

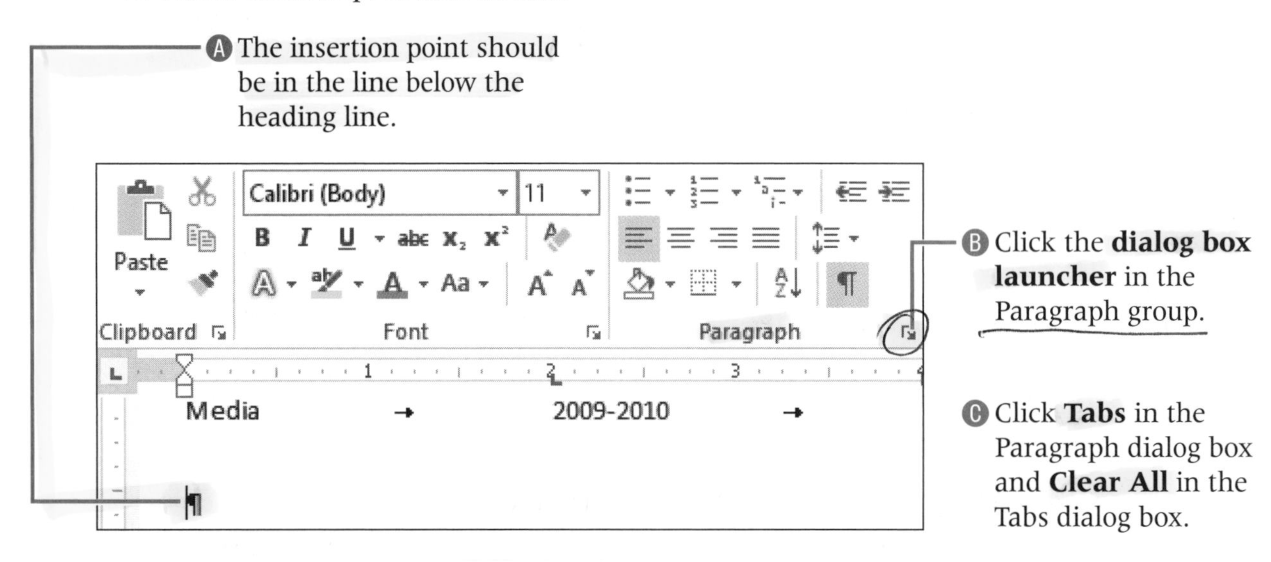

3. Follow these steps to set new tabs for the rest of the table:

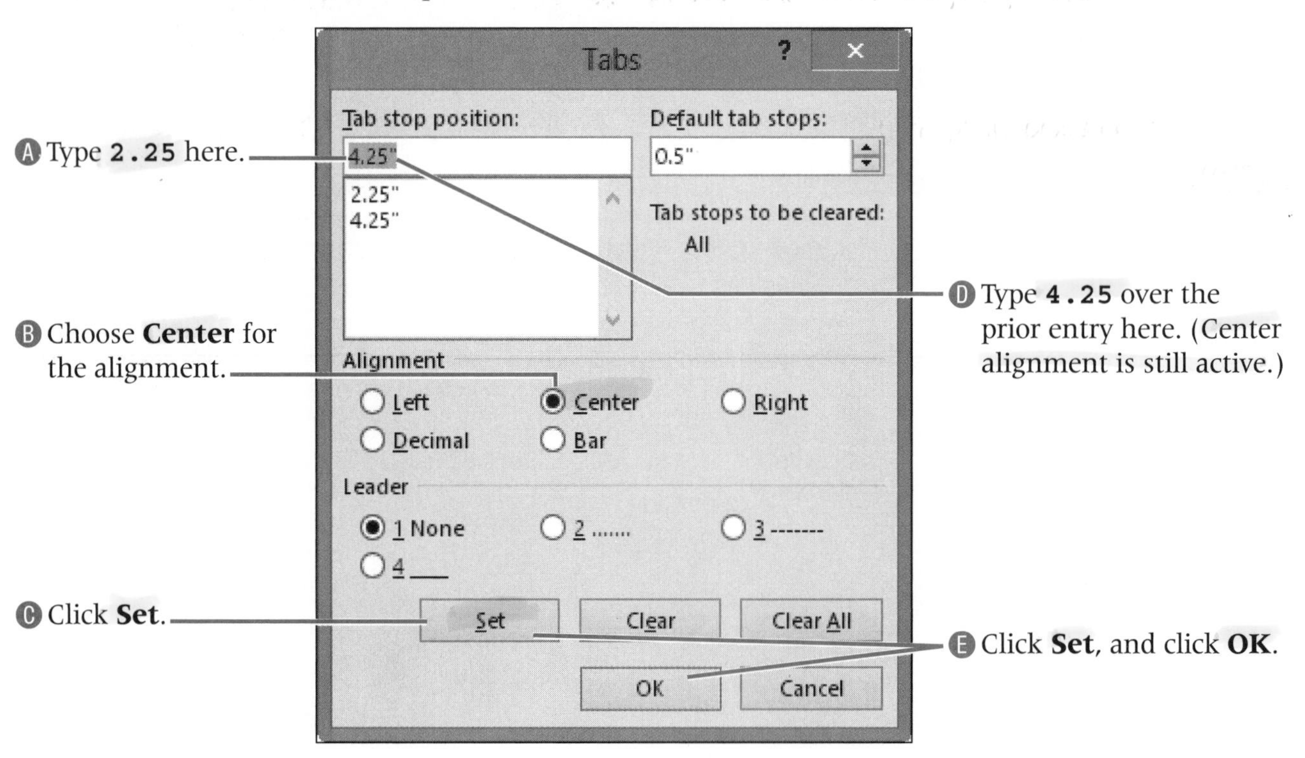

4. Type the rest of the table, tapping [Tab] wherever an arrow appears, and tapping [Enter] at the end of each line.

Media →	2009–2010 →	2010–2011¶
Facebook →	87% →	98%¶
Twitter →	59% →	84%¶
Blogs →	51% →	66%¶
Podcasts →	22% →	41%¶

5. Select the first line in the table and choose **Home→Font→Bold** [B].
6. Save the file.

Modifying Tab Stops with the Ruler

Video Library http://labyrinthelab.com/videos Video Number: WD13-V0408

To adjust a tab setting on the ruler, you select the paragraphs containing the tab stops you want to change, and then drag the tab to the new location. Delete a tab by dragging it off the Ruler.

If you accidentally drag a tab stop off the ruler while trying to move it, just click Undo.

DEVELOP YOUR SKILLS WD04-D08

✗ Modify and Delete Tab Stops from the Ruler

In this exercise, you decided the percentages could be better centered below the headings. You will use the ruler to modify the tab stops for the body of the table but not the heading line. Then you will delete a tab stop.

1. Save your file as **`WD04-D08-SocMediaRprt-[FirstInitialLastName]`**.
2. Follow these steps to adjust the tabs:

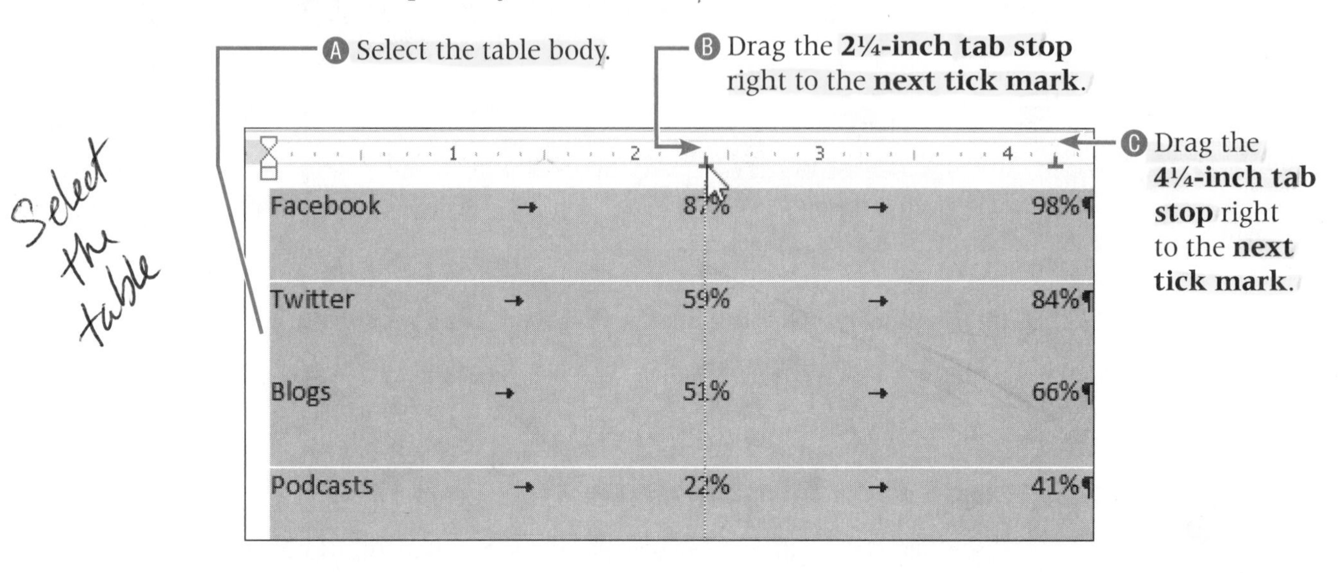

Now you will delete a tab stop. with the text still highlighted

3. Place the mouse pointer on the **4 3/8 inch tab** and drag it straight down off the ruler to remove the tab.
4. Click **Undo** on the Quick Access toolbar to replace the tab stop.
5. Save the report.

Show a dot leader tab stop

Using Numbered and Bulleted Lists

Video Library http://labyrinthelab.com/videos Video Number: WD13-V0409

Numbered and bulleted lists are effective in drawing your reader's attention to items of interest. You can turn them on before you begin typing or apply them after you type the list. Numbered lists are automatically renumbered if you insert or delete an item. A good example of when to use a numbered list is when sequence is important, as in a series of steps. Items in a bulleted list have no sequence.

FROM THE RIBBON

Home→Paragraph→Bullets

Home→Paragraph→Numbering

Promoting and Demoting List Items

Demoting an item increases the indent level by shifting it to the right. To promote an item decreases the indent level by moving it back to the left. When you demote items in a list, it creates an outline effect, indicating the level of importance of the items in the list.

FROM THE KEYBOARD

[Shift]+[Tab] to promote a list item

[Tab] to demote a list item

- Search for classes online
  - Locate desired subjects, dates, and times
  - Review syllabi
- Use course homepages

These two items were demoted by increasing the indent level.

QUICK REFERENCE | **WORKING WITH LISTS**

Task	Procedure
Convert text to a bulleted or numbered list	■ Select the text to be formatted, and choose Home→Paragraph→Bullets or Numbering.
Turn off bullets and numbering	■ Tap [Enter] twice at the end of the list; or, click the Bullets or the Numbering button.
Demote an item in a list	■ Select the item and choose Home→Paragraph→Increase Indent; or, tap [Tab].
Promote an item in a list	■ Select the item and choose Home→Paragraph→Decrease Indent; or, press [Shift]+[Tab].
Customize Bullets and Numbering	■ Choose Home→Paragraph→Bullets or Numbering menu button ▼ and choose Define New Bullet or Define New Number Format.
Remove a custom bullet or numbering from the gallery	■ Right-click the image and choose Remove.

DEVELOP YOUR SKILLS WD04-D09

Work with Bullets and Numbering

In this exercise, you will convert text to a numbered list, and then you'll create a bulleted list, promoting and demoting levels within the list.

1. Save your file as **`WD04-D09-SocMediaRprt-[FirstInitialLastName]`**.
2. Follow these steps to create a list:

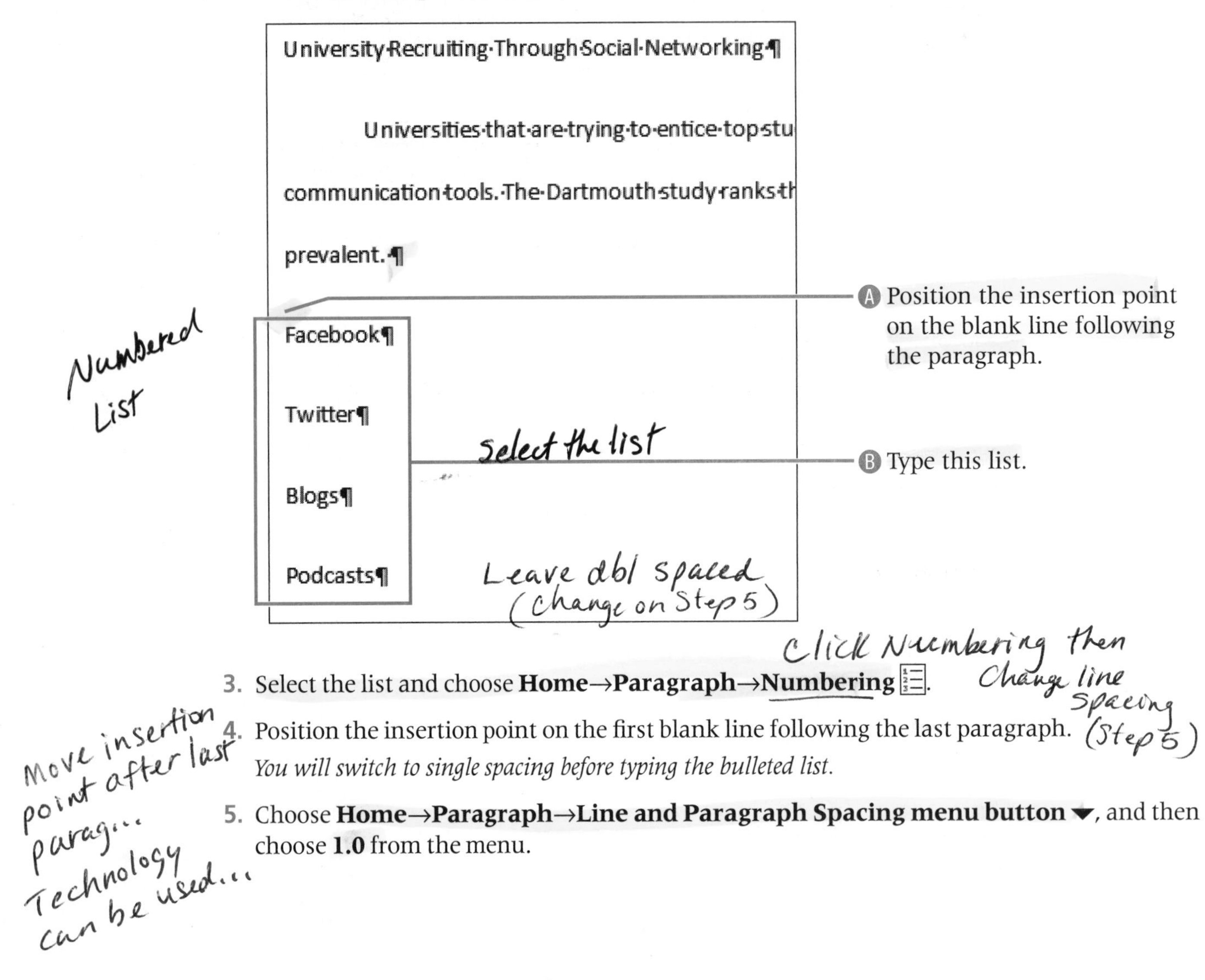

3. Select the list and choose **Home→Paragraph→Numbering**.
4. Position the insertion point on the first blank line following the last paragraph.
   You will switch to single spacing before typing the bulleted list.
5. Choose **Home→Paragraph→Line and Paragraph Spacing menu button ▾**, and then choose **1.0** from the menu.

6. Follow these steps to create a bulleted list:

Pg 2

Bulleted List

Ⓐ Click **Bullets**, type this text, and tap Enter.

Ⓑ Tap Tab to demote the bullet, and then type these two lines, tapping Enter at the end of each line.

Technology·can·be·used·to·reach·the·Net"Generation·

technology·a·natural·way·to·pursue·their·education,·to·study,

Click after "Classroom activities" ↑

- Search·for·classes·online¶
  - Locate·desired·subjects,·dates,·and·times¶
  - Review·syllabi¶
- Use·course·homepages¶ (See step 7)

Ⓒ Press Shift + Tab to promote this line, and then type this text.

7. Type the rest of the list as shown, demoting and promoting the bullet levels as needed.

- Use·course·homepages¶
  - Read·announcements¶
  - Get·student·handouts¶
  - Conduct·threaded·conversations·on·message·boards¶
  - Communicate·with·instructors·in·chat·rooms¶
- View·faculty·office·hours·online¶
- Review·academic·history·online¶

Press Enter 2xs to end bullets

8. Save the report.

Word 2013

Using the Bullets and Numbering Libraries

FROM THE RIBBON
Home→Paragraph→ Bullets menu button ▾

Home→Paragraph→ Numbering menu button ▾

Video Library http://labyrinthelab.com/videos Video Number: WD13-V0410

The Bullets and Numbering libraries enable you to choose a style for your bulleted or numbered list. You can also define your own custom formats.

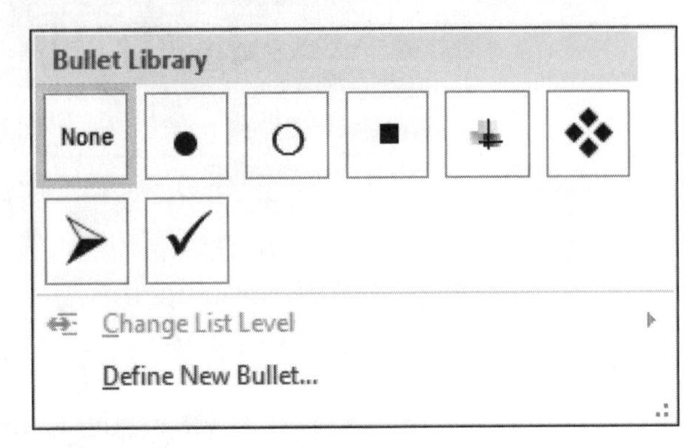

Bullet Library

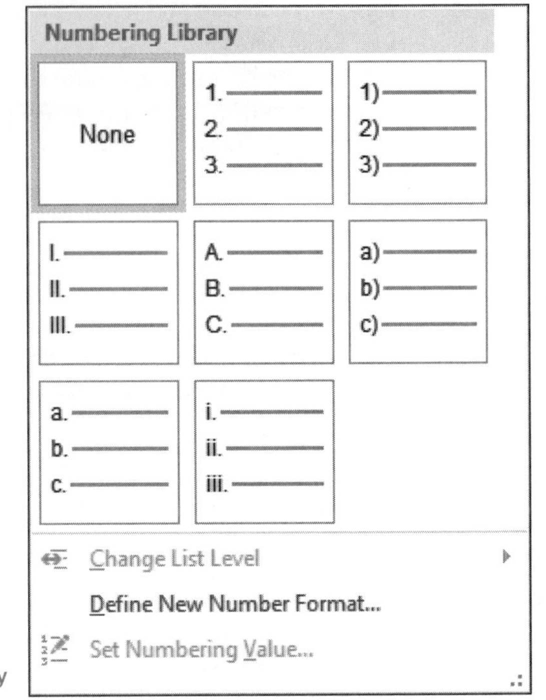

Numbering Library

DEVELOP YOUR SKILLS WD04-D10

Change the Bullet Style

In this exercise, you will choose a different bullet style for the first-level bullets from the Bullet Library.

1. Save your file as **WD04-D10-SocMediaRprt-[FirstInitialLastName]**.
2. Follow these steps to apply a different bullet:

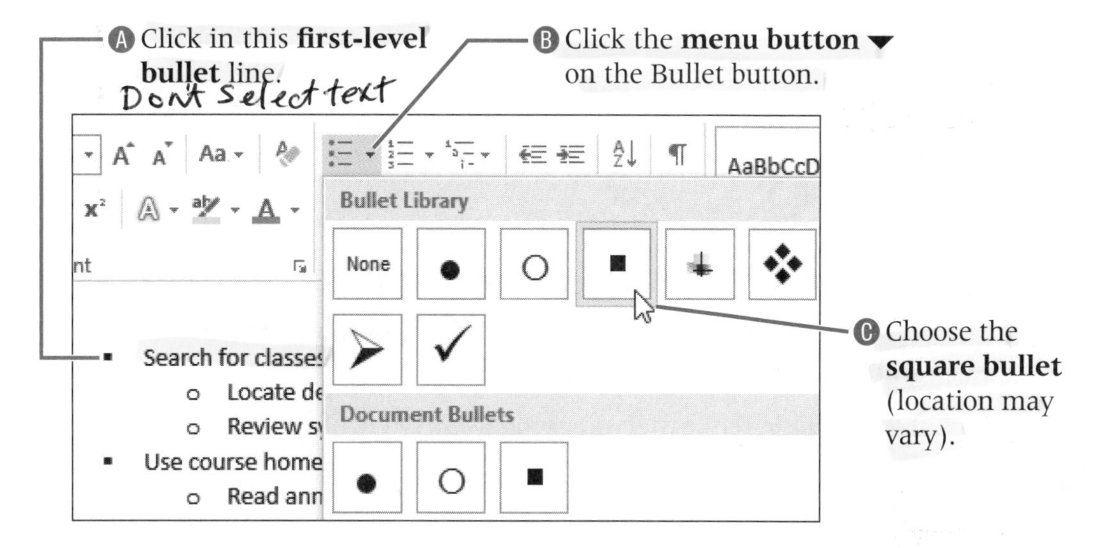

Notice that the bullet shape changed for all first-level bullets.

3. Save the report.

Customizing Bullet and Number Styles

Video Library http://labyrinthelab.com/videos Video Number: WD13-V0411

You can customize bullet styles by defining a symbol, picture, font, or alignment. You can customize the numbering style, font, format, and alignment.

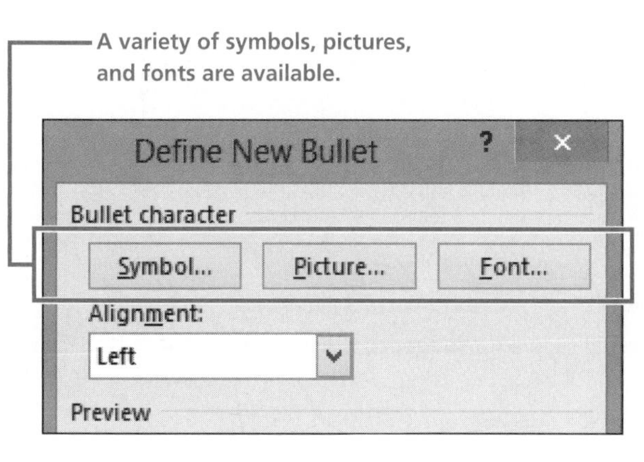

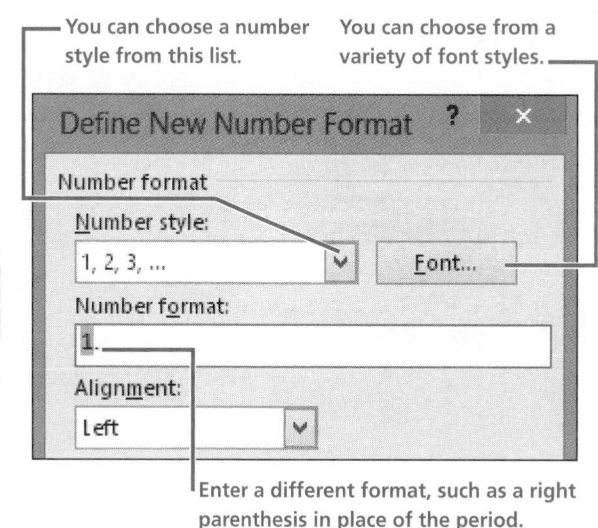

Restarting or Continuing Numbering

Many documents have more than one numbered list. You may want the numbering to continue sequentially from one list to the next. For example, if one list ends with the number 4 you may want the next list to begin with 5. If you type text after the first list, when you begin the next list, Word assumes you want to restart numbering at 1. If you want to continue numbering, Word provides an AutoCorrect smart tag where you can choose Continue Numbering.

DEVELOP YOUR SKILLS WD04-D11

Experiment with Custom Bullets

In this exercise, you will use the Define New Bullet dialog box to create a custom bullet. You will use a symbol as the new bullet style.

1. Save your file as **WD04-D11-SocMediaRprt-[FirstInitialLastName]**.
2. Click anywhere in a **first-level bulleted line** (such as *Search for classes online*).
3. Choose **Home→Paragraph→Bullets menu button ▾** and choose **Define New Bullet**.
4. Follow these steps to define a symbol as a new bullet:

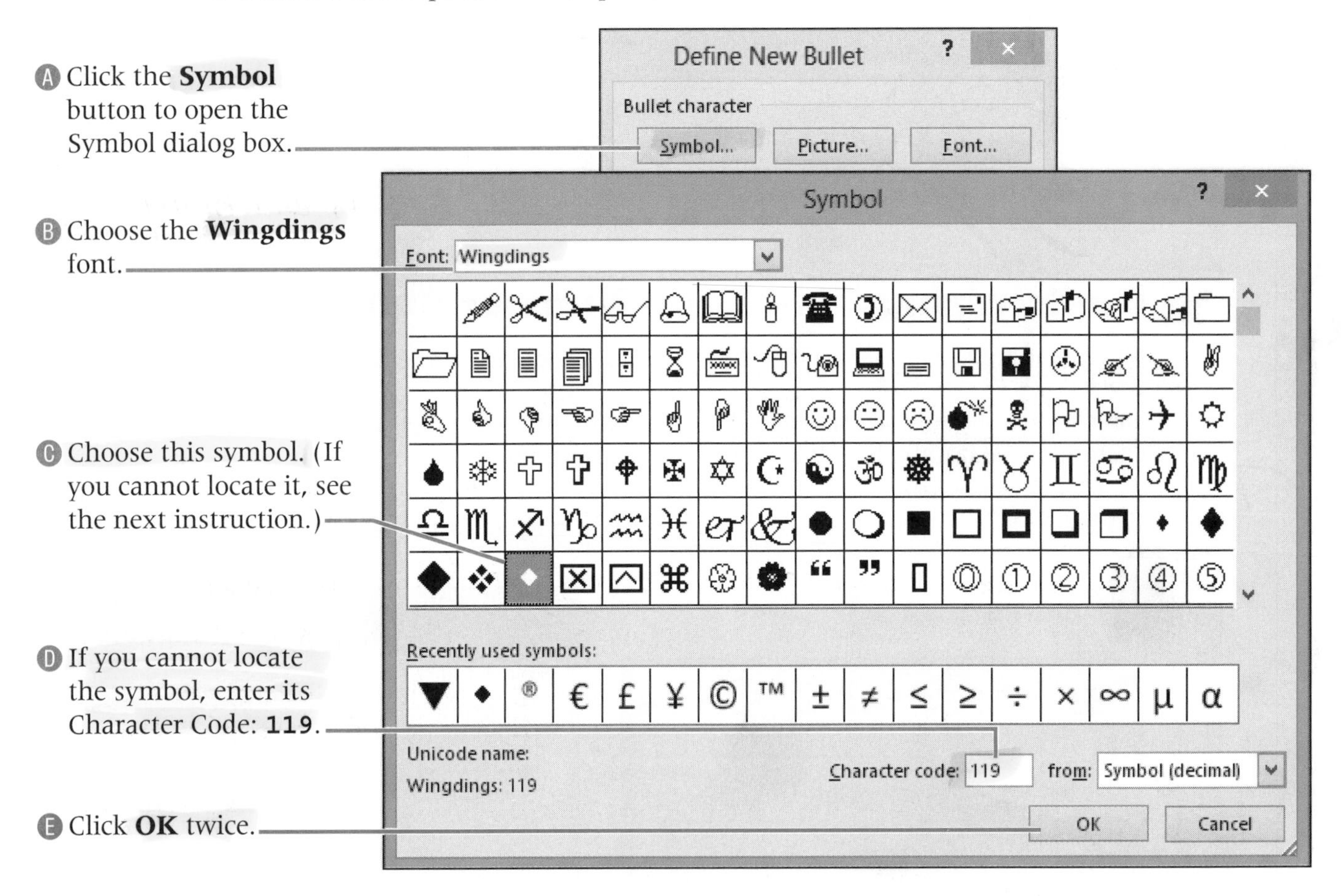

Notice that all the first-level bullets have changed to the custom bullet.

* Also show this, insert a picture "bullet". (Search online blue triangle)

5. Choose **Home→Paragraph→Bullets** ☰ **menu button ▾** to display the Bullet Library.

   The new bullet was added to the library. Now you'll remove the bullet so the next student who uses your computer will have the same experience.

6. Right-click the new bullet in the Bullet Library area, and choose **Remove**.
7. Display the **Bullet Library** again and notice that the new bullet was removed; close the menu.
8. Save the report.

Setting Line Breaks

Video Library http://labyrinthelab.com/videos Video Number: WD13-V0412

FROM THE KEYBOARD

[Shift]+[Enter] to create a line break

When working with bullets and numbering, tapping [Enter] generates a new bullet or number. What if you want to type something relative to a bulleted or numbered item on the next line(s) without generating a new bullet or number? A manual line break starts a new line (without inserting a paragraph mark) and continues the text on the new line. Line breaks are inserted with the [Shift]+[Enter] keystroke combination.

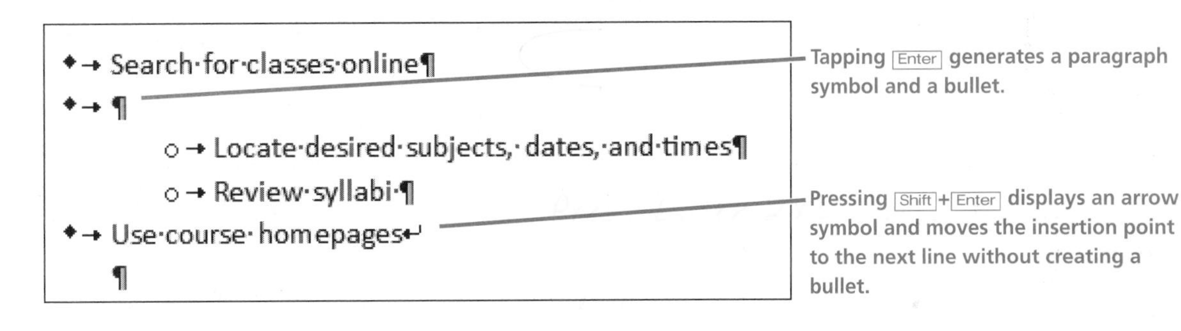

DEVELOP YOUR SKILLS WD04-D12

Insert Line Breaks in a List

In this exercise, you will use line breaks to add descriptive information about Facebook and Twitter. The line breaks will allow you to type additional information without generating a new number.

1. Save your file as `WD04-D12-SocMediaRprt-[FirstInitialLastName]`.
2. If necessary, choose **Home→Paragraph→Show/Hide** ¶ to display formatting marks.

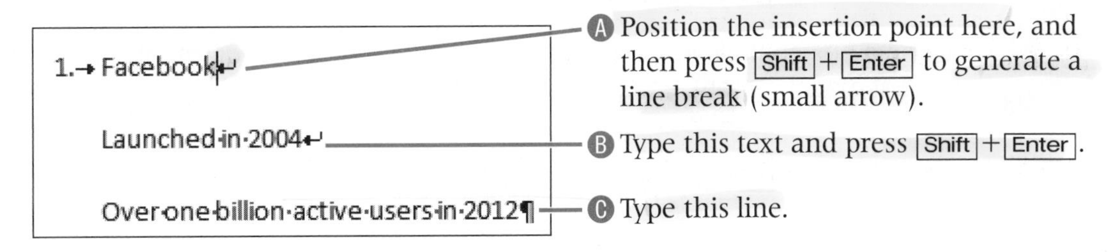

3. Position the insertion point to the right of *Twitter* in your numbered list.

4. Press Shift+Enter to generate a line break.
5. Type **Launched in 2006** and press Shift+Enter.
6. Type the following: **Over 500 million active users in 2012.**
7. Save the report.

Using Paragraph Space Settings

Video Library http://labyrinthelab.com/videos Video Number: WD13-V0413

The default spacing in Word 2013 is 1.08 rather than the traditional single spacing (1.0). Word adds 8 points (a little less than an eighth of an inch) of after-paragraph spacing when you use the Blank Document template. You can modify the amount of space that comes before or after a paragraph.

FROM THE RIBBON

Page Layout→Paragraph→Before

Page Layout→Paragraph→After

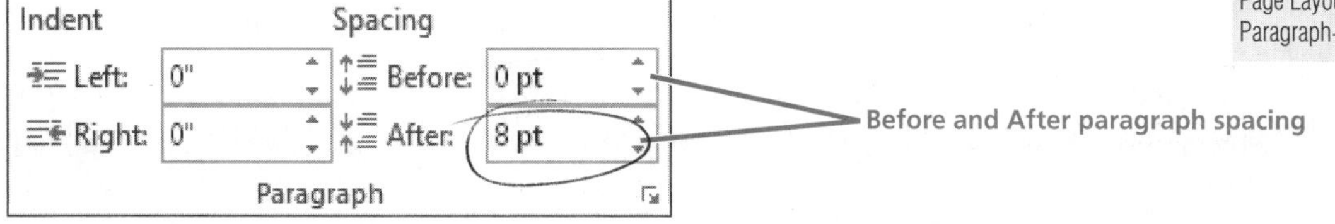

72 points = 1 inch

DEVELOP YOUR SKILLS WD04-D13

Set Paragraph Spacing

In this exercise, you will change the paragraph spacing between the headings and their following paragraphs.

1. Save your file as **WD04-D13-SocMediaRprt-[FirstInitialLastName]**.
2. Click in the heading *The Net Generation* on page 1.
3. Choose **Page Layout→Paragraph**, click the **After** box, type **2**, and tap Enter.
   Notice there is a little less space following the heading.

The spin box controls in the Spacing section use 6-point increments. If you want to use a different measurement, you must enter it manually.

4. Repeat the process for the remaining three headings.
5. Save the report.

Formatting with Borders and Shading

Video Library http://labyrinthelab.com/videos Video Number: WD13-V0414

You can apply borders and shading to selected text, paragraphs, and objects, such as tables. Page borders are also available to outline an entire page. In this lesson, you will apply borders to paragraphs. You can choose the style, color, and thickness of borders, and you can also select various shading colors and patterns.

Using Borders and Shading Buttons and the Dialog Box

FROM THE RIBBON

Home→Paragraph→Borders menu button ▾

Home→Paragraph→Shading menu button ▾

The Borders and Shading buttons have memory. The button face displays the last choice you made. That way you can apply the same type of border or shading several times in a row without opening the menu.

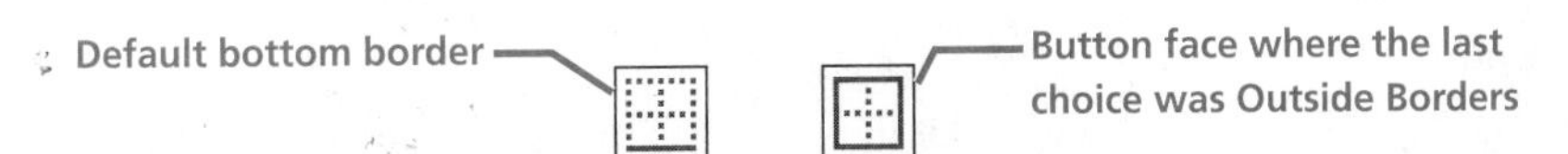

Choosing Borders and Shading from the Borders button menu displays the dialog box. The following illustrations show the features available in the Borders tab and Shading tab.

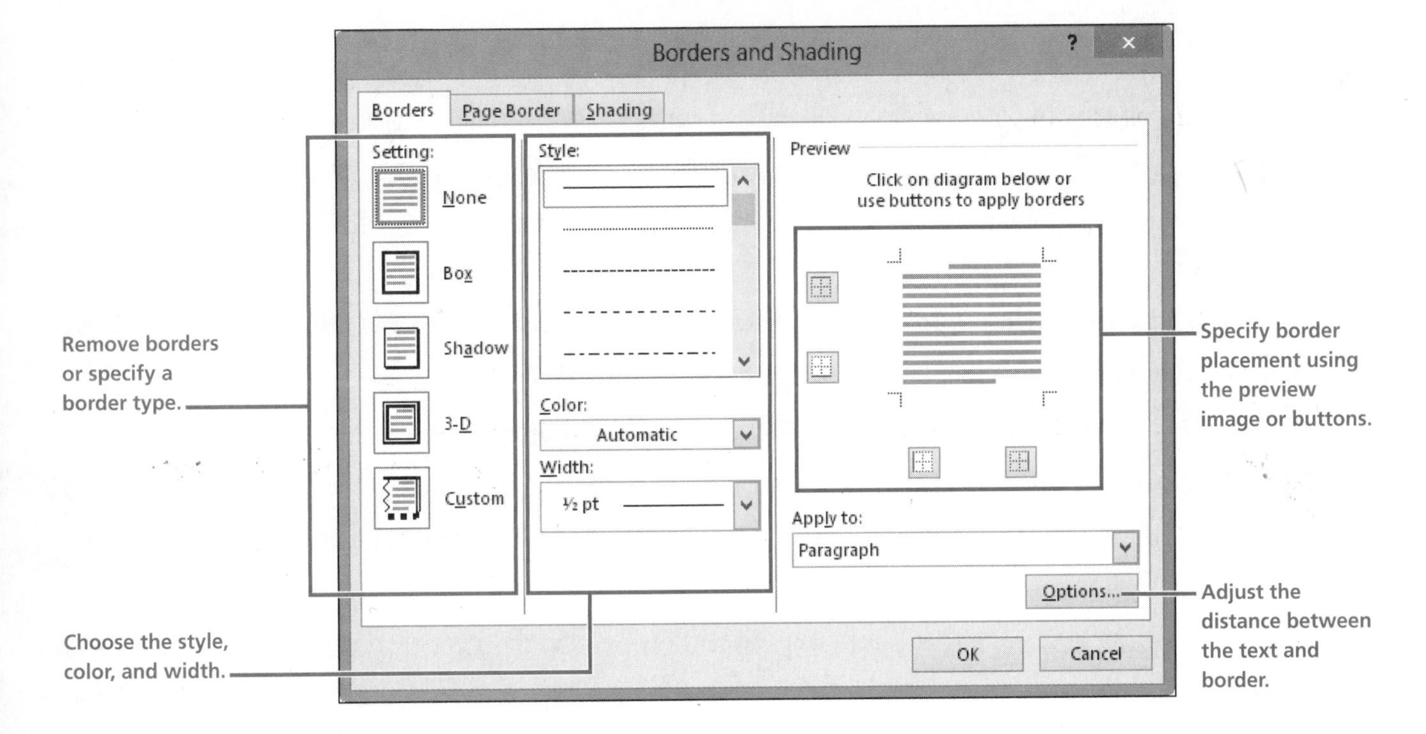

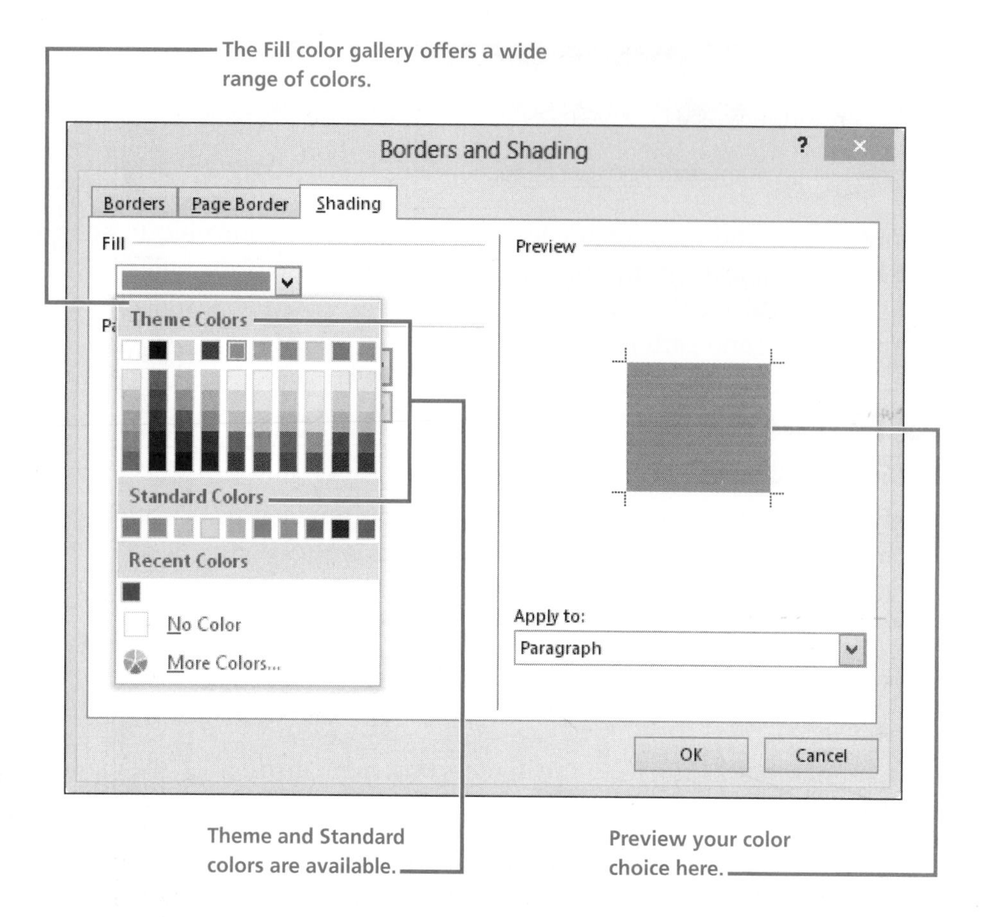

DEVELOP YOUR SKILLS WD04-D14

Apply Borders and Shading to Headings

In this exercise, you will apply borders and shading to the headings using the Borders and Shading dialog box.

1. Save your file as `WD04-D14-SocMediaRprt-[FirstInitialLastName]`.
2. Click anywhere in the heading **The Net Generation**.
3. Choose **Home→Paragraph→Borders** **menu button ▾**.
4. Choose **Borders and Shading** at the bottom of the menu to open the dialog box.
5. If necessary, click the Borders tab to bring it to the front of the dialog box.

6. Follow these steps to apply a border to the heading:

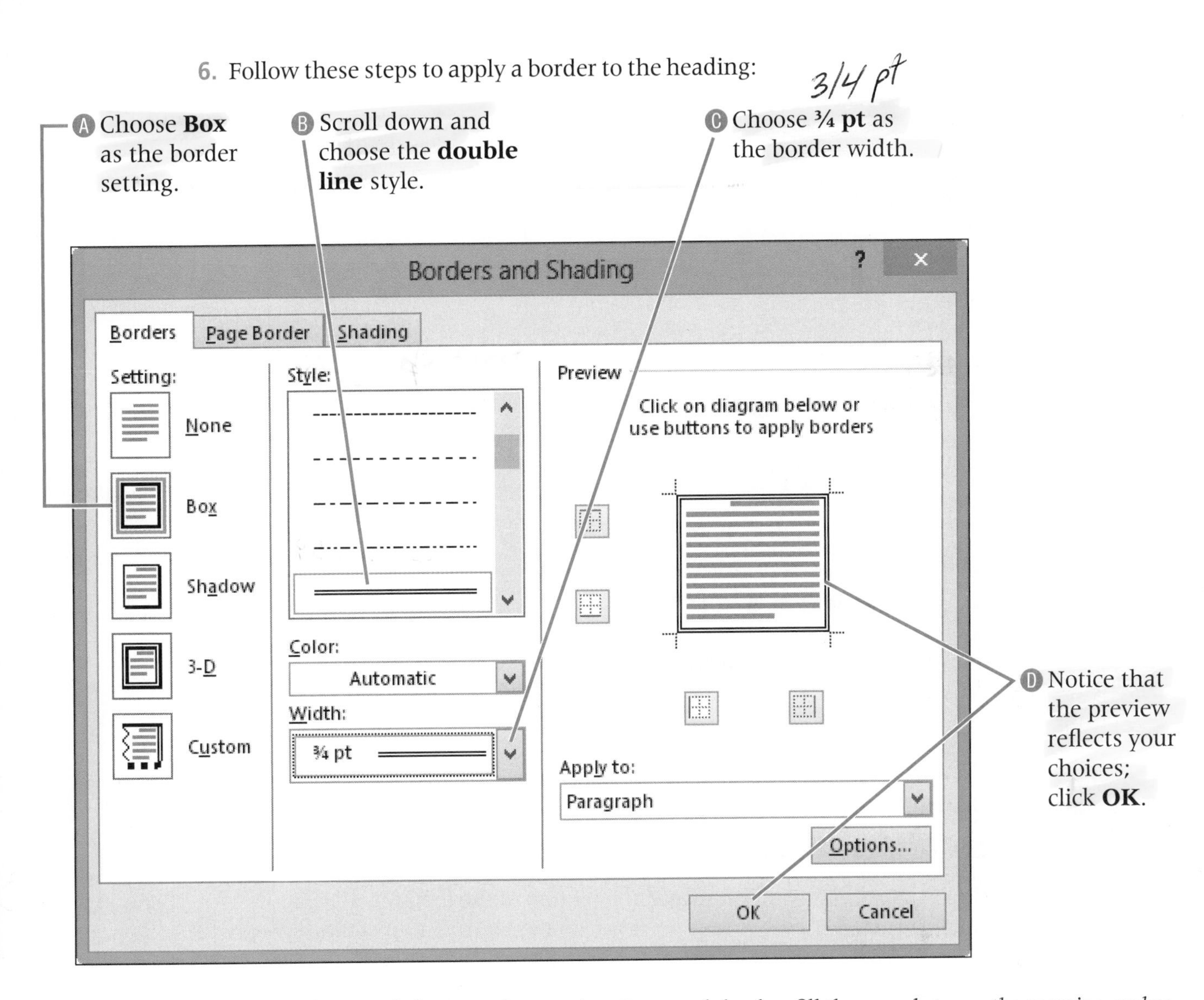

The border extends between the margins. Paragraph borders fill the space between the margins, unless the paragraph(s) is indented or a specific amount of text is selected.

7. Follow these steps to apply shading:

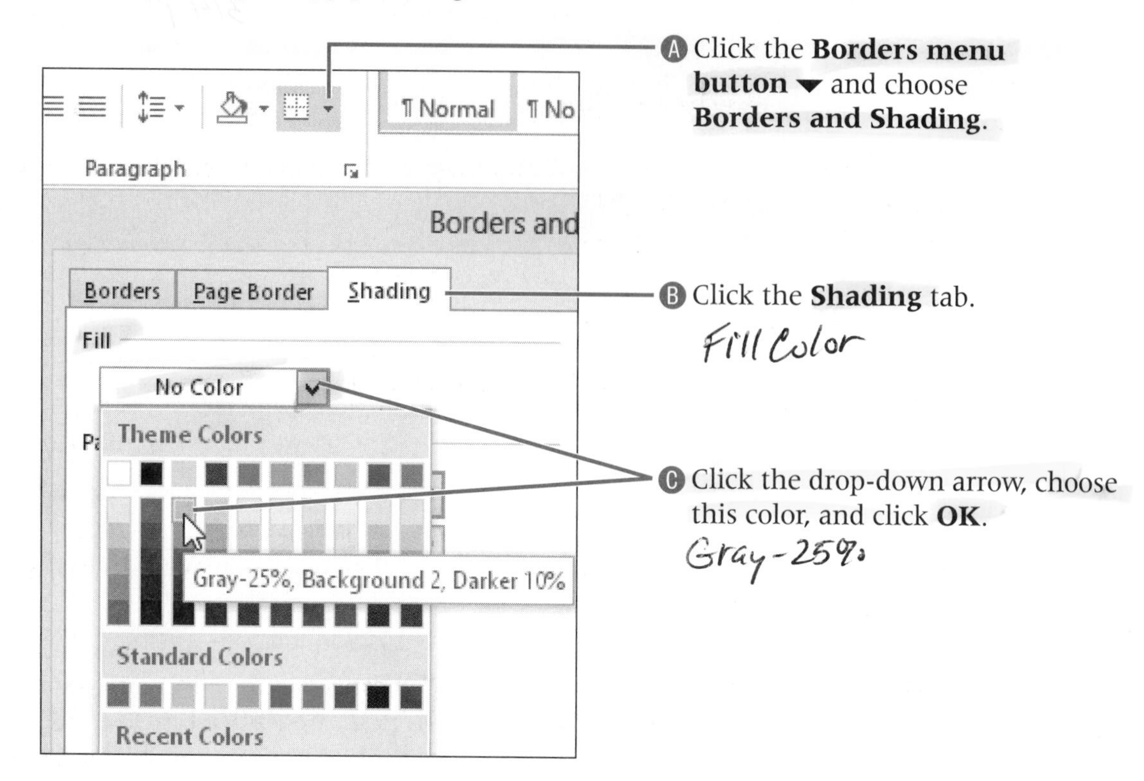

The text appears too close to the top border. Next you will adjust the spacing between the text and the top border.

8. Choose **Home→Paragraph→Borders** **menu button** ▾.
9. Choose **Borders and Shading** at the bottom of the menu.
10. Click **Options** in the Borders tab.
11. Enter **8** in the **Top** box, and then click **OK** twice.
    Eight points of space were added between the text and the border.

Use the Format Painter to Copy the Heading Formats

12. Make sure your insertion point is still positioned in *The Net Generation* heading.
13. Double-click the **Format Painter** in the Clipboard group of the Home tab.
    Remember, double-clicking keeps the Format Painter turned on.
14. Select the following headings to format them:
    - Rapid Increase in the Use of Social Media
    - University Recruiting Through Social Networking
    - Social Media Benefits for Students
15. Click the **Format Painter** to turn it off.
16. Save the report.

Formatting Text with Styles

Video Library http://labyrinthelab.com/videos Video Number: WD13-V0415

A style is one of the most powerful formatting tools in Word. It is a *group of formats* enabling you to apply multiple formats to a block of text all at once. Styles are based on the current template's theme, which is a set of colors, fonts, and graphic effects. Word contains styles for document elements, such as headings, titles, and special character formats, providing consistent formatting throughout a document.

Understanding Types of Styles

Word has many built-in styles, and you are always working within a style in Word. There are two basic types of styles: character and paragraph.

- Character styles: Character styles are applied to the word the insertion point is in or a selected group of words. Character styles only contain character formats, not paragraph formats. You can apply character styles to text *within* a paragraph that is formatted with a paragraph style.
- Paragraph styles: Paragraph styles are applied to all text in selected paragraphs or to the paragraph containing the insertion point. You can use any character or paragraph formats in a paragraph style. For example, you may want to format a heading with a large, bold font (character formatting) and apply paragraph spacing before and after the heading (paragraph formatting).

Using the Styles Gallery and the Styles Task Pane

Styles are located in the Styles gallery on the Ribbon and in the Styles task pane. Live Preview makes it easy to test a variety of styles in the gallery, while the Styles task pane provides style descriptions in ToolTips.

The gallery is limited to frequently used styles and is always at hand on the Ribbon. The Styles task pane is where you go if you need a more in-depth approach to styles.

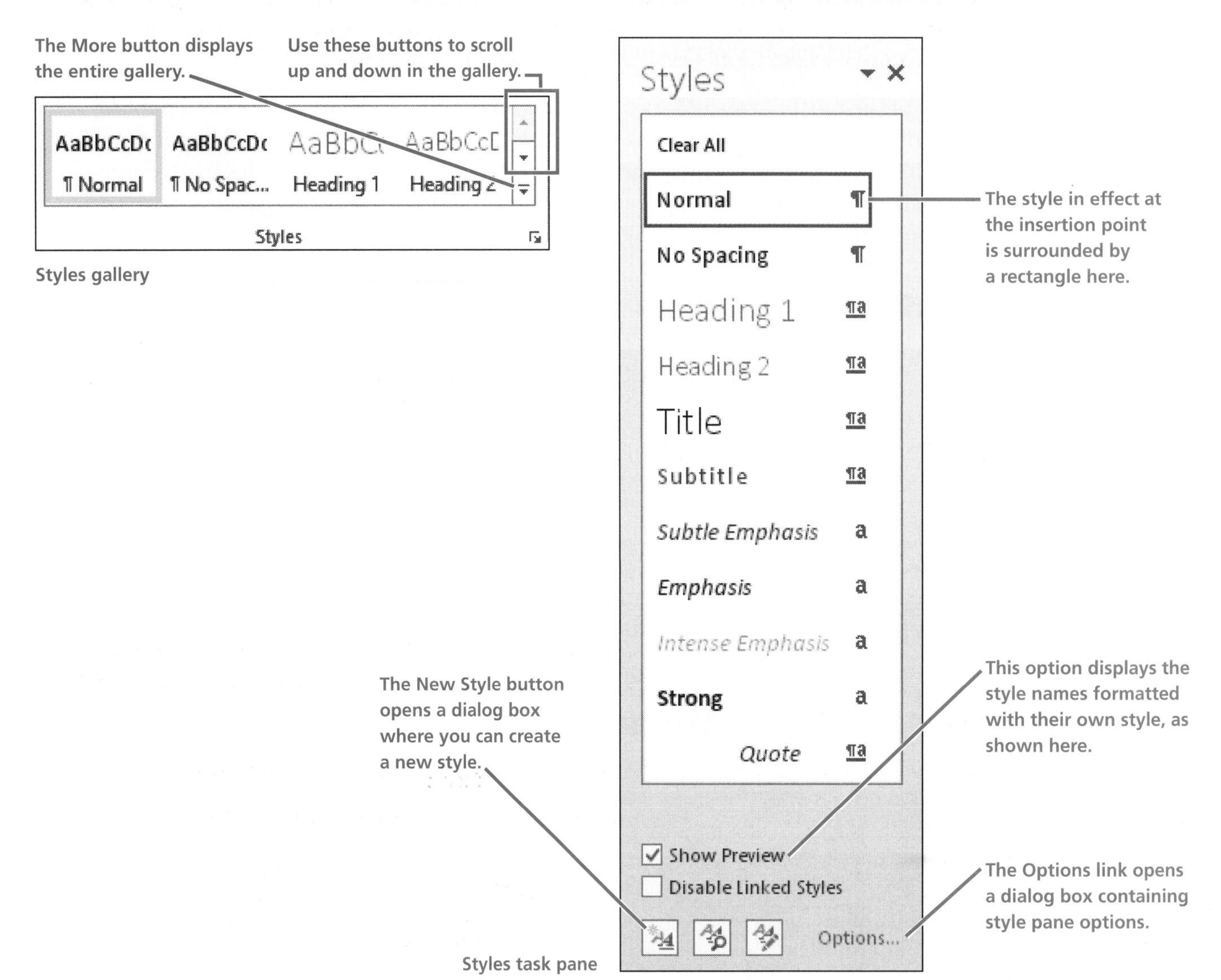

Collapsing Heading Topics

When you apply a heading style and then hover the mouse pointer over the heading, a small triangle marker appears at the left. You can click the marker to collapse and expand the text below it. This allows you to focus on certain portions of the document.

In this example, clicking the triangle marker collapsed the text below the heading.

The Net Generation

Rapid Increase in the Use of Social Media

A study at the University of Massachusetts, Dartmouth Center

that 100% of universities use social media today to communicate with

DEVELOP YOUR SKILLS WD04-D15

Apply Styles

In this exercise, you will use Live Preview in the Styles gallery to find styles that will give your report a professional, polished look. You will apply the Title style to the report's main heading and you will apply the Heading 1 style to the other headings.

1. Save your file as **WD04-D15-SocMediaRprt-[FirstInitialLastName]**.
2. Click anywhere in the report's main heading, **Social Media in Universities**.
3. Follow these steps to view and apply the Title style to the main heading.

4. Follow these steps to apply the Heading 1 style to the next heading:

Ⓐ Click to place the insertion point here.

Ⓑ Click **More** in the bottom-right corner of the Styles gallery.

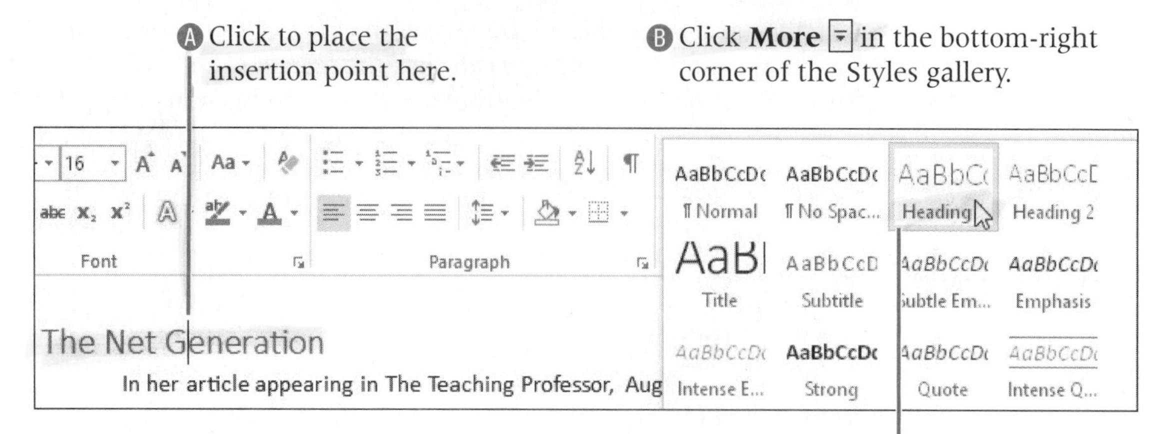

Ⓒ Click **Heading 1** to apply the style.

The Styles task pane includes all the styles that are in the Styles gallery. Now you will use the task pane to apply the Heading 1 style to the next heading.

5. Follow these steps to apply the Heading 1 style from the Styles task pane:

Ⓐ Click the Styles group **dialog box launcher**. Do this on pg 4.36

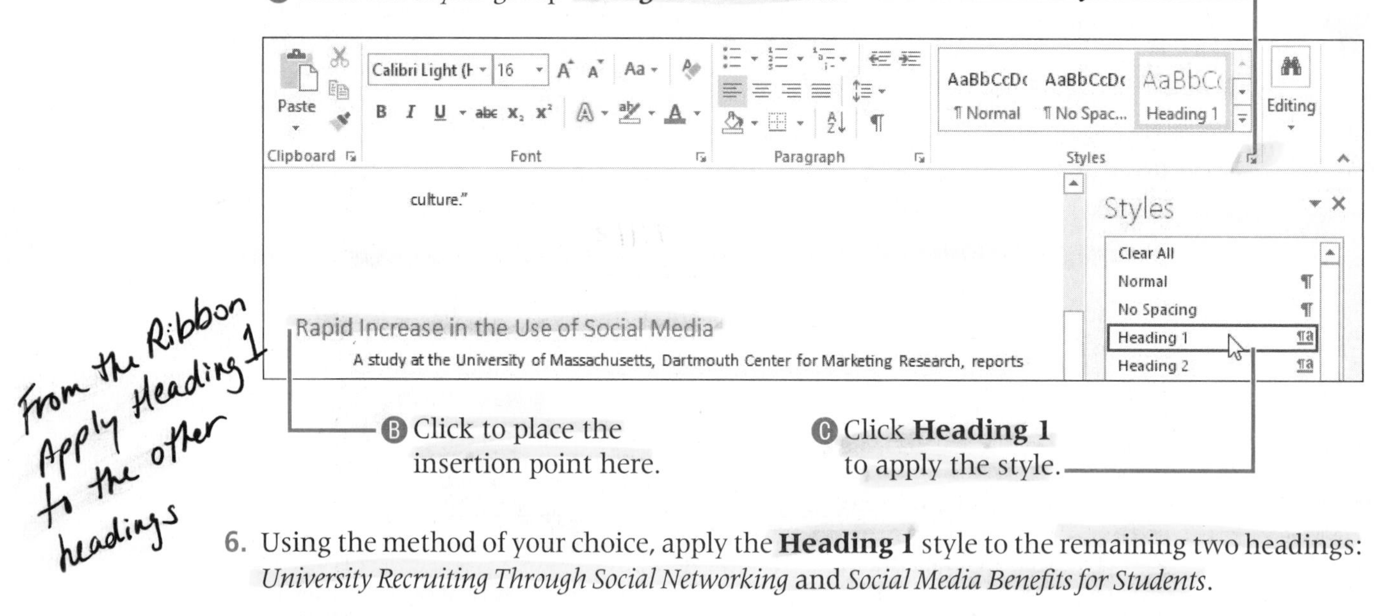

Ⓑ Click to place the insertion point here.

Ⓒ Click **Heading 1** to apply the style.

6. Using the method of your choice, apply the **Heading 1** style to the remaining two headings: *University Recruiting Through Social Networking* and *Social Media Benefits for Students*.

Collapse and Expand Text

7. Scroll up to *The Net Generation* heading.
8. Hover the mouse pointer over the heading to display the **triangle marker** to the left of the heading.
9. Click the marker to collapse the text below the heading.
10. Click the marker again to expand the text.
11. Save the report.

Creating a New Custom Style

Video Library http://labyrinthelab.com/videos Video Number: WD13-V0416

Thus far, you have applied built-in styles. However, there may be situations where the built-in styles do not meet your needs. For example, you may have corporate formatting standards set for different types of documents. You can create custom styles to meet those standards.

There are two approaches you can take to create custom styles. The method you choose is a matter of personal preference; both are equally effective.

- **Style by definition:** Choose all formats in the Create New Style from Formatting dialog box.
- **Style by example:** Format a block of text with the formats you wish to include in your style. The Create New Style from Formatting dialog box is able to copy the formats in your formatted text.

The following illustration points out the important elements in the Create New Style from Formatting dialog box.

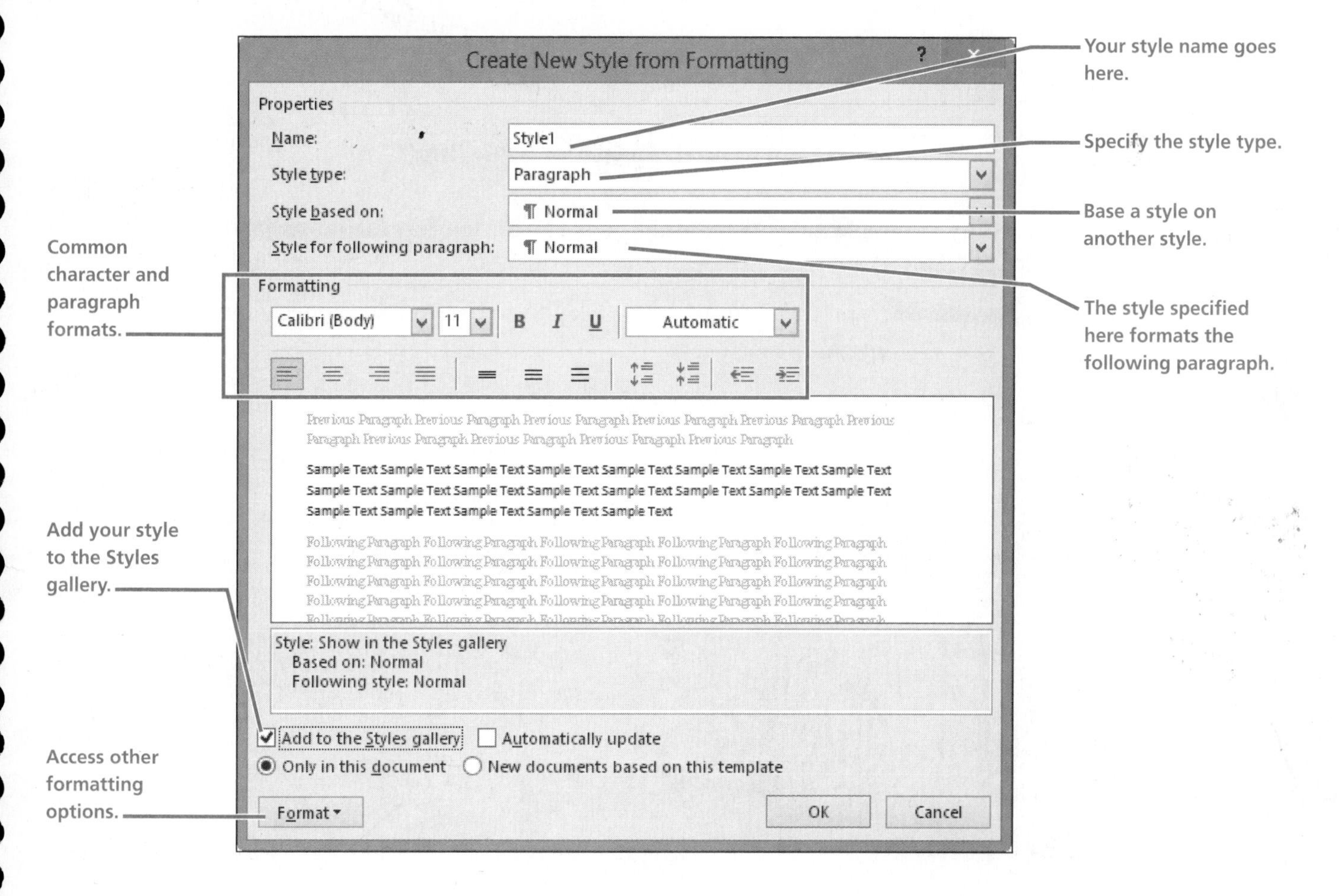

DEVELOP YOUR SKILLS WD04-D16

Create a New Style

In this exercise, you will create a new "style by example." It will be a character style, and you will apply the style to selected blocks of text.

1. Save your file as **WD04-D16-SocMediaRprt-[FirstInitialLastName]**.
2. Follow these steps to format the "style by example" text:

Ⓐ Select **Facebook** in the table and keep the mouse pointer in the selected text to display the Mini toolbar.

Calibri (Body) 11 Styles

Facebook → 87%

Ⓑ Apply **Bold** and **Underline**.

3. If necessary, choose **Home→Styles** and click the **dialog box launcher** to open the Styles task pane.
4. Click **New Style** in the bottom of the task pane. (Use ToolTips if necessary.)

5. Follow these steps to complete the new style:

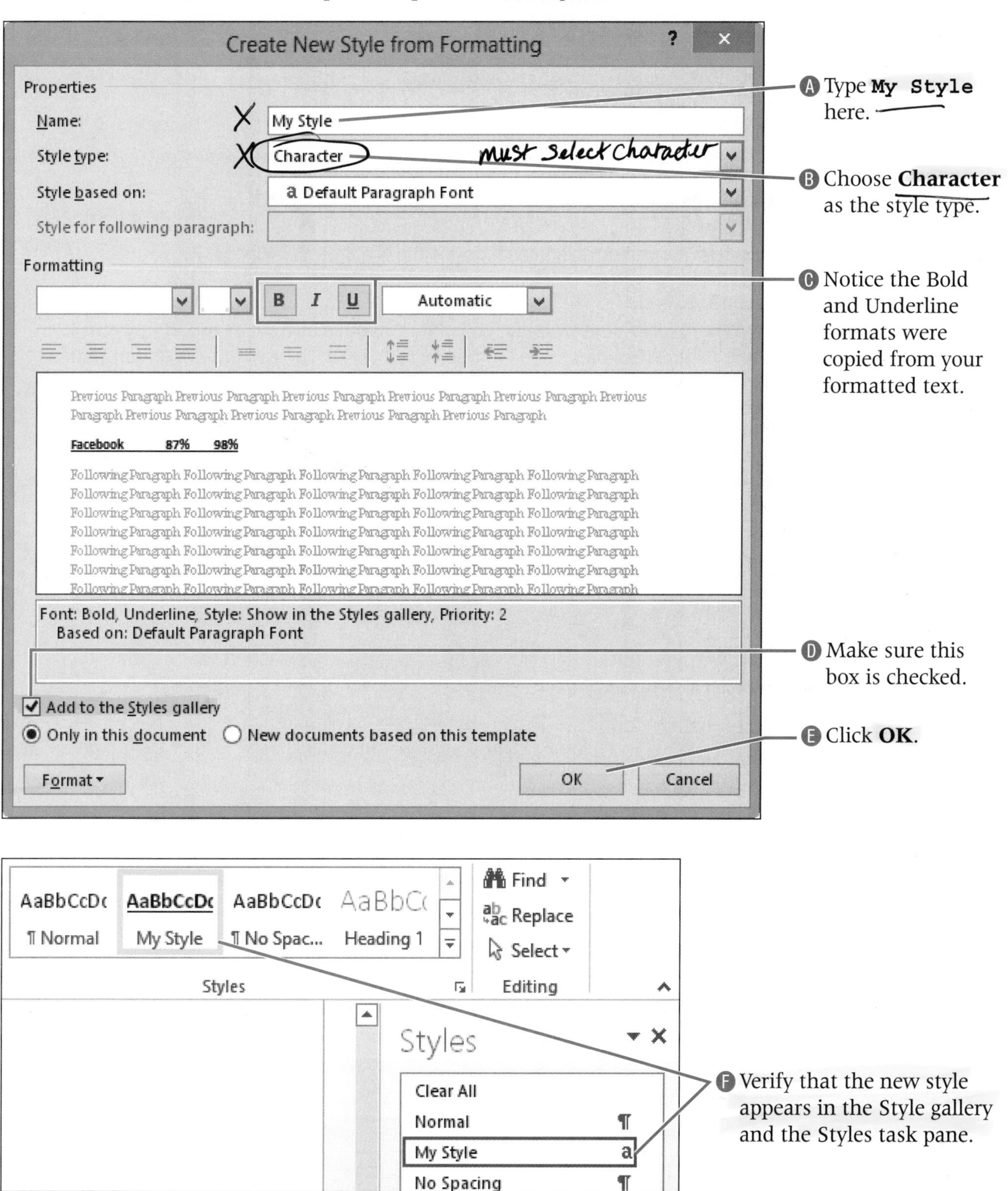

Now you will apply the style to the rest of the row headings.

6. Select **Twitter** and choose **Home→Styles→My Style**.
7. Select **Blogs** and click **My Style** in the Styles task pane.
8. Use either method to apply the style to **Podcasts**.
9. Save the report.

Modifying, Removing, and Deleting Styles

Video Library http://labyrinthelab.com/videos Video Number: WD13-V0417

You can modify built-in styles as well as styles that you create. The ability to modify styles is one of the great powers of Word. You can make global formatting changes by modifying a style. When you change a style, the changes are applied to all text in the current document that is formatted with the style.

You can remove a style from the Styles gallery without removing it from the Styles task pane. You can leave it in the task pane for future use, or if you prefer, you can delete it from the task pane. Completely deleting a style removes its formatting in the document.

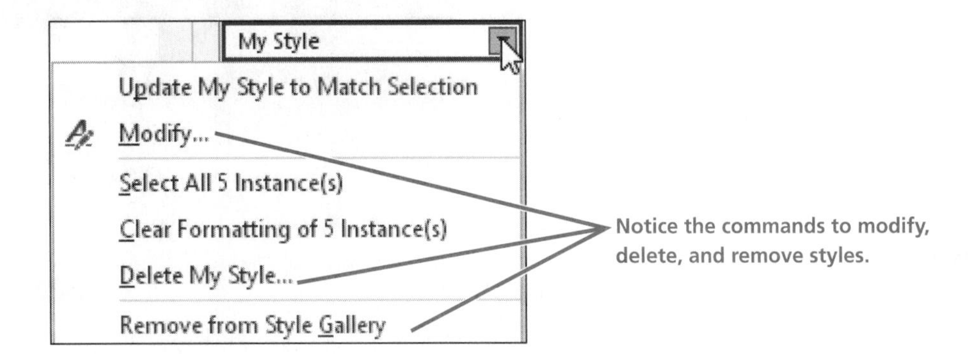

QUICK REFERENCE	USING WORD STYLES
Task	**Procedure**
Apply a style	■ **Character Style:** Select the text and choose a style from the Styles gallery or the Styles task pane. ■ **Paragraph Style:** Click in the paragraph and choose a style from the Styles gallery or the Styles task pane. To apply a style to more than one paragraph, select at least part of each paragraph.
Create a new style by definition	■ Click the New Style button, choose all desired formats from within the dialog box, and then click OK.
Create a new style by example	■ Format a block of text and click the New Styles button. ■ Name the style and click OK.
Modify a style	■ Choose Modify from the style's menu, make the desired changes, and then click OK.
Add a style to the Styles gallery	■ Choose Add to Style Gallery from the style's menu.
Remove a style from the Styles gallery	■ Choose Remove from Style Gallery from the style's menu, or right-click the style in the gallery and choose Remove from Style Gallery.
Delete a custom style	■ Choose Delete [style name] from the style's menu.

DEVELOP YOUR SKILLS WD04-D17

Modify and Remove a Style

In this exercise, you will modify a style to see how it impacts all text formatted with that style. Then you will remove the style from the Styles gallery and the Styles task pane.

1. Save your file as `WD04-D17-SocMediaRprt-[FirstInitialLastName]`.
2. Hover the mouse pointer over **My Style** in the Styles task pane and click the **menu button▼**.
3. Choose **Modify** from the menu to open the Modify Style dialog box.
   This dialog box contains the same elements as the Create New Style from Formatting dialog box.
4. Click **Italic** *I* to add that format, and click **OK**.
   The row headings are italicized. Now you will remove the style from the Styles gallery and the Styles task pane.
5. Hover the mouse pointer over **My Style** in the Styles task pane and click the **menu button ▼**.
6. Choose **Remove from Style Gallery**.
   My Style no longer appears in the gallery.
7. Open the menu for **My Style** in the task pane, and choose **Delete My Style**.

8. When the message appears verifying the deletion, click **Yes**.

   The style is removed from the task pane and the style formatting is removed from the row headings in the document.

9. **Close** [×] the Styles task pane, and save your report.

Navigating with the Navigation Pane

Video Library http://labyrinthelab.com/videos Video Number: WD13-V0418

The Navigation pane provides a great way to navigate through your document using heading styles. This gives you a bird's-eye view of your document so you can easily see the overall flow of topics.

FROM THE RIBBON
View→Show→ Navigation Pane

FROM THE KEYBOARD
[Ctrl]+[F] to open the Navigation pane

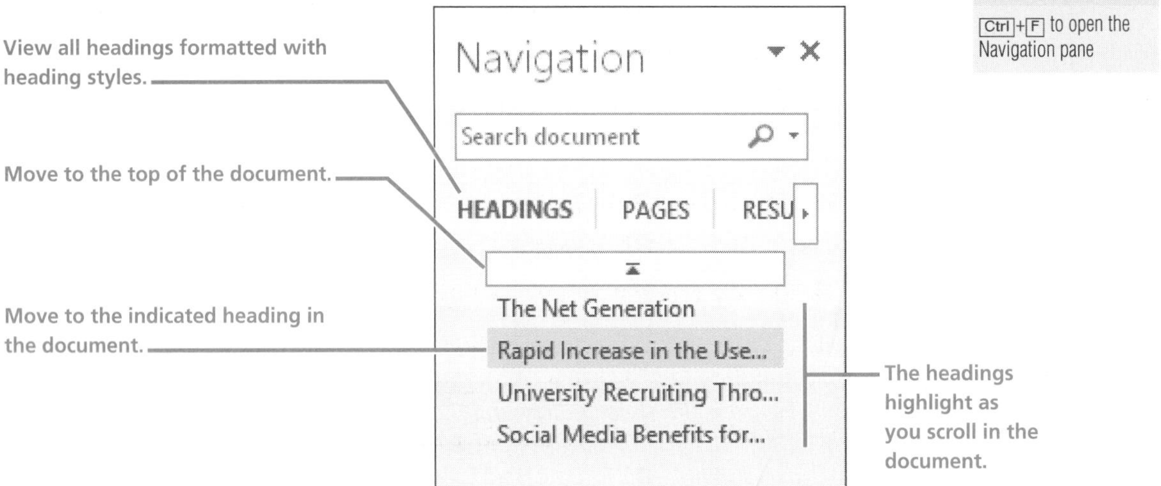

Rearranging Topics

Rearranging parts of your document is one of the most powerful uses of the Navigation pane. When you drag a heading to a new location, all of its lower-level headings and associated text move with it.

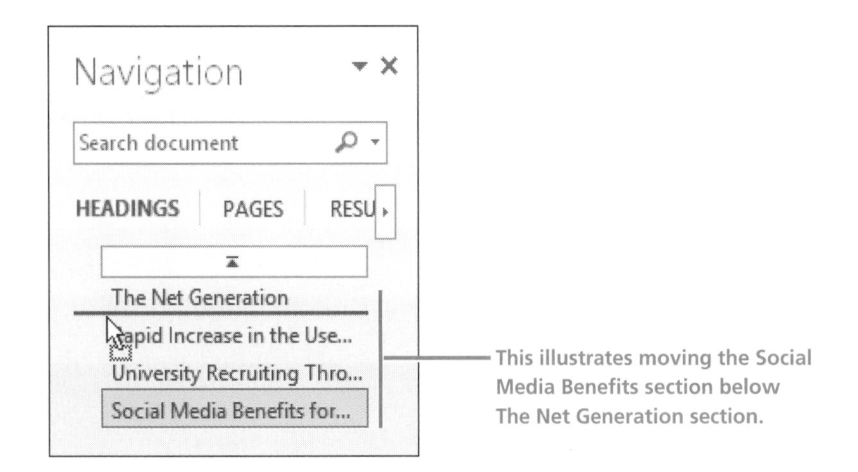

QUICK REFERENCE	REARRANGING A DOCUMENT USING THE NAVIGATION PANE
Task	**Procedure**
Display headings in the Navigation pane	■ Choose View→Show→Navigation Pane and click the Headings button at the top of the pane.
Rearrange a section	■ Click and drag a heading up or down to a new location.

DEVELOP YOUR SKILLS WD04-D18

Navigating and Rearranging Topics

In this exercise, you will use the Navigation pane to move through the report using heading styles. Then, you will use the Navigation pane to move a topic.

1. Save your file as `WD04-D18-SocMediaRprt-[FirstInitialLastName]`.
2. Choose **View→Show→Navigation Pane**, and click **Headings** at the top of the pane.
3. Click the **Social Media Benefits for Students** link in the pane to jump to that topic.
4. Scroll to the top of the report and notice that the highlighting in the pane changes as you scroll to show you where you are in the document.
5. In the Navigation pane, drag the **Social Media Benefits** topic below **The Net Generation** topic.
6. Scroll in the document to see how the topics were rearranged.
7. Delete the extra blank line below The Net Generation topic and, if necessary, below Social Media Benefits for Students topic to tighten up the text.
8. Close [×] the **Navigation pane** and save the document.

Introducing Headers and Footers

Video Library http://labyrinthelab.com/videos Video Number: WD13-V0419

Headers and footers appear at the top and bottom of every page in a document, respectively, above and below the margins. You can place text, page numbers, dates, and other items in the header and footer areas. When you enter information in these areas, it is repeated on every page of the document.

Word offers a variety of header and footer formatting styles, or you can create your own.

FROM THE RIBBON

Insert→Header & Footer→Header/Footer

Insert→Header & Footer→Page Number

Rapid Increase in the Use of Social Media

A study at the University of Massachusetts, Dartmouth Center for Marketing Research, reports that 100% of universities use social media today to communicate with students, up from 61% in the 2007–2008 academic year. Most universities have Facebook and Twitter accounts. The study reports these increases:

1

One of Word's built-in page number designs.

QUICK REFERENCE **WORKING WITH HEADERS, FOOTERS, AND PAGE NUMBERS**

Task	Procedure
Insert a built-in header/footer/page number	■ Choose Insert→Header & Footer→Header/Footer/Page Number and choose a built-in style.
Create or modify header/footer	■ Choose Insert→Header & Footer→Header/Footer and choose Edit Header/Footer.
Format page numbers	■ Choose Insert→Header & Footer→Page Number and choose Format Page Numbers.
Delete a header/footer/page number	■ Choose Insert→Header & Footer→Header/Footer/Page Number and choose Remove Header/Footer/Page Numbers.
Open/close header/footer	■ Double-click the header/footer areas to open them. ■ Double-click the main document to close the header/footer.

DEVELOP YOUR SKILLS WD04-D19

Add a Header and Page Numbers to the Report

In this exercise, you will add headers and page numbers to the report. You will use Word's built-in formats.

1. Save your file as `WD04-D19-SocMediaRprt-[FirstInitialLastName]`.
2. Choose **Insert→Header & Footer→Header** and choose the **Sideline** format from the gallery.
3. Click **Document Title** and type **`My Virtual Campus`** in its place.
4. Double-click in the document to close the header.
5. Choose **Insert→Header & Footer→Page Number** and slide the mouse pointer down the menu to **Bottom of Page**.
6. Scroll down in the gallery and choose **Large Color 3**.
7. Double-click in the document to close the page-number footer.
   You can open the header/footer area by double-clicking anywhere in the header/footer area.
8. Double-click in the footer area to open it, and then double-click in the document again to close the footer area.
9. Scroll through the report and observe the headers and page numbers.
10. Save the report.

Using the Resume Reading Bookmark

Video Library http://labyrinthelab.com/videos Video Number: WD13-V0420

When you close a document and then reopen it, Word remembers your last editing point and presents a pop-up bookmark offering to let you pick up where you left off. This Resume Reading feature provides a fast startup if you don't recall exactly where you were when you last worked in the document.

Welcome back!
Pick up where you left off:

Social Media Benefits for Students
A few seconds ago

DEVELOP YOUR SKILLS WD04-D20

Use the Resume Reading Bookmark

In this exercise, you will make an editing change to your report, and then save and close it. When you reopen the report, the Resume Reading Bookmark will let you quickly jump to where you left off.

1. Save your file as `WD04-D20-SocMediaRprt-[FirstInitialLastName]`.
2. Scroll to the **University Recruiting Through Social Networking** heading.
3. In the first line below the heading, change *top* to `the best`.
4. Save and close the report.
5. Follow these steps to display the Resume Reading Bookmark:

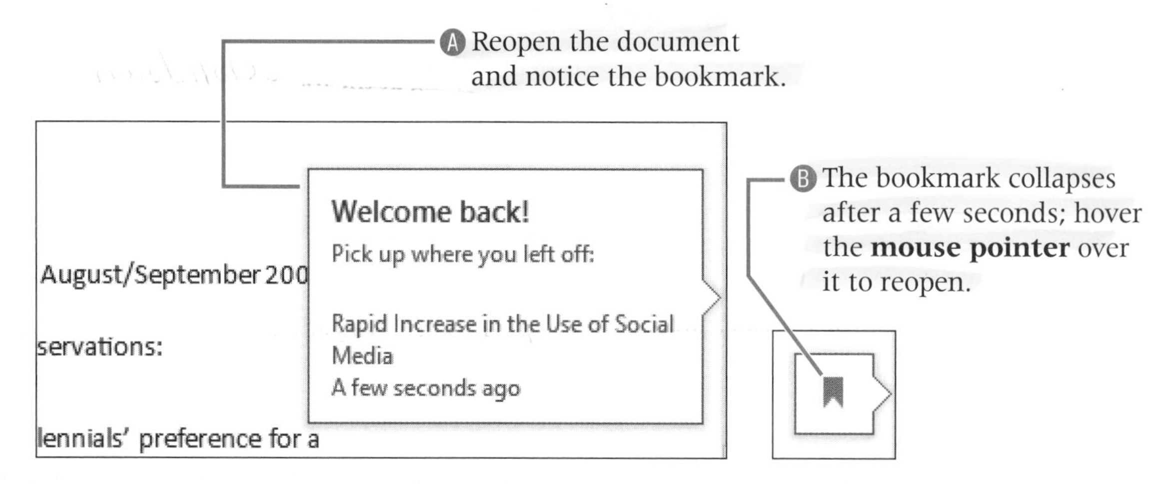

6. Click the **bookmark** to jump to your last editing location.
7. Save and close the report. Exit **Word**.

Concepts Review

To check your knowledge of the key concepts introduced in this lesson, complete the Concepts Review quiz by choosing the appropriate access option below.

If you are...	Then access the quiz by...
Using the Labyrinth Video Library	Going to http://labyrinthelab.com/videos
Using eLab	Logging in, choosing Content, and navigating to the Concepts Review quiz for this lesson
Not using the Labyrinth Video Library or eLab	Going to the student resource center for this book

Reinforce Your Skills

REINFORCE YOUR SKILLS WD04-R01

Format a Recycling Report

In this exercise, you will polish a report that Kids for Change members researched. You will use paragraph alignment, hyphenation, and indents. You will set custom tabs on the ruler to use in a tabular table, and finally, you will add after-paragraph spacing to several paragraphs.

Format Reports and Paragraphs

1. Start **Word**. Open **WD04-R01-ElecRecyc** from your **WD2013 Lesson 04** folder and save it as `WD04-R01-ElecRecyc-[FirstInitialLastName]`.
2. Position the insertion point in the heading at the top of the document.
3. Choose **Home→Paragraph→Center**.
4. Keep the insertion point at the top of the document.
5. **Choose Page Layout→Page Setup→Hyphenation**, and choose **Manual** from the menu.
6. When the message appears to hyphenate *following*, click **Yes**.
7. Click **Yes** to hyphenate *replaced*.
8. When the Hyphenation Is Complete message appears, click **OK**.

   Now you will insert a nonbreaking hyphen and nonbreaking space so terms will stay together if future editing repositions them.
9. Position the insertion point after *earth* in the first paragraph and tap Delete to remove the hyphen.

Kids for Change realize that society today is drowning in electronic de
ing reasons to recycle and guidance to help you when electronic equi
placed by newer models. Disposing of electronics in an earth-healthy

10. Choose **Insert→Symbols→Symbol** and choose **More Symbols**.
11. Click the **Special Characters** tab and choose **Nonbreaking Hyphen**.

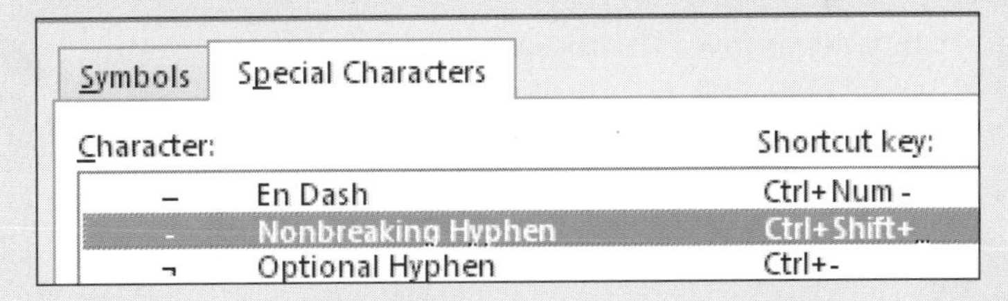

12. Click **Insert**, then **Close**.
13. Position the insertion point after *Agency* in the second paragraph and tap [Delete].

The United States Environmental Protection Agency(EPA) points out the following recycling benefits on their website:

14. Choose **Insert→Symbols→Symbol** [Ω] and choose **More Symbols**.
15. When the Symbol dialog box opens, click the **Special Characters tab** and choose **Nonbreaking Space**.
16. Click **Insert**, then **Close**.

Indent Text

17. If necessary, choose **View→Show→Ruler** to turn on the ruler.
18. Position the insertion point in the third paragraph.
19. Place the mouse pointer on the **Left Indent marker** (the rectangle) and drag it to the **half-inch mark**, and then place the mouse pointer on the **Right Indent marker** and drag it to the **6-inch mark**.

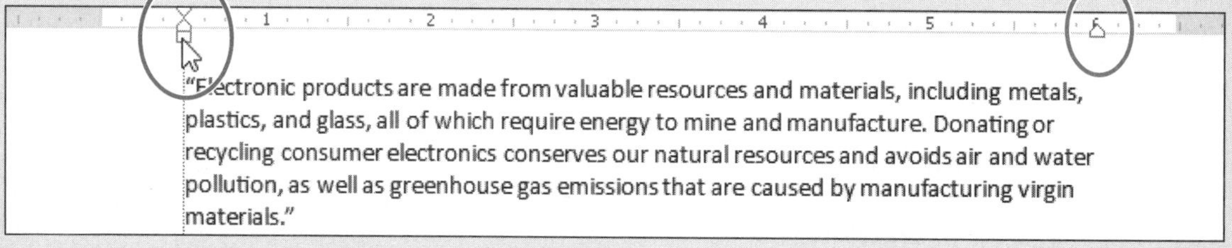

"Electronic products are made from valuable resources and materials, including metals, plastics, and glass, all of which require energy to mine and manufacture. Donating or recycling consumer electronics conserves our natural resources and avoids air and water pollution, as well as greenhouse gas emissions that are caused by manufacturing virgin materials."

Notice where the indent markers are now positioned.

Work with Tab Stops

20. Position the insertion point at the bottom of the document.
21. Type the following heading line using the default tab grid, tapping [Tab] where you see small arrows, and then tap [Enter] at the end of the line.

Ellsworth·Electronics → → → Arlington·Electronics → → → Wilson·Appliances¶
¶

22. Select the heading line and choose **Home→Font→Bold** [B].
23. Position the insertion point in the blank line below the heading line where you will set custom tabs.
24. Click the tabs box to display the **Center Tab**. (It looks like an upside down T.)

25. Perform these actions to set the following tab stops:
    - Click the ruler one tick mark to the right of a ½-inch.
    - Click one tick mark to the right of the 3-inch mark.
    - Click at the 5½-inch mark.

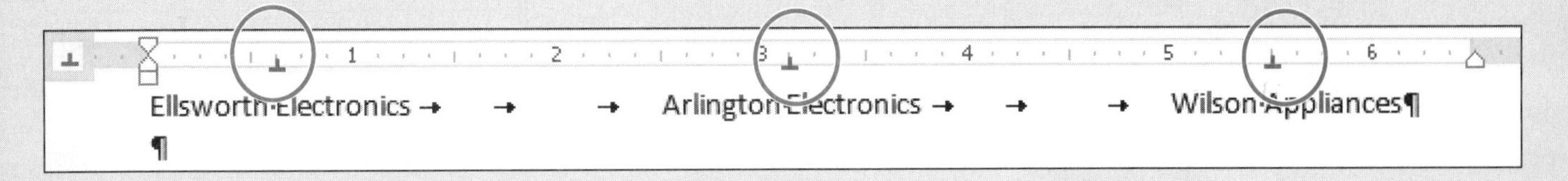

26. Type the following table, tapping Tab where you see a small arrow.

Now you will adjust the last tab stop so it is better centered.

27. Select all lines to which the tab stop applies and drag the tab one tick mark to the right of 5½ inches.

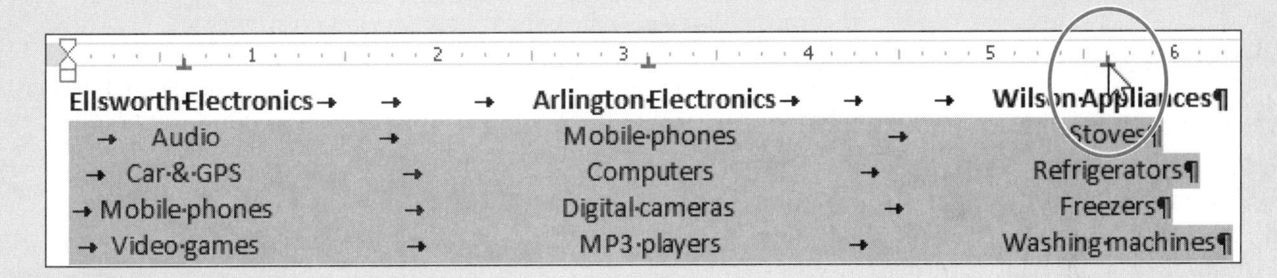

Apply Bullets and Numbers

28. Select the lines highlighted below and choose **Home→Paragraph→Bullets**.

The EPA provides the following examples of energy saved and metals retrieved:
- Recycling one million laptops saves the energy equivalent to the electricity used by more than 3,500 US homes in a year.
- For every million cell phones we recycle, 35 thousand pounds of copper, 772 pounds of silver, 75 pounds of gold, and 33 pounds of palladium can be recovered.

29. Make sure the text is still selected; choose **Home→Paragraph→Bullets menu button ▾**, then **Define New Bullet**.

30. Click **Symbol** in the Define New Bullet dialog box.

31. Choose **Webdings** in the Font list, and then choose the symbol shown here. (If you cannot locate it, type **52** in the Code field at the bottom of the dialog box.)

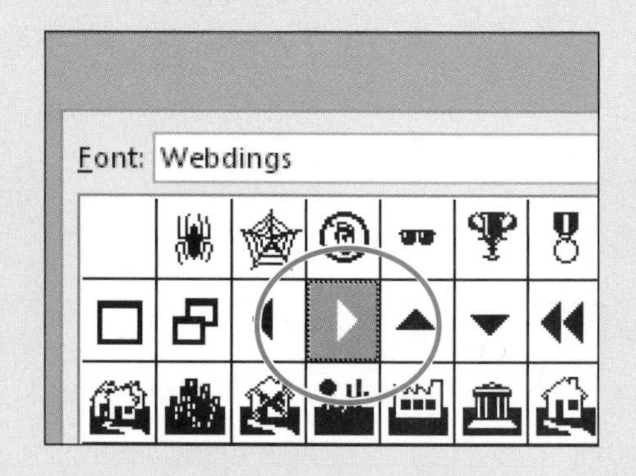

32. Click **OK** twice to set the new bullet symbol.
33. Select the lines shown below in the fifth paragraph.

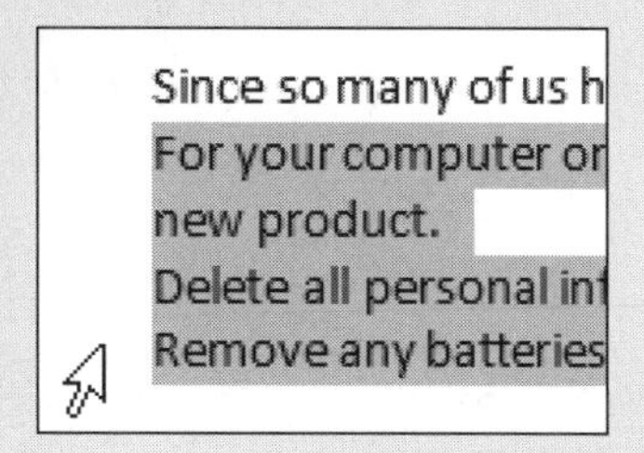

34. Choose **Home→Paragraph→Numbering**.

Apply Paragraph Space Settings

35. Position the insertion point in the second paragraph.

36. Choose **Page Layout→Paragraph**, type **2** in the Spacing After field, and tap Enter.

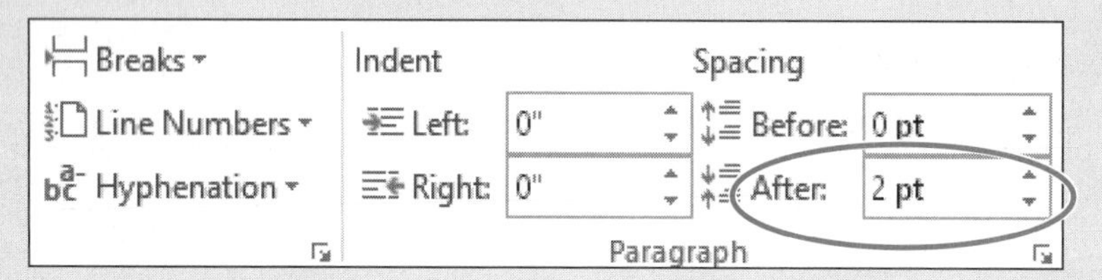

37. Use the same process to apply additional space to both the paragraph starting with *The EPA provides* and the paragraph starting with *Since so many*.
38. Save and close the file; exit from **Word**.
39. Submit your final file based on the guidelines provided by your instructor.

To view examples of how your file or files should look at the end of this exercise, go to the student resource center.

REINFORCE YOUR SKILLS WD04-R02

Format a Composting Report

In this exercise, you will format a composting research document, transforming it into a professional-looking report.

Format with Borders and Shading

1. Start **Word**. Open **WD04-R02-ActLocally** from your **WD2013 Lesson 04** folder and save it as `WD04-R02-ActLocally-[FirstInitialLastName]`.
2. Position the insertion point in the heading at the top of the document.
3. Choose **Home→Paragraph→Borders menu ▼**, and then choose **Borders and Shading**.
4. Choose **Shadow** as the border Setting, choose the sixth color in the last column (a dark green), and then set the Width to **2 ¼ pt**.

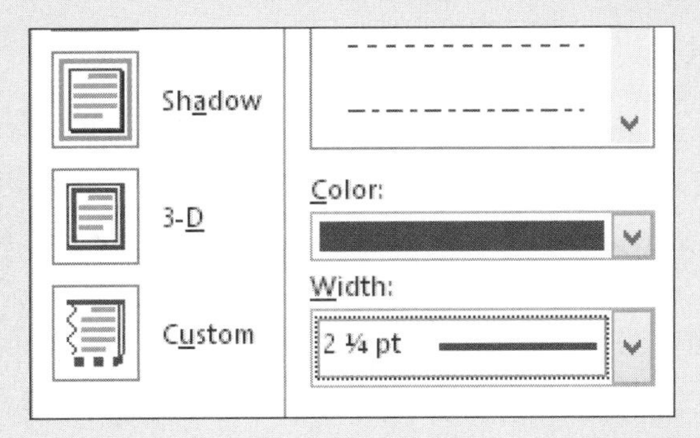

You will now apply shading to the area within the border.

5. Click the **Shading tab**.
6. Click the **Fill drop-down arrow**, choose the **second color** in the **last column**, and click **OK**.

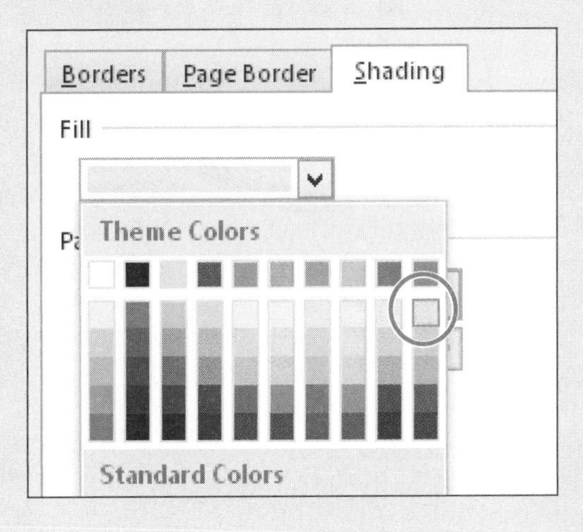

Use and Modify a Style and Collapse Headings

7. Select the *Obtain a Composting Bin* heading and choose **Home→Styles→Heading 2**.

8. Apply the **Heading 2** style to the rest of the headings in the document.
   Now you will modify the style so it will blend with the heading at the top of the document.
9. Click in one of the headings formatted with the **Heading 2** style.
10. Right-click the **Heading 2** style in the Styles group and choose **Modify** from the menu.

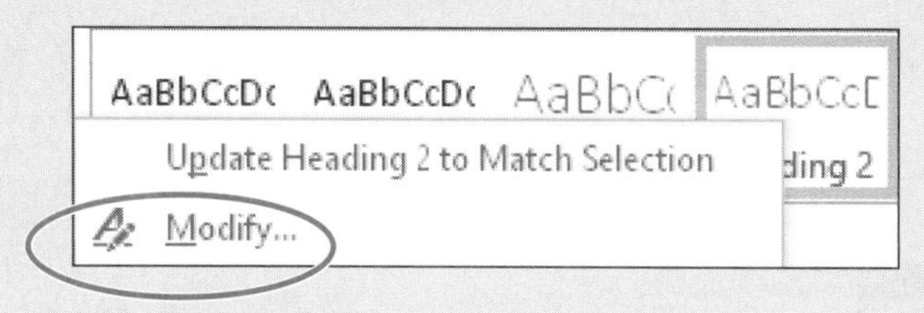

11. Click the **Bold** button, and then click the drop-down arrow and choose the darkest green theme color.

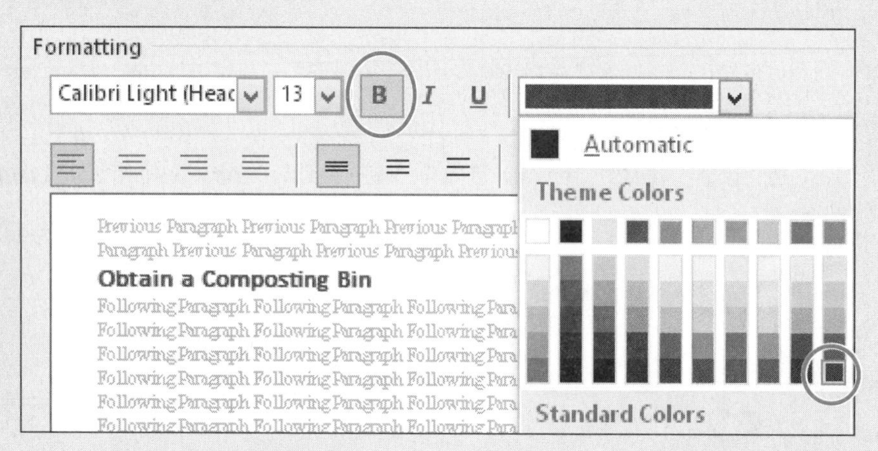

12. Click **OK** to save the changes to the heading style.
    Notice that all headings formatted with Heading 2 are now green and bold. Now you will collapse some of the headings.
13. Hover the mouse pointer over the *What Materials Can You Compost?* heading and notice the little triangle to the left of the heading.

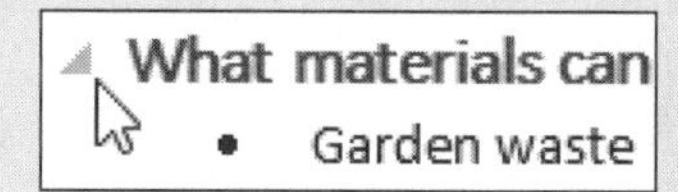

14. Click the triangle to collapse the text below the heading, and then click it again to expand the text.
15. Try expanding and collapsing some other headings, and then expand all headings.

Use the Navigation Pane to Rearrange Topics

16. Choose **View→Show→Navigation Pane**.
17. If necessary, click the **Headings tab** toward the top of the task pane.
18. Select the *Become a Composting…* topic, drag it to just above *Summary*, and drop it.
19. Close the **Navigation pane**.

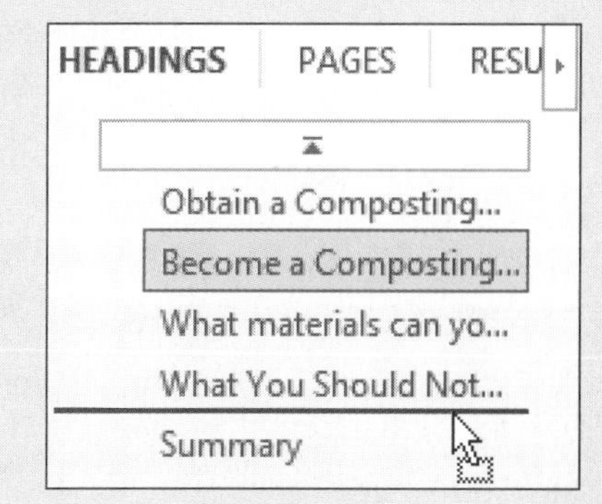

Insert a Page Number Footer

20. Choose **Insert→Header & Footer→Page Number menu ▾**.
21. Choose **Bottom of Page→Plain Number 1**.

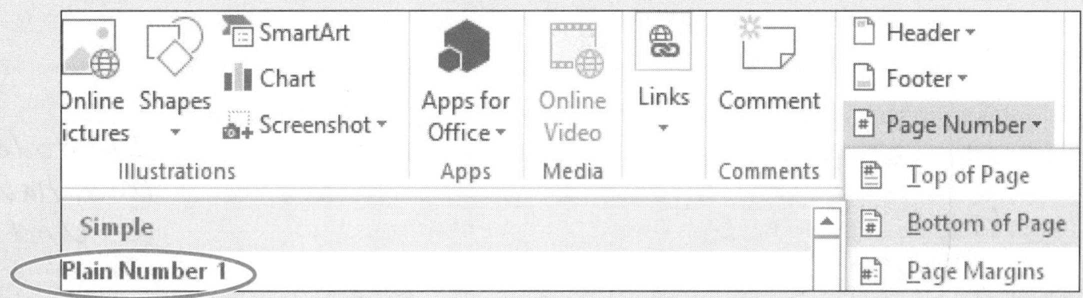

The chosen page number style appears in the footer of the document.

22. Double-click the body of the document to close the footer area.

Use the Resume Reading Bookmark

Now you'll save and close the file so when you open it again, the bookmark will appear. First, however, you will make an editing change so you can see how the bookmark guides you to your last location.

23. Go to page 2 and position the insertion point to the right of *ratio* in the *Carbon-nitrogen ratio* bullet point.
24. Tap [Enter] to generate another bullet and type `Inocula`.
25. Save and close the document; reopen it.
26. Click the **bookmark** and notice how it jumps you to the area where you were last working. (If the bookmark collapses, hover the mouse pointer over it to open it.)
27. Close the file and exit from **Word**.
28. Submit your file based on guidelines provided by your instructor.

    To view examples of how your file or files should look at the end of this exercise, go to the student resource center.

Do this if time allows

REINFORCE YOUR SKILLS WD04-R03

Format a Groundwater Report

In this exercise, you will work with paragraph formats, indents, and custom tab stops. You will create a numbered list and add after-paragraph spacing to headings. You'll work with borders and styles, and add a header, and then you'll use the Resume Reading bookmark.

Align Paragraphs and Hyphenate Text

1. Start **Word**. Open **WD04-R03-Groundwater** from your **WD2013 Lesson 04** folder and save it as `WD04-R03-Groundwater-[FirstInitialLastName]`.
2. Position the insertion point in the heading at the top of the document.
3. Choose **Home→Paragraph→Center** [icon].

   Next you will hyphenate the document.

Skip?

4. Choose **Page Layout→Page Setup→Hyphenation**, and then choose **Manual**.
5. Click **Yes** when Word prompts you to hyphenate *atmosphere*.
6. Click **Yes** to hyphenate *below*.
7. Click **No** when prompted to hyphenate *hazardous*.
8. Click **OK** when the Hyphenation Is Complete message appears.

If students do this, have them do an Undo

Indent Text

9. Select the lines at the bottom of the document starting with *Reduce Household chemical* through the last line of text.
10. Choose **Home→Paragraph→Increase Indent** [icon].

Work with Tab Stops

The kids have decided to conduct further research into groundwater contamination. You will create a table listing the kids and the topics each is assigned to.

11. If necessary, choose **Home→Paragraph→Show/Hide** [¶] to turn on formatting marks.
12. Position the insertion point on the last paragraph symbol at the bottom of the document.
13. Type the following heading line, tapping [Tab] wherever you see a small arrow, and tap [Enter] at the end of the line.

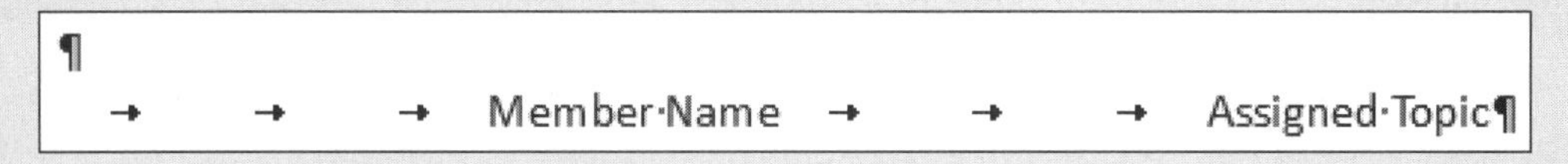

14. Select the heading line and choose **Home→Font→Bold** [B].
15. Position the insertion point on the line below the heading line.
16. Choose **Home→Paragraph→dialog box launcher** [icon].
17. Click **Tabs** in the bottom-left corner of the dialog box.

18. Type **2** in the **Tab Stop Position** box, click the **Center** option in the Alignment area, and then click **Set**.

19. Type **4.5** in the **Tab Stop Position** box, click **Set**, and then click **OK** to accept both of the new tabs.

20. If necessary, choose **View→Show→Ruler** to turn on the ruler, and then observe your custom tabs.

21. Type the following table, tapping [Tab] wherever you see a small arrow. Tap [Enter] at the end of the table.

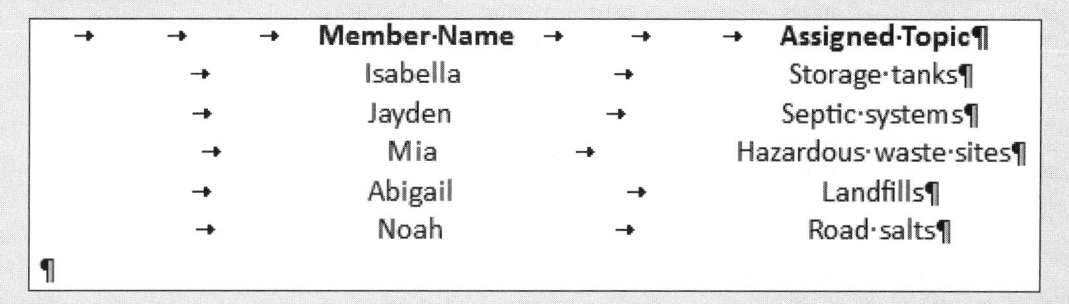

Member·Name	Assigned·Topic¶
Isabella	Storage·tanks¶
Jayden	Septic·systems¶
Mia	Hazardous·waste·sites¶
Abigail	Landfills¶
Noah	Road·salts¶

¶

Next you will remove the tabs from the ruler. It's good practice to confine custom tabs to the area where they are used.

22. Position the mouse pointer on the **tab at the 2"** mark and drag it down off the ruler.

23. Use the same process to remove the **tab at the 4.5"** mark.

Create a Numbered List

24. Select the lines that you indented earlier, starting with *Reduce household* and continuing through *water education*.

25. Choose **Home→Paragraph→Numbering**.

The first item might look better if it didn't extend so far to the right. If you use [Enter] *to shorten it, you will create a new number. So instead, you'll use a line break, which will shorten the line without generating a number.*

26. Scroll up, position the insertion point to the left of *chemicals* in item 1, and press [Shift]+[Enter].

Use Paragraph Space Settings

27. Position the insertion point in the *What is Groundwater?* heading.

28. Choose the **Page Layout** tab, type **2** in the Spacing After field, and then tap [Enter].

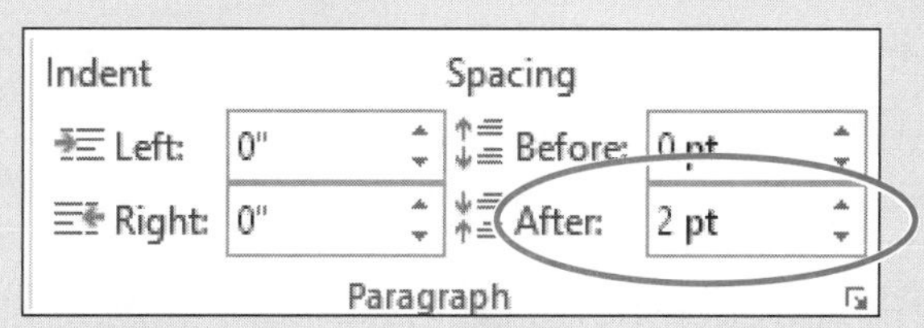

29. Repeat the process in steps 27 and 28 to add **2** points below the *How Can We Help?* heading.

Apply Borders and Styles

30. Position the insertion point in the heading at the top of the page and choose the **Home→Styles→dialog box launcher**.
31. In the Styles task pane, click the **Title** style to apply it to the heading.
32. Keep the insertion point in the heading, and choose **Home→Paragraph→Borders menu button ▾**.
33. Choose **Bottom Border**.
34. Position the insertion point in the *What is Groundwater?* heading.
35. Click **Heading 2** in the Styles task pane.
36. Choose **Page Layout→Paragraph**.
    Notice that the 2 points after-paragraph spacing is back to 0. The Heading 2 style overrode your formatting. Leave the spacing as it is.
37. Click in the *How Can We Help?* heading and apply the **Heading 2** style.
38. Keep the insertion point in the heading, hover the mouse pointer over **Heading 2** in the task pane, click the **drop-down arrow**, and choose **Modify**.
    You will now change the font color for the Heading 2 style.
39. Click the **drop-down arrow** to open the color gallery, choose the **Black, text 1** theme color, and then click **OK**.
    The color changes for both Heading 2 items.

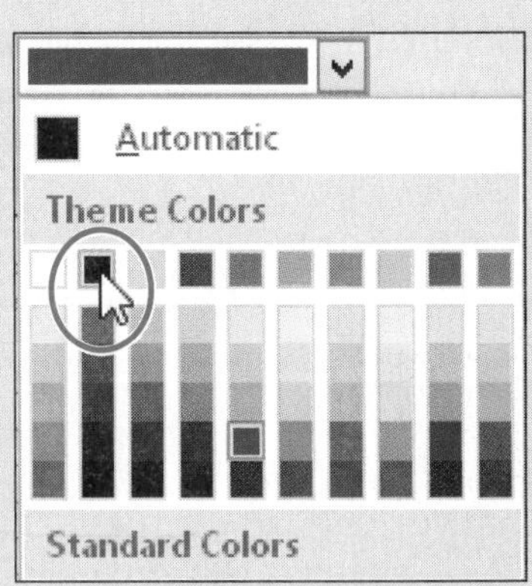

40. Close the **Styles** task pane, and choose **View→Show→Ruler** to turn off the ruler.

Use the Navigation Pane

41. Position the insertion point at the top of the document.
42. Choose **View→Show→Navigation Pane**.
43. Click **Headings** to display the document's heading list, if necessary.
44. Click *How Can We Help?* in the Headings list.
    Word jumps down to the heading selected.

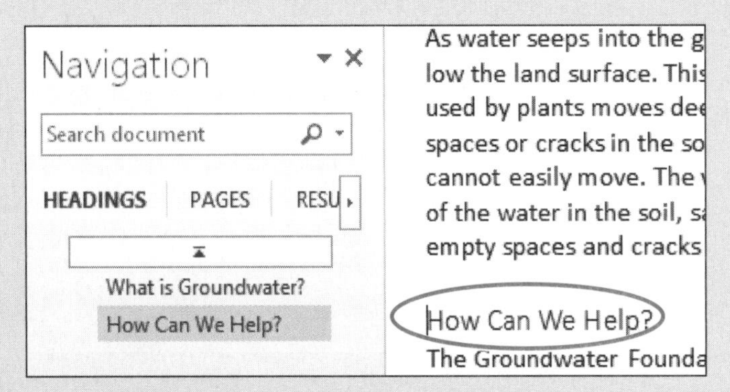

45. Close the **Navigation pane**.

Add a Header

46. Choose **Insert→Header & Footer→Header** and choose **Blank** at the top of the list.
47. Type `Groundwater` and double-click in the document to close the header area.
    Next you will make an editing change, and then close and reopen the document. Then you will use the Resume Reading bookmark to go to the last location where you were working in the document.
48. Click to the left of the left-most tab symbol in the first line of your table. Member Name
49. Press Ctrl + Enter to insert a page break and move the entire table to the next page.

Use the Resume Reading Bookmark

View Print Preview

50. Save and close the document, and then reopen it to display the Resume Reading bookmark.
51. Click the **bookmark** and Word jumps to the area where you last worked in the document.
52. Choose **Home→Paragraph→Show/Hide** ¶ to turn off formatting marks.
53. Save and close the document; exit from **Word**.
54. Submit your final file based on guidelines provided by your instructor.

Apply Your Skills

APPLY YOUR SKILLS WD04-A01

Format a Trip Report

In this exercise, you will create a report using paragraph alignment, hyphenation, and indents. You will then set custom tabs, apply bullets, and add after-paragraph spacing.

Format Paragraphs

1. Start **Word**. Open **WD04-A01-Belize** from your **WD2013 Lesson 04** folder and save it as `WD04-A01-Belize-[FirstInitialLastName]`.
2. Center-align the heading at the top of the document.
3. Choose **Page Layout→Page Setup→Hyphenation**, and then choose **Manual**.
4. When prompted to hyphenate *ambergriscaye* in the URL, click **No**.
5. Click **No** when prompted to hyphenate *Caribbean*.
6. Click **Yes** for all of the remaining hyphenation prompts.
7. Click **OK** when the Hyphenation Is Complete message appears.
8. Insert a **nonbreaking space** in all occurrences of *San Pedro*.
   Hint: There are four occurrences; you might want to use the Find feature to locate all of them.

Indent Text and Set Custom Tabs

9. Turn on the ruler, if necessary.
10. Click in the paragraph below the *Overview* heading.

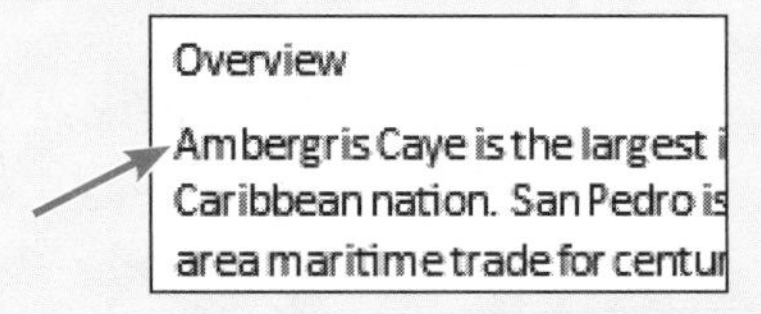

11. Use the **indent markers** on the ruler to indent the paragraph **¼ inch**.
12. Use the same process to indent the *Diving and Snorkeling* paragraph, the *Ruins* paragraphs, and the *Artists* paragraph.
13. If necessary, turn on the **Show/Hide** [¶] feature.
14. Position the insertion point at the second paragraph symbol at the end of the document.
15. Type the following heading row, using the formatting marks as a guide. Be sure to tap [Enter] at the end of the heading line.

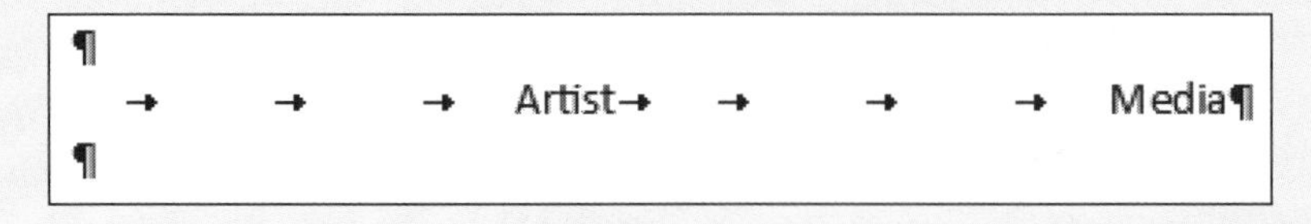

16. Apply **Bold** [B] to the heading line.

17. Position the insertion point in the line below the heading and set custom **Center tabs** at **1.75"** and **3.75"**.

18. Type the rest of the table as shown, using the formatting marks as a guide.

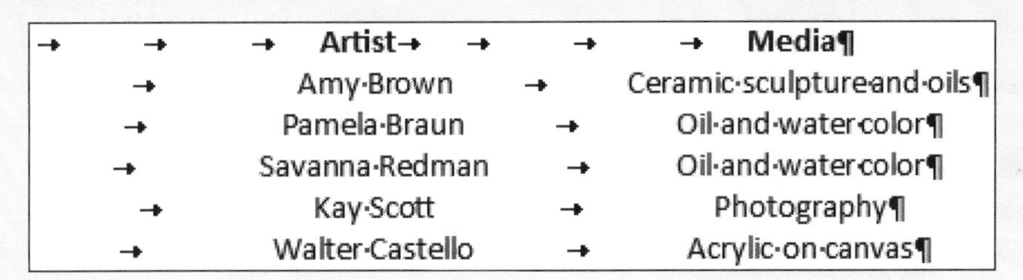

Artist	Media
Amy·Brown	Ceramic·sculpture·and·oils¶
Pamela·Braun	Oil·and·water·color¶
Savanna·Redman	Oil·and·water·color¶
Kay·Scott	Photography¶
Walter·Castello	Acrylic·on·canvas¶

Use Bullets and Paragraph Spacing

19. Scroll to the top of the document and select the four lines shown here.

¶
Overview¶
Diving·and·Snorkeling¶
Ruins¶
Artists¶
¶

20. Apply bullets to the selected lines and customize the bullets using a symbol of your choice.

21. Apply **6 points of after-paragraph** spacing to the headings *Overview, Diving and Snorkeling, Ruins,* and *Artists*.

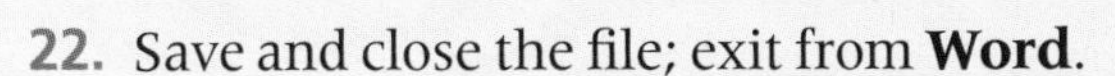

22. Save and close the file; exit from **Word**.

23. Submit your final file based on guidelines provided by your instructor.

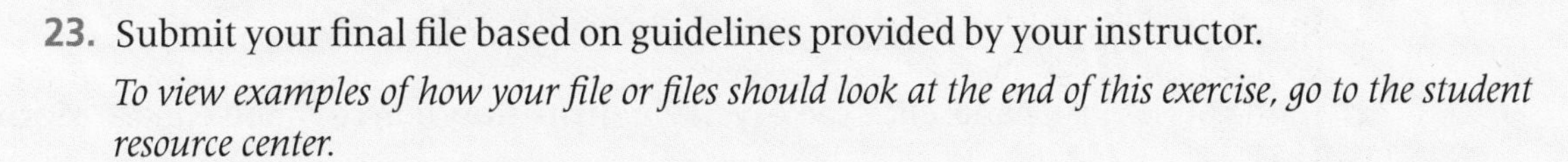

To view examples of how your file or files should look at the end of this exercise, go to the student resource center.

APPLY YOUR SKILLS WD04-A02

Format an Itinerary

In this exercise, you will create a document using borders and styles. You will use the Navigation pane to rearrange topics, and you will add headers and footers to the document. Finally, you will use the Resume Reading bookmark.

Use Borders and Styles

1. Start **Word**. Open **WD04-A02-Tahiti** from your **WD2013 Lesson 04** folder and save it as `WD04-A02-Tahiti-[FirstInitialLastName]`.

2. Open the **Styles task pane** and format the heading at the top of the document with the **Title** style.

3. Apply a **Bottom Border** from the **Borders** **menu button ▾**.

4. Format the headings for each day (Day One – Tahiti, Day Two – Tahiti, and so on) with the **Heading 2** style.

   Now you will use the small gray triangle to the left of a Heading 2 style to collapse and expand the text under it.

5. Hover the mouse pointer over the *Day One – Tahiti* heading and click the **triangle** to collapse the text below it.
6. Click the **triangle** again to expand the text.

   Now you will create a "style by example" to use on the subheadings for each day's schedule.
7. Select the subheading *Discover the Real Papeete* and format it with **10 point Verdana** font.
8. Apply the font color shown.

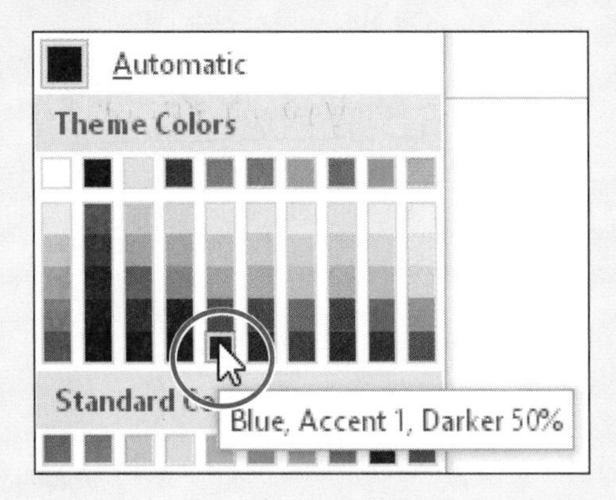

9. Click **New Style** at the bottom of the Styles task pane.
10. Name the style `My Style` and click **OK**.
11. Apply the style to all the subheadings in the itinerary.

    Next you will modify the style and all of the subheadings will automatically update.
12. In the Styles task pane, click the **My Style drop-down arrow** and choose **Modify**.
13. Click **Italic** *I* in the dialog box, and then click **OK**.

    All of the subheadings are italicized.
14. Close the **Styles task pane**.

Use the Navigation Pane and Add a Header and Footer

15. Choose **View→Show→Navigation Pane** to open it, and if necessary, click **Headings** at the top of the pane.
16. Drag and drop the **Day Two** heading above **Day One**; close the **Navigation pane**.
17. Rename the first heading `Day One - Tahiti` and rename the second heading `Day Two - Tahiti`.
18. Choose **Insert→Header & Footer→Header**, and then scroll down the gallery and choose **Sideline**.
19. Click in **Document Title**, type `Universal Corporate Events`, and close the header area.
20. Choose **Insert→Header & Footer→Footer**, scroll down the gallery, choose **Sideline**, and then close the footer area.

Use the Resume Reading Bookmark

Now you'll make an editing change so when you reopen the document, Word will provide a bookmark to return you to the area where you were last working in the document.

21. Scroll down to **Day Seven**. In the subtitle, replace *a Perfect* with **an Ideal**.
22. Save and close the document; reopen it.
23. Click the **bookmark** to jump to the location where you were last working in the document.
24. Close the file and exit **Word**.
25. Submit your final file based on guidelines provided by your instructor.

    To view examples of how your file or files should look at the end of this exercise, go to the student resource center.

APPLY YOUR SKILLS WD04-A03

Format a Sales Report

In this exercise, you will align text, use indents, and type a table using custom tab stops. You will customize bullets, insert a line break, and add after-paragraph spacing. After using the Navigation pane to reorganize text, you will add header text, and then you will use the Resume Reading bookmark.

Format Paragraphs and Indent Text

1. Start Word. Open **WD04-A03-SalesRpt** from the **WD2013 Lesson 04** folder and save it as **WD04-A03-SalesRpt-[FirstInitialLastName]**.
2. Center the *Sales Report* heading.
3. Use **Increase Indent** to indent the paragraph that begins with *The following table*.
4. Use manual hyphenation and accept any proposed hyphenations.
5. Click at the end of the paragraph you just indented and tap Enter twice.
6. Click **Decrease Indent** to position the insertion point at the left margin.

Apply Bullets and Set Custom Tab Stops

7. Type **Pending Deals** and tap Enter.

   Next you will set tabs for your Pending Deals table.

8. Use the Tabs dialog box to set **Left tabs** at **2.5"** and **4.5"**.
9. Type this table.

Pending·Deals¶

Company →	Destination →	Dates¶
Rogers·Electronics →	Hawaii →	Sept·2·through·7¶
Wilson·Construction →	Miami →	Sept·11·through·17¶
Milltown·Mortgage →	New·York·City →	October·11·through·17¶

10. **Bold** the heading row.
11. Select the entire table, and use the ruler to move the 2½" tab to **2¾"** and the 4½" tab to **4¾"**.

12. Select the six lines below *Mega Storage Devices* and apply **bullets**.
13. Add bullets to the lines below the other companies: **Springer Business College**, **Martin Medical Supplies**, and **Citizens Bank**.
14. Customize all of the bullets using a symbol of your choice. (Use the same symbol for all bullets.)
15. Click at the end of the *Accommodations* line below *Springer Business College* and insert a line break.
16. Type this text: `The owner's cousin works for a hotel chain.`
17. Select the heading line in your table and add **4 points of after-paragraph spacing**.

Apply Borders and Styles

18. Format the *Sales Report* heading with the **Heading 1** style.
19. The style overrode your centering, so center the heading again.
20. Choose **Home→Paragraph→Borders** and apply a **Bottom Border**.
21. Format the *Pending Deals* and *Bookings* headings with the **Heading 2** style.
22. Modify the **Heading 2** style by adding **Bold**.
    Notice that both headings update.
23. Format the company names (such as Mega Storage Devices) in the Bookings section with the **Heading 3** style.

Use the Navigation Pane and Insert a Header

24. Use the Navigation pane to move *Martin Medical Supplies* above *Springer Business College*.
    You may need to click the triangle to the left of Bookings to expand the text below it.
25. Insert a header using the **Blank style**, and type `Universal Corporate Events` as the header.

Make Use of the Resume Reading Bookmark

26. Position the insertion point at the end of the last bullet point below the Citizens Bank heading.
27. Tap Enter and type `Fuentes Imports` and apply the **Heading 3** style to that line.
28. Save and close the document, and then reopen it and use the **Resume Reading bookmark** to navigate to the area where you were last working in the document.
29. Close the file and exit **Word**.
30. Submit your final file based on guidelines provided by your instructor.

Extend Your Skills

In the course of working through the Extend Your Skills exercises, you will think critically as you use the skills taught in the lesson to complete the assigned projects. To evaluate your mastery and completion of the exercises, your instructor may use a rubric, with which more points are allotted according to performance characteristics. (The more you do, the more you earn!) Ask your instructor how your work will be evaluated.

WD04-E01 That's the Way I See It

As the owner of a small business in your community, you want to improve your business acumen so you can grow your business further. Therefore, you are taking night classes at your local community college. Your professor assigned the following research project.

- List three types of business reports. Format the names of the reports with a built-in heading style. Customize the style with borders and shading.
- Type a brief paragraph describing each type of report below each of the headings; use the indent feature to indent the paragraphs below the headings.
- List three elements included in each type of report, making them bulleted items. Then customize the bullets using a symbol or picture of your choice. Add after-paragraph spacing to the bulleted items.

Save your findings in a Word document named `WD04-E01-BizReports-[FirstInitialLastName]` and saved to your **WD2013 Lesson 04** folder. You will be evaluated based on the inclusion of all elements specified, your ability to follow directions, your ability to apply newly learned skills to a real-world situation, your creativity, and the relevance of your topic and/or data choice(s). Submit your final file based on the guidelines provided by your instructor.

WD04-E02 Be Your Own Boss

You belong to a small business breakfast club that meets monthly. Members support each other by sharing knowledge and experiences. Your business, Blue Jean Landscaping, has been very successful, and you've been asked to present a report detailing your success.

Provide a heading for the report and format it with a built-in heading style. Customize the heading style with formatting of your preference. Write a brief introductory paragraph, and then use the First Line Indent marker to indent the first line of the paragraph. Use a numbered list to point out the top five elements that are most responsible for your success. Add several points of after-paragraph spacing to the numbered items.

As a result of your success, you are planning to expand your business to three new locations. Create a tabular table using custom tab stops to list the names of the locations, the number of employees for each location, and the opening dates. Provide a heading above the table using a built-in heading style. Include a page-number footer for the report.

Compose a report in Word and save it as `WD04-E02-BizSuccess-[FirstInitialLastName]` in your **WD2013 Lesson 04** folder.

You will be evaluated based on the inclusion of all elements specified, your ability to follow directions, your ability to apply newly learned skills to a real-world situation, your creativity, and your demonstration of an entrepreneurial spirit. Submit your final file based on the guidelines provided by your instructor.

Transfer Your Skills

In the course of working through the Transfer Your Skills exercises, you will use critical-thinking and creativity skills to complete the assigned projects using skills taught in the lesson. To evaluate your mastery and completion of the exercises, your instructor may use a rubric, with which more points are allotted according to performance characteristics. (The more you do, the more you earn!) Ask your instructor how your work will be evaluated.

WD04-T01 Use the Web as a Learning Tool

Throughout this book, you will be provided with an opportunity to use the Internet as a learning tool by completing WebQuests. According to the original creators of WebQuests, as described on their website (WebQuest.org), a WebQuest is "an inquiry-oriented activity in which most or all of the information used by learners is drawn from the web." To complete the WebQuest projects in this book, navigate to the student resource center and choose the WebQuest for the lesson on which you are currently working. The subject of each WebQuest will be relevant to the material found in the lesson.

WebQuest Subject: Design elements of a well-formatted report.

Submit your file(s) based on the guidelines provided by your instructor.

WD04-T02 Demonstrate Proficiency

Stormy BBQ has been losing business lately. There is a new restaurant in town, and you suspect your customers are migrating to the competition. Create a report, which you will share with your employees, researching the competition.

Provide a heading for the report and format it with a border and shading. Add after-paragraph spacing to the heading.

Include three reasons you believe the competition is attracting your customers. Each of the reasons should be a heading formatted with a built-in heading style, customized with the heading formatting style of your choice. Write a short paragraph below each of the headings describing your reasons in more detail. Use the indent markers on the ruler to indent the paragraphs ¼".

Using the Numbering feature, list three steps you intend to take to win back your customers. Add your company name as a header and provide a page number in the footer area.

Save the report as `WD04-T02-Competition-[FirstInitialLastName]` in your **WD2013 Lesson 04** folder. Submit your file based on the guidelines provided by your instructor.

WORD 2013

Working with Tables

LESSON OUTLINE

LEARNING OBJECTIVES

After studying this lesson, you will be able to:

- Insert a table in a document
- Modify, sort, and format tables
- Apply built-in table styles
- Perform calculations in tables
- Insert and size columns and rows

A table is one of Word's most useful tools for organizing and formatting text and numbers. Tables are flexible and easy to use. Word provides a variety of features that let you set up, modify, and format tables. In this lesson, you will merge and split table cells, sort rows, quickly apply table styles, and perform calculations within tables.

CASE STUDY

Creating Tables for My Virtual Campus

You are an administrative assistant for the product development team at My Virtual Campus. The team is always looking for new ideas to enhance the websites. You have a few ideas of your own that may be useful for students: a list of typical expenses with totals, and a simple layout for viewing class schedules. You decide to create tables to present your ideas at the next product development meeting.

Personal Expenses	Estimate	Actual	Difference
Food	425	435	$ 10.00
Entertainment	100	150	$ 50.00
Transportation/Gas	50	55	$ 5.00
Cell Phone	75	85	$ 10.00
Totals	650	725	$ 75.00

You can insert formulas in tables.

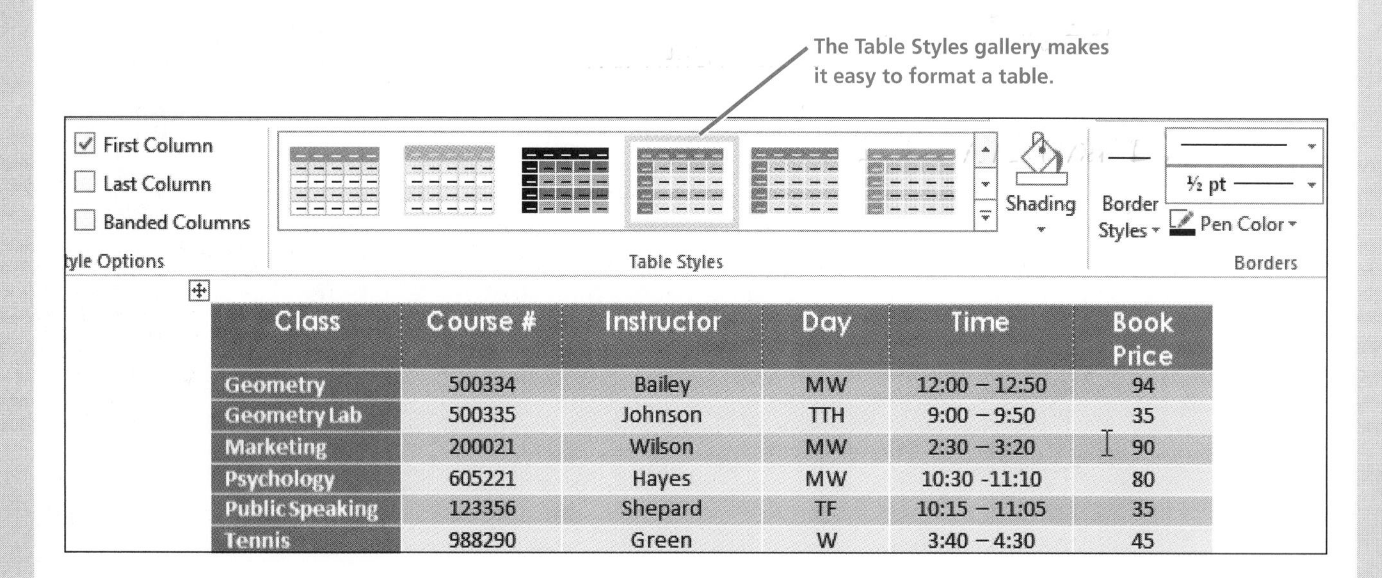

Class	Course #	Instructor	Day	Time	Book Price
Geometry	500334	Bailey	MW	12:00 – 12:50	94
Geometry Lab	500335	Johnson	TTH	9:00 – 9:50	35
Marketing	200021	Wilson	MW	2:30 – 3:20	90
Psychology	605221	Hayes	MW	10:30 -11:10	80
Public Speaking	123356	Shepard	TF	10:15 – 11:05	35
Tennis	988290	Green	W	3:40 – 4:30	45

Introducing Tables

Video Library http://labyrinthelab.com/videos Video Number: WD13-V0501

Tables provide a convenient method of organizing and aligning data in an easy-to-read format, and they are a nice way to break up a text-heavy document. Using Word's table styles adds flair to your documents, and tables draw your reader's attention to key items.

Tables are organized in columns and rows. Where columns and rows intersect, they form a rectangle known as a cell. You can type text or numbers in cells, and you can even perform simple calculations.

Column — Cell — Row

Personal Expenses	Estimate	Actual	Difference
Food	425	435	$ 10.00
Entertainment	100	150	$ 50.00
Transportation/Gas	50	55	$ 5.00
Cell Phone	75	85	$ 10.00
Totals	650	725	$ 75.00

Contextual Tabs

Contextual tabs appear in context with the task you are performing. The Tables feature, as well as other Word features, uses contextual tabs. They appear on the Ribbon when the insertion point is in a table. The following illustration shows the Table Tools' Design and Layout tabs, where you can format tables.

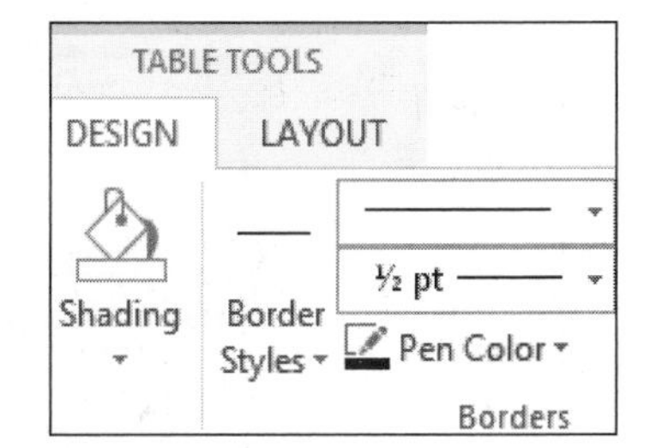

Navigating in a Table

You can move the insertion point by clicking in a cell, or you can use a variety of keystrokes for navigating.

TABLE NAVIGATION KEYSTROKES	
Move To	**Keystroke**
Next cell	Tab
Previous cell	Shift+Tab
Next row	↓
Previous row	↑
Beginning of row	Alt+Home
End of row	Alt+End
Top of column	Alt+Page Up
End of column	Alt+Page Down

DEVELOP YOUR SKILLS WD05-D01

Navigate and Enter Data

In this exercise, you will navigate in a table and enter data.

1. Open **WD05-D01-StdntTables** from your **WD2013 Lesson 05** folder and save it as `WD05-D01-StdntTables-[FirstInitialLastName]`.

   Replace the bracketed text with your first initial and last name. For example, if your name is Bethany Smith, your filename would look like this: WD05-D01-StdntTables-BSmith.

2. Position the insertion point in the first cell of the **Expense Table** on the first page.
3. Tap [Tab] twice to move to the end of the first row.
4. Tap [Tab] again to move the beginning of the second row.
5. Press [Shift]+[Tab] three times to move back one cell at a time.
6. Press [Alt]+[End] to move to the end of the row.
7. Press [Alt]+[Home] to move to the beginning of the row.
8. Test some other keystrokes.

   Refer to the preceding table as necessary for navigation keystrokes.

9. Enter the following data in your table.

Personal Expenses	Estimate	Actual
Food	425	435
Entertainment	100	150
Transportation/Gas	50	55
Cell Phone	75	85

10. Save the file and leave it open; you will modify it throughout the lesson.

Inserting Tables

Video Library http://labyrinthelab.com/videos Video Number: WD13-V0502

You can insert a table using the Table button, the Insert Table dialog box, and the Quick Tables gallery. You can even draw a table with the mouse pointer.

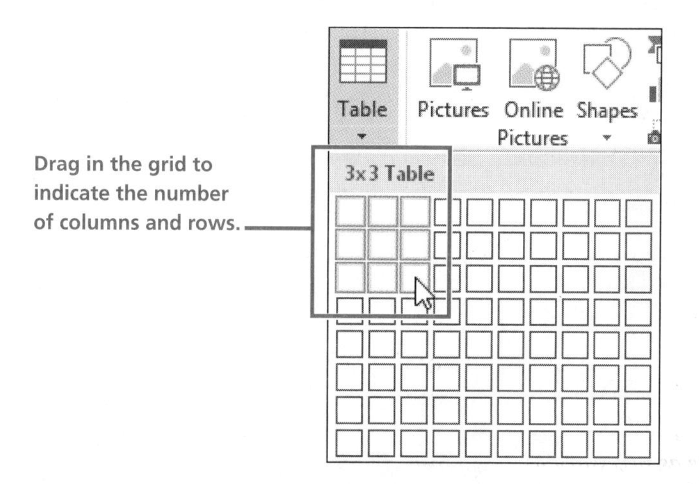

Using the Insert Table dialog box, you can choose various options for the table.

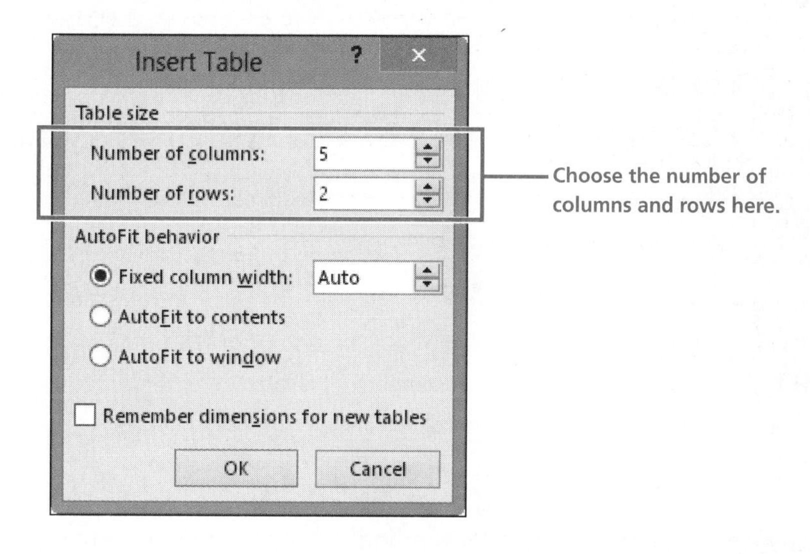

The Quick Table gallery lets you choose predesigned tables, such as calendars and various table layouts.

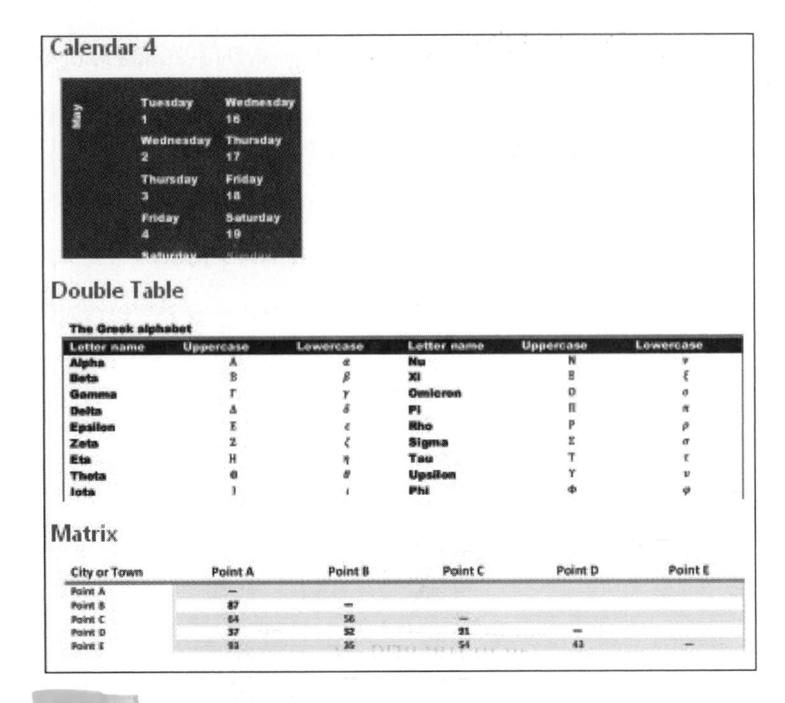

QUICK REFERENCE	INSERTING A TABLE
Task	**Procedure**
Insert a table	■ Choose Insert→Tables→Table and drag in the grid to select the number of columns and rows.
Insert a table using the Insert Table dialog box	■ Choose Insert→Tables→Table and choose Insert Table. ■ Set the number of rows and columns.
Insert a Quick Table	■ Choose Insert→Tables→Table and choose a Quick Tables style.
Draw a table	■ Choose Insert→Tables→Table and choose Draw Table. ■ Click and drag to draw a rectangle for the table. ■ Drag to draw the row and column lines inside the rectangle.

You can add a row to the bottom of a table by tapping [Tab] when the insertion point is in the last table cell.

DEVELOP YOUR SKILLS WD05-D02

Insert Tables

In this exercise, you will create a 3x3 table and enter data. You will also add rows to the bottom of the table. Then you will insert a Quick Table.

1. Save your file as `WD05-D02-StdntTables-[FirstInitialLastName]`.
2. If necessary, choose **Home→Paragraph→Show/Hide** ¶ to display formatting marks.
3. Position the insertion point on the blank row below the *Schedule Planning* heading on page 2.
4. Follow these steps to insert a table:

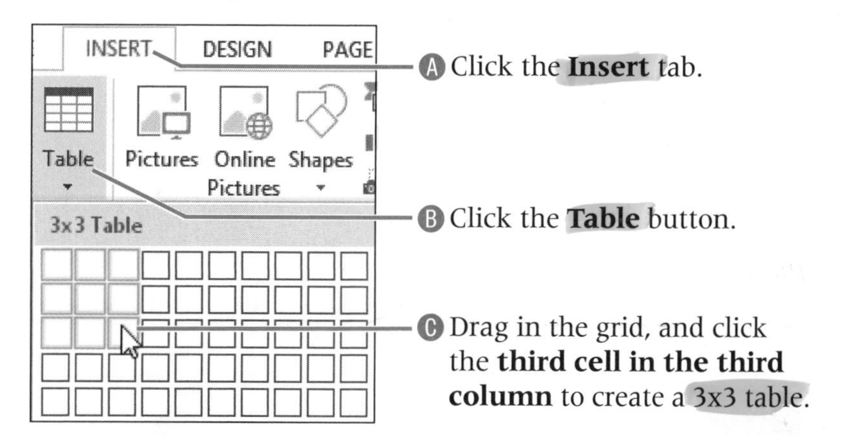

A Click the **Insert** tab.

B Click the **Table** button.

C Drag in the grid, and click the **third cell in the third column** to create a 3x3 table.

5. Enter the text shown, tapping Tab when you need to add a new row.

Course	Days	Units
Math	MWF	3
Science	MWF	3
International Tourism	TTH	2
Biology	TH	3
Biology Lab	W	1

Insert a Quick Table

Because you are hoping to join a fraternity/sorority, you will insert the Greek Alphabet table to help you learn the characters. You can use this table for any purpose by deleting the text and replacing it with your own data.

6. Navigate to the top of page 4, and choose **Insert→Tables→Table**.
7. Follow these steps to insert the table:

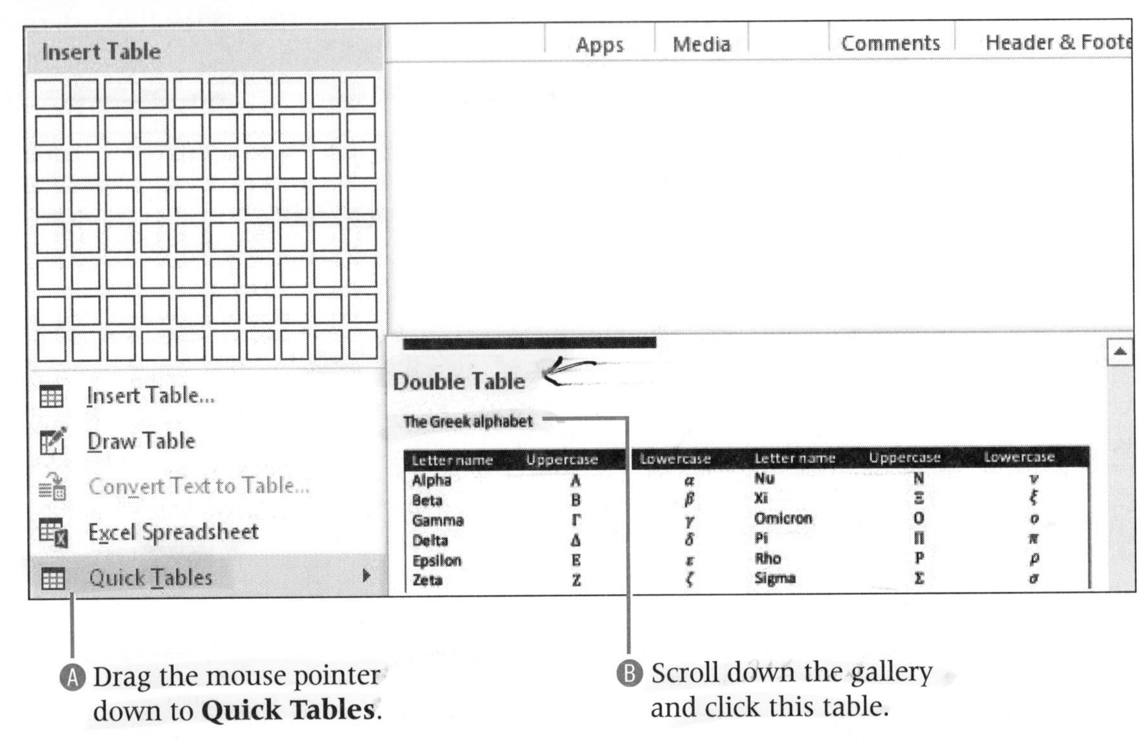

The Quick Table is added to your document.

8. Save your file.

Converting Tables

Video Library http://labyrinthelab.com/videos Video Number: WD13-V0503

Sometimes data is best set in tabular columns and sometimes it's best in a table. When you first begin laying out your data, you may not know which options to choose. Word's ability to convert from one to the other prevents you from having to start over.

Converting Text to a Table

Tabs are commonly used as separators in columnar tables. Note that there must only be one tab between columns for the conversion to work properly. When you convert, you are telling Word to replace each tab with a new table column.

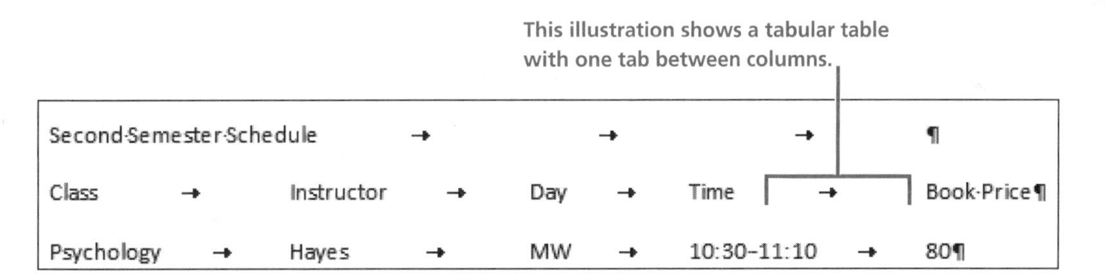

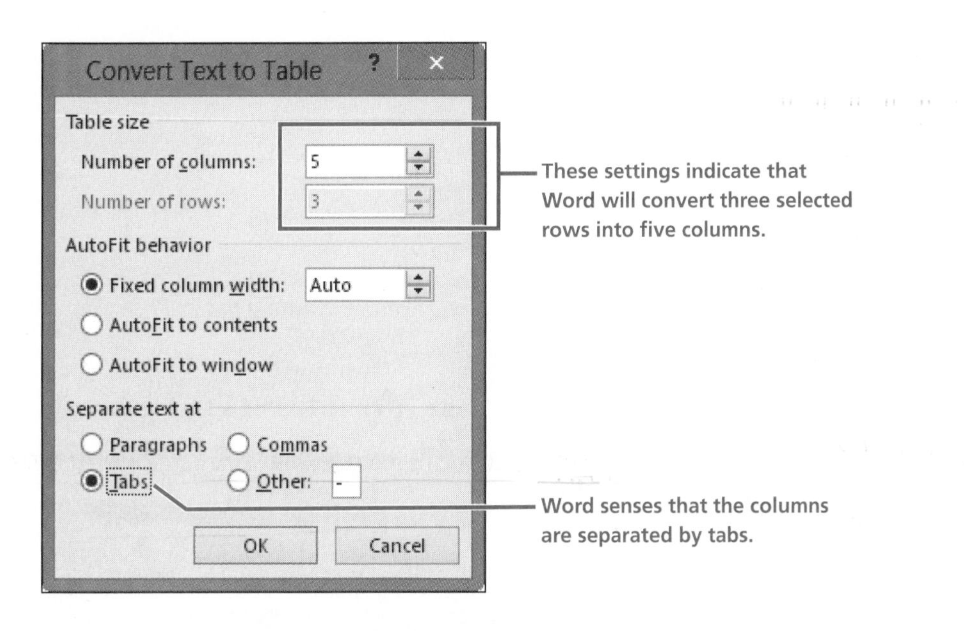

Converting a Table to Text

You can specify whether the converted text should be separated by paragraph marks, tabs, commas, or another character that you specify.

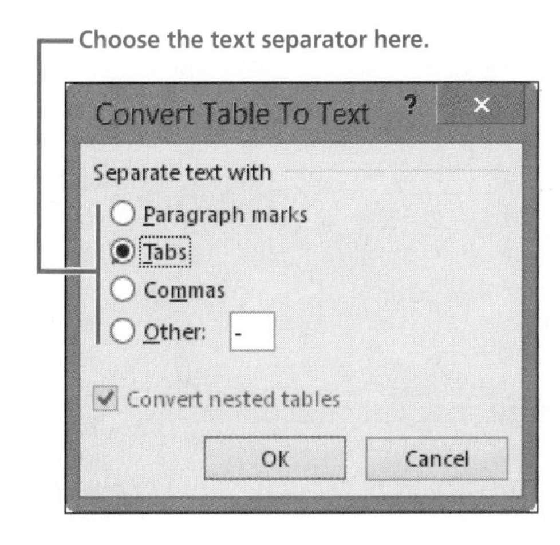

QUICK REFERENCE	CONVERTING TEXT TO TABLES AND TABLES TO TEXT
Task	**Procedure**
Convert text to a table	■ Turn on formatting marks and ensure there is only one tab separating the columns. ■ Select all lines to be converted, and choose Insert→Tables→Table→Convert Text to Table. ■ Choose the text separator and the number of columns.
Convert a table to text	■ Click in any table cell and choose Table Tools→Layout→Data→Convert to Text. ■ Choose the desired text separator.

DEVELOP YOUR SKILLS WD05-D03

Convert Text to a Table

In this exercise, you will convert text currently in tabular columns into a table. Then you will convert the table back to regular text.

1. Save your file as `WD05-D03-StdntTables-[FirstInitialLastName]`.
2. Scroll to page 3 and select all the rows, including the *Second Semester Schedule* heading.
3. Choose **Insert→Tables→Table**, and choose **Convert Text to Table**.
4. Follow these steps to create a table from the selected text:

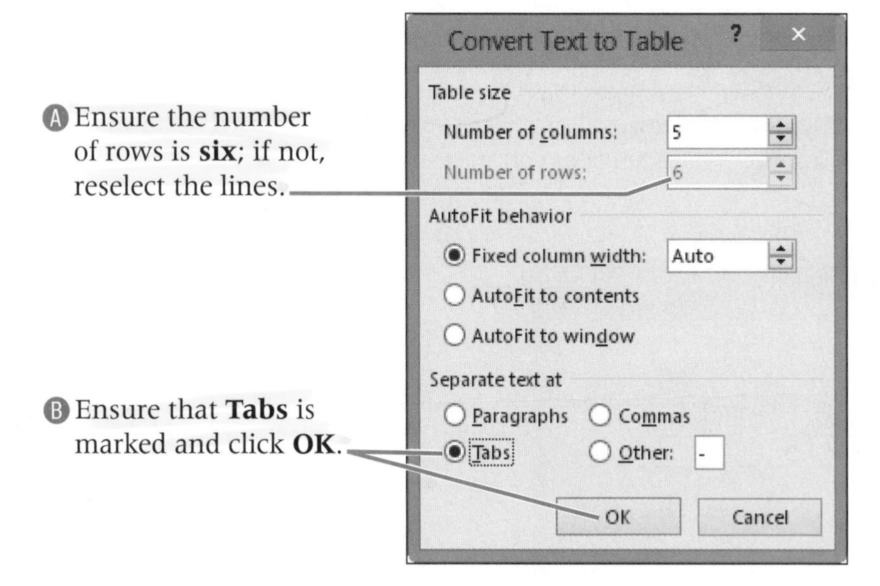

The text is now in a five-column table. Don't worry about the heading being in one cell. You'll fix that a little later.

Convert a Table to Text

5. Click in any table **cell**.

Notice the two new Table Tools tabs, Design and Layout, have been added to the Ribbon. These are contextual tabs, meaning they appear in context with what you are working on, in this case, when the insertion point is in a table.

6. Choose **Table Tools→Layout→Data→Convert to Text** . When the dialog box appears, verify that **Tabs** is chosen and click **OK**.

   The table is converted back to a tabular table.

7. Click **Undo** to return the text to table format.
8. Save the file.

Selecting Data in a Table

Video Library http://labyrinthelab.com/videos Video Number: WD13-V0504

The mouse pointer changes shape depending on whether you're selecting a cell, row, column, or the entire table. The following illustrations display the various pointer shapes when selecting in a table.

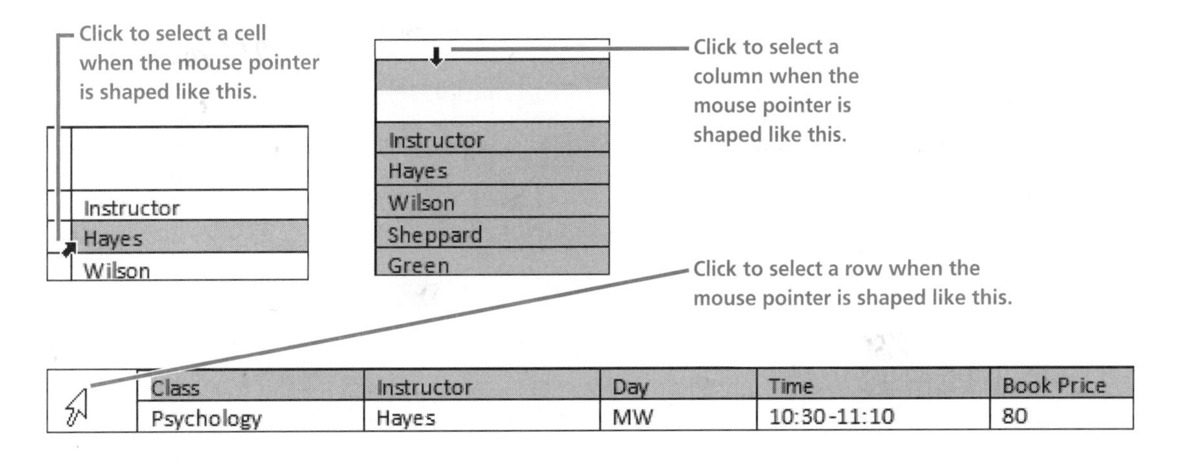

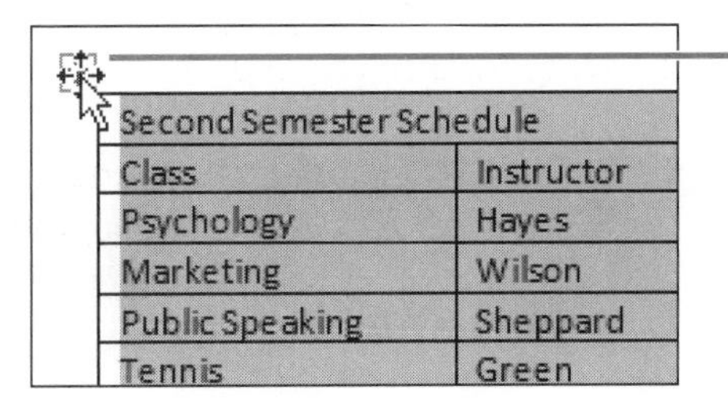

Click the square move handle to select the entire table. (The insertion point or mouse pointer must be in the table for the handle to appear.)

Customizing Alignment, Direction, and Cell Margins

Data can be aligned horizontally or vertically, and you can change the direction of text. You can also modify the cell margins. These commands are found in the Alignment group on the contextual Layout tab that appears when the insertion point is positioned in a table.

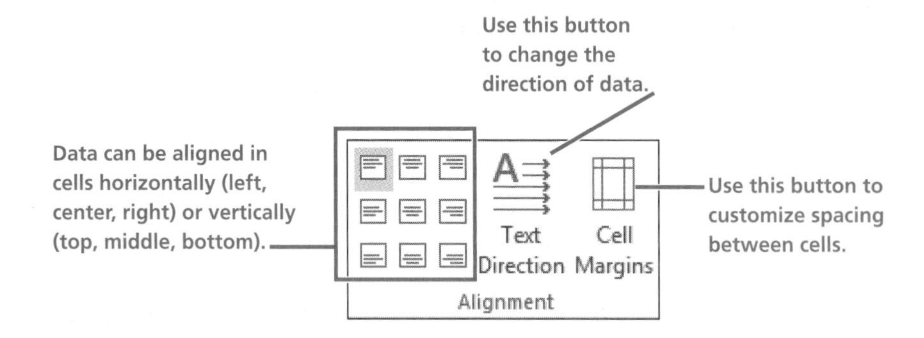

DEVELOP YOUR SKILLS WD05-D04

Select and Align Data, and Modify Cell Margins

In this exercise, you will center-align data, change text direction, and increase cell margins.

1. Save your file as **`WD05-D04-StdntTables-[FirstInitialLastName]`**.
2. Follow these steps to center the heading row data:

Ⓐ Position the mouse pointer in the margin left of the second row and click when the mouse pointer looks like this.

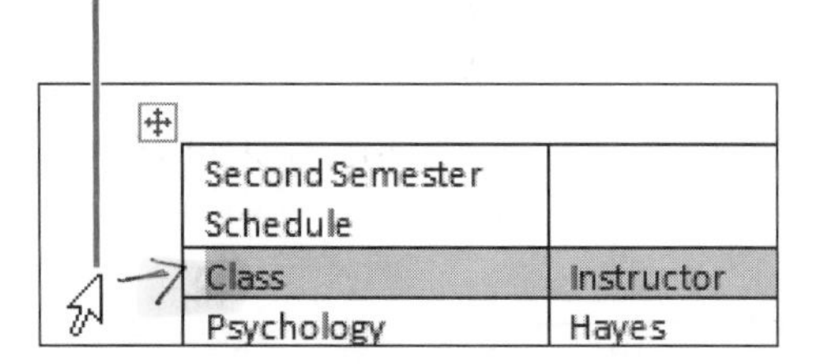

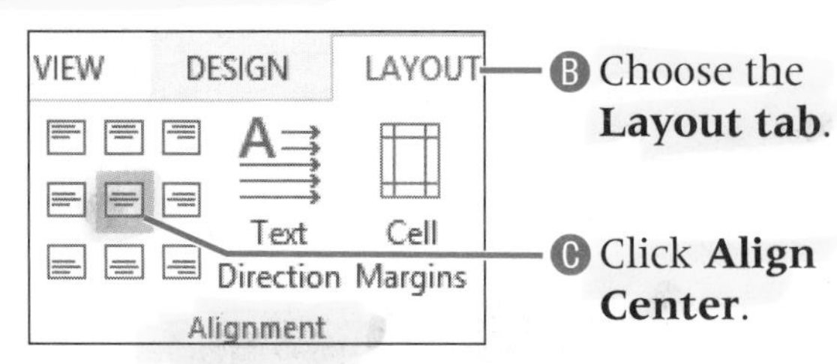

Ⓑ Choose the **Layout tab**.

Ⓒ Click **Align Center**.

3. Follow these steps to center the data in a range of cells:

Ⓐ Click and drag to select these cells.

Hayes	MW	10:30-11:10	80
Wilson	MW	2:30–3:20	90
Sheppard	TF	10:15–11:05	35
Green	W	3:40–4:30	45

Ⓑ Choose **Table Tools→Layout→Alignment→Align Center**.

Change Text Direction

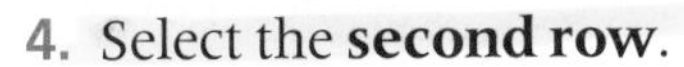

4. Select the **second row**.

5. Choose **Table Tools→Layout→Alignment→Text Direction** twice to change to vertical with the text facing to the right.
6. Click **Undo** twice to change back to horizontal alignment.

Change Cell Margins

7. Follow these steps to increase the distance between the text and cell borders:

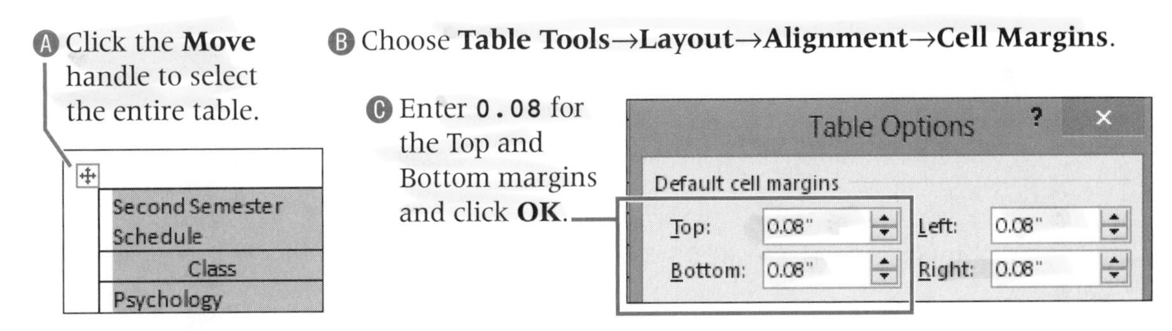

8. Save your file.

Merging and Splitting Cells

Video Library http://labyrinthelab.com/videos Video Number: WD13-V0505

You can merge two or more adjacent cells in the same row or column into a single cell. The merge option is often used to center a heading across the top of a table. You can also split a single cell into multiple cells.

A dialog box, shown in the following illustration, appears when you click the Split Cells button so you can determine the specifics of your split.

The contextual Layout tab containing the Merge Cells and Split Cells commands appears when the insertion point is in a table.

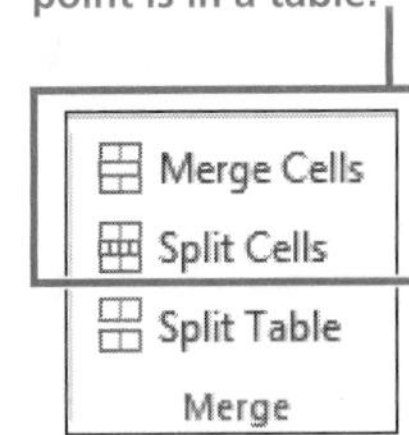

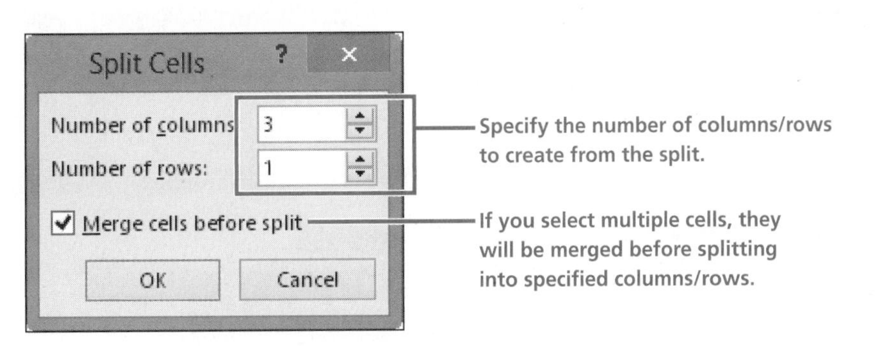

QUICK REFERENCE	MERGING AND SPLITTING TABLE CELLS
Task	**Procedure**
Merge cells	■ Select the cells to merge, and choose Table Tools→Layout→Merge→Merge Cells.
Split cells	■ Select the cell to split, and choose Table Tools→Layout→Merge→Split Cells. ■ Choose the number of rows and/or columns.

DEVELOP YOUR SKILLS WD05-D05

Merge and Split Cells in a Table

In this exercise, you will merge the cells in the first row to create one cell, where you will center the title across the width of the table. You will practice splitting cells, and then you will convert the title to regular text.

1. Save your file as **`WD05-D05-StdntTables-[FirstInitialLastName]`**.
2. Follow these steps to merge the table row and center the title:

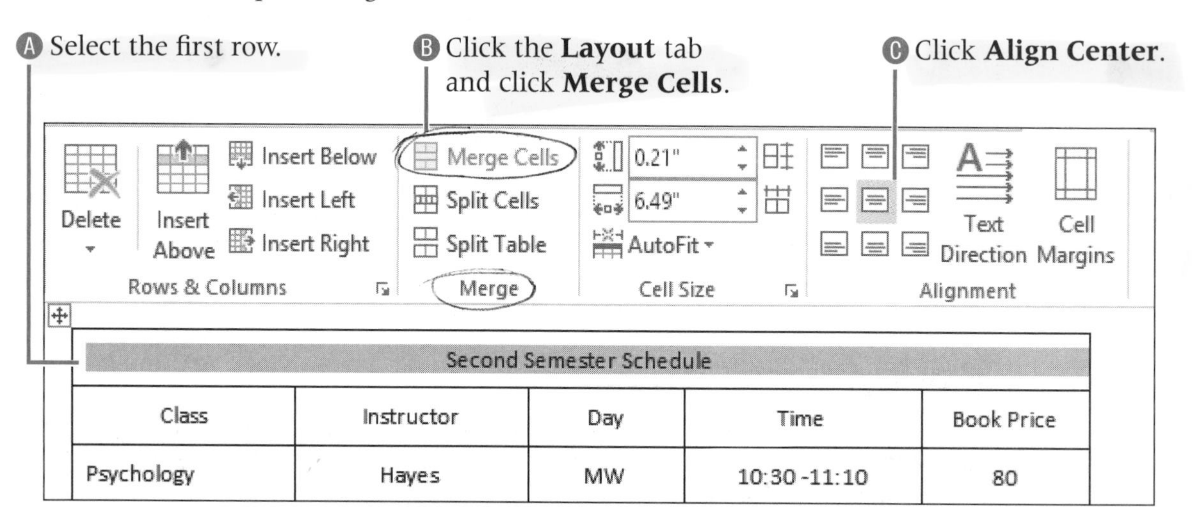

3. With the first row still selected, choose **Table Tools→Layout→Merge→Split Cells** .
4. When the dialog box opens, choose **three columns** and **one row**; click **OK**.
5. Click **Undo** to merge the cells again.
6. With the first row still selected, choose **Table Tools→Layout→Data→Convert to Text**.
7. Verify that **Paragraph Marks** is chosen and click **OK**.
8. Save the file.

Formatting with Borders, Shading, and Styles

Video Library http://labyrinthelab.com/videos Video Number: WD13-V0506

Borders, shading, and styles can enhance the readability of a table, and they add pizzazz. These tools are conveniently located on the contextual Design tab that appears when the insertion point is in a table. The Borders and Shading buttons have memory, meaning they reflect the last option chosen in the current session. This is convenient if you want to apply the same effect multiple times. Newly created tables have borders by default.

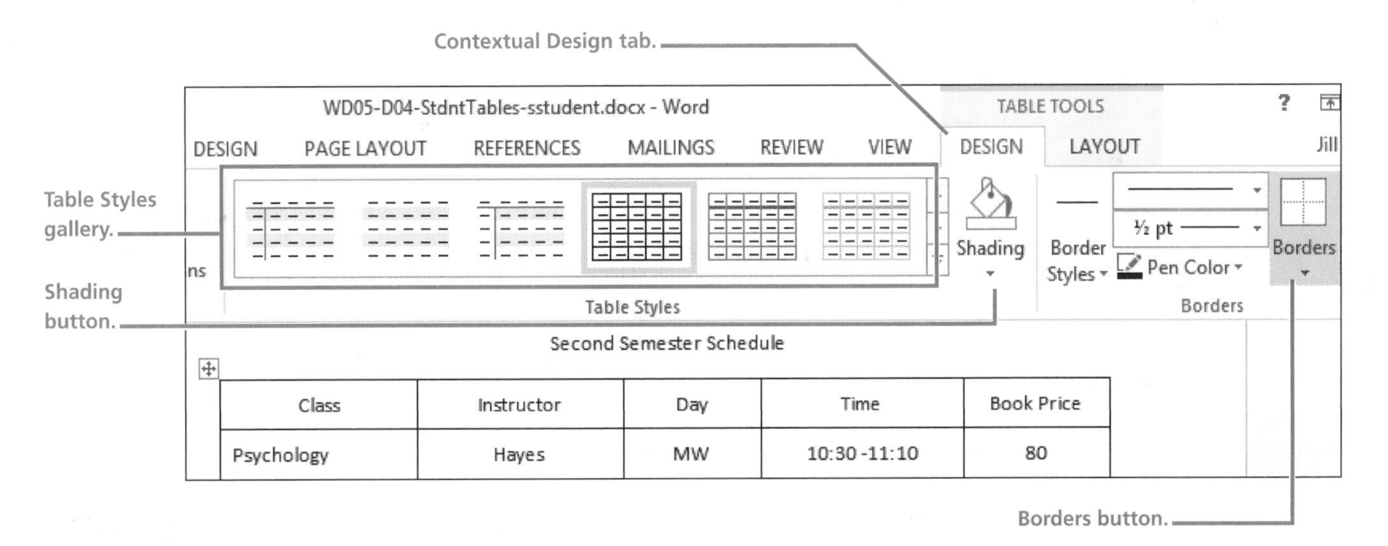

Modifying Formats

Just like regular text, you can easily modify table formats using the formatting tools on the Home tab. Or use the *Mini toolbar*, which provides convenient formatting tools right at your mouse pointer when you select data.

DEVELOP YOUR SKILLS WD05-D06

Use Borders, Shading, and Styles

In this exercise, you will remove all borders from your table, and then apply borders and shading to the first row. Then you will choose a table style to format your table.

1. Save your file as `WD05-D06-StdntTables-[FirstInitialLastName]`.
2. Click the **move handle** in the upper-left corner of the Second Semester Schedule table to select it.

   Remember, the insertion point has to be in the table or you have to hover the mouse pointer over the table for the move handle to appear.

3. Choose **Table Tools→Design→Borders→Borders** ⊞ **menu button ▼** and choose **No Border**.

   You may see gridlines within the table, but they won't print; they are just there to guide you. The Borders button menu on the Design tab provides the option to turn gridlines on or off.

4. Select the **first table row**, choose **Table Tools→Design→Borders→Borders** ⊞ **menu button ▼**, and choose **Outside Borders**.

5. Keep the first row selected and choose **Table Tools→Design→Table Styles→Shading** **menu button ▼**.

6. Choose the third color in the third column, **Tan, Background 2, Darker 25%**.

Use Table Styles

7. Make sure the insertion point is in the table, and choose **Table Tools→Design→Table Styles**.

8. Click the **scroll buttons** to look through the gallery, and then hover the **mouse pointer** over several styles to see a **Live Preview** of the styles.

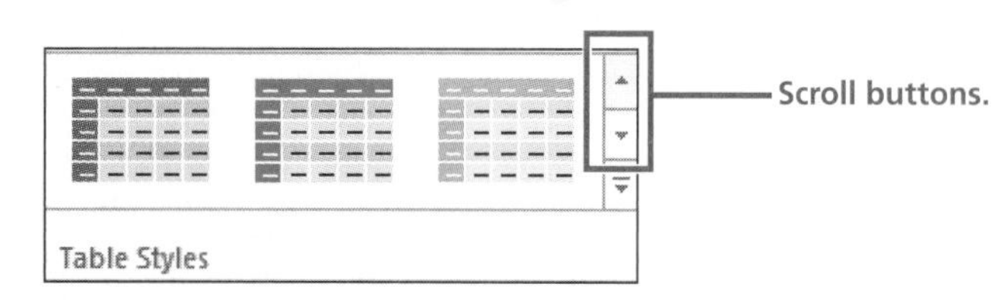

9. Click the **More** button below the scroll buttons to open the gallery and choose **Grid Table 5 Dark – Accent 1** (toward the bottom of the gallery).

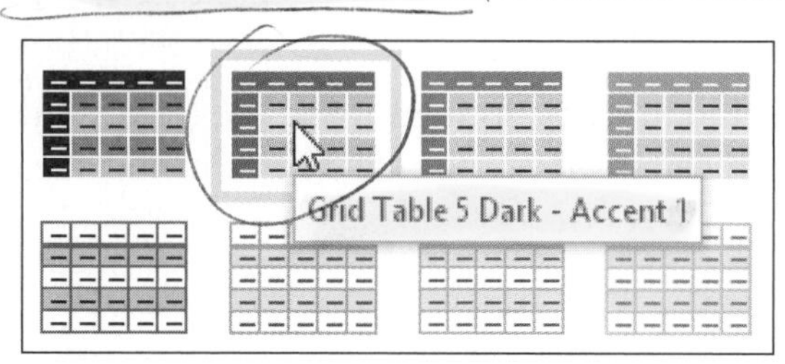

   The style overrides your cell margin spacing and borders and shading. In turn, you can override Table Styles formatting.

10. Select the first row of the table; choose **Home→Font→Font menu button ▼** and choose **Century Gothic**.

11. With the first row still selected, choose **Home→Font→Font Size menu button ▼** and choose **12 points**.

12. Save the file.

Sorting Data in a Table

Video Library http://labyrinthelab.com/videos Video Number: WD13-V0507

The Sort button in the Data group on the contextual Layout tab opens the Sort dialog box, which provides options to sort one or more columns in ascending or descending order, and choose whether the first row of the table contains column headings.

You can choose to sort a table by up to three levels. For example, say you have a table containing column headings for city, state, and zip. You can have Word sort the table first by state, then by city within state, and then by zip code within city for a three-level sort.

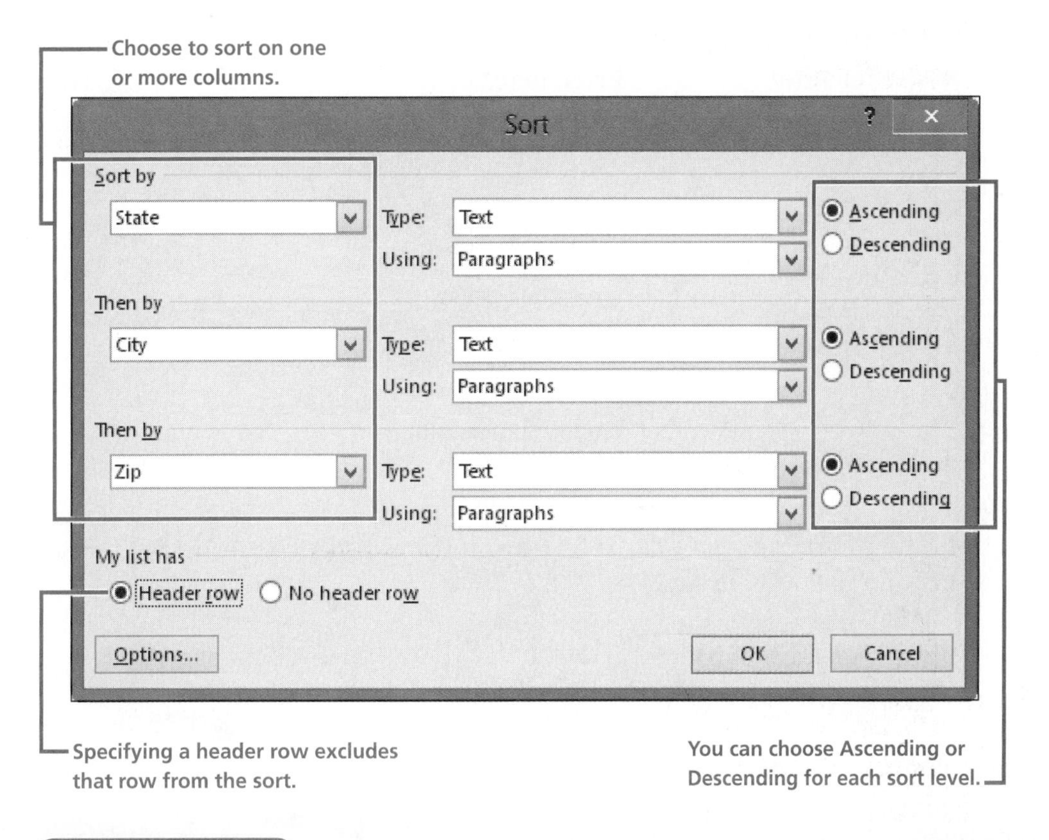

QUICK REFERENCE	SORTING TABLES
Task	**Procedure**
Sort a table	■ Click in the table and choose Table Tools→Layout→Data→Sort. ■ Choose Header Row or No Header Row, and select the columns to sort by. ■ Choose the Type of data and choose Ascending or Descending for each sort level.

DEVELOP YOUR SKILLS WD05-D07

Sort Table Rows

In this exercise, you will practice sorting the Second Semester Schedule table.

1. Save your file as `WD05-D07-StdntTables-[FirstInitialLastName]`.
2. Position the insertion point in any cell in the **Second Semester Schedule** table.
3. Choose **Table Tools→Layout→Data→Sort** .
   Word displays the Sort dialog box.
4. Follow these steps to sort the table:

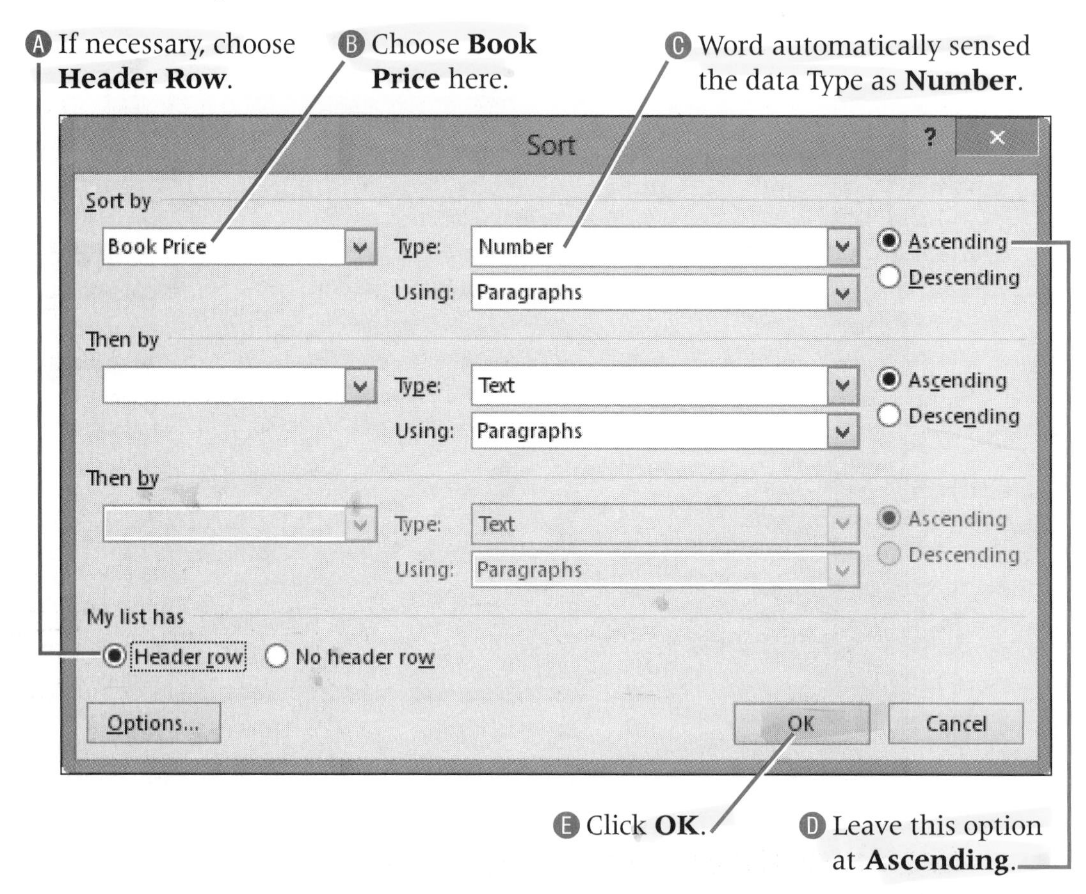

Word sorts the table numerically by book price.

5. Choose **Table Tools→Layout→Data→Sort** again.
6. In the Sort dialog box, make sure **Header Row** is chosen, choose **Class** from the Sort By list, and click **OK**.
   The table is now sorted in ascending order by Class.
7. Save your file.

Inserting Rows and Columns

Video Library http://labyrinthelab.com/videos Video Number: WD13-V0508

You can insert columns and rows in an existing table. If you wish to insert multiple columns or rows, you must first select the same number of existing columns or rows as you wish to insert. For example, to insert two new rows, select two existing rows.

You can use the buttons in the Rows & Columns group on the Layout tab to insert columns and rows, or you can use the drop-down menu that appears when you right-click a selected column or row.

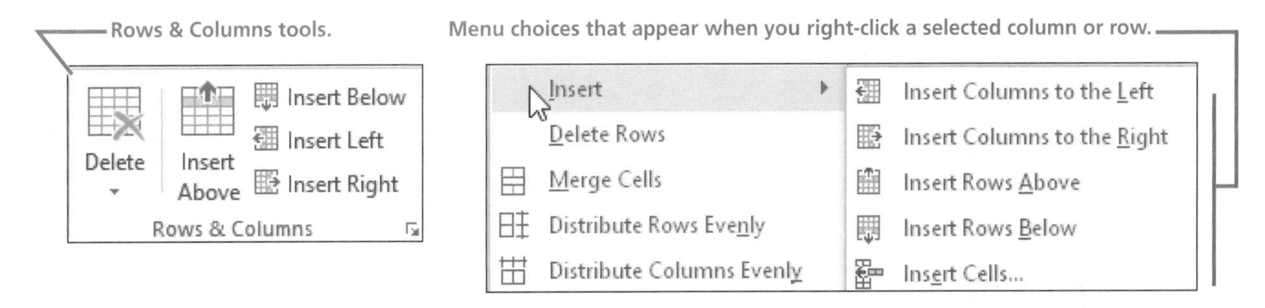

A quick and easy way to insert a column or row is with the Insert Control that appears when the insertion point is in the table and you move the mouse pointer between two columns or rows, as shown here.

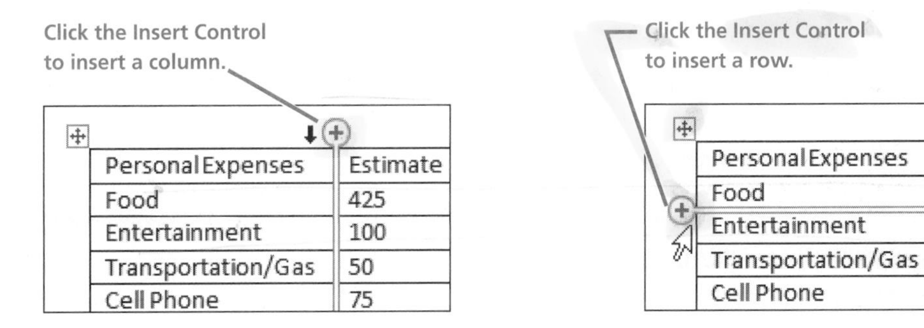

Moving Rows and Columns

You can move a row or column by using the Cut and Paste commands or by using the mouse to drag and drop. When you select the entire row or column and move it to another location, Word automatically makes room for the selection by moving the other rows down or the other columns to the right.

If you select an individual cell within a row or column, when you paste, Word replaces any existing data in the cell. You can prevent data loss by inserting a blank row or column prior to moving.

QUICK REFERENCE	WORKING WITH COLUMNS AND ROWS
Task	**Procedure**
Insert rows or columns	■ Click in the desired row/column or select the same number of rows/columns you wish to insert. ■ Choose Table Tools→Layout→Rows & Columns, and then choose Insert Above/ Below or Insert Left/Right. Or, position the mouse pointer between two rows/ columns and click the Insert Control.
Delete table elements	■ Select the desired row(s), column(s), or cell(s). ■ Choose Table Tools→Layout→Rows & Columns→Delete and choose the item to delete.
Move a row or column using Cut and Paste	■ Select the entire row(s) or column(s) and choose Home→Clipboard→Cut. ■ Select the row to paste the data above or the column to paste the data to the left of. ■ Choose Home→Clipboard→Paste.
Move a row or column using drag and drop	■ Select the entire row(s) or column(s) and drag to the first cell in the desired row or column.

DEVELOP YOUR SKILLS WD05-D08

Insert Rows and a Column

In this exercise, you will insert multiple rows and a new column in the table.

1. Save your file as `WD05-D08-StdntTables-[FirstInitialLastName]`.
2. Position the mouse pointer to the left of the **Marketing** row until it becomes the white arrow.
3. Click and drag down to select the **Marketing and Psychology** rows.
4. Choose **Table Tools→Layout→Rows & Columns→Insert Above** to insert two new rows above the Marketing row.
5. Add the following data to the new blank rows:

Geometry	Bailey	MW	12:00 – 12:50	94
Geometry Lab	Johnson	TTH	9:00 – 9:50	35

6. Follow these steps to insert a new column:

Ⓐ Position the mouse pointer here to display the Insert Control.

Ⓑ Click the **Insert Control**.

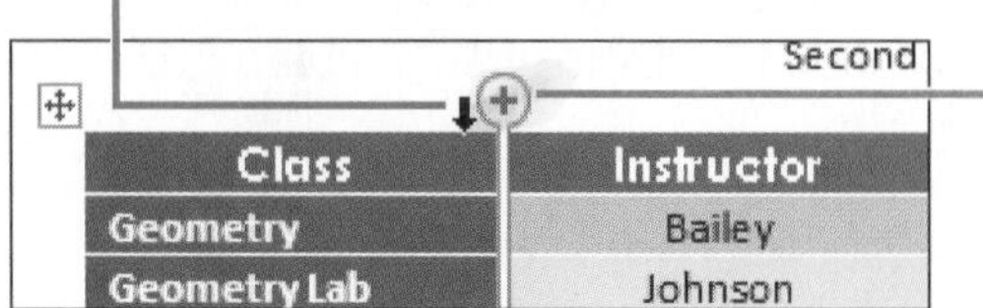

A new column is inserted to the right of the Class column.

7. Type **`Course #`** as the new column heading.
8. Enter the following data in the column.

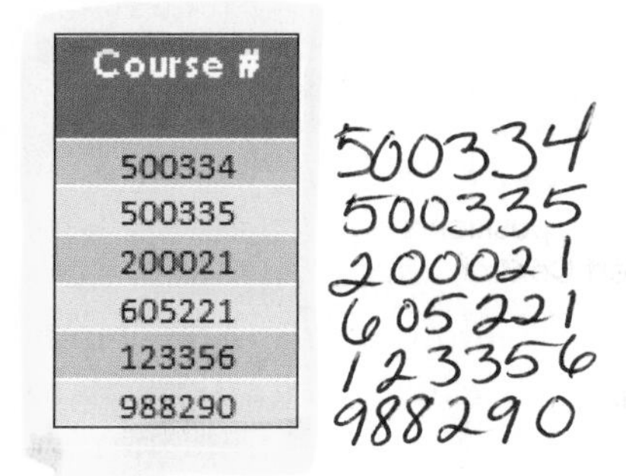

Course #
500334
500335
200021
605221
123356
988290

9. Scroll back up to the *Expense Table* on page 1 and position the insertion point in the **Actual** column.
10. Choose **Table Tools→Layout→Rows & Columns→Insert Right** .
11. Type **`Difference`** as the new column heading; save the file.

Performing Calculations in Tables

Video Library http://labyrinthelab.com/videos Video Number: WD13-V0509

When the Formula dialog box opens, it displays the Sum function. The Sum function recognizes whether there are numbers in the cells above or to the left of the formula cell and indicates that in the formula automatically. However, sometimes you may need a formula for something other than addition. In that case, you use cell addresses in the formula. Although the columns and rows are not lettered or numbered as they are in Excel, which is the Microsoft application designed to "crunch numbers," you must use cell addresses for certain calculations in a table. The first cell in a table is considered to be cell A1 (first column, first row).

Word's formulas are not nearly as sophisticated as Excel's; however, they are adequate for simple calculations.

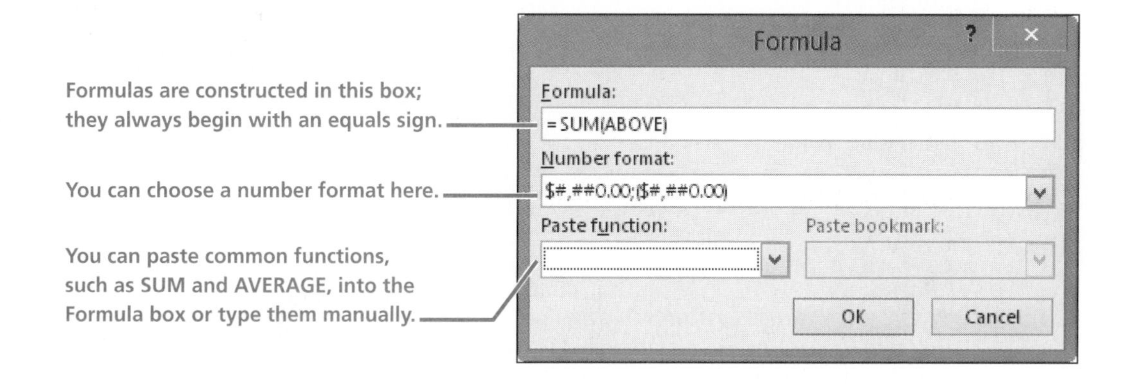

Constructing Formulas

You construct formulas by typing directly into the Formula dialog box. In Word, formulas can contain a combination of the following elements.

- **Arithmetic operators:** The most common arithmetic operators are + (addition), – (subtraction), / (division), and * (multiplication). For more complex formulas, use Microsoft Excel and copy and paste into Word.
- **Cell addresses:** In Word tables, columns are labeled A, B, C, etc., and rows are numbered 1, 2, 3, etc. Each cell has an address formed by the column letter and row number. For example, cell A1 refers to the cell in column A and row 1. You can use cell references in formulas. For example, the formula =D2–C2 subtracts the number in cell C2 from the number in cell D2.
- **Functions:** Functions are predefined formulas that perform calculations on cells. The most common functions are SUM, AVERAGE, MIN, and MAX.

  A function is followed by a set of parentheses in which you enter arguments. Arguments include numbers, cell addresses, a range of cells, or direction references (see next bullet).

  A range of cells is separated by a colon. For example, to include cells C2, C3, and C4 only in a formula, you would type C2:C4.
- **Direction references:** In Word, functions can use direction references to indicate cell ranges. The direction references are ABOVE, BELOW, LEFT, and RIGHT. As an example, the formula =SUM(ABOVE) would sum all numbers above the cell containing the formula.

If a number relating to a formula changes, right-click the cell containing the formula and choose Update Field to recalculate the formula.

QUICK REFERENCE	CONSTRUCTING FORMULAS
Task	**Procedure**
Create a formula	■ Choose Table Tools→Layout→Data→Formula and delete the formula in the formula box. ■ Type an equals (=) sign and construct the formula using cell addresses. ■ Use the appropriate operator: + (add), – (subtract), * (multiply), / (divide).
Calculate with a function	■ Choose Table Tools→Layout→Data→Formula and delete the formula in the formula box. ■ Type an equals (=) sign and choose a function from the Paste Function list. ■ Enter the arguments within the parentheses.

DEVELOP YOUR SKILLS WD05-D09

X Construct Formulas

In this exercise, you will use formulas to calculate the difference for each expense item and calculate the totals for the Estimate, Actual, and Difference columns.

1. Save your file as **WD05-D09-StdntTables-[FirstInitialLastName]**.
2. Click in the **second row** of the *Difference* column. D2

   This cell is named D2 because it is the fourth column (D) in the second row (2).

3. Choose **Table Tools→Layout→Data→Formula** *fx*.
4. Follow these steps to create a formula to subtract the *Estimate* from the *Actual* expense:

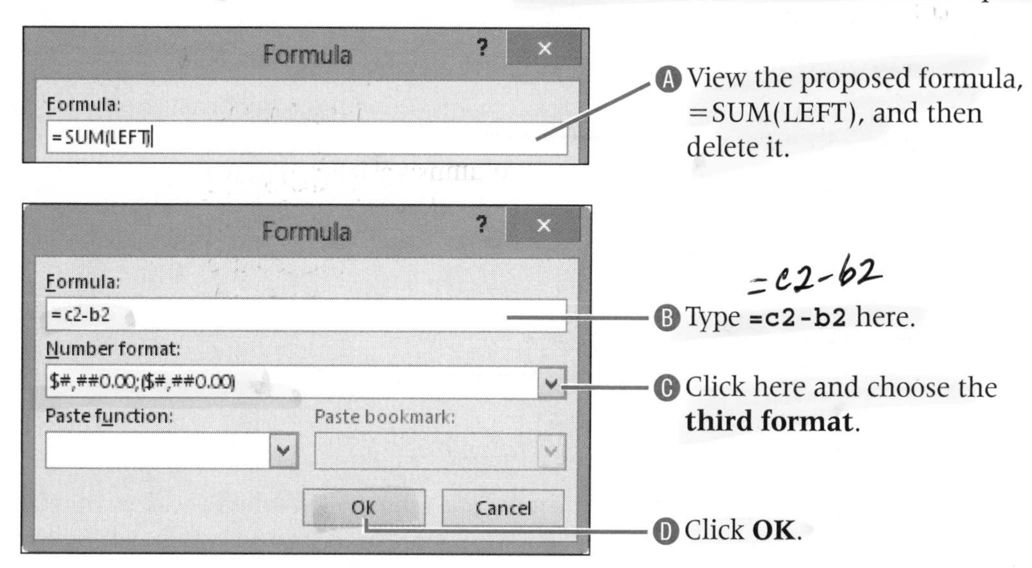

This formula subtracts the estimated food expense (column b, row 2) from the actual food expense (column c, row 2). Notice that the result, $10.00, displays with a dollar sign and two decimal places because of the dollar format chosen.

If you wish to display the dollar format without the two decimal places, you must delete them manually from each cell.

5. Click in the cell beneath the formula.
6. Choose **Table Tools→Layout→Data→Formula** *fx*.
7. Remove the proposed formula and type `=c3-b3`. =c3-b3
8. Click the **Number Format** menu arrow, choose the **third format**, and click **OK**.
9. Enter formulas in the remaining rows in the *Difference* column choosing the same format as before. Transp/

Create a Formula to Total the Columns

10. Position the insertion point in the last table cell and tap Tab to create a new row.

Personal Expenses	Estimate	Actual	Difference
Food	425	435	$ 10.00
Entertainment	100	150	$ 50.00
Transportation/Gas	50	55	$ 5.00 =c4-b4
Cell Phone	75	85	$ 10.00 =c5-b5

11. Type `Totals` in the first cell and tap Tab to move to the next cell.
12. Choose **Table Tools→Layout→Data→Formula** *fx*.

Word assumes you want to add the numbers above the formula cell.

13. Click **OK**.

The result should be 650. Notice that the total does not have the dollar sign or decimals, since you did not specify any special formatting.

14. Calculate the total for *Actual* column with no formatting.
15. Calculate the total for the *Difference* column and add the same formatting as the other numbers in the column.
16. Save the file.

Sizing Rows and Columns

Video Library http://labyrinthelab.com/videos Video Number: WD13-V0510

You can easily resize columns and rows in a table. Word offers a variety of techniques for this. The adjust pointer, a double-headed arrow, appears whenever you position the mouse pointer on a row or column gridline. You can adjust the column width and row height by dragging the gridline.

Dragging a gridline adjusts column width or row height.

Expense Table

Personal Expenses	Estimate	Actual	Difference
Food	425	435	$ 10.00
Entertainment	100	150	$ 50.00
Transportation/Gas	50	55	$ 5.00
Cell Phone	75	85	$ 10.00

Dragging a column or row marker on the ruler also adjusts column width and row height.

The Cell Size group in the contextual Layout tab provides handy tools for working with column and row sizes.

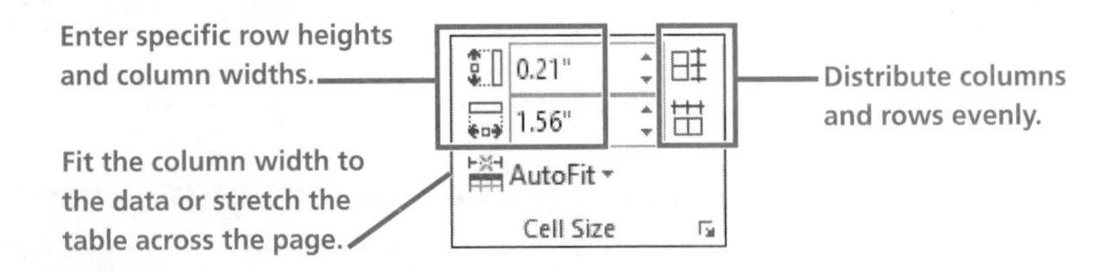

DEVELOP YOUR SKILLS WD05-D10

Adjust Column Widths

In this exercise, you will adjust column widths using the adjust pointer and the tools in the Cell Size group on the Layout tab.

1. Save your file as **`WD05-D10-StdntTables-[FirstInitialLastName]`**.

2. Follow these steps to change the width of the first column:

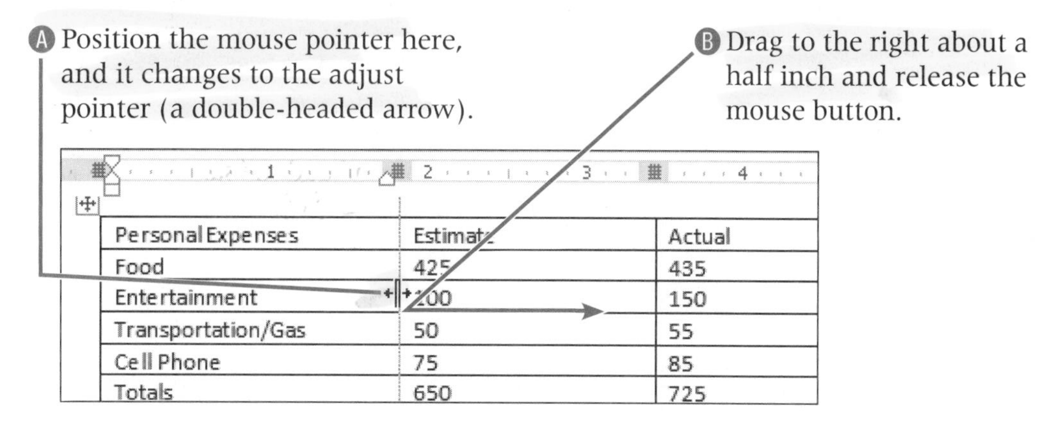

3. Follow these steps to distribute the last three columns evenly:

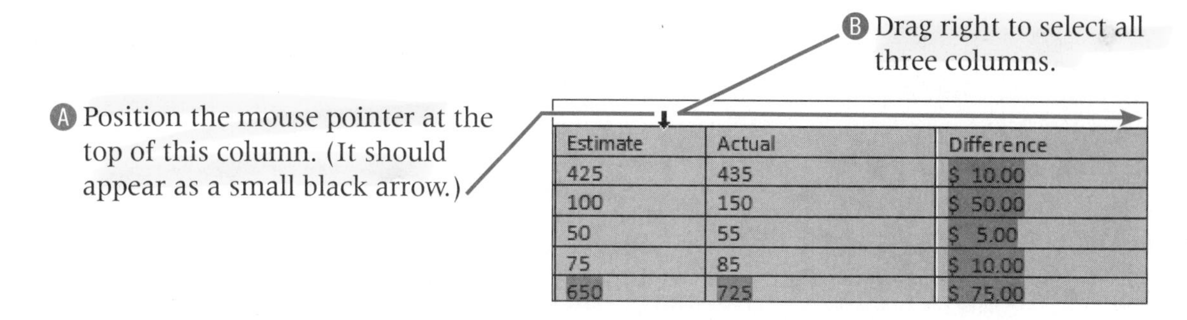

4. Choose **Table Tools→Layout→Cell Size→Distribute Columns** to make the selected columns the same size.

AutoFit Columns

5. Scroll to the **Schedule Planning table** on **page 2** and select the **entire table**.
6. Choose **Table Tools→Layout→Cell Size→AutoFit**, and choose **AutoFit Contents**.
   All columns are now as wide as they need to be based on the width of their contents.
7. Save and close the file. Exit **Word**.

Concepts Review

To check your knowledge of the key concepts introduced in this lesson, complete the Concepts Review quiz by choosing the appropriate access option below.

If you are...	Then access the quiz by...
Using the Labyrinth Video Library	Going to http://labyrinthelab.com/videos
Using eLab	Logging in, choosing Content, and navigating to the Concepts Review quiz for this lesson
Not using the Labyrinth Video Library or eLab	Going to the student resource center for this book

Reinforce Your Skills

REINFORCE YOUR SKILLS WD05-R01

Insert Tables and Align Data

Kids for Change are partnering with the local Center for Environmental Health to identify products in the home that present a risk to babies. In this exercise, you will create, enter data in, and navigate a table. You will convert a tabular document to a table and format alignment, text direction, and cell margins. Finally, you will merge and split cells.

Navigate in a Table

1. Start **Word**. Open **WD05-R01-RiskTeam** from your **WD2013 Lesson 05** folder and save it as `WD05-R01-RiskTeam-[FirstInitialLastName]`.
2. Position the insertion point in the first table cell and tap ↓.
3. Tap Tab to move to the right one cell.
4. Press Shift+Tab to move to the left one cell.
5. Press Shift+Tab again to move to the end of the previous row.
6. Press Alt+Home to move to the beginning of the row.
7. Press Alt+End to move to the end of the row.
8. Press Alt+Page Down to move to the bottom of the column.
9. Press Alt+Page Up to move to the top of the column.

Insert Tables

10. If necessary, choose **Home→Paragraph→Show/Hide** to display formatting marks.
11. Position the insertion point on the second blank line below the table.
12. Insert a **3x6 table** and enter the data shown here.

Remember, you can add rows to the bottom of a table by tapping Tab when you reach the last table cell.

Product	Risk factor	Risk
Foam products	Chlorinated Tris	Gene mutations
Drop-side cribs	Side can drop	Suffocate or strangle
Sleep positioners	Face against positioner	Suffocate or strangle
Blankets	Baby becomes entangled	Suffocate
Crib tents	Baby becomes entangled	Strangle
Changing tables	Baby can fall	Injury
Bath seats	Can tip	Drown

Next you will insert a calendar quick table so you can keep track of meetings with the Center for Environmental Health.

13. Position the insertion point at the end of the document and tap [Enter].
14. Choose **Insert→Tables→Table** and slide the mouse pointer down to **Quick Tables**.
15. Insert **Calendar 2**.
16. Position the insertion point at the end of the document and tap [Enter].

    Now you will copy a tabular table from another file and paste it into your document.
17. Open **WD05-R01-FoodRisk** from your **WD2013 Lesson 05** folder.
18. Copy the contents of the document and paste it at the end of your **Risk Team** document.
19. Close the **Food Risk** file.

Convert Text to a Table

20. Select the entire tabular table.
21. Choose **Insert→Tables→Table→Convert Text to Table**.
22. Accept the defaults in the dialog box and click **OK**.

Select Table Data

23. Click in the **food risk** table to deselect.
24. Position the mouse pointer at the top of the middle column, and when the mouse pointer appears as a black down-pointing arrow, click to select the column.

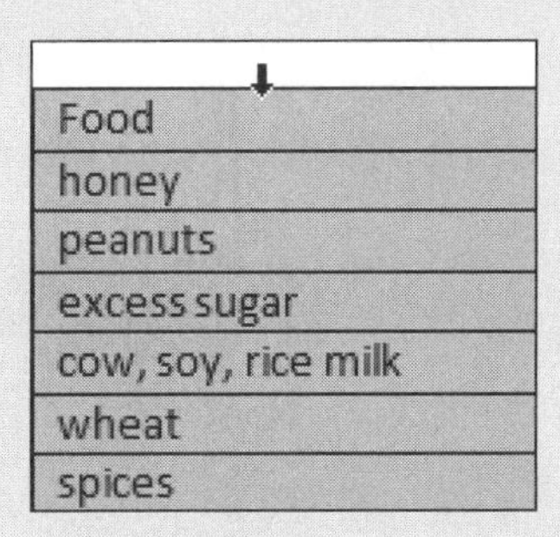

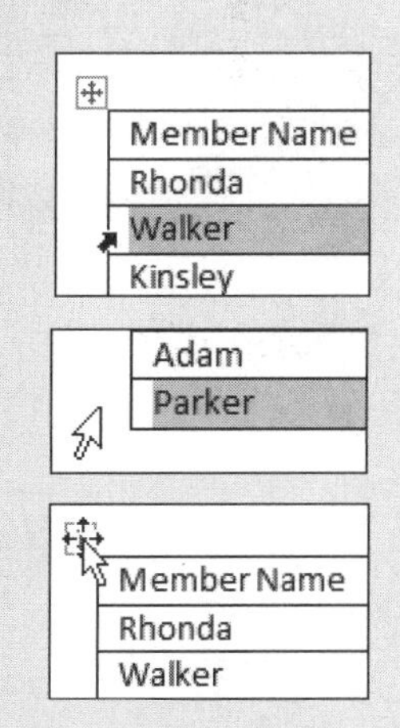

25. Position the insertion point just inside the left edge of the **Walker** cell, and when the mouse pointer appears as a black-tilted arrow, click to select the cell.
26. Position the mouse pointer in the margin to the left of the **Parker** row, and when the mouse pointer appears as a white-tilted arrow, click to select the row.
27. Click the insertion point in the table to display the move handle, then position the mouse pointer over the move handle. When the mouse pointer appears, click to select the entire table.

Align Data, Change Text Direction, and Modify Cell Margins

28. Select the **Food and Risk Factor columns**.
29. Choose **Table Tools→Layout→Alignment→Align Center**.
30. Select the first column and choose **Layout→Alignment→Align Center Right**.
    The first column should still be selected.
31. Choose **Table Tools→Layout→Alignment→Align Center Left**.
32. Select the first row and choose **Table Tools→Layout→Alignment→Text Direction**.
33. Click **Text Direction** again.
34. Click **Undo** twice to return to horizontal alignment.
35. Select the entire table and choose **Table Tools→Layout→Alignment→Cell Margins**.
36. In the Table Options dialog box, change the **top and bottom margins** to `0.04` and click **OK**.

Merge and Split Cells

37. Click in the first table row.
38. Choose **Table Tools→Layout→Rows & Columns→Insert Above**.
    The new row should be selected.
39. Choose **Table Tools→Layout→Merge→Merge Cells**.
40. Click in the new row and type `Food Risk`.
41. Choose **Table Tools→Layout→Merge→Split Cells**.
42. Accept the default number of columns and rows and click **OK**.
43. Click **Undo** to merge the cells again.
44. Save and close the file; exit from **Word**.
45. Submit your final file based on the guidelines provided by your instructor.
    To view examples of how your file or files should look at the end of this exercise, go to the student resource center.

REINFORCE YOUR SKILLS WD05-R02

Format, Organize, and Calculate Tables

In this exercise, you will use borders, shading, table styles, and font formatting. You will sort a table, work with columns and rows, and perform calculations. Finally, you will adjust column widths.

Format with Borders, Shading, and Styles

The Kids for Change members are planning a demonstration of safe cleaning products at the Community Center. They need to figure out how much salt, lemon, vinegar, and baking soda they will need.

1. Start **Word**. Open **WD05-R02-SafeClean** from your **WD2013 Lesson 05** folder and save it as `WD05-R02-SafeClean-[FirstInitialLastName]`.
2. Position the insertion point in the table on page 1 and choose **Table Tools→Design→Table Styles**.

3. Open the gallery and choose **Grid Table 4 – Accent 6**.
   Hint: It's a green style.
4. Select the table, choose **Table Tools→Design→Borders→Borders** **menu button ▾**, and then choose **Outside Borders**.
5. Select the first row, choose **Table Tools→Design→Borders→Borders** **menu button ▾**, and then choose **Bottom Border**.
6. With the first row still selected, choose **Table Tools→Design→Table Styles→Shading** **menu button ▾**.
7. Choose the last green color in the right-hand column, **Green, Accent 6, Darker 50%**.
8. Select the entire table, choose **Home→Font→Font menu button ▾**, and then choose **Comic Sans MS**.
9. Select in the first column starting at *Clean coffee pot* through the end of the column.
10. Choose **Home→Font→Italic** .

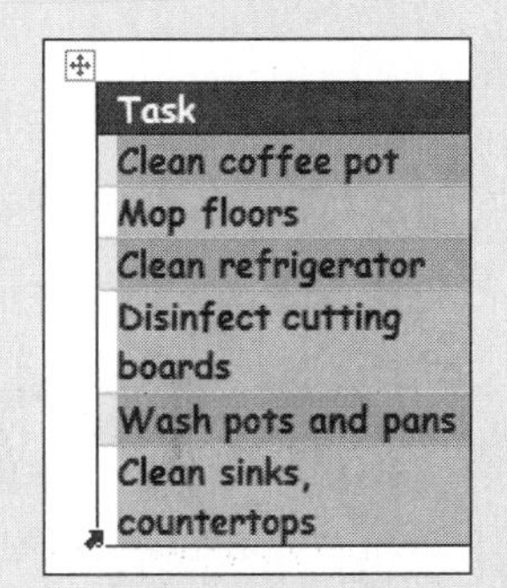

Sort Table Data

Dylan, a Kids for Change member, volunteers at a green cleaning supplies company so he can become familiar with safe cleaning products. He has been asked to complete the Order Tracking Sheet.

11. Go to page 2 of the **Safe Clean** file and select the entire table.
12. Choose **Table Tools→Layout→Data→Sort** and, if necessary, choose the **Header Row** option in the Sort dialog box.
13. Click the **Sort By field drop-down arrow** and choose **Item #**; click **OK**.
    The Item # column is now in ascending numeric order.
14. Use the same process to sort by the **Customer ID column** in ascending order.

Insert a Column and Row

15. Position the insertion point in the **Price column**.
16. Choose **Table Tools→Layout→Rows & Columns→Insert Right** .
17. Position the insertion point in the last cell of the new column and tap Tab to add a row.
18. Type `Total` in the first cell of the new row, and then type `Total` at the top of the new column.

Perform Calculations in a Table

19. Position the insertion point in the second cell of the last column.
20. Choose **Table Tools→Layout→Data→Formula** .
    You will multiply Quantity by Price to calculate the total price for the first customer.
21. Delete the contents of the **Formula box** and type `=d2*e2` in the box.
    Remember, the asterisk (*) is the multiply sign.

22. Choose the **dollar** format (third format) from the Number Format drop-down list, and then click **OK**.
23. Repeat the process to calculate the total and apply the currency format for the rest of the customers.

    Now you will total the last column.
24. Position the insertion point in the last cell of the Total column.
25. Choose **Table Tools→Layout→Data→Formula** fx

    The formula defaults to =SUM(ABOVE), which is what you want.
26. Choose the **dollar** format, and then click **OK**.

Size Columns

27. Select the entire table.
28. Choose **Table Tools→Layout→Cell Size→AutoFit** and choose **AutoFit Contents**.

    The width of the columns is adjusted based on the widest entry in each column.
29. Save and close the file; exit from **Word**.
30. Submit your final file based on the guidelines provided by your instructor.

    To view examples of how your file or files should look at the end of this exercise, go to the student resource center.

REINFORCE YOUR SKILLS WD05-R03

Insert and Format Tables

This holiday season, Kids for Change members are working with the local fire department to collect toys for needy kids. The members will be assigned to different neighborhoods for collecting. In this exercise, you will format a table that tracks how many toys each member collects.

Navigate in a Table

1. Start **Word**. Open **WD05-R03-Toys** from your **WD2013 Lesson 05** folder and save it as `WD05-R03-Toys-[FirstInitialLastName]`.
2. Position the insertion point in the first table cell (page 1) and press [Alt]+[End] to move to the end of the row.
3. Press [Alt]+[Page Down] to move to the bottom of the column.
4. Press [Alt]+[Home] to move to the beginning of the row.
5. Tap [Tab] twice to move two cells to the right.
6. Press [Shift]+[Tab] to move to the left one cell.
7. Tap [↑] to move up one row.

Insert a Table

Kids for Change members decided to take up a collection from friends and family to purchase additional toys. You will insert a Quick Table to track the donations.

8. Scroll to the end of the document and press [Ctrl]+[Enter] to insert a page break.
9. Choose **Insert→Tables→Table** and slide the mouse pointer down to **Quick Tables**.
10. In the submenu, scroll down and choose **Tabular List**.
11. Select the *ITEM* heading and type **MEMBER** in its place.
12. Select the *NEEDED* heading and type **AMOUNT** in its place.
13. Select the remaining rows and tap [Delete].
14. Enter the new data as shown.

MEMBER	AMOUNT
Ella	$20
Tom	$17
Roger	$32
Stella	$15
Jennifer	$22
Max	$29
Jose	$35
Albert	$40

Convert Text to a Table

15. Scroll to page 2 and select the rows in the tabular table from *Exposure* through *Lacerations*.
16. Choose **Insert→Tables→Table** and choose **Convert Text to Table**.
17. When the Convert Text to Table dialog box appears, click **OK**.

Select Table Data

18. Position the mouse pointer in the margin to the left of the third row and click to select the row.
19. Position the mouse pointer at the top of the Danger column, and when the mouse pointer appears as a black down-pointing arrow, click to select the column.
20. Position the mouse pointer in the bottom-left corner of the Pull toys cell, and when the mouse pointer appears as a tilted black arrow, click to select the cell.
21. Click the move handle in the upper-left corner of the table to select the entire table.

Align Data, Change Text Direction, and Modify Cell Margins

22. Scroll to the table on page 1.
23. Select the second and third columns.
24. Choose **Table Tools→Layout→Alignment→Align Center Right**.
25. Choose **Table Tools→Layout→Alignment→Align Center**.

26. Select the first table row.
27. Choose **Table Tools→Layout→Alignment→Text Direction** .
28. Click **Undo** to return to horizontal alignment.
29. Select the entire table.
30. Choose **Table Tools→Layout→Alignment→Cell Margins** .
31. Change the **top and bottom margins** to `0.06`, then click **OK**.

Merge Cells

32. Select the four Sycamore cells in the third column.
33. Choose **Table Tools→Layout→Merge→Merge Cells** .
34. Delete three of the Sycamore entries.
35. Use the same technique to merge the Homestead Valley and Middle Ridge cells, and then delete three Homestead Valley and three Middle Ridge entries.

Use Borders, Shading, and Table Styles

36. Select the entire table.
37. Choose **Table Tools→Design→Borders→Borders menu button ▾**, and then choose **No Border**.
38. Choose **Table Tools→Design→Table Styles**, click the More button on the Styles gallery, and then choose the **Grid Table 4 – Accent 5** style.

    Hint: It's a blue style.

Sort Data

Several Kids for Change regional directors plan to meet following the toy collection to discuss plans for next year's collection. They compiled a mailing list of directors who will be notified of the meeting.

39. Scroll to the table on page 3 and position the insertion point in the table.
40. Choose **Table Tools→Layout→Data→Sort** .
41. If necessary, choose **Header Row** in the Sort dialog box, then choose sort by **State**, then by **City**, then by **Zip**, and then click **OK**.

    The California cities sorted in ascending alphabetic order within State, and the Dallas zip codes sorted in ascending numeric order within City.

Insert Rows and Resize Columns

42. Scroll to the table on page 4.

    Region 5 was accidentally omitted.

43. Position the mouse pointer to the left of the last two rows until the **Insert Control** appears.

Region¤
1¤
2¤
3¤
4¤
6¤

44. Click the control to insert a blank row between the last two rows, and then enter the following data in the new row.

5	1,951	2,543

45. Select the entire table, choose **Table Tools→Layout→Cell Size→AutoFit**, and choose **AutoFit Contents**.

Perform Calculations

46. Position the insertion point in the last table cell and tap [Tab] to insert a new row at the bottom of the table.

47. Type `Totals` in the first cell of the new row and tap [Tab] to move to the next cell.

    Now you will calculate the totals for all regions for both years.

48. Choose **Table Tools→Layout→Data→Formula** *fx*.

49. Accept the default Sum function in the Formula box and click **OK**.

50. Use the same process to calculate this year's total.

51. Save and close the file and exit from **Word**.

52. Submit your final file based on the guidelines provided by your instructor.

Apply Your Skills

APPLY YOUR SKILLS WD05-A01

Insert Tables, and Align and Merge Cells

In this exercise, you will navigate in a table, insert a new table, and convert a table to tabular text. You will select and align data and use cell margins. Then you will merge cells to create a table heading.

Navigate in and Insert a Table

1. Start **Word**. Open **WD05-A01-CorpEvents** from your **WD2013 Lesson 05** folder and save it as `WD05-A01-CorpEvents-[FirstInitialLastName]`.
2. Navigate in the table on page 1 using the keystrokes shown in the *Navigating in a Table* section of the main lesson.
3. If necessary, choose **Home→Paragraph→Show/Hide** ¶ to display formatting marks.
4. Scroll to page 2 and position the insertion point on the first blank line below *Oceanic Cruise Lines*.
5. Insert a **4x5 table** and enter the data shown.

Date	Itinerary	Ship	From
03/18/2013	4-night Bahamas Cruise from Miami	Oceanic Star	$279
03/22/2013	3-night Bahamas Cruise from Miami	Oceanic Jewel	$289
03/24/2013	7-night Bahamas Cruise from New York	Oceanic Star	$1159
03/25/2013	7-night Bahamas Cruise from New York	Oceanic Jewel	$599

Convert a Table to Text, Select Data, and Customize Alignment

6. Scroll to page 3 and select the table.
7. Choose **Table Tools→Layout→Data→Convert to Text**.
8. Make sure **Tabs** is chosen in the Convert Table to Text dialog box and click **OK**.
9. Scroll to page 1 and select data using the selection techniques described in this lesson.
10. Select the second and third columns and click **Align Center** on the Layout tab.
11. Select the second row and click **Text Direction** on the Layout tab.
12. Click **Undo** to return to horizontal alignment.

Use Cell Margins and Merge Cells

13. Select the page 1 table and use the **Cell Margins** on the Layout tab to set the top and bottom margins at `0.08"`.
14. Merge the first row and type `Travel Special` as the table heading.
15. Save and close the file; exit from **Word**.
16. Submit your final file based on the guidelines provided by your instructor.
    To view examples of how your file or files should look at the end of this exercise, go to the student resource center.

APPLY YOUR SKILLS WD05-A02

Format, Organize, and Calculate Tables

In this exercise, you will format with borders, shading, and table styles, and then you will sort data. You will insert columns and rows, and finally, you will perform calculations and size columns.

Apply Borders, Shading, and a Table Style

1. Start **Word**. Open **WD05-A02-Universal** from your **WD2013 Lesson 05** folder and save the file as `WD05-A02-Universal-[FirstInitialLastName]`.
2. Select the table on page 1; choose **Table Tools→Design→Borders→Borders menu button ▼** and choose **No Border**.
3. Select the first row, and use **Borders** to apply a **bottom border**.
4. Apply a bottom border to the last row of the table.
5. Select the first row, then choose **Table Tools→Design→Table Styles→Shading menu button ▼** and choose **Gold, Accent 4, Darker 25%**.
6. Select the third row and apply **Gold, Accent 4, Lighter 60%**.
7. Apply the same color you used in the third row to the **fifth row**.
8. Scroll to page 2, position the insertion point in the table, choose **Table Tools→Design→Table Styles**, and open the Table Styles gallery.
9. Choose the **Grid Table 6 Colorful – Accent 4** style; it's a yellow style.

Sort Data and Insert a Row and Column

10. Using the page 2 table, sort by the **Travel Package column** in ascending order, specifying that the table has a header row.
11. Scroll to the page 1 table and sort by the **Group Travel column** in descending order, specifying that the table has a header row.
12. Using the same table, sort by the **Visa/Passport column** in ascending order, specifying that the table has a header row.
13. Using the page 1 table, insert a **blank row at the top** of the table, **merge** the cells in the **first row**, and type `Universal Corporate Events`.

14. Use **Align Center** to center the heading.

15. Scroll to page 3 and add a **column** at the end of the table and a row at the bottom of the table.

Perform Calculations and Size Columns

16. Type `Totals` in the blank cell at the bottom of the first column.

17. Insert a formula using the **Sum function** and **dollar** format to total columns two through four.

18. Delete the **decimal point and zeros** at the end of each total.

    Hint: Position the insertion point to the left of the decimal point before deleting.

19. Type `Totals` in the first cell of the last column and insert a formula using the **Sum function** and **dollar** format to total the rows for the three plans. Be sure to check that the formula is correct before clicking OK.

20. Delete the **decimal point and zeros** at the end of each total.

21. Scroll to page 2 and use the **AutoFit** feature to autofit the contents of the table.

22. Save and close the file; exit from **Word**.

23. Submit your final file based on the guidelines provided by your instructor.

    To view examples of how your file or files should look at the end of this exercise, go to the student resource center.

APPLY YOUR SKILLS WD05-A03

Create and Format Tables

In this exercise, you will navigate in a table, insert a new table, and convert a table to text. You will change cell margins, merge cells, and apply borders and shading. You will also sort data, delete and add columns/rows, perform calculations, and resize cells.

Navigate in and Insert a Table; Convert a Table to Text

1. Start **Word**. Open **WD05-A03-Travel** from your **WD2013 Lesson 05** folder and save the file as `WD05-A03-Travel-[FirstInitialLastName]`.

2. If necessary, position the insertion point in the first table cell on page 1.

3. Tap ↓ twice to move to the third row.

4. Press Shift + Tab to move to the end of the second row.

5. Press Alt + Home to move to the beginning of the row.

6. Press Alt + Page Down to move to the bottom of the column.

7. Press Alt + Page Up to move to the top of the column.

8. If necessary, choose **Home→Paragraph→Show Hide** ¶ to display formatting marks.

9. Scroll to page 2 and position the insertion point next to the first paragraph symbol at the top of the page.

10. Insert a **4x5 table** and enter the data shown.

Day Tours	From	When	Duration
Versailles	$70	Daily except Mon	4 hrs.
Eiffel Tower	$75	Daily	3 hrs.
Louvre Museum	$65	Daily except Tue	2.5 hrs.
Moulin Rouge Show	$153	Daily	4.5 hrs.

11. Scroll to page 3 and select the table.
12. Convert the table to text; ensure that **Tabs** are chosen to separate text.

Select Data, Customize Alignment, and Modify Cell Margins

13. Scroll to page 1 and use the **move handle** to select the table.
14. Select the **Bangkok** row.
15. Select the **Thailand** and **Vietnam** cells.
16. Select columns two through five and click **Align Center** on the Layout tab.
17. Select the table and change all cell margins to `0.04`.
18. Select the table and change the top and bottom cell margins to `0.06`.

Merge Cells, and Use Borders and Shading

19. Scroll to page 2 and insert a blank row at the top of the table.
20. Merge all cells in the first row, type `Universal Corporate Events` in the row, and center align the row.
21. Select the table, remove all borders, and select the **first row**.
22. Apply **outside borders** to the row, and apply a **blue shading** color of your choice.

Sort a Table, and Work with Columns and Rows

23. Scroll to page 1, sort by the **price column** in ascending order, and indicate that the table has a Header Row.
24. Sort the **Dates column** in ascending order indicating a Header Row.
25. Delete the **Duration column**.
26. Add a row to the bottom of the table and enter the data shown.

Hong Kong	6/9/2013	2438	10%

27. Add a **column** at the end of the table and type `Discount Amount` as the column header.

Perform Calculations and Size Columns

28. In the **second cell** in that column, enter the formula, **`=c2*d2`**, choosing the **second format** in the Number Format field.
29. Enter **formulas** to calculate the discount amount for the remaining rows using the second number format.
30. Add a **new row** to the bottom of the table and type **`Maximum Price`** in the first cell.
31. Position the **insertion point** at the bottom of the **Price column**, enter the formula, **`=MAX(c2:c7)`**, and do not use any special number formatting.

    The formula determines the highest tour price in the column.
32. Select **columns two through five** and position the **adjust pointer** (double-headed) arrow between two of the selected columns.
33. Double-click to autofit the columns to the width of the longest entry in each column.
34. Save and close the file; exit from **Word**.
35. Submit your final file based on the guidelines provided by your instructor.

Extend Your Skills

In the course of working through the Extend Your Skills exercises, you will think critically as you use the skills taught in the lesson to complete the assigned projects. To evaluate your mastery and completion of the exercises, your instructor may use a rubric, with which more points are allotted according to performance characteristics. (The more you do, the more you earn!) Ask your instructor how your work will be evaluated.

WD05-E01 That's the Way I See It

You are the owner of a small store. You have a few corporate customers who order from you in large quantities and you plan to keep track of their orders in a table. Start a new Word document named `WD05-E01-CorpCustomers-[FirstInitialLastName]` and saved to your **WD2013 Lesson 05** folder. Create a 5x6 table with the following column headings: Order Date, Item, Units, Cost, and Total.

Enter five rows of order data for the first four columns. In the Total column, enter formulas for all five rows to multiply Units by Cost. Add a row at the end of the table and use the Sum function to add the Cost and Total columns to determine total costs and sales to date. Add another row to the bottom of the table and enter formulas at the bottom of the Cost and Total columns to determine the maximum cost and maximum total. Enter labels in the last two rows to appropriately describe the data.

Add a row to the top of the table, merge the cells, and enter your company name. Apply a table style of your choice to the table and, if necessary, center-align your company name and right-align the last three columns. AutoFit the last three columns.

You will be evaluated based on the inclusion of all elements specified, your ability to follow directions, your ability to apply newly learned skills to a real-world situation, your creativity, and the relevance of your topic and/or data choice(s). Submit your final file based on the guidelines provided by your instructor.

WD05-E02 Be Your Own Boss

Your company, Blue Jean Landscaping, is offering a spring flower planting special. Start a new Word document named `WD05-E02-SpringFlowers-[FirstInitialLastName]` and saved to your **WD2013 Lesson 05** folder. Create a 3x8 table with the following column headings: Flower Name, Price, and Discount Percent.

Enter data that you decide on in the rows below the heading row. Add a column at the end of the table and enter formulas to calculate the discount amount for each row. Use the dollar format for the numbers. Supply an appropriate column heading for the new column. Sort the table in ascending, alphabetic order by the Flower Name column. Add a row at the bottom of the table and enter a formula in the Price column that determines the highest priced flower and add a suitable label to the row. Apply borders and shading to the table to enhance its readability and make it attractive.

You will be evaluated based on the inclusion of all elements specified, your ability to follow directions, your ability to apply newly learned skills to a real-world situation, your creativity, and your demonstration of an entrepreneurial spirit. Submit your final file based on the guidelines provided by your instructor.

Transfer Your Skills

In the course of working through the Transfer Your Skills exercises, you will use critical-thinking and creativity skills to complete the assigned projects using skills taught in the lesson. To evaluate your mastery and completion of the exercises, your instructor may use a rubric, with which more points are allotted according to performance characteristics. (The more you do, the more you earn!) Ask your instructor how your work will be evaluated.

WD05-T01 Use the Web as a Learning Tool

Throughout this book, you will be provided with an opportunity to use the Internet as a learning tool by completing WebQuests. According to the original creators of WebQuests, as described on their website (WebQuest.org), a WebQuest is "an inquiry-oriented activity in which most or all of the information used by learners is drawn from the web." To complete the WebQuest projects in this book, navigate to the student resource center and choose the WebQuest for the lesson on which you are currently working. The subject of each WebQuest will be relevant to the material found in the lesson.

WebQuest Subject: How tables are used in business.

Submit your final file(s) based on the guidelines provided by your instructor.

WD05-T02 Demonstrate Proficiency

A new chef has just been hired at Stormy BBQ. He is placing the weekly food order for the first time, and the owner has asked you to work with him to be sure his order makes sense. Start a new Word document named `WD05-T02-ChefOrder-[FirstInitialLastName]` and saved to your **WD2013 Lesson 05** folder. Set up a table for the order that includes elements such as the name of the food item, the price, the quantity, and total costs, and then insert the formulas to calculate the total costs.

Assume that it is summer and order fruits and vegetables that are in season and in quantities that guarantee freshness for the week. Sort the table in an order that you think will make sense for the food seller. Add a row at the top of the table, merge the cells, and enter Stormy BBQ, centered, as the heading. Size the table in a way that ensures that it is easy to read, and apply a table style of your choice that also enhances readability.

Submit your final file based on the guidelines provided by your instructor.

Index

Notes

Notes

Notes

Notes

Notes

Notes

Notes

Notes

Notes

Notes

Notes

Notes

Notes

Notes